THE LION AND THE UNICORN

THE LION AND THE UNICORN

Gladstone vs Disraeli

Richard Aldous

W. W. Norton & Company
New York   London

For information about permission to reproduce selections from this book,
write to Permissions, W. W. Norton & Company, Inc., 500 Fifth Avenue,
New York, NY 10110

For information about special discounts for bulk purchases, please contact
W. W. Norton Special Sales at specialsales@wwnorton.com or 800-233-4830

Manufacturing by The Haddon Craftsmen, Inc.
Production manager: Anna Oler

Library of Congress Cataloging-in-Publication Data

Aldous, Richard.
The lion and the unicorn : Gladstone vs Disraeli /
Richard Aldous. — 1st American ed.
p. cm.
Includes bibliographical references and index.
ISBN-13: 978-0-393-06570-1 (hardcover)
ISBN-10: 0-393-06570-7 (hardcover)
1. Gladstone, W. E. (William Ewart), 1809–1898. 2. Disraeli, Benjamin,
Earl of Beaconsfield, 1804–1881. 3. Prime ministers—Great Britain—Biography.
4. Great Britain—Politics and government—1837–1901. 5. Great Britain—History—
Victoria, 1837–1901. I. Title.
DA562.A53 2007
941.081092'2—dc22   2006103106

W. W. Norton & Company, Inc.
500 Fifth Avenue, New York, N.Y. 10110

W. W. Norton & Company Ltd.
Castle House, 75/76 Wells Street, London W1T 3QT

1 2 3 4 5 6 7 8 9 0

To Kathryn

Contents

Illustrations

Preface

The story of Gladstone and Disraeli is a familiar one: it needs retelling.

'There has never been a generation better informed about "now", with so little sense of how we came to be here,' Richard Chartres, Bishop of London, recently observed about our appreciation of the nineteenth century. Behind this statement lies a widely held unease that Britain has lost a grip on the events, characters and ideas that have shaped its past. At a time of fundamental debate about patriotism, liberal values, cultural identity and tradition, there is growing consensus about a need to reclaim the national story. This is not so that it might provide examples of individual and collective virtue – although often it does – but because its drama, controversy and complexity tell us something about the road Britain has travelled and the choices made. The past may well be a foreign country, but in truth they don't do everything differently there.

The clash between Gladstone and Disraeli is part of that national story. In fact, such is its centrality to a time when Britain was the world's leading power, it is surprising that there has been no earlier attempt to write a book on their relationship. Victorians and post-Victorians usually approached Gladstone and Disraeli in one of two ways: either in partisanship, or to achieve synthesis. Many were confirmed Gladstonians or Disraelians, who refought the battles of their champions. Others merged the two men almost into one, as emblematic of an age of equipoise. For both sides the rivalry itself was so clear-cut, it hardly needed to be stated. As belief in the superiority of the British system faded, however, so too did the collective appreciation of that relationship.

Now it is possible to retell the story in a modern way. Recent scholarship and technological innovation have made papers relating to the two men widely available. The process of combing the archives for new material, whilst never complete, long ago became subject to the law of diminishing returns. As the leading Disraeli scholar, Paul Smith, wrote in 1996, 'It seems improbable that new caches of evidence of first-rate significance will appear, and likely that, while research will continue to extend our grasp of the detail and context, . . . advance in understanding will come primarily by more sensitive reflection on what has, for the most part, been long familiar.' The wheel has turned full circle. Emphasising the relationship between Gladstone and Disraeli offers a new approach for a contemporary audience; telling the story because it is both seminal and dramatic is something the Victorians themselves would have applauded.

That the two protagonists loathed each other from an early stage and could hardly bear to be in the same room was obvious even in their own time. Yet, while personal discord gave an edge to political rivalry, their divergence was about more than mismatched tempera-ments. Gladstone and Disraeli were engaged in a turbulent battle of ideas. They collided on great national and international questions: globalisation and free trade, wars of religion and ideology between Christians and Muslims, liberal internationalism, humanitarianism and *realpolitik*, constitutional liberty and the rights of the individual, national identity, imperial expansion, and the role of government in raising the condition of the poor. In their struggles on these and many other topics, they wanted supremacy not just in parliament, but also among the people. For Gladstone and Disraeli there were no focus groups: their political wills battled to instruct rather than to follow public opinion.

'I love fame, I love reputation,' Disraeli said. It was true for each of the rivals. But their quest for both became much more: a clash of mighty opposites.

For help in a variety of ways, I wish to thank: Michael Adams, Tom Bartlett, Kathleen Burk, Judy Brett, Peter Clarke, Padraic Conway, Mary Daly, Sue Freestone, Patrick Geoghegan, Theo Hoppen, Alistair Horne, the late Lord Jenkins of Hillhead, William Mulligan, Cormac Ó Gráda, Jayne Ohlmeyer, Andrew Roberts, Jay Sexton, Peter Stafford, and A.N. Wilson; colleagues in the UCD School of History & Archives, particularly Maurice Bric, and Ronan Fanning, John McCafferty and

James McGuire; Harry White, who provided a G & S soundtrack for G & D; David Reynolds, ever the supportive mentor; Simon Ball, friend and intellectual sparring partner since Cambridge. He, along with Alvin Jackson, Mark Lytle and Kathryn Aldous, read and commented upon the full manuscript: for putting aside their own work to improve mine, I am profoundly grateful. I also thank Anthony Whittome, my splendid editor at Hutchinson (assisted by James Nightingale, Lucie Jordan and Cecilia Duraes), for his constant support at every stage in the conception and writing of this book; Bob Weil and his assistant Tom Mayer, whose rigour and energy have made the Norton experience a real joy; Georgina Capel, who always makes life so much easier; my mother and late father, who encouraged me from my earliest years to enjoy tales of the great figures of history; my daughter, Elizabeth, thankfully more concerned with Dora the Explorer than the Victorians; and my wife, Kathryn, to whom *The Lion and the Unicorn* is dedicated in love and gratitude.

Richard Aldous, Dublin 2006

Prologue

The Funeral

William Gladstone was at home in Flintshire, North Wales, when the news came early that morning. Benjamin Disraeli was dead. It was hardly unexpected, but Gladstone immediately recognised the implications for himself and the country. 'It is a telling, touching event,' he confided to his diary. 'There is no more extraordinary man surviving him in England, perhaps none in Europe. I must not say much, in the presence as it were of his Urn.'

Gladstone's uncharacteristic reticence came because Disraeli's death would 'entail upon me *one* great difficulty: but God who sends all, sends this also'. Gladstone was understating the problem. The specific difficulty was the tribute to his great rival that, as prime minister, he would have to make in the House of Commons. His wider problem was that all society would be watching and waiting for him to slip up in the coming weeks. And nowhere would scrutiny be greater than from the very top. Queen Victoria had revered Disraeli. She reviled Gladstone. If he put so much as a foot wrong, she would make his life intolerable.

Gladstone, who understood this, acted fast. Lord Granville, the foreign secretary, had urged him during Disraeli's last illness to retain the initiative when the moment came. There should be no hint of churlishness or lack of respect. Gladstone must offer a grand public funeral at Westminster Abbey before anyone, the Queen in particular, demanded it of him. So when the telegram came at 8 a.m. on that Tuesday after Easter Gladstone was shocked, but prepared. He immediately wired Disraeli's executors with the offer. He followed it with a letter of

I

condolence to Monty Corry, Disraeli's private secretary, on a death 'which will be regarded with so much mournful interest throughout the country & beyond its limits'.

The letter to the Queen came less easily. Gladstone was a prodigious letter writer, but he delayed writing to Victoria. He was aware of his reputation for cant. Perhaps he believed an early letter would have seemed disingenuous. Maybe he struggled with the necessary words of tribute. The monarch herself lost no time in telegraphing to Gladstone her desire for a public funeral. 'I am in deep grief at this irreparable loss of a most devoted and valued friend,' she told him.

Prompted finally to confront the reality of his relationship with Disraeli by the one person he could not circumvent, Gladstone responded immediately. 'Mr Gladstone would not seek, nor could he earn, Your Majesty's regard by dissembling the amount or character of the separation between Lord Beaconsfield [Disraeli] and himself,' he wrote. 'But it does not in any degree blind him to the extraordinary powers of the deceased statesman, or to many remarkable qualities, in regard to whom Mr Gladstone, well aware of his own marked inferiority, can only desire to profit by a great example.' The Queen no doubt endorsed the last point.

For the next few days at home in Hawarden Castle Gladstone fretted about what was to come. Each of his decisions would seem redolent with meaning. There would be much talk of the personal animosity that fuelled their five-decade struggle for power. It was not something that gave him any pleasure. 'I am not and never was his rival, so far as it depended on my will or intention,' he protested to his son Harry: 'I have been most widely and sharply severed from him but by something totally different from personal hatred, and I am bound to say I do not think he felt any hatred towards me.'

Few, if any, would have believed him.

Disraeli's London House, 19 Curzon Street, Mayfair

Monty Corry must have smiled when he received Gladstone's letter. Disraeli had discomforted the prime minister in life. Now he would wrong-foot him still in death.

In the days that followed Disraeli's passing all deferred to Corry, including the executors and even the Queen. He had been more like

a son than a secretary. During the final days of illness, Corry had minis-
tered to him. He was there at the very end, holding the dying man's
hand and offering words of comfort. Promotions and sinecures had
been turned down to stay after the election defeat in 1880, but Disraeli
had rewarded his loyalty. Corry had lacked the money and estate necessary to be raised to the peerage. The outgoing prime minister had
used his charms on the Queen to persuade her to ennoble Corry,
who became Lord Rowton. Gladstone had compared it to Caligula
making his horse a Roman senator.

Now Corry would perform a last duty: burying Disraeli according
to his instructions. Those could hardly have been clearer: he was to
be buried at the church at Hughenden, next to his wife, Mary Anne,
and in a service that should match the simplicity of her funeral. A
letter from his late wife found among Disraeli's private papers reinforced this. It implored that husband and wife should lie together
in the same grave. The Queen ended any dispute about the matter.
After a visit from Corry on 20 April, she wrote to Granville that
Disraeli's 'wishes to be laid by the side of his devoted wife should be
considered as sacred, and that he should rest at Hughenden, which he
was so fond of'. It was, she later observed on the day of Disraeli's
funeral, so typical of him to avoid the 'gloomy pomp' and 'dismal
dreariness of a grave in the great Metropolitan Abbey'.

Disraeli's Country House, Hughenden Manor, Buckinghamshire

On Tuesday 26 April, to the sound of peacocks screeching on the
terrace, the coffin of Benjamin Disraeli, 1st Earl of Beaconsfield, was
removed to the twelfth-century local church. For more than thirty
years, he had attended St Michael and All Angels as lay rector. He had
paid for its renovation. His beloved sister, Sarah, had made the
communion kneelers and matching Sedilia with her own hands. He
had presented the vicar, Henry Blagdon, who would conduct the
service. In all senses, wrote Corry, the burial would be 'just a village
funeral, no more'.

Except that everything else made this a spectacular occasion. All the
shops in nearby High Wycombe closed to allow thousands to line the
route of the cortege. Green-clad ranks of the Buckinghamshire
Volunteers provided a guard of honour. The coffin was covered in wild
primroses from the Queen with an inscription in her own hand. Walking

behind were three of her sons, including the Prince of Wales, along with bishops, ambassadors from France, Russia, Germany and Turkey, six dukes, and myriad marquesses, earls and other peers. All but one of Disraeli's last cabinet attended, as did Lords Hartington, Harcourt and Rosebery for the Liberals. Even his one-time friend, but latterly bitter enemy, Lord Derby came.

Disraeli had died rich, garlanded in honours that included an earldom and the Order of the Garter, had twice been prime minister and was hailed throughout Europe. Much more than a state funeral – as he had surely known – this straightforward burial at Hughenden confirmed his pre-eminence in history over all who attended. By dragging everyone out to Buckinghamshire on a special train from London, he forced them to concede the point famously made by Bismarck at the Congress of Berlin: 'Der alte Jude, das ist der Mann.'

There were two notable absentees at Hughenden that day. The first was Queen Victoria. Protocol forbade the monarch from attending (a custom not broken until 1965 when Queen Elizabeth II attended the funeral of Winston Churchill at St Paul's Cathedral). Yet in all other respects she was chief among the mourners. The flowers from her gardens at Osborne that adorned Disraeli's coffin were no obligatory token. 'I hardly dare trust to speak of myself. The loss is so over-whelming,' she had written to Corry, abandoning the customary 'royal we', on hearing the news: 'Never had I so kind and devoted a Minister and very few such devoted friends.' Just days after the funeral, on 30 April, she would make a private pilgrimage to Hughenden to retrace on foot the route of the cortege and place a wreath of china flowers in the vault. On her instruction, Lord Beaconsfield's banner and insignia of the Order of the Garter were taken from Windsor for display in the church. Later, she would erect a personal memorial in his honour.

The other absentee was William Gladstone.

The Royal Academy of Arts, Piccadilly

Gladstone moved briskly enough up the staircase of Burlington House hours after the Queen's visit to Hughenden, but he was feeling old. Now in his seventies, the prime minister had begun to show his age. His hair was white. Never a snappy dresser, he had recently come to look positively dishevelled. His eyesight was failing and his back increas-ingly stiff. From this point he could add a new complaint. Since Disraeli's death, he had been unable to sleep. Chronic insomnia would dog him the rest of his life.

The previous days had been difficult for Gladstone. There had been criticism of his decision not to reconvene parliament immediately so that tributes might be paid. Instead this would have to wait a staggering three weeks. He had not gone to Disraeli's funeral because to pay respects to his greatest personal rival would have been, in his secretary's words, 'a humbug'. That choice prompted national outrage, not least from the Queen, who interpreted it as a personal slight. When it was announced that Gladstone had failed to attend due to overwork, outrage turned to derision. *The Times* pointedly remarked that the special train from Paddington, with the Prince of Wales already on board, 'was delayed for some little time while waiting for Mr Gladstone'. Bizarrely his decision had been well meant. Disraeli's rejection of a public funeral had moved Gladstone. 'There is something touching in his determination to be buried by the side of his wife,' he told his son. In keeping with the 'private' nature of the occasion, he had stayed away. By putting sincerity above propriety and common sense, he had contrived to establish the one impression he had wished to avoid: graceless disrespect.

When Gladstone entered the anteroom to the dining hall for the Royal Academy annual banquet he could feel eyes subtly turning towards him. There was nothing unusual in that. But there was a special inquisitiveness that evening. Perhaps he could even detect a hint of mischief around the mouths of some guests. When he looked up, he understood why.

Staring down at him was a magnificent four-foot oil portrait of Disraeli by the brilliant society artist Sir John Millais. The picture was a work in progress, which gave it an added poignancy. More to the point, it was an obvious partner for a portrait of Gladstone completed two years earlier. Gladstone had been painted in right profile. Now Disraeli, in left profile, would catch his eye in artistic perpetuity.

Speaker after speaker at the dinner referred to Millais' painting, and to its pair. Gladstone, who often struggled with social off-the-cuff remarks, was not prepared to speak on Disraeli. When he rose, he astonished the audience by remarking coldly of the portrait that 'it is, indeed, an unfinished work. In this sense it was a premature death.'

'Made my speech,' Gladstone wrote in his diary when he returned home: 'this year especially difficult.' Worse was to come the following day. At a packed Westminster Abbey, Gladstone attended Disraeli's memorial service. The dean, Arthur Stanley, who had attended the same prep school as Gladstone, gave the address. His text was Judges 16: 30: 'So the dead which he slew at his death were more than they which he slew in his life.' In the middle of his peroration, the dean unexpectedly combined Disraeli with (the still very much alive) Gladstone. They were, observed Stanley while the prime minister flushed and squirmed, the 'Great Twin Brothers' of British political life.

It was all too much for Gladstone. By the next day he was 'confined to bed with diarrhoea', from where he unhappily prepared his speech to parliament on his great sibling rival.

10 Downing Street

William Gladstone was on his knees. Mind and body were in distress. As the hour of tribute to Disraeli approached on Monday 9 May, he threw himself at the mercy of the Almighty in the face of 'my very difficult task'. He had endured a week of wretched health. After days of chronic diarrhoea, he had finally returned to the House of Commons on 5 May, only to find MPs in fractious and factional mood. 'This latter visit thoroughly upset me again after my three days of struggle,' he wrote, before returning immediately to bed. Over the weekend, the doctor was called out several times each day. All the while, he worried about framing 'the difficult motion for the Beaconsfield Monument'. His daughter Mary did not help matters by carping about the 'first rate nonsense' that had been written about Disraeli. Gladstone was barely well enough to go to the House that Monday, but his absence was unthinkable. The unwelcome task simply had to be faced. 'I commit myself to God, who has ever helped,' he remarked stoically before setting out.

In the end Gladstone performed brilliantly. He was a magnificent actor in the theatre of parliament. From the moment he went on show the habits acquired over almost half a century kicked in. Heads craned from all sides of the House as Gladstone emerged from behind the Speaker's Chair. What they saw was a prime minister who was erect and composed as he moved quickly to his place on the front bench. He was an animated Commons performer, but on this occasion when he rose to speak there was only composure and deference.

Neither was there any humbug. He acknowledged that he had been 'separated from Lord Beaconsfield by longer and larger differences than, perhaps, ever separated any two persons brought into constant contact in the transaction of Public Business'. Yet in spite of the divide there was much to praise: Disraeli's 'extraordinary intellectual powers', 'his long-sighted persistency of purpose' linked to a 'remarkable power of self-government', the 'strong sympathies with his race, for the sake of which he was always ready to risk popularity and influence', and, touchingly, 'his profound, devoted, tender, and grateful affection for his wife'. Above all else, Gladstone celebrated 'his great Parliamentary courage, which I . . . have never seen surpassed'.* Only one note rang false: Gladstone's 'firm conviction that, in all the judgements ever delivered by Lord Beaconsfield upon myself, he never was actuated by sentiments of personal antipathy'.

A generous and faithful speech resonated in parliament and beyond. Even the Queen approved, writing to Gladstone later 'to express to him that she has been *much gratified* by it, and by the tribute he has paid to the great qualities of Lord Beaconsfield.'

Gladstone did not leave the House of Commons until almost two o'clock in the morning. Exhausted by sickness and nervous energy, he felt a profound sense of relief that 'all went better than I could have hoped'. Yet in the days that followed he could not shake off his sense of disjuncture. Ill health continued, with many days spent in bed. And he was pensive, even maudlin. He read a commentary on the desolate vision of the Book of Job, perhaps reflecting that 'Great men are not always wise'.

By 17 May, more than a fortnight after the onset of his diarrhoea, he remained 'not well'. Perhaps the 'fund of vital force is . . . not enough for the very heavy calls upon it,' he ruminated in his diary. 'So nature murmurs and resents from time to time.' He began to think of retirement, telling his son that he was 'ever brooding upon the desire' of escaping public life.

And Gladstone raged against Disraeli. The great showman had outwitted him at the last. 'As he lived, so he died,' Gladstone fulminated. 'All display, without reality of genuineness.' While confined to bed his mind wandered back across the six decades of their relationship. They had tussled to define the very nature of Britain itself. Like heavyweight fighters, they had punched and parried in the ring to win the ultimate prize: leadership of the world's most powerful nation.

---

* Disraeli's official biographer, W. F. Monypenny, records this differently: 'his great parliamentary courage – a quality in which I . . . have, I think, never known but two whom I could pronounce his equal'. The 'two' almost certainly would have been Sir Robert Peel and Lord John Russell.

Yet as Gladstone reflected, did he even remember that first meeting with Disraeli in 1835? Few then would have foreseen the battle to come, least of all young William Gladstone.

As so often, it was a feud that began over dinner.

1

The Dinner Party

17 January 1835

Lord Lyndhurst looked down the table with a certain satisfaction. He had organised this dinner to put two men together, and it had worked brilliantly. His young protégé, Benjamin Disraeli, was performing with the cool, witty assurance expected of a society novelist. But the young man also wanted political success. The connection made that night would help to forge his reputation in a new arena. It would help Lyndhurst, too, in the difficult fights ahead that year. Yes, he reflected, the meeting of Benjamin Disraeli and Winthrop Mackworth Praed was going to work out very well indeed.

Praed was a regular contributor to the *Morning Post*. He was severing his ties with the newspaper to join Lyndhurst in the Tory government of Sir Robert Peel. Lyndhurst had identified Disraeli as a perfect replacement. During the coming summer Disraeli would write a series of fourteen damning leading articles for the paper as the (now out of office) Tories battled to scupper the contentious Municipal Corporations Bill in the House of Lords.

Lyndhurst was the most important political contact Disraeli had made. It was a happy relationship. They were separated by thirty-two years, but seemed cut from the same cloth. The two men enjoyed many common interests, not least the bed of Lady Henrietta Sykes (whom they shared with the artist Daniel Maclise). Lyndhurst was an outsider operating within the British elite. His father was an American artist, John Singleton Copley, famous for grand historical paintings such as *Chatham's Last Appearance in the Lords*. Unlike many Americans in nineteenth-century England, Lyndhurst's way was not eased by vast personal wealth. His rise came conventionally through the law. He would hold the position of Lord Chancellor in every Tory government from Canning in 1827 to Peel in 1846. He was a brilliant lawyer and political opportunist, but never lost his reputation as an unmistakably disreputable creature.

Lyndhurst and Disraeli had met the previous year at a dinner given, appropriately enough, by Henrietta. They hit it off immediately. Personal liking was sustained by political necessity. Lyndhurst needed the brilliance of Disraeli's pen; Disraeli needed Lyndhurst's patronage.

The dinner party that night was part of Lyndhurst's plan to kick-start Disraeli's already stuttering political career. Patronage was important. Yet Disraeli also needed to make contacts and build alliances with politicians of his own generation. He needed someone to befriend him, identify with him, to share his triumphs and disappointments while plotting and scheming together, looking out for each other's backs, and re-enforcing each other's claims for power.

No one was coming faster than another guest at the table. William Gladstone was a junior lord of the Treasury, protégé of the prime minister, Peel, and destined for cabinet. The historian Thomas Babington Macaulay would famously describe him as 'a young man of unblemished character, and of distinguished parliamentary talents, the rising hope of those stern and unbending Tories . . .'. In the week following the dinner, Gladstone would be promoted to undersecretary of state for war and the colonies. He was only twenty-five years old.

Lyndhurst recognised the strength that an alliance and friendship between Gladstone and Disraeli would generate. Gladstone was gifted, earnest, impassioned and connected, but lacked glamour. Disraeli was witty, alluring and clever, but was not *un homme sérieux*. During the evening, Lyndhurst discoursed on politics for the younger men. 'Never defend yourself before a popular assembly, except with and by retorting the attack,' he told them. 'The hearers, in the pleasure which the assault gives them, will forget the previous charge.' It was entirely characteristic that Gladstone should have stored away the advice word for word while Disraeli refashioned it as a brilliant epigram: 'Never complain and never explain.' The combination of their talents would have been formidable. But that aspect of the dinner party was not going well.

Gladstone and Disraeli loathed one another from the beginning. There was no empathy between the two men. Disraeli was a cold if brilliant dinner companion. It was part of his Byronic pose to appear both Romantic and cynical at the same time. His air was sardonic, urbane and always a little bored. Gladstone's manner, on the other hand, came with a rush of fervour. He drank copiously at dinner, revelled in discussion and took a genuine interest in anything and everything. He might dominate the conversation, but talk always flowed.

When Gladstone was introduced to Disraeli he discovered one of the few men who could make him dry up. Both men pronounced the same judgement on each other. Disraeli wrote to his sister shortly afterwards of meeting 'young Gladstone' at dinner. 'Rather dull,' he recorded dismissively, 'but we had a swan, very white and tender, and stuffed with truffles, the best company there.' Gladstone, never a clotheshorse even as a bachelor, later remembered his amazement at the foppery of Disraeli's dress. The man himself he also found to be 'dull'.

The worst indictment of all came in Gladstone's diary for that night in January 1835. He recorded the dinner with Lyndhurst and listed the important guests. Disraeli was not mentioned even in passing.

For Benjamin Disraeli was a man of little importance. A minor Jewish novelist struggling to enter parliament was of limited interest to a future prime minister.

Gladstone's Diary, Three Weeks Earlier: 29 December 1834

My birthday. Twenty five years have passed over my poor head: the body they say is now compact & firm: but my mind at least remains incoherent and disjointed: void of the power to realise its desires & thoughts, and of the courage to seize upon occasion in its flight: though I think its mechanical aptitude for labour may have grown. But . . . I am still one of that Body to whom the promises are assured: to whom God is a Father, and Jesus Christ an elder brother: O joy! that in our embers, Is something that doth live!

When Benjamin Disraeli met Gladstone for the first time just a few weeks after these words were written, it had been a confrontation with his worst nightmare: a pious, Evangelical Christian both younger and more successful than himself. Disraeli was a minor celebrity, but was not generally esteemed. Gladstone, by contrast, was already held in high regard within the governing circle to which Disraeli aspired. The glittering prizes of youth had been his, won by natural brilliance allied to a prodigious capacity for hard work. Now Westminster and society acknowledged him as the rising man, the

brightest hope of his generation and destined for the highest eche-
lons. And all this achieved at just twenty-five. No wonder Gladstone
was smug. He was in every sense 'one of that Body to whom the
promises are assured'.

William Gladstone was a child of England's moneyed elite. He was
born in Liverpool at the end of 1809. His father, John, had turned a
modest family fortune into great wealth by investment in property,
shipping, West Indian sugar and slavery. This delivered great advantages
to his children, not least his youngest and favourite son, William. The
boy was sent to Eton and then Christ Church, Oxford, hothouses for
the governing classes. By the time he was just twenty-two, he had
been elected to parliament at Newark – a seat in the gift of the Duke
of Newcastle, whose son, Lord Lincoln, was a friend from Eton and
Oxford. Everything was in place for a brilliant career.

Yet the young Gladstone was not a cheerful man. The tone of his
diary entry for his twenty-fifth birthday is a typical mixture of the
self-satisfied and mortified. He wanted and enjoyed worldly success,
but saw his life primarily in religious terms. For if continental
Romanticism obsessed Disraeli, so Christianity preoccupied Gladstone.

William's religious temperament was essentially that of an Evangelical.
During the 1830s, he increasingly came under the influence of the
mainly Anglo-Catholic Oxford Movement, but his personal observ-
ance, with its emphasis on private prayer, Bible study and frequent
church attendance, remained that of a low-church protestant. Childhood
Evangelicalism produced in him an apparently contradictory mixture
of shame and self-satisfaction. His parents had encouraged him towards
introspection about the inherent sinfulness of his life; constant self-
examination was the principal bulwark against Satan. Alongside this
existed a certain arrogance that a sinner, once he had received salvation as a gift from God, might take pride in his place among the saved.
When added to the self-righteous anger that Gladstone learnt directly
from his abrasive father, the combination was a Christian faith that
was both contemplative and aggressively high-handed.

For much of his early life Gladstone had thought he would become
a Church of England priest. As late as 1830, he told his father that 'the
work of spreading religion has a claim infinitely transcending all others
in dignity, in solemnity, and in usefulness'. What changed his mind was
the national debate that preceded the 1832 Reform Act. Gladstone
was passionately opposed to reform of the franchise (the 'vote'). He
organised anti-reform meetings at which he shouted himself hoarse

and jostled with pro-reformers. His forty-five-minute speech in the Oxford Union established him as a brilliant orator in the eyes of his influential contemporaries.

The reform debate politicised Gladstone. Increasing the vote had profound implications for the recognised order, not least the Church. Gladstone believed it would end in 'the destruction of the Church Establishment, to the overthrow of our kingly government in this country . . .; to the degradation of its national character and through the depredation of the British Nation, to wide and irreversible ruin throughout the world'. This was a grave situation, and Gladstone was a young man of sufficient seriousness to respond. Only by rejecting the contemplative priestly life to engage as a public man of action could he join the fight to save the Church and nation from annihilation.

Gladstone left England in February 1832 for a grand tour of Europe. In Milan on 6 July he received the 'stunning and overpowering' offer from Lord Lincoln of a constituency. 'I think I may call it the most remarkable of my life,' he told his diary. The implications were clear to him. He would now join the battle 'to forward those merciful purposes, with which God sent me and every other being into the world — and for the effectuation of which in us all Jesus Christ shed his precious blood upon the Cross. May the great gift of that sacrifice, even the presence of the heavenly comforter, be with me, support me, succour me, enlighten me . . . May I feel my weakness, mine utter and infantile weakness — and then indeed, and then only, there is hope that it may be made strength.'

The 1832 Reform Act had transformed Newark from a constituency in Newcastle's 'pocket' to a competitive election for 1600 votes. Nevertheless the duke's political machine continued to dominate, and Gladstone topped the poll on 14 December.

When he entered parliament as a Tory MP early in 1833, he did so 'provided unquestionably with a large stock at least of schoolboy bashfulness'. London quickly knocked that out of him. Parliament provided a focus and purpose to Gladstone's life around which a social network fitted easily. He rapidly became a young 'man around town', although not in the sense that Disraeli would have understood. Agreeable rooms were acquired at Albany, just off fashionable Piccadilly. The cut of his suits became more stylish. He joined the Carlton Club, as well as the Oxford and Cambridge. He enrolled at Lincoln's Inn to enjoy the company of old school and college friends. Only dinner parties on

Sundays, even at the request of Sir Robert Peel, were refused. At other times he was a regular and sociable guest at the capital's dining tables, often drinking copiously. He particularly enjoyed musical evenings for which he prepared by taking extra singing lessons. He continued to read widely and voraciously. Church attendance remained as keen as ever. He walked regularly in nearby Green Park. All in all, it was a pleasant bachelor's life.

Gladstone would later become England's most famous Liberal, but as a young Tory MP he won his reputation as the rising hope of the 'stern and unbending' by resisting change of any kind. He had already fought against franchise reform. Now in his first parliament he opposed reform to working conditions, the poor law, local government, the Church of England, tariffs, the army and navy, and even the House of Commons. His maiden speech was a defence of West Indian plantation owners, of which his father was one, against government attempts to abolish slavery.

Gladstone quickly gained the reputation as a 'die-hard' Conservative opposed to reform, but he also got noticed for his hard work. He revelled in his duties as an MP. When so many dissolute members were tardy in their obligations, this made him stand out. He adored listening to debates in the chamber. If he missed a division, which was rare, he expressed himself 'excessively disgusted'. He immersed himself in the detail of the great debates of the day, particularly on the West Indies. Meetings were attended and petitions received with terrific enthusiasm.

This active engagement with the nitty-gritty of politics meant that no one was surprised when, in late 1834, he was given a junior office in the new Conservative administration.

'May God guide me,' he wrote in his diary on receiving an offer from Peel. 'Much has He done for me: surely this is providentially ordered.'

Contarini Fleming

I tell you what, my friend, the period has arrived in your life when you must renounce meditation. Action is now your part . . . Act, act, act; act without ceasing, and you will no longer talk of the vanity of life.

Disraeli gave these words of advice to the hero of his novel *Contarini Fleming*. In June 1832, the month after it came out, he had taken his own instruction by jumping into the political arena at his local constituency of High Wycombe (electorate: thirty-two). He began his campaign flamboyantly by addressing a crowd while standing on the portico of the Red Lion. He lost. The following December, he lost again. Ten days before that first meeting with Gladstone in 1835, now aged thirty, he lost for a third time. Disraeli tried his luck in Taunton a few months later. Another defeat. And all the time he fretted about his greying hair and lack of either prospects or money. Time and fate, it seemed, were leaving Disraeli behind. He was not, unlike Gladstone, on an obvious road to success, but then little about his life to that point had been straightforward.

Disraeli enjoyed an unconventional background, but it was not the humble one he subsequently liked to portray in his tale of rags to riches. His Jewish grandfather, Benjamin D'Israeli, had emigrated from Italy, south-west of Venice, to England in 1748. He prospered as a stockbroker and merchant in London, leaving on his death a considerable legacy of £35,000 to Isaac, his son. Isaac married Maria Basevi, the daughter of another wealthy Italian Jewish immigrant in 1802. They had five children. Their second child and eldest son was Benjamin, born in Holborn on 21 December 1804.

Books defined young Ben's world. His father was a successful man of letters who enjoyed an appealing life in the Reading Room of the British Library, the dining room of the Athenaeum Club (of which he was among the earliest members), and the comfort of his own private library. Isaac achieved celebrity in his mid-twenties with the first volume of *Curiosities of Literature*, which brought together anecdotes and character sketches of great writers. *The Literary Character*, a reflection on the nature of literary genius, confirmed his status. In 1809 he helped found the *Quarterly Review*, which became among the most respected and influential Conservative journals of the age. Highly strung, obsessed with genius and fame, with a ready eye for moneymaking opportunities, Isaac D'Israeli was recognisably the father of the man that his eldest son would become.

Ben grew up inside the loop of fashionable, literary society, but he was not a secure child. His upbringing combined the eccentric with the dysfunctional. He did not get the affection from his mother that a fragile temperament demanded. This might at least in part explain why for all his adult life Disraeli would crave the maternal embrace of older women.

The boy's education was unusual. His brothers would later attend

Winchester, but he was sent to a school in Higham Hill run by a self-taught Unitarian minister. Isaac had met him in a bookshop. It was a progressive school that eschewed the traditional emphasis on the classics. Instead it encouraged a love of European literature, history and philosophy. Ben supplemented this with long hours of reflection in his father's ample library. What it did not provide was the often brutal 'bugger-me-with-a-toasting-fork' male initiation rites that nearly all public school boys of the English governing class endured. This left him less institutionalised than most, but with few male friends of his own generation and an enduring dislike of the rituals of masculine company.

By the time he reached his twenties, Benjamin Disraeli had determined on a future: he wanted to be a genius; he wanted to be famous; and he wanted to be rich. After a disastrous foray into the stock market, Disraeli turned to a more obvious route to quick success for a young man of his temperament and connections. The first volume of his novel *Vivian Grey*, published in 1826, was written in an astonishing three weeks. Vital, excoriating and funny, it was an immediate sensation. 'Silver-fork' novels, which portrayed high society as brittle and corrupt, were at the height of fashion. The publisher, Henry Colburn, persuaded Disraeli not to have his name on the cover. It was puffed as an insider's account of the London social scene. This led to a frenzy of speculation as to the identity of the well-bred writer who had exposed the iniquities of the upper classes. When the author was finally revealed as Mr Benjamin Disraeli, an upstart Jew, disappointment quickly turned to vitriolic abuse.

The sharks were waiting when the conclusion of *Vivian Grey* was published. Their verdict matched that of Gladstone who, on reading it almost half a century later, condemned it as 'trash'. The critics tore Disraeli to pieces. 'With what horror, with what supreme, appalling astonishment, did I find myself for the first time in my life a subject of the most ruthless, the most malignant, and the most adroit ridicule,' he would write. 'I was sacrificed, I was scalped . . . The criticism fell from my hand, a film floated over my vision; my knees trembled. I felt that sickness of heart that we experience in our first serious scrape. I was ridiculous, it was time to die.'

Disraeli's humiliation and failure were so overwhelming that, at just twenty-two, he suffered a full nervous collapse. He disappeared completely for almost three years. The 'cold, dull world', he wrote later in *Contarini Fleming* (1832), could not imagine the 'despondency' of 'youthful genius' aware of 'the strong necessity for fame', yet with 'no simultaneous faith in [its] own power'. Disraeli did not fully recover until the age of twenty-seven, at which point he resolved to abandon his introspective life of the mind to enter the public arena, presumably on the grounds that it was safer.

This commitment to a life of action came only after Disraeli had refashioned himself in line with his two most important intellectual and cultural influences: Romanticism and Judaism.

Disraeli viewed himself as a quintessential Romantic hero. His mental and physical collapse he understood as part of the suffering any true Romantic must endure for the sake of self-knowledge and authenticity. Like so many of his generation, he revered the poet Lord Byron. Disraeli had been in awe since childhood. Isaac D'Israeli and Byron were both published by John Murray. Byron greatly admired *Curiosities of Literature*, telling Murray, 'I don't know a living man's book I take up so often, or lay down more reluctantly, as [D']Israeli's.' Benjamin Disraeli slavishly copied Byron in dress and manner, including the air of disdainful melancholy that he kept up for the rest of his life. 'When one is young [one] chooses one's poet and abides by him,' Disraeli reflected towards the end of his life. Byron was that 'one'.

Disraeli's love of Byron also encouraged him to reflect intensely on continental Romanticism. 'Destiny is our will,' he proclaims in *Contarini Fleming*, 'and our will is our nature.' That quest for self-knowledge was part of the process of *Bildung* so integral to German Romanticism: the discovery, liberation and demonstration of our true nature. Alongside it went a distancing irony. Theatrical, affected, sarcastic, knowing, and with the tongue always firmly in the cheek, this sense of detachment allowed the Romantic Disraeli to say or do almost anything without it ever being entirely clear whether or not he was being serious.

The process of discovering his true nature and masking it with irony took on a new manifestation in the immediate years after his breakdown. Suddenly Disraeli came to understand and define himself as Jewish. The catalyst for this redefinition was a trip to the 'Near East' (now the 'Middle East') made between May 1830 and October 1831. The tour was part of the process of recuperation from his illness. Whatever it did for his physical wellbeing, it certainly had a powerful spiritual and intellectual effect.

Disraeli had shown very little interest in his Jewish roots until this point. He had been baptised into the Church of England when aged twelve. His father had hoped this 'conversion' might help his progress in English society. Young Ben seems not to have cared one way or another. Throughout his twenties, his Jewishness barely featured in his writings, either private or public. When he visited Italy in 1826, including Venice with its famous ghetto, he mentioned Jews only once in letters home. In London he encountered little more than casual anti-Semitism. In fact, the literary circles within which he moved positively welcomed an element of the exotic in their writers. Oxford University's award of an honorary doctorate to Isaac D'Israeli seemed to demonstrate that a Jewish writer could be taken seriously (even if Jews were not allowed to be admitted as undergraduates).

Perhaps Ben's early attitude to his background is best demonstrated in his choices about what to call himself as a writer. He anglicised his surname by dropping the apostrophe – D'Israeli became Disraeli – but he did not opt to drop altogether an obviously Jewish name. His 'new' name represented exactly what he was: an English baptised Jew.

Disraeli's 1830s tour of the Near East awakened a new appreciation of the Orient. He was captivated by the Ottoman Empire, on which he would later clash so severely with Gladstone. After meeting the Turkish Grand Vizier in Yanina, Albania, he gleefully wrote home to his sister of his 'delight at being made much of by a man who was daily decapitating half the province'. The highlight of the journey came in Jerusalem. He was 'thunderstruck' on first seeing the 'gorgeous city' from the Mount of Olives, but tellingly wrote to his sister that his 'mind is full of the sublime, not the beautiful'.

The trip to Jerusalem aroused a fascination with the Near East that transformed Disraeli's sense of identity. His response to the Jews was more intellectual and cultural than religious. His letters home make no reference to the Jewish population, or famous sites such as the 'Wailing' Wall. He was fascinated by Arabs as much as by Jews (who both co-existed fairly easily in the 1830s). By spurring his imagination the visit offered a new way for Disraeli to explore his Romantic vision. Rather than shy away from his Jewish origins he now embraced them. Even as he travelled, he began sketching out a new work. It was based on the life of a twelfth-century Jewish prince who conquered much of western Asia before eventual defeat and martyrdom at the hands of the Islamic majority. The resulting novel, *The Wondrous Tale of Alroy*, proclaims from every page the magnificent splendour and fantastical richness of oriental life. It also seems to proclaim Disraeli's own ambition to be a strong, visionary leader in a land that was alien to him. Alroy's epitaph in the novel comes from his sister Miriam: 'You have shown what we can do and shall do,' she tells him before his death. 'By what Man has done, we learn what Man can do; and gauge the power and prospects of our race.'

There is little doubt that Disraeli, at the end of his twenties, took Alroy as an inspiration to great things. The novel had portrayed 'my ideal ambition' and 'a secret history of my feelings'. Now there was a call to action. 'I wish to act what I write,' he confided to his diary in 1833. 'I shall write no more about myself.'

Disraeli's Jewish awakening only added to his appearance as an exotic creature. Since childhood he had cultivated a reckless Byronic exhibitionism, which had been most obviously demonstrated in his dress. In his teens Disraeli had affected wearing velvet coats with flamboyant ruffles and silk stockings with red clocks. As a young man about town this developed quickly into full-blown dandyism. A contemporary described him in his twenties coming up Regent Street 'when it was crowded, in his blue surtout, a pair of military light blue trousers, blue stockings with red stripes and shoes!'

Disraeli understood exactly the impression he was able to create. 'The people quite made way for me as I passed,' he wrote of a walk through town. 'It was like the opening of the Red Sea . . . Even well-dressed people stopped to look at me.' He favoured sensuous material in bright, contrasting colours. His waistcoats were embroidered with gilt flowers. Pockets overflowed with golden chains. His ivory cane was held in hands gleaming with sparkling rings worn on top of white kid gloves. It was all calculated to make an immediate and lasting impact on those he encountered. 'I love fame; I love reputation,' he proclaimed.

Disraeli's dandified Romanticism got him noticed. He self-consciously pushed at the boundaries of taste wherever he went. This often made him unpopular. During his trip to the Near East he had offended sensibilities at the British garrisons in Malta and Gibraltar with his manner and dress. Young officers were astonished both by the variety of the buttons on his waistcoats and the excessiveness of his conversation. He was the first visitor to bring two canes – one for the morning, one for the evening – which he changed ostentatiously as the guns fired at noon. (It was a mannerism later copied by Oscar Wilde.) He immediately adopted foreign dress, turning up to meet the governor of Gibraltar in an embroidered Andalusian jacket, white trousers and a multicoloured sash. When he left Malta, he was dressed as a Greek pirate, with blood-red shirt, huge silver buttons, a sash crammed with knives, a red cap, red slippers and sky-blue pantaloons trimmed with ribbons. By that stage the officers' mess had long stopped asking him to dinner.

Disraeli returned from the Near East in the autumn of 1831 having picked up many things, most of them somehow connected to his worship of the late Lord Byron. He had, like the poet, begun to exaggerate oriental touches to his appearance, most obviously Jewish curls at his temples. These served to embellish his already mysterious image. He was now attended by Byron's former servant, Tita, found in Malta and soon to be installed at Isaac's house in Buckinghamshire. The poet's dissolute nature was mirrored in a painful dose of the clap, which required a nasty course of mercury treatment. And then there was his reputation: it was no great surprise that Disraeli's Byronic manner also brought with it claims that he was gay.

The suggestion of homosexuality was all part of a dandy's pose. Fashionable Georgian and Regency society, particularly in the literary salons of London, encouraged homoerotically charged friendships not least for their sense of danger. Sodomy remained illegal. Punishment was brutal, often ending in lynching or, theoretically, death. Evidence was always difficult to come by. Most enjoyed witnessing the public affectation without caring about the reality of private inclinations. The situation only became damaging if sly, amused whispers became direct accusations.

Claims about Disraeli's homosexuality centred on one man: Edward Bulwer Lytton. The two men took to each other immediately when they met in 1830. Lytton was a successful author and dandy. His 1828 bestseller, *Pelham*, was in a similar vein to Disraeli's *Vivian Grey*. He would enjoy even greater success with *The Last Days of Pompeii*. The two men quickly established a rapport. They regularly dined together. Each puffed the other's reputation, not least through good book reviews. They shared and promoted each other's ambition to get into parliament. Both revelled in the life of young men about town, and feared the approach of middle age. They attended parties, where they would feed each other lines and compete to be the most outrageous. Together they would visit 'the Naughty House' to be 'shampooed and vapour-bathed'. Theirs was a meeting of minds and temperaments that would last a lifetime. Lytton was the only direct contemporary Disraeli counted as a friend.

Some contemporaries questioned whether their relationship went further. Certainly Lytton's wife believed it did. Rosina Wheeler had married Lytton in 1827 after being introduced to him by Byron's lover,

Lady Caroline Lamb. The marriage would end in bitter divorce with Rosina committed to a mental asylum. She was a possessive wife who did not like her husband to have friends. To become a companion of Bulwer Lytton was to become an enemy of Rosina. Her attacks on Disraeli were vehement and unremitting: the onslaught would last more than fifty years.

Disraeli was for Rosina 'a facsimile of the Black Princely Devil'. She made persistent accusations about his sexuality. In Lytton's library at Knebworth she wrote 'queer' in Disraeli's books. She tried to persuade the future Mrs Disraeli not to marry. Her doctor recorded that she 'talked incessantly and vehemently, denouncing Sir Edward and Mr d'Israeli, accusing them of monstrous crimes'. Letters were sent to 'colleagues and friends' of the two men making similar claims. She even wrote to Queen Victoria, telling her that Disraeli and Lytton were like 'two inhabitants of Sodom and Gomorrah'.

No evidence supported Rosina Lytton's stream of poisonous invective, but it added to Disraeli's already louche reputation. For a young man in the hunt for a career in politics, that reputation was becoming damaging. This became clear in the events surrounding his unsuccessful attempt to win Taunton at the general election in April 1835.

The man who turned up to fight that election was every inch the exhibitionist. He arrived 'very showily attired in a dark bottle-green frock coat, a waistcoat of the most extravagant pattern, the front of which was covered with glittering chains, and in fancy-pattern pantaloons'. His speeches, a local journalist noted, were delivered 'in a lisping, lackadaisical tone of voice', and he 'minced his phrases in apparently the most affected manner'. Only the political content of those speeches was uncompromising.

Standing at his first election as an official Tory candidate, Disraeli was determined to show that he was a worthy protégé of Lord Lyndhurst. The Whigs and Irish MPs under the leadership of Daniel O'Connell had combined to bring down the government in which Lyndhurst was Lord Chancellor. Now Disraeli attacked both. 'The Whigs [have] seized the bloody hand of O'Connell,' he declared. They were in power only 'by leaguing themselves with one whom they had denounced as a traitor'.

Garbled reports of the speech, misquoting Disraeli calling O'Connell 'a traitor', soon reached Dublin. The Irish politician responded with a vicious anti-Semitic attack. 'He has just the qualities of the impenitent thief on the Cross, and I verily believe, if Mr Disraeli's family herald were to be examined, and his genealogy traced, the same personage would be discovered to be the heir at law of the exalted individual to whom I allude,' O'Connell observed. 'I forgive Mr Disraeli now, and as the lineal descendant of the blasphemous robber who ended his career beside the Founder of the Christian Faith, I leave the gentleman to the enjoyment of his infamous distinction and family honours.'

This shameful attack was widely reported in England. Honour, along with Disraeli's sense of the theatrical and Romantic, demanded immediate satisfaction. Disraeli issued a challenge; O'Connell declined. Disraeli followed it up with another to O'Connell's son, who had recently fought a duel on his father's behalf. He also declined. 'We shall meet at Philippi,' Disraeli wrote to the elder O'Connell (referring to parliament), 'and rest assured that . . . I will seize the first opportunity of inflicting upon you a castigation which will make you remember and repent the insults that you have lavished upon Benjamin Disraeli.'

Disraeli would not win a seat at Westminster until two years later, so that 'opportunity' had to be put on hold. The row with Daniel O'Connell had brought Disraeli political notoriety to match his literary reputation. 'I greatly distinguished myself,' he noted of the affair in his diary. Certainly he was admired for his courage in facing down a most ferocious and skilled politician. The publicity fed the sense of him as a man who could not be ignored. It also confirmed him as a man of suspect character: bombastic, arrogant, self-serving and flashy.

Disraeli had lived his whole life under the influence of Byron. Now in 1835, the year he met Gladstone, he was dismissed by society as a sensationalist without either temperament or prospects. He was, at best, an amusement, or, at worst, an ostentatious Jewish upstart. He was famous, but greatness seemed beyond him. Disraeli had stretched every sinew of his character to emulate his hero.

Instead most dismissed him as mad, bad and dangerous to no one.

2

Young Englishmen

Williiam Gladstone perched on the opposition front bench, just down from Sir Robert Peel, appraising the scene in the gloaming of the gas-lit chamber. For a man of his natural sense of purpose it was a welcome sight. Row after row of serious men in dark frock coats and tall silk hats sat crushed together on the benches. Here among them were the players who in succession would dominate British politics. All those, with the exception of Lord Aberdeen, who would hold the office of prime minister for almost half a century were there, including Melbourne, Russell and Palmerston. And he was one of their number. William Gladstone, not yet twenty-eight, had already been a Conservative MP for five years and held junior office. He would go on to be prime minister four times. As he turned his head to look at the mass of backbench MPs, he could not help but notice immediately behind Peel the inappropriately flamboyant new Conservative member for Maidstone. This was the first parliament of Victoria's reign. As Gladstone eyed Benjamin Disraeli, it surely never crossed his mind that he was looking at another future prime minister, the Queen's favourite, and the man who would become his greatest rival.

Disraeli had taken five years and five elections to become a Member of Parliament. He would remain one for another forty years. Any early reservations that serious men like Gladstone might have had about Disraeli's merits were quickly confirmed by a notorious maiden speech on 7 December. 'D'Israeli made his first exhibition this night,' recorded the diarist and 'man about town' Charles Greville, 'beginning with florid assurance, speedily degenerating into ludicrous absurdity, and being at last put down with inextinguishable shouts of laughter.'

First speeches by new MPs were traditionally received indulgently. Disraeli, however, was determined to make a mark from the outset. His target, again, was Daniel O'Connell. Now 'at Philippi' together, Disraeli took his first opportunity to renew their quarrel during a debate on the validity of Irish returns at the recent election. O'Connell attacked the Conservatives for their impertinence at raising the matter. Lord Stanley, heir to the Earl of Derby, was to have replied, but Disraeli managed to catch the Speaker's eye as soon as the Irish leader sat down.

Dressed with his usual panache, Disraeli began in a theatrical, sarcastic manner intended to provoke the Irish MPs. He ridiculed O'Connell's 'rhetorical medley', and made the House laugh by referring to one of his charities as 'a project of majestic mendicancy'. Then things got nasty. Irish intimidation and corruption, Disraeli charged, had 'only assumed a deeper and darker hue' since the Reform Act. Irish MPs, who had been mildly jeering, now began open aggression by hissing, shouting, catcalling, stamping their feet and making animal noises. Opposition backbench MPs took this as an opportunity to abuse the Irish members, whose support for Melbourne had denied the Tories office.

Disraeli tried to struggle on, but could barely make himself heard above the noise. His rhetoric became more high-blown, with much awkward classical imagery. The Conservative front bench looked mortified, although Peel tried valiantly to cheer him on. Eventually Disraeli was forced to give up, not before shouting across the floor of the House: 'I will sit down now, but the time will come when you will hear me.' When Lord Stanley, who detested the Irish, stood to follow he made no reference to their treatment of Disraeli. The new member for Maidstone had embarrassed himself and the party. Even John Hobhouse, who as Byron's executor was not a man easily surprised, thought the speech 'such a mixture of insolence and folly as I never heard in my life before'.

'I wish your debut had been more auspicious,' his father wrote to him afterwards, 'but I am always fearful that the "theatrical games" will not do in the English Commons'. It was a lesson that was now dawning on Disraeli. A few days later he dined with his friend Bulwer Lytton, who brought along Richard Lalor Sheil. Although a senior Irish MP, Sheil had a testy relationship with O'Connell, and felt sufficiently moved by Disraeli's 'crush' to offer some worldly advice about the Commons. 'Be very quiet, try to be dull,' he warned, re-enforcing Isaac's opinion, 'and in a short time the House will sigh for the wit and eloquence which they know are in you.'

If Disraeli needed a lesson on how to present a difficult case to the Commons, he soon recognised it in a speech by Gladstone a few weeks later. Gladstone opposed his own party on a bill concerning the governance of Canada. According to *The Times* he gave a measured, well-argued speech 'evincing considerable research'. Disraeli was certainly impressed. 'Gladstone spoke very well,' he told his sister Sarah, noting that he drew a response from a government minister and Peel.

The seriousness of purpose needed in the House of Commons was finally making an impression on Disraeli. His next intervention after his disastrous first outing was a short, bare statement about changes to copyright, a subject on which he, as an author, might have expected to be heard. He did not speak again until March, when he mounted a defence of the Corn Laws that won favour with Tory squires. By April he was on a roll, reporting to Sarah 'a most brilliant and triumphant speech' during another debate on the Copyright Bill, which drew praise from all sides of the House. 'The whole day,' he boasted, 'has been passed in receiving compliments on my speech.'

Disraeli was at last finding his place at Westminster. 'I have begun several things many times, and I have often succeeded at the last,' he had predicted in his maiden speech. He was always likely to remain a maverick, but now Disraeli was on his way to becoming a House of Commons 'character'. It seemed the best for which he could hope.

Gladstone and Disraeli were now together in parliament, their lives running in parallel, and occasionally touching. Both men enjoyed a reputation, although of a very different nature. History would say that they entered British politics at the dawn of the modern era. The 1832 Reform Act was perhaps the defining constitutional landmark on the long road to democracy — it 'set men athinking', Disraeli would later say — yet the lives of these two young MPs remained governed by the traditions of the eighteenth century. Their world was a small one. The novelist Henry Fielding had plausibly defined the word 'nobody' as 'all the people of Great Britain except about 1200'. Byron concurred, but thought the number was 1500. The prime minister, Lord Melbourne, went so far as to suggest that the few thousand who read the *Morning Chronicle* might be included. The attitude of this elite to those outside was summed up by Lord Chesterfield's aphorism that where two or three were gathered together, there was a mob.

Two parties dominated politics. Each had its own distinctive tradition. The Whigs, broadly speaking, were the party of the city, and held themselves to be the elite of the elite. Their sybaritic activities, not least prodigious gambling, centred on the magnificent houses of great aristocratic families – notably the Russells and the Cavendishes (the Dukes of Bedford and Devonshire). They judged themselves, perhaps with good reason, as protectors for more than six hundred years of English parliamentary government. It was not a claim anyone was allowed to forget. The central lobby at the Earl of Leicester's Holkham Hall, for example, displayed a frieze of panels illustrating the triumph of liberty over despotism. King John signs the Magna Carta surrounded by barons, each of whom bears the face of a member of the 1830 Whig cabinet. Yet for all this veneration of tradition, the Whigs were constant meddlers in the political and social system. Their maxim, said one Tory historian, was 'Whatever is, is wrong'. For Whigs, reform was an argument in itself. This explained their admiration for the French Revolution, which won them an unpopular reputation in the country as an 'un-English' party. No one understood this better than Disraeli. 'In order to accomplish their object of . . . concentrating the government of the state in the hands of a few great families, the Whigs are compelled to declare war against all those great national institutions, the power and influence of which present obstacles to the fulfilment of their purpose', he had written in an 1835 polemic, 'It is these institutions which make us a nation.' He would continue to throw this insult at the Whigs and their Liberal successors for almost half a century.

Standing against the Whigs were the Tories, labelled by their rivals as 'the stupid party'. Lord John Russell, who had steered the Reform Act through the Commons, dismissed them as unfit to hold 'the higher offices of state'. Even brilliant Tories, such as Pitt, Canning and Peel, had for generations winced on surveying row after row of dim country squires interested only in field sports. Novelists and playwrights cruelly lampooned these rural MPs. Thomas Love Peacock's 'Sir Simon Steeltrap', for example, fights a relentless campaign against his own tenants: he 'committed many poachers, shot a few; convicted one third of the peasantry; suspected the rest; and passed nearly the whole of them through a wholesome course of prison discipline'. These were not men with whom either Gladstone or Disraeli shared much affinity. For the younger man – protégé of Peel and part of that group which would redefine Toryism as 'Conservatism' – this mattered less; for Disraeli, apparently fated to a life on the backbenches, the phrase 'fish out of water' could hardly ever have seemed more apt.

What both men had to endure together in 1837, however, was the inevitable frustration of opposition. This was not helped by Peel's statesman-like view that government legislation should be assessed on its merits rather than rejected as a matter of course. For Peel, opposition was a question of principle not party. It often made parliament a dull, conciliatory place not the cruel bear pit in which young MPs might make their reputations by taking on the big beasts of government. This relatively quiet life on the opposition benches at least gave Gladstone and Disraeli time to concentrate on affairs of the heart. For both men, this was rapidly becoming a major preoccupation.

Gladstone's ascent in public life had been swift, but it was accompanied by much private angst. Much of this was to do with religion; the rest had more to do with sex. By 1838 Gladstone was close to crisis. 'The world outside me seems somehow dismantled now, because of the icy coldness of my heart,' he wrote. 'I walk among the splendours of the world like a dead man, and in business like one bound to death, with a heart of stone.' All of this might have been avoided, he believed, 'had I been married'.

For all Gladstone's political skill, he lacked both diplomacy and charm with women. Gladstone's was predominantly a male world. His own father had been a dominant, angry head of household who bullied Mrs Gladstone. William had been bred in the world of Eton and Christ Church, where women were matrons, cooks or bedders. He was easy in male company, even developing a number of homoerotic friendships. The most infamous of these was with Arthur Hallam, an Eton contemporary who in death became the subject of Tennyson's elegy, *In Memoriam* (1850). No sooner had Gladstone left Oxford than he plunged into London's political milieu with its masculine bastions of the Commons, the clubs of St James's, and high-church Anglicanism. He became almost inseparable from James Hope, a university friend and fellow Anglo-Catholic. Whatever sexual frustrations he had were satisfied, according to his diary, by 'vigorous' masturbation, 'which returns upon me again & again like a flood'. This was not a lifestyle into which women intruded. It certainly was not one to which many were attracted.

Although Gladstone knew very little about women, he was fairly sure that he wanted one of his own. Early marriage was part of the

Evangelical tradition from which he came. Even after he determined to find himself a wife, beginning in 1835, his initial attempts ended in disaster. First he courted Caroline Farquhar, the sister of Walter, an Eton and Christ Church friend. The project was embarked upon rather as one might buy a house or a horse. Many letters were sent and visits paid, but most of them were to Miss Farquhar's father and brother. How to interest the lady herself was beyond him. 'The barrier you have to overcome is the obtaining of my sister's affections,' the frustrated Walter told him after eight months of courtship. 'No Mama!' Caroline had exclaimed on seeing Gladstone walking across her family's park at Polesden Lacey, 'I cannot marry a man who carries his bag like that.' Fifty years later, finding herself at the communion rail of the Savoy chapel next to Gladstone, she immediately stood up and left.

Rejected by Caroline, Gladstone immediately turned his attentions to Lady Frances Douglas, teenaged daughter of the Earl of Morton. Here the humiliation was even greater. He courted her during a short trip to her father's estate near Edinburgh in 1837. She found him earnest and dull. When he persisted in the chase, the Earl of Morton was forced to deliver a 'crushing' rejection along with an instruction to end all correspondence. 'I live almost perpetually restless and distressed,' Gladstone complained shortly afterward (having contemplated throwing himself into the grave at a funeral that day).

'Active duty brings peace' became Gladstone's motto after his romantic rejection by the Mortons. He pitched himself into parliamentary life and scholarship. By the summer of 1838 he had produced a massive draft of *The State in Its Relations with the Church*, a powerful but uncompromising book on the Anglican Church as the conscience of the British nation. Exhausted physically, emotionally and mentally, Gladstone took off in August for Italy, where finally he met his match.

Gladstone had arranged to meet there Sir Stephen Glynne, MP for Flintshire and a distant relation of the great Tory prime minister Pitt the Younger. While in Rome his now weary eye fell on Glynne's eldest daughter, Catherine – 'soft face, high-coloured as a girl's, and tremulous mouth', a contemporary wrote – whom he began to court immediately. After four nervy months, he came close to proposing at the Coliseum on a moonlit January evening. A few days later he did it instead by letter. It was not a proposal to sweep a young girl off her feet. 'I seek much in a wife in gifts better than those of our human pride, and am also sensible that she can find little in me,' he wrote, in a single long-winded sentence, 'sensible that, were you to treat this note as the offspring of utter presumption, I must not be surprised: sensible that the life I invite you to share, even if it be not attended, as I trust it is not, with peculiar disadvantages of an outward kind, is one, I do not say unequal to your deserts, for that were saying little, but liable at best to changes and perplexities and pains which, for myself, I contemplate without apprehension, but to which it is perhaps selfishness in the main, with the sense of inward dependence counteracting an opposite sense of my too real unworthiness, which would make me contribute to expose another – and that other!' On receiving the letter Catherine pleaded for time, no doubt hoping it would give her the opportunity to work out exactly what Gladstone meant.[*]

Gladstone returned to England without an answer, and reproached himself for 'incorrigible stupidity' in again being 'precipitate'. Once more he slumped into despair. 'The truth is I believe my affections are more worthless than ever,' he wrote in his diary, reviewing the previous unhappy twelve months. 'I am so deadened and exhausted by what has taken place.' He need not have worried. On 8 June they walked together along the Thames at Fulham, where his 'blessed creature' finally accepted the proposal.

There was an element of convenience about the marriage: Gladstone needed a wife; the Glynnes needed his wealth. She also added class to his 'new' money. But at least their characters were complimentary. Catherine, two years younger, shared his depth of faith, but in all other ways helped to lighten his emotional load. She was straightforward, natural, and not particularly intellectual. She was full of jokes, often speaking in made-up slang. While William was obsessed about order and punctuality, she was perpetually disorganised and late. Her dress sense was scruffy, a characteristic that the previously impeccable William would quickly adopt. Less endearing was her anti-Semitism, in which terms she would later encourage her husband to think about Disraeli, whom she loathed. Their marriage lasted almost sixty years, until his death in 1898, and produced eight children. Catherine would go on to be one of the first overtly 'political' wives: she regularly sat on the platform at her husband's rallies, waved to crowds from windows and trains while he slept, and even alerted reporters when a speech was about to begin. On visiting London she would sit for hours behind

---

[*] 'He really was a frightful old prig,' wrote Clement Attlee, prime minister between 1945 and 1951, on reading this letter reprinted in a biography of Gladstone: 'Fancy writing a letter proposing marriage including a sentence of 140 words all about the Almighty. He was a dreadful person.'

the Grille of the Ladies' Gallery in the House of Commons nervously listening to her husband's (long) speeches. At other times she remained uncomplainingly at Hawarden. Catherine, commented one political observer, was 'intent on one thing only in this life – her husband'.

The wedding took place at Hawarden, the Glynne country seat, on 25 July; a few weeks later Benjamin Disraeli also married, no less relieved than Gladstone to have found a wife.

Throughout the 1830s Disraeli had acquired a notorious reputation for affairs with older, married women. He was able to brazen out gossip about his love affairs. What he could not run away from were his considerable debts, which, thanks to his costly lifestyle, were spiralling out of control. Most of his correspondence was now taken up with angry creditors. He was often unable to leave home for fear of arrest. This he tried to alleviate by throwing off a couple of novels, *Henrietta Temple* and *Venetia*, which were moderate successes. Part of his relief in being elected to the House of Commons was the fact that members could not be arrested while parliament was in session. That looked a short reprieve. Hardly a year into his first term, Disraeli was faced with the stark truth that his debts had become so bad he would not be able to fight any subsequent election.

The obvious solution for a man in Disraeli's serious financial jeopardy was to marry for money. Fate seemed to intervene when his fellow constituency member at Maidstone died suddenly in March 1838. Wyndham Lewis left a forty-five-year-old widow, Mary Anne, and no children. Disraeli several years earlier had described her as 'a pretty little woman, a flirt and a rattle'. Now he pursued her for her wealth.

By the time he discovered that Mary Anne was not as rich as he had imagined, Disraeli had half fallen in love with her. Rather than dump her, he laid himself bare, writing to tell the truth. 'I avow when I first made my advances to you, I was influenced by no romantic feelings,' he told her frankly. Now her fortune had 'proved to be much less than I, or the world, imagined it', and would not 'benefit me in the slightest degree'. Yet despite her more modest circumstances, Disraeli's heart had been touched. 'I found you, as I thought, amiable, tender, yet acute and gifted with no ordinary mind; one whom I could look upon with pride as the partner of my life, who could sympathise with all my projects and feelings, console me in moments of depression, share my hour of triumph, and work with me for our honour and our happiness.'

They married on 28 August 1839 at fashionable St George's, Hanover Square. Mary Anne's verdict on her new husband was unequivocal: 'He is a genius.'

Whitehall Gardens

On the last day of the summer of 1841, the new prime minister, Sir Robert Peel, waited in his London house, just off Horse Guards Parade, for the arrival of William Gladstone. He had decided on a strong cabinet that already included one former premier – the Duke of Wellington – and two future ones – Lords Aberdeen and Stanley. The question now was what to do with his young men.

The Conservatives had won the recent general election with a tidy majority of seventy-six. It was an undoubted personal triumph for Peel, who had dragged his party back to the middle ground of British politics. Tory opposition to the 1832 Reform Bill had seen them condemned as opponents to compromise of any kind. Moderate opinion, including among traditional Tory supporters – the Crown, the Church of England, Oxford and Cambridge, and older trading interests such as sugar – had decisively turned against them. Peel's success had been to win back most of these habitual followers while also reaching out to a new constituency. In short, this meant recon-ciliation with the middle class, particularly new commercial interests such as cotton and coal. Harmony between the classes, he argued, was the best way to avoid revolution and increase prosperity. 'If the spirit of the Reform Bill,' he had famously declared in his 1834 Tamworth Manifesto, 'implies merely a careful review of institutions, civil and ecclesiastical, undertaken in a friendly temper, combining with the firm maintenance of established rights the correction of proved abuses and the redress of real grievances – in that case I can for myself and my colleagues undertake to act in such a spirit and with such inten-tions.'

Peel's image as moderniser had been vital to the Conservative victory, but his character and personality would ultimately prove a liability. For the prime minister's command as an efficient adminis-trator could not hide the fact that he was neither charming nor charis-matic. He worked incredibly hard and demanded a similarly high standard of others. Although happily married, and passably affable company when shooting or gambling, his manner was cold when dealing with matters of state. He offered little in the way of small talk and was often curt, even rude. Cabinet ministers would find themselves abrasively ticked off. Relations with backbench MPs were perfunctory. What mattered to Peel was an efficient despatch of business. That ensured he was admired even when he was not loved. If difficult times came, as they surely must for any government, there were plenty within his own party happy to see a proud man humbled.

Peel's arrogance stemmed from an intriguing cocktail of insecurity, intellectual conceit and great wealth. He was a product of 'new' money equipped with all the accoutrements of 'old' money other than natural ease. His father had been the first authentic cotton manufacturing millionaire of Britain's industrial revolution. When the old man died in 1830, Peel inherited the title, lands and money. Yet riches and political success had not brought contentment. Peel was uncomfortable in company, and defensive about his Lancashire origins. He never lost his northern accent, despite attempts to flatten his vowels. 'He had managed his elocution like his temper,' Disraeli later quipped: 'neither was originally good.'

It is hardly surprising, then, that when Gladstone arrived for his interview on 31 August 1841, this severe young man should both have repelled and attracted Peel. For here was his spitting image. Twenty-one years separated them, but their lives showed an eerie symmetry. Both were northerners whose money came from trade. Each of their fathers had been a self-made businessman who had used his money to acquire titles and parliamentary seats, and to educate his children among the elite. Peel and Gladstone both went to Christ Church, Oxford, and achieved Double Firsts. Each was elected to parliament aged just twenty-one. Both became government ministers in their twenties yet neither had much in the way of social graces. They shared a dedication to hard work and a contempt for inefficiency. Gladstone was in every way Peel's apprentice.

Yet the new prime minister was worried that his most gifted pupil was going off the rails. Since 1832, Peel had been working to create a less reactionary Conservative party. Now Gladstone had established himself, in Macaulay's words, as 'the rising hope of those stern and unbending Tories who follow, reluctantly and mutinously, a leader [Peel] whose experience and eloquence are indispensable to them, but whose cautious temper and moderate opinions they abhor'. Peel himself had been appalled by the argument in Gladstone's *State and Church*.

'This young man will ruin his fine political career if he persists in writing trash like this,' he had exclaimed on reading the book, before throwing it to the floor. Peel appreciated that Gladstone had talent but was beginning to wonder if he had judgement.

Though Gladstone arrived hoping for a cabinet position, he was disappointed. Peel instead offered Gladstone a junior post that would enable him to demonstrate his administrative skill while keeping him clear of controversy. It was a difficult meeting lasting just a quarter of an hour. Peel told him that financial questions would be the government's 'chief importance'. Gladstone was to go to the Board of Trade as vice president, taking the lead in the Commons. Even though Peel assured him that it was 'an office of the highest importance', Gladstone was deeply unhappy. 'It really is an apprenticeship,' he protested. Peel retorted that 'it will be a good arrangement both with a view to the present conduct of business and to the brilliant destinies which I trust are in store for you.' The subtext was clear: work with me and the glittering prizes await. Gladstone came away from the meeting like 'a reluctant schoolboy'.

If Gladstone was an unenthusiastic pupil at Peel's academy, then Disraeli felt as if he had failed the entrance exam. He spent most of those late summer days at the Carlton Club trying to divine from every whisper of gossip whether or not he would be invited to join the government. Eventually, in desperation, he wrote directly to Peel on 5 September begging for office. 'I have had to struggle against a storm of political hate and malice, which few men ever experienced,' he wrote, 'and I have only been sustained under these trials by the conviction, that the day would come when the foremost man of this country would publicly testify, that he had some respect for my ability and my character.'

Unbeknown to Disraeli, his wife Mary Anne had also written to the new prime minister the previous evening. No doubt her husband would have been mortified by this humiliating intervention if he had ever found out. Mary Anne, a friend of Peel's sister, hoped this last-ditch effort might save her husband's career. She had spoken to Peel at a social occasion the previous spring when he had given her hope that Disraeli might be promoted. Now she tried the same tactic again. 'My husband's political career is for ever crushed, if you do not appreciate him,' she wrote. 'Literature he has abandoned for politics. Do not destroy all his hopes, and make him feel his life has been a mistake.'

Neither letter made the slightest impression on Peel. He had not entertained even for a moment the idea of Disraeli as a minister. Nor was there a compelling reason why he should. Disraeli was not only a marginal figure still tainted by sexual and financial scandal, but also a loose cannon on the backbenches whose devotion to self was greater than that to his party or its leader. There was certainly no personal rapport between a dull dog like Peel and the flamboyant peacock Disraeli. All in all, the only surprise in this exclusion was that Disraeli should have been flabbergasted by it.

Peel dismissed Disraeli in a cold reply to the plaintive letter of 5 September, rebuking the aspirant for his presumption. That same day the newspaper published a full list of ministerial appointments. 'All is over,' Disraeli wrote mournfully to his sister. In reality it was simply the beginning. Peel would be made to regret his decision to exclude Disraeli.

Robert Peel had reservations about both Gladstone and Disraeli. Only in Gladstone, however, did he see that huge ability compensated for a recalcitrant nature. Even though he would remain slightly bemused by his young protégé, Peel stuck with him. Few doubted Gladstone's talent or aptitude. Sir James Graham, home secretary and Peel's closest cabinet ally, maintained that 'Gladstone could do in four hours what it took any other man sixteen to do, and he worked sixteen hours a day'. What he needed was direction. By appointing him as vice president of the Board of Trade, Peel hoped that religion would be pushed firmly to the back of his over-eager mind. Peel had given him the opportunity to find a new passion: government money.

Gladstone now threw himself into the detail of public finance, habitually working all day and much of the night. His immediate boss was the Earl of Ripon (who as Viscount Goderich had briefly and disastrously been prime minister in 1827). The two men enjoyed an uneasy relationship, but it was another important tutelage for Gladstone. Tariff reform, which fell within the purview of the Board of Trade, was at the heart of the government agenda. Gladstone by instinct was a protectionist, supporting the system by which goods, notably food, were taxed coming into Britain. A few years working in detail on trade questions under Ripon changed his mind. In 1843 he wrote an article for the *Foreign and Colonial Quarterly* magazine that celebrated the huge reductions in tariffs that he had made. Tariff reform signified the 'natural and proper consequences of [Britain] possessing, in a superior degree, the elements of industrial greatness'. The policy also had a moral basis.

'Religion and Christian virtue,' he wrote, 'like the faculty of taste and the perception of beauty, have their place, aye and that the first place, in political economy, as the means of creating and preserving wealth.'

Peel worked closely with Gladstone on trade matters, but also took the opportunity to teach him a few political home truths. When Gladstone (always the zealous convert) threatened to resign in 1842 because the pace of reform was too slow, Peel subjected him to a dressing down, 'the negative character of [which] had a chilling effect on my feeble mind' and left him 'sick at heart'. The lesson was straightforward enough: 'that it was impossible for every one to have precisely that which he thought best'.

Peel had saved him, Gladstone would write at the end of his career, from one of 'the most palpable errors of my political life'. Even so he remained an exasperating pupil. In 1843, Peel offered him the top job at the Board of Trade when Ripon became secretary for India. This would bring Gladstone into cabinet for the first time. But at the meeting with Peel on 13 May, rather than confine himself to a simple 'thank you', Gladstone produced a list of demands. These included reversing the decision to merge the North Wales bishoprics of Bangor and Asaph. 'I have to consider with God's help by Monday whether to enter the Cabinet, or retire altogether,' he told a bemused prime minister. Even Gladstone's Anglo-Catholic friends urged him not to sacrifice his political career for Welsh Anglicanism. In the end, common sense prevailed. Less than two years later, Gladstone was playing up again. The issue was still Anglicanism – this time across the Irish Sea.

After an initial period of repression in Ireland, Peel had come to believe by 1842 that a conciliatory policy would facilitate the more efficient running of the country. The government dithered on exactly how to do this before turning its attention to the Roman Catholic national seminary at Maynooth in County Kildare. The key to administrative calm in Ireland, Peel thought, was the position of the Catholic clergy: keep them happy and everything else would follow. He therefore proposed a permanent, increased government subsidy to Maynooth, with vastly improved salaries, new scholarships and a building grant. In January 1845, Peel told the cabinet that a bill would be presented to the House in a matter of weeks.

The increased grant to Maynooth presented Gladstone with a dilemma, although no one, including it seems even the man himself, understood why. In *State and Church* he had written at great length on why the government should not offer succour to any religion that might challenge the Church of England. To provide money to aid the educational mission of Roman Catholicism was in direct contradiction to that principle. So Gladstone resigned. The decision, noted one journalist, was as ridiculous as a man jumping off 'the Great Western train, going forty miles an hour, merely to pick up his hat'. Having vacated his cabinet seat on the matter, Gladstone then proceeded to vote for the legislation when it was debated in the Commons on 11 April. His 'deliberate and even anxious support', he told a bemused House, was 'in opposition to [my] most deeply cherished predilections'.

'I really have great difficulty sometimes in comprehending what Gladstone means,' the weary Peel told Graham. Even Gladstone recognised that he had ruined a brilliant political future. 'I could not but know,' he wrote mournfully, 'that I should inevitably be regarded as fastidious and fanciful, fitter for a dreamer or possibly a schoolman, than for the active purposes of public life in a busy and moving age.'

Observing from the backbenches Disraeli put it more bluntly: 'Gladstone's career is over.'

When Gladstone sat down after his speech during the Maynooth debate on 11 April, Disraeli leapt immediately to his feet to reply. He was disappointed. The Speaker, with due deference, called the heir to the Duke of Norfolk. When he had finished, Disraeli again came to his feet. This time the Speaker recognised him, not least because Tory backbench MPs were shouting for him. Disraeli's speech was a denunciation of Peel and the Maynooth bill. And to needle Peel, he attacked his vulnerable apprentice. This was the first time that Disraeli took aim at Gladstone and landed a palpable blow.

Disraeli had turned immediately to Gladstone's sophistry. He expressed 'surprise' that the member for Newark had not simply delivered his speech from the government benches. Gladstone, 'subtle a casuist as he may be', could not disguise the absurdity of his position in backing the government on exactly that conviction for which he had resigned. What is his argument, taunted Disraeli: 'It is this: that the principle upon which the State has hitherto been connected with the ecclesiastical affairs of this country is worn out. We must seek a new principle, says the right honourable gentleman, and the Government which I have left because I support it – that Government has discovered a new principle.' This was, remarked Disraeli to scornful, appreciative laughter, 'a little vague'.

Gladstone returned in the early hours to his elegant London house on Carlton House Terrace, depressed that he had performed 'most defectively'. The whole question of Maynooth and his resignation, he lamented in his diary, 'lies heavily on my mind'. What surely must also have been on his mind was the matter of his taunter-in-chief. Just how had Benjamin Disraeli – a laughing stock in the House only a few years earlier – transfigured himself into the leader of those Tory backbench rebels who now threatened to bring down the government?

The man who had commanded the House that night was far removed from the laughing stock of his maiden speech in 1837. Disraeli had learnt well Sheil's instruction to appear dull. To begin with, his dress was transformed. The florid waistcoats, gaudy jewellery and colourful trousers had gone. In their place were sombre black frock coats, with conventional charcoal striped trousers and square-toed boots. His curls were more subdued. He had no need to wear a hat in the Commons chamber to hide his emotions, because he showed none. His face had become a mask, displaying little other than general sardonic amusement, most often at his own wit.

And he had begun to attract a fan club in the House. This was made up, he told his wife with evident satisfaction, 'chiefly of the youth, and new members'. In October 1842, two of those new MPs, George Smythe and Alexander Cochrane-Baillie, had visited Disraeli in Paris to ask if, along with their friend Lord John Manners, they might follow his lead in parliament. This was the beginning of the group known as 'Young England'. Their origins were rooted in Eton and Oxford, where Manners and Smythe had honed a nostalgic vision that rejected the materialism and utilitarianism of the industrial age. They gloried in the splendours of the medieval church, the feudal system and the Stuart monarchy. Their admiration of Disraeli was based on his cynical yet idealistic romanticism, and his reputation as a man of letters. Gladstone had been Manners' running mate at Newark in 1841, but loftily dismissed his and his friends' ideas as 'mournful delusions'. Disraeli on the other hand, flattered by their attentions, had immediately responded to their potent mixture of youth, aristocratic blood and romantic ideals. No doubt it also appealed to him that others, including their fathers, the prime minister and Gladstone, all disapproved of his influence. They acted in concert until 1845, before breaking over Maynooth, by which stage Disraeli had no need of the alliance. Manners, however, would always remain among his most trusted friends and advisers. The Oxford don Frederick Faber (author of the hymn 'Faith of Our Fathers') observed Manners' 'delicate holiness'. He also had a vivid and romantic imagination. Those qualities plus his aristocratic pedigree ensured a lifelong place in Disraeli's affections.

Young England also provided Disraeli with the context for a sweeping 'state of the nation' trilogy of novels. These laid out a Conservatism to rival that of Peel. It was the first time since his election to parliament that Disraeli had returned to fiction. He did so because he recognised that a flamboyant vision required an imaginative setting. Disraeli, moreover, remained a fascinating but marginal figure in politics; on the other hand a new novel was guaranteed to attract attention in influential literary and social circles. The three novels – *Coningsby, or The New Generation, Sybil, or The Two Nations,* and *Tancred, or The New Crusade* – were published between 1844 and 1847. The first, he later wrote, considered 'the origin and condition of political parties', the second 'considered the condition of the people' and the last examined 'the position of the descendants of that race who had been the founders of Christianity'. In *Sybil,* Disraeli introduced his most pervasive and long-lasting contribution to the language of English politics – 'one-nation' Conservatism.

Together these novels offered a vision that combined idealism, fantasy and surprising elements of social realism. They set out the moral and political principles by which England might flourish. Judaism is recognised as central to Western civilisation. Heroism triumphs over small-mindedness. In each story the central protagonist – Coningsby, Egremont or Tancred – overcomes anxiety to offer a new kind of leadership that draws strength from the examples of the past. That leadership is rooted in a desire to serve the Crown and the common people. This crusade takes place against a background of pettiness and malice. The political expedience of Tadpole and Taper, the wilful self-indulgence of Marney and Monmouth, the spiritual vacuum of entire communities such as Wodgate, and recurring material poverty: all are tackled by imagination, courage, selflessness and enlightened guidance. Typical of Disraeli's enemies of the nation is the Gladstonian character of Vavasour in *Coningsby*. He is 'the quintessence of order, decency, and industry' who smugly articulates the utilitarian creed that civilisation is 'the progressive development of the faculties of man'. This in contrast to the narrator, Disraeli's surrogate self, who proclaims himself the kind of 'primordial and creative mind' who can 'say to his fellows: Behold! God has given me thought; I have discovered truth, and you shall believe!'

Disraeli's trilogy was imaginative and heroic, but it was also waspishly political. The principal target for his sting was the prime minister. In *Coningsby*, Disraeli criticises Peel's 1834 Tamworth Manifesto, to which he had happily subscribed earlier, as 'an attempt to construct a party without principles'. He reserved his full firepower until *Sybil*. Britain under Peel was in political and social decay. The country was made up of 'two nations' of rich and poor, who knew little of each other. One enjoyed the privileges of power, wealth and prestige; the other lived in squalor, misery and poverty. To create 'one nation' required imagination, a quality Disraeli believed Peel singularly lacked.

Peel appears in *Sybil*, not even disguised, as the 'gentleman in Downing Street'. He is complacent, devious and cynical. To emphasise the point, his secretary is Mr Hoaxem. With two delegations waiting outside to make representations on free trade, Hoaxem gets his instructions. First up would be the farmers. 'Well you know what to say,' says the gentleman in Downing Street. 'Prove to them particularly that my only objective has been to render protection more protective, by making it practical, and divesting it of the surplussage of odium.' 'I see,' says Hoaxem admiringly, 'and what am I to say to the deputation of manufacturers of Mowbray, complaining of the great depression of trade, and the total want of remunerating profits?' 'You must say exactly the reverse,' says the gentleman in Downing Street.

To hammer the point home, Disraeli gives the 'gentleman' a final declaration of cant that incorporates one of Peel's favourite phrases. 'I have no doubt you will get through the business very well, Mr Hoaxem, particularly if you be "frank and explicit",' he says, 'that is the right line to take when you wish to conceal your own mind and to confuse the mind of others.' It was a devastating character assassination, but it was only the beginning. By late 1845, Benjamin Disraeli was intent on destroying Peel.

Gladstone read *Sybil* with enough apprehension to bother writing two pages of notes about it. There was a lofty disdain for the characters spending too much time 'chattering on subjects of which it is impossible that they can know anything'. Yet Gladstone was forced to admit that the political scenes were 'capital'.

And of the barely concealed attack on the prime minister, Gladstone admitted that it brilliantly exposed 'the two-faced effects of the Peel legislation'.

3

Strangers

Colonial Office, 23 January 1846

Gladstone sat in his new department reading with horror the previous night's proceedings in the Commons. A few weeks earlier he had told an old school friend that 'something is in the wind – and something serious'. Now he knew that the Conservative government was in grave trouble. A cabinet minister had already resigned. Many of those who remained sat not in the Commons but in the House of Lords, which left Peel curiously unprotected on the front bench of the lower house. For the incoming colonial secretary the frustration at not being at his chief's side was overwhelming.

Peel had not waited even a year before returning Gladstone to the government after the Maynooth incident. Within the year Gladstone was back, promoted to the Colonial Office. The prime minister had increasingly come to rely on him for advice in all areas of economic and financial policy. His mastery of financial detail was renowned. More importantly, Gladstone's ferocious debating skills and his ability to cast economic argument in moral terms would shore up Peel's position in the fight to come. For the prime minister had set his mind on repealing the Corn Laws. Gladstone's technical facility and his commitment to the cause of reform made him indispensable. Peel had been uncharacteristically demonstrative when offering him a post on 22 December 1845, as if bestowing a benediction. 'Peel was most kind, nay fatherly,' Gladstone wrote in his diary that night: 'we *held* hands instinctively and I could not but reciprocate with emphasis his "God bless you"'. The prodigal son had returned.

But Gladstone's rehabilitation had come at a cost: he lost his parliamentary seat. Tradition until well into the next century demanded that any MP appointed to cabinet should immediately offer himself to his own constituency for re-election. More often than not this mechanism was a formality with the new minister given a clear run by all parties. Things were rarely that simple for Gladstone.

The Duke of Newcastle, who had Gladstone's Newark constituency in his gift, despised Peel and free trade. So strongly did he feel about the matter that he stopped talking to his own son, Gladstone's close friend and cabinet colleague, Lord Lincoln. Over Christmas 1845, Newcastle made it clear to Gladstone that he would use all his influence to prevent his re-election. In the end Gladstone did not even bother contesting the seat. Holding power but no longer an MP, the new minister then began a desperate search for a parliamentary seat. 'Somewhere or other I must woo again as soon as possible,' he wrote in January. Advances were made to North Nottinghamshire, Wigan, Liverpool, Dorchester, Chester, South Lancashire, Oxford City, Scarborough, Aberdeen and Montrose Burghs. None amounted to anything. There was no reason, he complained six months later, why any of them 'should not have had me if they liked it'.

The problem was that Gladstone was not a likeable young man; most constituencies decided he was more trouble than he was worth. He did not find another seat until August 1847 when his old university, Oxford, elected him back to parliament. This absence left Gladstone an anxious spectator during the six brutal months of parliamentary debate in 1846 when the Conservative party was split asunder.

On that fateful night of 23 January 1846, Sir Robert Peel had staked his political future on a policy of free trade. Few would have guessed it from the tone of his address to the House. In the fevered atmosphere of a chamber sensing a defining moment, Peel gave a dull, enervated performance. His tedious statement was short on principle and long on the prices of flax and wool, salt beef and domestic lard. Only at the very end did Peel finally rally himself. Turning to his own MPs, he denounced those who would challenge his authority. 'I see constantly put forth allusions to the power of those men to remove me from office,' he exclaimed. Let them be warned: he would fight. When Peel sat down, his own party received him in dead silence.

Lord John Russell, the Whig leader of the opposition, followed the prime minister. Russell supported repeal and took his cue on this occasion from Peel. He delivered an equally dull statement that concentrated on detail not principle. What had seemed likely to be an explosive debate had turned into a damp squib. The House was bored.

Conservative MPs were disheartened especially since Peel had been let off the hook.

Just as the debate looked set to fizzle out, a Tory backbencher leapt to his feet to begin a ferocious attack on his leader. Disraeli's speech was as colourful and funny as it was wounding. Peel was compared to the admiral of the Ottoman fleet who, on taking command, had steered the Sultan's entire navy into the enemy's port. 'I have an objection to war,' he reported the admiral as saying, amid gales of laughter. Peel was just such a traitor. The prime minister's own supporters had been treated 'with contempt and disdain'. He had shown appalling conceit in coming to the House to say, 'I will rule without respect of party, though I rose by party; and I care not for your judgement, for I look to posterity.' That appeal to posterity was itself fraudulent, because Peel was 'a man who never originates an idea'. Instead he was 'a watcher of the atmosphere, a man who, as he says, takes his observations, and when he finds the wind in a certain quarter, trims to suit it'. In short, 'such a person may be a powerful minister, but he is no more a great statesman than the man who gets up behind a carriage is great whip'.

This brutal attack on Peel finished with a call to arms. 'Do not then, because you see a great personage giving up his opinions – do not cheer him on; do not yield so ready a reward to political tergiversation,' Disraeli insisted. 'Above all, maintain the line of demarcation between the parties; for it is only by maintaining the independence of party that you can maintain the integrity of public men, and the power and influence of Parliament itself.'

With that he sat down. All around him, fellow Tories shouted and waved their order papers in the air. On the front bench, Peel sat stony faced amid the chaos as the cheers went on for several minutes. Before they had subsided, it was obvious to all in the House that the issue of free trade was now set to be a defining issue in British politics.

Back at the Colonial Office, the minister laid down the report of the debate. 'The skies are dark enough,' he grimly observed. Gladstone had just missed his first crucial set-piece engagement with Disraeli.

Protectionism was an issue that divided families and friends. Newcastle, for example, broke off all relations with his Peelite son, Lord Lincoln, and used his local power to unseat him at the next election. The two men were only reconciled years later at the duke's deathbed. Yet for all the controversy the technicalities of the scheme make it difficult to understand from a distance why such passions were aroused. The tariff on wheat was levied under the Corn Laws of 1828, which had introduced a sliding scale of duties. Under this arrangement, wheat was imported almost without duty if the price at home remained above seventy-three shillings a quarter. When that price fell below fifty-four shillings, there was a stiff duty of twenty shillings per quarter. Between those two prices was a sliding scale of duties. It was a fairly practical scheme to balance the needs of farmers with the desire to keep food, especially bread, at a price affordable even by the very poorest.

During the late 1830s a great popular movement had grown up to campaign for the abolition of protection. This was the Anti-Corn Law League. Its most famous leaders were John Bright and Richard Cobden, whose radicalism was matched by natural eloquence and the kind of zeal more usually associated with religious preachers. The power of the organisation lay in its simple aim – the repeal of the Corn Laws – and its ability to project that message across class barriers, especially in urban areas. In general terms, industrialists supported an end to protection because it would lower costs; industrial workers were in favour because it would mean cheaper food. From 1843 onwards a brilliant campaign of political agitation pushed the issue to the top of the national agenda. In Manchester, where campaigning was at its most vigorous, a venue was even built for mass rallies – the Free Trade Hall.

By the time Peel had become prime minister for the second time in 1841 he was fully committed to reform of the Corn Laws. This was part of his mission to modernise the national economic and financial system, which included the reintroduction of income tax in 1842 and the Bank Act of 1844. Given that Peel's own tremendous wealth came from manufacturing, it was no great surprise that he should move to promote manufacturing above agricultural interests. Catastrophe in Ireland reinforced his own inclination for reform. By 1845 the potato blight, which eventually would kill around a million of the eight million population, had begun to manifest itself. Famine would be a human tragedy, but it also had the potential to be a political disaster both in Ireland and with British public opinion. So Peel moved not to reform the Corn Laws but to repeal them. Cheaper food, he hoped, would head off the worst excesses of famine in Ireland.

His Corn Importation Bill was introduced at the beginning of the 1846 parliamentary session. At the core of the proposition was the abolition of all duties on imported corn after February 1849. In the three-year intervening period, tariffs would be phased out. In addition, Peel announced an immediate end to duties on salt and fresh pork, live cattle and all vegetables. Other foodstuffs, such as cheese and butter, were to have reduced levies. Duties were also abolished or reduced on a significant number of manufacturing goods. The landed classes were promised hefty compensation and investment in the rural economy to soften the blow.

Peel thought he had presented a moderate package of reform that offered something to everyone, and balanced the needs of the poor, farmers and manufacturers. He offered the promise of a happier, more stable Britain. 'I have seen the effect of a moderate price of provisions,' he told a friend: 'Improved manufactures – extended employment – buoyant Revenue – decrease of crime – Social Contentment – and I do honestly and sincerely dread the consequences of advanced prices, and a resolute maintenance of the present Corn Laws.'

It was a vision of the future that convinced parliament, but not his own party.

'In the lobby, all the Squires came up to shake hands with me, and thank me for the good service,' Disraeli had written after an earlier debate on the Corn Laws. 'They were so grateful, and well they might be, for they certainly had nothing to say for themselves.'

Most of the 'protectionists' were Tories of this kind determined to defend the landed interest at any cost. A minority had engaged in a critical way with the ideas of Cobden and the Anti-Corn Law League, contesting the free-market theories of Adam Smith and David Ricardo that underpinned them. Free trade, they argued, was flawed by its inability to overcome the central weakness of a manufacturing economy: the propensity to produce beyond the means of consumption. Protection acted as a pressure valve to spread national income and employment by preventing overspecialisation. These protectionists did not dispute the importance of the manufacturing interest to Britain's wealth. They simply wanted to moderate its social consequences and defend Britain against foreign competition. Other protectionists, like Bentinck, simply resented the way in which Peel had treated his party. 'What I cannot bear is being sold,' he pithily observed, a remark that was much repeated by his supporters. For Disraeli, there was little or no principle involved at all. Later he would drop protectionism almost as quickly as he adopted it. His interest in 1845/6 was one of simple ambition. Here was an opportunity to confront a prime minister who would not promote him. Lord Stanley, a future Tory premier, later told

Queen Victoria that 'he did not think Mr Disraeli had ever had a strong feeling, one way or the other, about Protection'.

It was the brilliance of Disraeli's oratory that had established him as the most effective spokesman of the anti-Peelite Conservatives. Throughout 1845 he had undermined Peel's commanding authority in the House by a potent mixture of ridicule and character assassination. Yet for all the power of argument, Disraeli had lacked any real friends in parliament. That changed during the debates on repeal. The unlikely character that emerged to act with him was a Tory MP who in his previous eight years in the House had never even bothered to speak in a debate.

Lord George Bentinck was the second son of the Duke of Portland, but unlike many second sons was a wealthy man. His passion was racing. The owner of one of the most successful stables in the country, he had won the Oaks and been instrumental in rooting out corruption in the sport. It was the ethics of 'playing the game' that led him to make a principled stand against Peel's betrayal of his own party. For eight years Lord George had sat quietly. Now, during the first reading of the Corn Laws bill, he stood to address his fellow MPs for the first time. It was well past midnight, and many of the honourable members were asleep. When they woke to hear Bentinck speak, no doubt some thought they were dreaming. What they heard was a denunciation of Peel's policy, and, in particular, the prime minister's decision to invite Prince Albert to hear the debate, which implied royal approval. The speech was long-winded, including a sentence that ran to several hundred words. A few weeks afterwards he wrote to Disraeli asking for help with his speeches. Disraeli's way with words and Bentinck's pedigree would combine to bring down Peel and create a new political party.

While Disraeli was making new friends, Gladstone did his best to rally support for Peel. He sat prominently in the gallery of the Commons on 27 January as the prime minister opened the debate on the Corn Laws. A few days later, he organised an 'evening party at home attended by all Young England' (with which Disraeli had broken) to 'con[verse] on the Corn and Govt.' Such social gatherings were repeated frequently in the coming months. He began a voluminous correspondence with wavering MPs. He dined with senior Protectionist Tories such as Lord Stanley to prevail upon them to rally behind the leader for the sake of the party. 'Long Corn discussion' became a frequent diary entry. And all the time he wrote detailed letters to his father, who was a passionate supporter of Protection. But his sense of frustration at being away from the thick of the action was palpable. 'A most gracious purpose of God has spared me the most wearing part of the labours that my resumption of office should have brought: the bitter feuds of Parliament,' he wrote in his diary at the end of March, 'but my heart does not answer as it should in lively thankfulness.'

For all Gladstone's agitation at being away from the fight, his attitude towards Peel was not uncritical. Peel was an arrogant man who believed the wisest counsel was his own. Even close supporters were not taken fully into his confidence. 'I [have] not the smallest idea, beyond mere conjecture, of the views and intentions of Sir R. Peel with respect to himself or to his government,' Gladstone complained. 'Only we had been governed in all questions, so far as I knew, by the determination to carry the corn bill and to let no collateral circumstances interfere with that main purpose.' If Peel had taken him into his trust more freely, then Gladstone surely would have convinced him to take the one opportunity he was offered to destroy Disraeli for ever.

This defining moment for Disraeli, when he left his political jugular exposed, came in the midst of his greatest parliamentary triumph to date. He had brilliantly coordinated the Protectionist campaign against repeal, causing maximum discomfort to the prime minister. The most wounding attack he saved for the third reading of the bill on 15 May. He spoke for more than three hours in a speech that combined economic detail with withering personal invective. Whereas the younger Disraeli might have played to the gallery with extravagant gestures, this new incarnation was restrained in manner and elegant in delivery. This made the attack all the more devastating.

Disraeli laid out an extremely detailed argument on why the measure 'would be fatal to our agricultural interests' and 'sap the main energies of our manufacturing prosperity'. He attacked talk of the measure leading to cheaper bread as 'claptrap'. After more than two and three-quarter hours of figures and learned opinions, keeping the House playfully on tenterhooks, Disraeli finally turned his guns on his own leader. Peel had 'humiliated' the country. He had abandoned his own political party, leaving it to be 'annihilated'. He led a government of 'political peddlers that bought their party in the cheapest market and sold us in the dearest'. There was 'no statesman who [had] committed political petty larceny on so great a scale'. The result of Peel's treachery was that 'all confidence in public men is lost'. The common people would never forgive them. Disraeli could only hope that at 'the dark and inevitable hour' to come, the people might remember 'those who, betrayed and deserted, were neither ashamed nor afraid to struggle for the "good old cause" – the cause with which are associated principles the most popular, sentiments the most entirely national, the cause of labour, the cause of the people – the cause of England!'

Disraeli sat down to a thunderous ovation from the Tory back-benches. His disastrous maiden speech must have seemed an eternity away. This was a triumph of the highest order, destined to be celebrated as one of the most famous attacks of parliamentary history. In the midst of success, overconfident and pumped with adrenalin, Disraeli contrived to self-destruct.

Peel had dealt with Disraeli's attacks, Gladstone said, with a kind of 'righteous dullness'. Now finally the prime minister's stentorian manner broke to reveal his anger towards this outrageous attack on his character by a mere backbencher. He told the House that he was not going to trade personal insults with the MP, and then promptly did so. If his whole career had been nothing more than an act of political larceny, Peel inquired, why had Disraeli asked him for a job in the government? Surely this desire 'to unite his fortunes with mine in office [implies] the strongest proof which any public man can give of confidence in the honour and integrity of a Minister of the Crown'.

Disraeli had scored such a hit with his speech that he might easily have ignored the taunt (not least because it was true). Instead he jumped to his feet to protest. He assured the House that 'nothing of the kind' had taken place. To ask for preferment would have been 'totally foreign to my nature'. Certainly if a position had been offered 'I dare say I should have accepted it, [but] with respect to my being a solicitor of office, it is entirely unfounded'.

This was a barefaced lie. Disraeli had begged Peel for office in 1841, telling him that 'to be unrecognised at this moment by you appears to me to be overwhelming' and concluding with a desperate 'appeal to your own heart . . . to save me from an intolerable humiliation'.

Peel had since endured several years of scorn from Disraeli. He had been ridiculed, taunted, branded a deceiver and a cheat, and condemned as the destroyer of a great party. Here now was Peel's chance to exact brutal revenge. As he stood at the despatch box, some MPs thought they saw him finger a piece of paper in his pocket. Was it the letter? Produced and read now, it would reveal Disraeli as a liar driven by an ungentlemanly desire for personal revenge. Lying to the House was a serious transgression – and one from which a member might never recover. Here was Peel's chance to plunge the knife in deep.

And he missed it. Rather than finish off Disraeli, he reverted to good manners. He had not meant to suggest that Disraeli was motivated by disappointment in office. He had merely wondered why, if Disraeli thought him a political reprobate, he had 'intimated to me that he was not unwilling to give me that proof of confidence that would have been implied by the acceptance of office'. On Disraeli's claim never to have solicited office, Peel remained inexplicably silent.

Perhaps Disraeli knew his man well enough to guess that a gentlemanly code would see him through. Doubtless he understood Peel sufficiently well to calculate that producing the letter was simply beneath his dignity. Nevertheless it had been an appalling risk. Though Peel demurred in reading out the letter in parliament he might easily have released it to *The Times* with similarly devastating effect. Gladstone's friend Lord Lincoln, who had walked to the House for the debate with Peel, frustratedly complained that he had seen the letter in the PM's despatch case that morning. Peel's sense of fair play, it seems, had saved Disraeli. If so, it was a lucky escape, but one already typical of this high-wire political artist.

The fact that Peel had pulled his punch did not stop Disraeli from exacting full revenge on this 'Arch-Traitor'. The combination of Peelite loyalists and Whig opposition saw the Corn Importation Bill safely through its third reading with a comfortable majority. Yet only 106 of the 328 Conservatives who voted did so with their leader. The hardcore rebels, led by Disraeli and Bentinck, resolved to bring down the government. Their first opportunity came on the Protection of Life Bill, a measure introduced by Peel with the wearily familiar aim of pacifying Ireland.

A division on the second reading of the bill in the Commons took place on 25 June, the same night that the Corn Importation Bill passed its final stage in parliament. Peel had succeeded in repealing the Corn Laws; now die-hards in the party exacted their revenge. Bentinck, in a speech drafted by Disraeli, charged that Peel had 'insulted the honour of parliament and of the country, and it is now time that atonement should be made to the betrayed'. More than seventy Conservative MPs joined Disraeli and Bentinck in voting against the government and another eighty abstained. It was enough to defeat the bill. The next day, Peel called his ministers to 10 Downing Street to announce his intention to resign. It was the 'shortest cabinet' Gladstone had ever known.

'The Ministry have resigned,' Disraeli crowed triumphantly from the Carlton Club to his wife on 29 June. 'All "Coningsby" and "Young England" the general exclamation here.' Nobody understood this better than Gladstone. 'Dizzy's parliamentary brains' had brought down the government. His performances in the House 'were quite as wonderful as the report makes them'. Disraeli, Gladstone conceded, was a man he had underestimated. During the six months that his new rival had been in the ascendancy, Gladstone had lost both his seat in the Commons and a ministerial position, and was alienated from his own party. Peel, his great mentor, was destroyed. Faced with this catalogue of disappointment a despairing Gladstone considered withdrawing from public life altogether. His world, he forlornly concluded on 7 July, was 'in chaos'.

4

The Game

The Summer Exhibition

On Saturday 4 May 1850, William Gladstone spent a contented afternoon in the East Wing of the National Gallery on Trafalgar Square. He was there to view the Royal Academy's Summer Exhibition. 'There was much to see,' he noted after wandering among the pictures. A few hours later he was back at the Academy to attend a formal dinner. It was typical of Gladstone that he should have bothered to view the exhibition before enjoying the hospitality of the Academy. That evening he joined an eclectic gathering of painters, writers, politicians, judges, bishops and nobility all gossiping and intriguing happily together.

This annual banquet was always a magnificent occasion, not least for a man who enjoyed conversation as much as Gladstone. He would be seated on the 'politicians'' table, which would include his mentor Sir Robert Peel. Yet he had almost declined the invitation. 'It is not as if I had to make any speech there,' he told Catherine, his wife, before setting out, 'still I do not feel quite sure whether I was right in accepting.' Principal among his reservations was the seating plan. For Gladstone had been placed next to Benjamin Disraeli. Worse still, on his other side Sir James Graham had not turned up. So not only was Gladstone sitting next to Disraeli, he would have to talk to him all evening. Perhaps determined to make the best of things, he headed toward the dining room with little expectation of a good night ahead.

Watching him, Disraeli's face revealed nothing. In reality he was no more enthusiastic about the evening ahead than his dinner companion.

For all his brilliance as a raconteur Disraeli often struggled with the gossamer threads of social conversation on these occasions. Catch him on bad form, even at home, and discomforted guests might find themselves barely able to raise a word out of him. All-male gatherings were worst. Perhaps it was the absence of a public school and university education that had left Disraeli unable to master the banter and 'jocks' humour of boys when gathered together. The previous year he had been seated with the writers; now he had joined the politicians. 'R.A.s were puzzled how to place me,' he complained afterwards to his sister Sarah. 'They took me out of the wits . . . and placed me among the statesmen.'

In the event, the evening was a delightful one. Both men, no doubt prepared for the worst, were surprised that the other made such an effort. 'It went off very well,' Disraeli told Sarah, 'Gladstone being particularly agreeable.' Uncannily, in the privacy of his journal, Gladstone similarly recorded the 'dinner at the Royal Academy: there I sat by Disraeli who was very easy and agreeable.' The next day, he reported to his wife: 'Disraeli was very pleasant, has plenty to say, and sails near enough to politics without going too near.' Much of their conversation was about books. Disraeli was particularly charmed by Gladstone's self-effacing admission that he did not have a good memory for passages and 'never could command them'.

Both men left the Academy in good spirits. Disraeli was on his way to a glamorous party given by Katherine Lawrence, the sophisticated, fantastically rich wife of the American Minister in London. Most of those at the Academy dinner were drifting that way. But not Gladstone. Perhaps he told Disraeli that he needed to walk off the effects of the banquet. As Disraeli strolled up Piccadilly to the party, a smile might have formed. The rumours, after all, had already started.

Gladstone instead was heading for Shaftesbury Avenue, on his way to a secret liaison. He had met the woman two nights earlier. This time they went to her rooms at 6 Duke's Court to talk long into the night. She shared her worries about money and providing for her son. 'Poor creature,' Gladstone wrote in his diary afterwards. What else happened Gladstone left unrecorded, but by the following week he was overcome with shame and remorse. 'I did not go to Holy Communion,' he wrote, 'for I have had much wicked negligence to reproach myself with of late as respects particular temptations and although desiring that heavenly food I thought reverence required a longer consideration.'

Many would have been surprised if such a prominent churchman as Gladstone had been conducting an affair. Fewer would have ventured to suggest that he was in the middle of an emotional and sexual crisis. Yet the gossip in London was beginning to gather intensity. Gladstone seemed powerless to stop the rumours or moderate his own behaviour. For the truth was straightforward enough: William Gladstone now habitually spent the late hours in the company of women of the night.

The political turmoil of the mid-1840s was accompanied by personal crisis for Gladstone. His involvement with prostitutes was but the most obvious symptom. By the 1850s his relationship with Catherine was efficient, often affectionate, but not without exasperation. Habitually she conversed in a made-up language – 'Glynnese' (after her maiden name of Glynne) – that Gladstone found irritating. She rarely read books or even newspapers, and could be shockingly uninformed. Catherine attended both church and parliament regularly, but had little interest in discussing either. When apart, the Gladstones wrote to each other most days. These letters were frank, but also contain more than a hint of emotional detachment. William, in a manner stiff even for the times, would sign off 'Ever yours affty, W. E. Gladstone' and scrawl 'Mrs W. E. Gladstone' across the bottom of the letter as if writing to his solicitor. Perhaps it was for treatment of this kind that Catherine in middle age exclaimed to him: 'Oh William dear, if you weren't such a great man you would be a terrible bore!'

Sex was one of many frustrations for the Gladstones. Between 1840 and 1854, Catherine bore William eight children and had at least one miscarriage. Her pregnancies were often very difficult; on at least one occasion she almost died giving birth. The convention of the day was that husbands did not sleep with their wives during pregnancy. Gladstone, between the births of his first and last children, was therefore excluded from the marital bed for prolonged periods in nine out of fourteen years. His late thirties and early forties thus entailed his own 'period of confinement'. The result was implosion.

Crisis revealed itself through a cycle of sexual temptation, sin and reproach. The young Gladstone had been tortured by guilt about his obsession with masturbation. Later he enjoyed a 'long and shameful experience of the snares of sin' after becoming fixated on pornography. This fascination was so overwhelming that in 1845, while in Baden-Baden in Germany, he had drawn up a memorandum of his own sexual depravity.

In painstaking if opaque detail Gladstone listed the ways in which he was open to 'my chief besetting sin'. The resulting self-portrait is of a man in the grip of a mania about sex. The 'channels' through which it came included '1. Thought, 2. Conversation, 3. Hearing, 4. Seeing, 5. Touch, 6. Company'. Temptation was irresistible when he was bored or else found himself confronted by the unfamiliar. He was particularly receptive, he deduced, in times of '1. Idleness, 2. Exhaustion, 3. Absence from usual place, 4. Interruption of usual habits of time, 5. Curiosity of knowledge, 6. Curiosity of sympathy'. The remedies he offered himself to be rid of this fixation included '1. Prayer for blessing on any act about to be done, 2. Realising the presence of the Lord crucified & Enthroned, 3. Immediate pain'.

This last instruction did not fully manifest itself until 1849 when Gladstone began whipping himself. By that stage pornography was the least of his worries. Gladstone's involvement with prostitutes, which he called 'rescue work', had begun innocently enough. He had joined in 1844 an Anglo-Catholic lay brotherhood that met regularly in the Margaret Chapel (later All Saints, Margaret Street). The group was subject to twelve rules, one of which was to engage in 'some regular work of charity'. Gladstone initially met this requirement by working with down-and-outs of both sexes in Soho. By 1849 he had become increasingly preoccupied with the women, particularly those working the streets. He was habitually 'out at all hours' to put himself 'in the way of contact with exciting causes' and tread 'the path of danger'. Over the next five years, Gladstone estimated, he 'conversed indoors or out' with '80 to 90' prostitutes. That time had not 'been purely spent on my part'. He knew well enough that 'though probably in none of these instances have I not spoken good words, yet so bewildered have I been that they constitute the chief burden of soul'.

A number of these women became favourites, particularly during the sexual frenzy that overtook him between 1849 and 1852. In July 1850 he became infatuated with a prostitute called Emma Clifton. He would loiter outside the Argyll Rooms in Great Windmill Street (near Piccadilly Circus) waiting for her. These premises, which housed the most notorious brothel in London, put Gladstone in constant danger of discovery. Yet he persisted night after night. Even when Gladstone left London for the summer, he felt compelled to return to see her. The following year his attentions turned to a P. Lightfoot. Here the risks became even greater, including the reckless step of taking her back to his new house in Carlton Gardens. Later that summer Elizabeth

Collins replaced Miss Lightfoot. A diary entry after an evening with her offers perhaps the most succinct evocation of the conflicted nature of Gladstone's emotions. 'Went with a note to E. C.'s – received (unexpectedly) and remained 2 hours: a strange and humbling scene – returned and ♌.' This was used by Gladstone to signal that he had scourged himself. Rescue work followed by self-mortification had become the pattern of Gladstone's life.

Trawling the streets of London was but the most extreme symptom of a life in disarray. Gladstone had turned forty in 1849. The diary entry for his birthday revealed a man caught in the depths of despair and self-abnegation. 'The retrospect of my inward life is dark,' he wrote. 'These decade birthdays are even greater than the annual ones. How blessed would it be if this should be the point from whence is to spring a lowlier and better life.' The simple truth was that William Gladstone was having a mid-life crisis.

Because Gladstone noted everything so painstakingly in his journal, the link between emotional stress and rescue work is recorded in meticulous detail. Typically for a man of his age, there were painful rites of passage to be endured. Shortly after his birthday he had to watch helplessly the traumatic death of his five-year-old daughter, Jessy, from meningitis. The following year his father died. Sir John Gladstone had been in many ways an austere parent, but he had provided the foundations on which William's career had been built. John's great wealth had provided a fine education, houses to match William's political and social aspirations, and a regular, significant income. To the end, he had been the undisputed head of the Gladstone family.

Between these two personal losses came the death of Gladstone's political mentor. In the summer of 1850 Sir Robert Peel was thrown from his horse while out riding on Constitution Hill and died soon afterwards. There had been a cooling between Gladstone and Peel during the last years. Yet Peel's influence on his young charge had been immense. Peel had offered the model of 'new money' success. During the crisis of 1839–43, Peel had persuaded the younger man not to abandon politics. He steered Gladstone away from theory towards the challenges of economic and fiscal policy, which became the bedrock of the latter's political career. They disagreed about many things, not least religion, but Gladstone recognised that Peel had given him an education in politics offered to few others. He was in every sense Peel's apprentice. Now the pupil-master was gone. On the night of Peel's death, Gladstone was discovered in the House 'unable to speak for tears'.

In the midst of these painful losses, a man must surely turn to his friends for comfort. Yet even here Gladstone found only anguish. In April 1851 his two closest friends, James Hope and Henry Manning, left the Church of England for Rome. It was a devastating shock. Manning later described the distressing scene when he and Gladstone separated in the little chapel off Buckingham Palace Road. Kneeling together for the last time as Anglicans, Manning rose from his seat and said, "I can no longer take the Communion in the Church of England." I rose up, and laying my hand on Mr Gladstone's shoulder, said, "Come." It was the parting of the ways. Mr Gladstone remained; and I went my way.'

'A day of pain! Manning and Hope!' Gladstone wrote on hearing the news formally announced, adding later: 'they were my two props. Their going may be a sign that my work is gone with them.' The conversion of these most intimate friends pushed Gladstone's sexual and emotional crisis to new levels. He had consorted with prostitutes in the months after the deaths of Jessy and Peel. The charitable nature of this rescue work had still been apparent at least to Gladstone himself. Now he recognised that the catastrophe of Hope and Manning had taken his motivations to something entirely different. 'Such terrible blows not only overset and oppress but I fear also demoralise me,' he wrote, 'which tends to show that my trusts are Carnal or the withdrawal of them would not leave such a void.'

Obsession with Elizabeth Collins – 'lovely beyond measure' – followed immediately afterwards. The scourging became more intense and diary entries self-denigrating. Gladstone understood that his meetings with Elizabeth were 'strange, questionable, or more'. Motivations seemed 'deluded'. Actions were 'unlawful'. By August 1851 Gladstone's nerves were shattered. After another meeting with Elizabeth he set down his worst fears. His two closest friends and 'only supports' had been 'wrenched away from me, leaving me lacerated, and I may say barely conscious morally'.

He understood only too well what this could mean. In 1845 he had seen the horror of a Gladstone unleashed when his sister Helen became addicted to laudanum. She was taken for a cure at Baden-Baden. When Gladstone visited her there he found a frenzied drug addict 'held down by force to have leeches put in'. It was this terrifying experience that impelled him to confront his own worst nature in the memorandum on temptation and how to avoid it.

Six years on, Gladstone was clear that he had failed to contain his carnal desires. Now he contemplated whether his own deepest instincts might 'succeed in bringing about my ruin, body and soul'.

Hughenden Manor, New Year 1849

While Gladstone fretted on turning forty, Benjamin Disraeli, five years older, surveyed his life with considerable satisfaction. Seeing in the New Year for the first time in his recently acquired house in Buckinghamshire, Disraeli could reflect on a dream fulfilled: he had at last become an English country gentleman. Disraeli enjoyed a reverence for notions aristocratic. He already understood his own heritage in-terms of an ancient, noble race; now he was adding to that inheritance a stake in the land of his birth.

The acquisition of Hughenden had been an important political as well as social step. No senior Conservative could prosper without a country seat. Yet for all its political resonance, Disraeli's pleasure in Hughenden was genuine. Its history went back to Edward the Confessor, whose wife Edith counted it among her possessions. A mile from High Wycombe, set in seven hundred and fifty acres, the house was a white-stuccoed, three-storey building of simple elegance. The pleasing gardens and lawns faced south, with woods on either side. For more than thirty years this graceful environment would offer a place of rest and escape for Disraeli, surrounded by 'birds, flowers, and running waters'.

While the broad course of Disraeli's life moved in the right direction, troubles lurked. As for Gladstone, there had been the crises of mid-life to confront. Almost exactly a year earlier, his beloved father, Isaac, had died. 'It will be conceded,' Disraeli wrote in a preface to a posthumous edition of *Curiosities of Literature*, 'that in his life and labours, he repaid England for the protection and hospitality which this country accorded to his father a century ago.' Benjamin was his father's sole heir and executor. He inherited a significant sum, but it was as nothing compared to his increasingly alarming debts. At the time of his father's death he owed around £20,000, even though Mary Anne had already paid off debts amounting to £13,000. Desperate for income, Disraeli made the agonising decision to sell off his father's antiquarian library – one of the finest collections in England. Significantly the volumes he kept to remove to Hughenden were mostly on Jewish history.

Six months later Disraeli's debts threatened to destroy his career. Precarious finances should have ruled out the purchase of Hughenden in the first place. On the market for £35,000 the property was simply beyond Disraeli's means. The only way he had been able to buy it was with a loan that by any other name was a gift. It was Disraeli's great friend and parliamentary protector Lord George Bentinck who organised the capital. This was a grand political gesture: by making Disraeli a country gentleman, Bentinck was formalising the association between this brilliant outsider and an ancient noble family. The sale had gone through on 6 September 1848. Two weeks later Bentinck, aged just forty-six, was dead. The Duke of Portland, his father, immediately called in the debt.

A few nervous months of negotiation had followed. Disraeli informed Bentinck's brother, Lord Henry, that he could not afford to repay the debt without selling the property. This would also force him to resign his seat as MP for Buckinghamshire. If the Portlands wanted him to play 'the high game in public life' they must accept that he 'could not do that without being on a rock'. Suddenly confronted with losing him, Henry declared to Disraeli that 'he was resolved I should play the great game'. It was an inspired moment of *noblesse oblige*. In fulfilling his brother's wishes, Henry Bentinck had put at the disposal of the English aristocracy a political and parliamentary genius who understood their interests far better than they did themselves. Disraeli would remain thereafter as master at Hughenden from where the great game would not only be played but also won.

The death of Lord George Bentinck had left Disraeli as the only viable leader of the Conservatives in the House of Commons. 'Disraeli was the only piece upon the board on that side of politics that was above the level of a pawn,' reflected the Duke of Argyll. 'He was like a subaltern in a great battle where every superior officer was killed or wounded.' The problem for this battle-scarred junior officer was that his commander in chief hated him.

Lord Stanley, a former cabinet minister and heir to the Earl of Derby, had emerged in 1846 as the acknowledged leader of the Conservatives (minus the Peelites). Handsome, witty and learned, he had the charisma and pedigree to act with the expectation that his instructions would be followed. For the next two decades, there would be no question of anyone else assuming the overall leadership of the party. He was a magnificent orator. His translation of *The Iliad* was a bestseller. Racing

– not least the 'Derby', which to his frustration he never won – was a passion on which he spent huge sums from his vast wealth. The Stanleys were among England's richest landowners, the 'Kings of Lancashire', where they reigned from Knowsley Hall, not far from Liverpool. Few, if any, Victorian aristocrats (even those senior in rank) enjoyed such a combination of prestige and riches as the Derbys.

The current heir to the title (which he inherited in 1851) had begun his political career as a conventional Whig aristocrat in the reforming government of Lord Grey. He had gradually drifted to the right, serving under Peel as secretary for war and the colonies. He resigned, to be replaced by Gladstone, when Peel finally converted to free trade. His overriding political philosophy combined an aversion to extremism (whether radical or ultra-conservative), contempt for popular politics and a determination that change of any kind should come only slowly.

More than any other anti-Peelite, including Disraeli, Stanley gave legitimacy and authority to the continuing Conservative party. He behaved in politics like the wealthy racehorse owner that he was: unlikely to work up a sweat by riding the horse himself, but very much the man in charge. He could often be charming, and was a master of the pointed jest. (Hearing the riddle posed 'Why is heaven like a bald head?', Stanley declined the usual response that both were shining places where no parting existed, suggesting instead that 'in neither place is a "Whig" in sight'.) Yet whatever his capacity for charm, Stanley rarely bothered to deploy it. He refused to undertake the frequent entertaining that went with political leadership, more often taking pleasure in discomforting his social inferiors. He 'made no pains to soothe irritated vanities', complained Bulwer Lytton. 'He thought he did the party a great favour to lead it at all.'

Lord Stanley directed his party from the House of Lords.* His difficulty was that Disraeli, after the death of Bentinck, had an unanswerable claim to leadership in the Commons – effectively making him Tory second-in-command. Stanley recognised that Disraeli was a man of talent. 'I am doing you a bare justice when I say that as a debater there is no one of our party who can pretend to compete with you,' he wrote at Christmas 1848, 'and the powers of your mind, your large

---

* Throughout the nineteenth century, the leader of a political party could operate from either the House of Commons or the House of Lords. When a party leader was in the Lords, the position of leader of the House of Commons assumed heightened importance. The last prime minister to lead from the Lords was Salisbury (1886–92, 1895–1902).

general information, and the ability you possess to make yourself both heard and felt, must at all times give you a commanding position in the House of Commons, and a commanding influence in the party to which you are attached.' An inevitable 'But' followed immediately afterwards.

That qualification came because Stanley neither liked nor trusted Disraeli. Much antipathy came from a misunderstanding during Disraeli's colourful earlier travels. Disraeli had returned with an eclectic mix from his visit to the Near East in 1831, including an exotic pirate's outfit, Lord Byron's butler and the clap. Among the intimacies that grew up on that trip was a friendship with Stanley's younger brother, Henry. The attraction between the two men was obvious: the snobbish Disraeli recognised an 'in' to one of the most powerful aristocratic families in England; Henry warmed to the cosmopolitan exoticism of this outrageous wit and novelist. They landed at Falmouth and travelled on together to London.

Once in the capital, Henry Stanley did not return to his family home but disappeared. Servants were despatched all over London to find him. Eventually he was run to ground at Effie Bond's, a notorious house of ill repute in St James's where he had taken rooms. Interrogated about how he had ended up in such a place, it emerged that one Benjamin Disraeli had introduced him there. Lord Stanley vowed to have his revenge. Ten years later, when Peel seemed on the verge of appointing Disraeli to government, he told the prime minister, 'if that scoundrel were taken in he would not remain himself'. At the time it had seemed a fatal blow to Disraeli's ambitions.

Now, through a series of frankly astonishing political circumstances, Stanley found this same man as his deputy. Worryingly, his own son Edward, a newly elected MP, seemed increasingly in Disraeli's thrall. And worse still, Disraeli showed no sign of renouncing his natural leadership in the Commons. The letter sent at Christmas 1848 had asked him to accept with 'manliness of character' that he would not lead the party in the lower house. He must 'waive a claim which your talents might authorise you to put forward, and, satisfied with the real eminence of your position, to give generous support to a Leader of abilities inferior to your own'.

Fine, Disraeli replied, but then you lose me. 'I am Disraeli the adventurer,' he told Stanley, 'and I will not acquiesce in a position which will enable the party to make use of me in debate, and then throw me aside.' Eventually a bizarre compromise was agreed that would see

Disraeli installed as one of three co-leaders in the House alongside the nonentities Lord Granby and J. C. Herries. This triumvirate, noted the amused Lord Aberdeen, was rather like the one that ruled France in the 1790s, comprising the inconsequential Sièyes and Ducos and Napoleon Bonaparte.

Stanley remained forever distrustful of Disraeli, never calling him by his first name. But he did come to value him. The Protectionists were in chaos. If they were ever again to form a government, fundamental change was needed. For this Stanley might provide the authority, but it was Disraeli who would supply ideas and strategy. Vital to Disraeli's vision of a new Conservatism was an unexpected source: Gladstone.

The 1847 general election had left the Conservatives in their worst position in a generation. Sir Robert Peel, a man generally admired in the country, was lost. Lord Stanley seemed a minnow in comparison. Few others, including Disraeli, had experience even of junior office. Almost the entire officer class of the Conservative party, including Aberdeen, Graham and Gladstone, had withdrawn into a Peelite clique that refused even to act in broad concert with MPs who had betrayed them.

The reputation of the Tories rested on their standing as the natural party of government. They had governed for almost thirty of the previous forty years. Now consisting mostly of duffers and plodders, the Tories had ceded that advantage to the Whigs. 'I am in despair about the elections,' wrote William Beresford, the party's chief whip. 'The lukewarmness and shiftiness of those I have to deal with is most disheartening.' Lord Palmerston put it more bluntly in 1850 as the hapless Whig government of which he was a member floundered: 'The Cabinet would have been broken up, if its successors were ready. But where are they?'

Disraeli understood only too well where these successors were, and resolved to get them back. On the morning after the death of Robert Peel, Lord Stanley's son, Edward, breakfasted with his mentor. He was astonished at how he found Disraeli. There was very little regret at the fate of Peel, but a genuine excitement at an obvious political opportunity. 'He speculated on the possibility of recovering Graham and Gladstone,' the young MP recorded in his diary. This would be achieved, Disraeli told him, by one audacious act: 'definitively abandoning a protective duty'. The country had spoken decisively in favour of free trade. 'Protection is not only dead but damned,' he explained. The policy needed to be dropped and party wounds healed.

Reconciliation would also require Disraeli's personal sacrifice, but there was only one man to whom he would give way. In February 1851 the Russell government finally collapsed under the weight of its own incompetence. The Queen invited Stanley to form a government. The putative premier called on Disraeli immediately afterwards to discuss a potential cabinet. It was at this meeting, according to Stanley's son, that 'D. expressed his willingness to serve under Gladstone if the latter could be brought over'. Poor Edward was shattered. How could one who 'had borne the burden and heat of the day . . . be set aside to make way for allies who only at that moment ceased to be enemies?' Disraeli insisted that Gladstone must be won over. Lord Stanley understood the point. Just a look to his son was enough. 'Without his having stated a positive opinion in words,' wrote the forlorn young man, 'it is now clear to me that he will not persevere, unless strengthened by the accession of Gladstone.'

Gladstone was out of the country when he received his invitation to see Stanley. He arrived back at Dover before dawn on the morning of 26 February after an appalling crossing of the Channel. As soon as he got back to Carlton Gardens he saw the Duke of Newcastle (his old friend Lord Lincoln). Newcastle pleaded with him not to serve under Stanley. 'Alliance with him would not be safe,' he warned. Yet even to this childhood confidant Gladstone would not reveal his intentions. 'I should have to consider my course carefully,' he told him noncommittally.

Gladstone went immediately to see Stanley who put the offer to him. 'He told me his object was that I should take office with him – *any* office (his being by implication out of the question) subject to the reservation that the Foreign Department was offered to Canning but if he declined it open to me,' recorded Gladstone. The leadership of the House of Commons was not mentioned explicitly, but was clearly enough implied. Gladstone got the message immediately. 'I [will] ask no question and make no remark on these points,' he told Stanley, 'as none of them would constitute a difficulty with me, provided no preliminary obstacle were found to intervene.'

Thus far Disraeli's plan had worked perfectly. Gladstone was surely on the brink of joining a Conservative government. Then Stanley turned away from Disraeli's advice. An astonished Gladstone listened as Stanley outlined his proposals to restore a duty on corn. 'I heard him pretty much in silence, with surprise, but with an intense relief feeling that if he had put Protection in abeyance I might have had a most difficult question to decide, whereas now I had no question at all,' wrote Gladstone afterwards. 'His announcement decided everything.'

The chance at reconciliation evaporated. 'The real question with me is this,' reflected Gladstone: 'why did he waste time in proposing to me to join a Cabinet which was to propose a fixed duty on Corn.' That same night he despondently slipped out alone into London's streets looking for someone to lift his spirits. 'Walked in search of E. Clifton without effect,' he wrote miserably on returning home.

Two days later Edward Stanley called to find Disraeli in similarly low spirits. Disraeli had 'counted on success, and felt the disappointment keenly'. The defeat, he said, was 'decisive'. There seemed little possibility to 'reunite the fragments' of the party. Any Conservative government would be weak and ineffectual.

My career is over, Disraeli told Edward. He would retire from public life, and return to literature 'leaving those who brought [me] and themselves into this trouble to find their own way out'.

5

Thunder and Lightning

T he old duke reclined somnolently on the crimson benches of the chamber with his chin lodged on his chest. He was a small man with a large, square head and a familiar, prominent nose. A striking white winter cape fell over his broad shoulders to fend off the cold. As he dozed, curious onlookers in the public gallery gazed down, taking this opportunity to observe perhaps the most famous man in the world. For this was not just any peer: this was Wellington – victor of Waterloo and vanquisher of Napoleon.

Wellington was now aged eighty-two with less than a year to live. He was stooped, profoundly deaf and prickly with it. Anyone, including a passer-by helping him across Hyde Park Corner, might find himself on the rough end of his tongue.

'My Lord, I have passed a long and not uneventful life,' the starstruck man had told him, 'but never did I hope to reach the day when I might be of some assistance to the greatest man that ever lived.'

'Don't be a damn fool!' the duke replied tartly.

As Wellington slumbered in the Lords, the 14th Earl of Derby (as we must now call Stanley) joined him on the Tory benches. This was an act of fealty and respect. Almost exactly a year earlier Derby's attempt to form a government had ended in failure. Now he had just accepted the Queen's invitation to become prime minister. The new premier had come in person to tell Wellington the names of his cabinet. As Derby read from his list, a look of bewilderment crossed the Iron Duke's face. He craned his neck forward to catch the names. 'Who? Who?' he roared. Even when Derby was able to get the duke to understand, it made little difference. 'Sir John Pakington,' shouted Derby. 'Who is he?' bellowed Wellington again. 'Never heard of him.'

It was an inauspicious beginning to Lord Derby's first administration. History forever afterwards would recall this as the 'Who? Who?' government. Most who served in cabinet were nonentities. Once in office they achieved very little.

Yet the 1852 Conservative government marked a turning point. For it was here that active hostilities began between the two men set to dominate British politics for the next thirty years.

The Conservative opportunity to seize power had come following the acrimonious collapse of Lord John Russell's government. The Whig leader had struggled on throughout 1851 after Derby's earlier failed effort to form an administration. In December he had rashly dismissed Lord Palmerston as foreign secretary for his unauthorised endorsement of Napoleon III's seizure of power in France. Palmerston had promised revenge and on 20 February 1852 he got it. Acting in concert with Disraeli, Palmerston inflicted his famous 'tit for tat' defeat of a Militia Bill. Russell, indignant and humiliated, immediately resigned. Where previously Derby had vacillated, now he resolved to take office. He swiftly accepted the Queen's invitation to form a government, but did not this time consult Gladstone and the Peelites. Instead he turned to Lord Palmerston.

The sixty-seven-year-old Irish peer was among Britain's most colourful politicians. For many years Palmerston had been known primarily as a 'man about town'. A wonderful conversationalist, he was in demand at every salon in London. Women in particular found it hard to resist his charms, winning him the nickname 'Lord Cupid'. He was also a great outdoorsman. Invitations to shooting parties at his estates, Broadlands in Hampshire and Brocket in Hertfordshire, were highly prized. In politics, he served both in Tory and Whig cabinets. His métier was foreign affairs, in which he developed a British policy of divide and rule among the great powers. In addition, he believed that Britain should, by force if necessary, 'extend, as far and as fast as possible, civilization'. It was this last attitude, when added to his personal charisma, that made him such a popular figure in the country.

Disraeli had offered to give way to him as leader of the House of Commons. Palmerston's natural, deep-rooted Tory views seemed an easy fit into a Derby government. He liked Disraeli and Lord Malmesbury, the new foreign secretary. Certainly the ministerial salary would be useful in keeping his debtors at bay. Yet while he flirted with the Conservatives, and enjoyed being chased by them, in the end he declined. Palmerston was an opportunist in many ways, but he had principles, of which free trade was one. He could not in conscience join a protectionist government, although he 'promised forbearance, even support if possible'.

With Palmerston declining, Disraeli was left as the clear second-in-command to Derby and undisputed leader in the Commons. He also, to his own surprise, became Chancellor of the Exchequer. It was not a position he wanted or to which he even felt well suited.

'Don't worry,' Derby noted laconically when Disraeli queried whether he was the right man for the job. 'They give you the figures.'

Disraeli's first action as chancellor was to play for more time. He made a deal with the Whigs, who were regrouping, that in the first instance he would introduce an interim financial statement. There simply was not time to prepare a full budget, which would now come instead at the end of the year. In between time, a general election was held to give greater clarity to the situation in the Commons.

In the event it only confirmed the death of Protectionism. To be sure, the Conservatives made gains of around twenty seats, but they failed to win a majority. There were many conservative-minded MPs outside the party, including the Peelites and Palmerston, who might vote with them on specific issues. On Protection, however, the free traders had an overwhelming majority in the Commons. It was this more than anything that released the Conservatives from any sense of obligation to restore protective duties. The people had spoken clearly; the Conservative party, to Disraeli's huge relief, now listened.

'We built up an opposition on Protection and Protestantism,' Disraeli observed immediately after the election. 'The first the country has positively pissed on.'

When MPs returned to the House of Commons in November 1852 it was to witness the historic opening by the Queen of the new Houses of Parliament. When Victoria had been crowned in Westminster Abbey in 1837, most of the Palace of Westminster had been a blackened shell after a calamitous fire three years earlier. (MPs since had been meeting in the old House of Lords.) From the ruin had emerged a magnificent new Gothic edifice by Charles Barry and Augustus Pugin that proclaimed the power, confidence and majesty of the British nation. Building work had run wildly over time and budget, and MPs complained that there were not enough seats, but the glorious new palace quickly became one of the world's iconic buildings.

Westminster now had a wonderful theatre of state. This was a stage that appealed at a profound level to at least one of its leading actors. In every detail Pugin had been keen to emphasise the drama and splendour of parliament. His flights of romantic fantasy projected images of politics and society as they should be (irrespective of the more earthbound reality). It was this above all that attracted Benjamin Disraeli. Pugin had been sympathetic to Young England, which had embraced medieval revivalism. Like Pugin, Disraeli hated the Reformation, industrialism and utilitarianism. In his novel *Coningsby*, he had included two characters based on Pugin's patrons, Lord Shrewsbury and Ambrose Phillipps de Lisle. The new House, with its ornate celebration of Britain's past, could hardly have been more appealing. Disraeli had his own aura of mystery and fantasy. Now he had a palace of Gothic enchantment in which to weave his magic.

Treasury Front Bench

Disraeli's pale face betrayed nothing. Waiting to move to the despatch box, he sat impassively, arms and outstretched legs crossed, hardly seeming to notice the fevered atmosphere swirling around him. In the ethereal, hissing gaslight he seemed a threatening, hazily sinister figure. Yet beneath the air of menace, Disraeli was seething with emotion. Tonight, 16 December 1852, he recognised as a pivotal moment in his career. He was about to wind up the budget debate. Everyone was predicting a crushing, humiliating loss.

Most on the opposition benches could barely conceal their delight at the chance to plunge the knife deep into one who had himself wielded the dagger with such relish. Few were more eager than the Peelites. 'What goes around comes around' might have been their motto. Finally revenge would be exacted for the political assassination of Sir Robert Peel. 'I fear we are in a great scrape,' Disraeli had told Lord Derby beforehand, 'and I hardly see how the Budget can live in so stormy a sea.'

Only the previous night Disraeli had poured out his fears and insecurities to a most unlikely source. John Bright, the Radical leader, had called at Disraeli's invitation to Grosvenor Gate, Mary Anne's London house. Bright had arrived to find an influenza-ridden chancellor alone, in his dressing gown, frantically working on papers. They talked cursorily about the budget. Then, as the midnight hour approached, Disraeli uncharacteristically let down his defences. He spoke of the hostility he encountered within the cabinet where mediocrities such as Sir John Pakington considered him 'not a gentleman'. Even Lord Derby was undermining his authority by criticising the budget, ironically, as too Peelite. Backbench MPs dismissed his chances of winning round the House because 'Jews make no converts'.

'No man knows what I have struggled against and overcome,' Disraeli told the astonished Bright. 'I have been a Minister, and am now about to be beaten.'

In the Commons chamber MPs crammed into every available space to hear Disraeli speak. While the chancellor sat stealthily in this overwrought environment, the member for Oxford University was engaged in constant commentary and eager banter with those around him. William Gladstone was rarely quiet in the House. Characteristically slouched on the opposition benches, his eyes occasionally darted towards the chancellor. Gladstone disliked the budget. ('I am convinced that Disraeli's is the least Conservative budget I have ever known.') He disliked Disraeli himself even more. He could admire his 'marvellous talent', and his 'brilliant buoyancy', but never 'would I go to him for conviction'. Only weeks earlier, Gladstone had informed Lord Derby that he would never join a Conservative government led in the Commons by Disraeli. Now he prepared himself for an assault, telling his wife, 'I have a long speech fermenting in me and I feel as a loaf might in the oven.'

The means of attack was a denunciation of the budget as an offence to Peelite principles of sound economic management. Such an approach had the dual advantage both of defending Peel's legacy and playing to the majority opinion in the House. The principal criticism came on the question of taxation. Peel had introduced income tax in 1842 as a (supposedly) temporary measure. Disraeli's imaginative new scheme was unacceptable, opponents argued, because it implied that taxation would be maintained for the foreseeable future.

Few doubted that the chancellor had initiated a radical budget, but most did not understand why. Disraeli's aim, suggestive of his later philosophy, was to broaden the party's appeal to include the urban middle class, and even the working class. This meant a fundamental reorganisation of the financial system to create a more integrated, stable equilibrium between competing interests. Farmers and landowners were offered compensation for the abandonment of Protection by a reduction in malt duties, which also appealed to poorer beer drinkers. He then proposed to ease the burden of urban, commercial and industrial interests by differentiating income tax. Those relying on 'earned' (or 'industrious') income would pay at a lower rate than those 'unearned' (or 'spontaneous') incomes. The other main development proposed was an increase in the inhabited house duty in order to pay for greater defence expenditure.

It was this last measure, forced on Disraeli by Derby at the last minute, which undermined the balancing of interests, as it fell mostly on those living in the cities. This made it easy for critics to claim that the government was imposing more taxes on urban interests than on its friends in the countryside. The overall thrust of the budget was in fact completely the opposite. This was an audacious play for the centre ground of British politics, and an early articulation of Disraeli's one-nation Conservatism. Gladstone recognised exactly what it represented – 'a most daring bid for the support of the liberal majority' – and resolved to kill it at birth.

Shortly after ten o'clock the Chancellor of the Exchequer rose to speak. His dark eyes surveyed the phalanx of opposition MPs who, having abused him so violently, were now surprisingly hushed. Into this sudden quiet, as if sensing the occasion, a crash of thunder exploded outside. Bolts of lightning traversed the mid-winter night sky, flashing through the windows and unexpectedly illuminating the Commons chamber. For the next three hours this dramatic phenomenon of nature would provide the special effects as Disraeli fought for his political life.

Amid this commotion Disraeli appeared a study in calm and poise, his only display of emotion a smirk at the corners of his mouth. When he began to speak, each word was articulated slowly and clearly with ringing, almost exaggerated, pronunciation. This was a man in control. Any wound would be intentional, his demeanour announced, not the result of opposition taunts. It was to be, in the words of E. M. Whitty, a watching journalist, 'the speech of wild genius'.

Disraeli began cleverly with an appeal to the Commons rank and file.

'I was not born and bred a Chancellor of the Exchequer,' he told them. 'I am one of the Parliamentary rabble.'

Cheers immediately rang round the chamber. It was a good start. Scornfully Disraeli turned on his critics. In this counterattack, recorded

Whitty, he was 'trampling, crushing, destroying all before him'. Political grandees were subject to particular assault, at first withering, later brutal. His first target was Sir Charles Wood, his predecessor as chancellor. Wood's mathematics tutor at Oxford had described him as the cleverest pupil he had ever had. This did not prevent him from going on to be among the most unpopular chancellors in living memory, a reputation Disraeli was happy to exploit.

Earlier in the debate Wood had called the chancellor 'reckless' on income taxation, apparently forgetting his own proposal to double that tax. 'Talk of recklessness!' Disraeli mocked. 'But then the right honourable gentleman tells *me* – in not very polished, and scarcely in Parliamentary language – that *I* do not know my business.' There were 'some other things' Wood also needed to learn, Disraeli continued, notably 'that scurrility is not sarcasm, and that insolence is not invective'.

At this the Conservative benches erupted with laughter and roars. 'Never did one parliamentary speaker receive a severer infliction at the hands of another,' the admiring Edward Stanley (now Lord Stanley, but retaining his seat in the Commons) told his sister. 'He attacked again and again, demolishing him at each onset, and closing with a personal invective which maddened the House with excitement.' The humiliated Wood, his face as thunderous as the sky outside, could only answer by gesticulating wildly at Disraeli.

Next the chancellor turned to Sir James Graham, another former chancellor and Peel's closest confidant. The frosty and high-minded Graham was an unpopular figure with both sides of the House. He therefore offered Disraeli a soft target. By now the atmosphere in the House had turned to pure poison. Disraeli happily stirred in some more venom. Graham was a man 'whom I will not say I greatly respect', he sneered, 'but rather whom I greatly regard'. If the figures on taxation were wrong, Disraeli noted, perhaps members would be glad to know that the chancellor had been much influenced by Graham's 1834 Superannuation Bill. 'I am perfectly willing not to lay too much stress on the *epea pteroenta* ['winged words'] uttered in the heat of debate,' Disraeli told Graham, 'but when I refer to public records, and when I look at a statute of the realm, then I have a right to suppose that I encounter . . . the better mind of a most able man.'

Earlier noise from the other side of the House had subsided into stunned quiet in the face of Disraeli's invective. 'The Opposition presented a most remarkable appearance, not speaking to each other, pale in the gaslight,' noted Sir William Fraser, a devotee of Disraeli. 'It reminded one of the scenes in the National Convention of the French Revolution.'

They were not quiet for long. As Disraeli wound up his reply, a furious crescendo of abuse swelled on the other side of the chamber, much of it virulently anti-Semitic. Disraeli in response, with finger pointing directly at Wood, swore 'not [to] submit to the degradation of others'.

'Yes! I know what I have to face,' Disraeli shouted to make himself heard in the commotion. 'I face a Coalition.' He paused studiedly to look first at the Whig benches, and then, particularly sourly, at the Peelites seated below the gangway. 'The combination may be successful,' he declared, now raising his right hand into the air. 'But coalitions have always been brief.' His hand came down hard on the despatch box. 'This, too, I know, that England does not love coalitions.' For himself, he would trust to 'the public opinion which governs this country – to that public opinion whose mild and irresistible influence can control even the decrees of Parliaments, and without whose support the most august and ancient institutions are but "the baseless fabric of a vision"'.

Disraeli dropped exhausted but triumphant back to his seat, his countenance uncharacteristically flushed by influenza. It had been a spellbinding speech, lasting almost until 1 a.m., and recognised immediately as a parliamentary masterpiece. 'He fought for his life and never man fought more desperately or with more skill and power,' recorded the approving John Bright in his diary. 'This speech was his greatest speech; he was in earnest; argument, satire, sarcasm, invective, all were abundant and of the first class.' The schoolboy George Trevelyan, later a cabinet minister under Gladstone, recalled that when the chancellor had finished 'a sigh of regret went up from his audience'. Prolonged cheering, stamping of feet, and waving of order papers on the government benches quickly followed. Suddenly a collective gasp rang through the House. Then savage hooting.

William Gladstone, inexplicably, was on his feet.

Traditionally it was the chancellor who had the last word in the budget debate. Now MPs expected to divide and vote. Yet here was Gladstone, trembling with rage at the despatch box, trying to make himself heard. 'Gladstone's look when he rose to reply will never be forgotten by me,' recalled Stanley. 'His usually calm features were livid and distorted with passion, his voice shook, and those who watched him feared an outbreak incompatible with parliamentary rules. So stormy a scene I never witnessed.'

Conservatives across the House screamed insults. The Speaker tried haplessly to calm them, while also telling Gladstone that he was out of order. Gladstone would not give way. Shouting against the cacophony of raised voices opposite, he began a personal assault on Disraeli.

'The speech we have just heard is a speech that ought to meet with a reply, and that, too, on the moment,' he bellowed into the tempest, which matched the electrical storm outside, 'and, Sir, I begin by telling the right hon. gentleman the Chancellor of Exchequer that I postpone for some minutes the inquiry whether he knows his business or not, that there are some things which he, too, has yet to learn.

'And I tell the right hon. gentleman more – that the licence of language he has used – the phrases he has applied to the character of public men (*loud cries of "Hear, Hear"*) – that the phrases he has applied to the characters of public men, whose careers – (*The remainder of the sentence is drowned out in renewed cries from both sides of the House*).'

With arm raised and fist clenched, Gladstone addressed screaming Tory backbenchers directly. 'I will tell them this,' he warned, 'that they must bear to have their Chancellor of the Exchequer, who is so free in his comments upon the conduct of others, brought to the bar of the opinion of this Committee, and tried by those laws of decency and propriety (*Cheers and confusion drown out the remainder of the sentence*).'

There remained only one point of calm in the House. Benjamin Disraeli sat impassive, arms and legs crossed again, as if enjoying a few moments of winter sunshine by the lake in St James's Park. As Gladstone now turned directly towards him, fierce eyes bulging, Disraeli ostentatiously moved forward on his bench. 'Placing his eyeglass, with forefinger of his right hand curved over it, to his right eye, he glanced for about three seconds at the clock over the entrance door,' observed Fraser. 'Replacing the glass in the breast of his coat, he again relapsed into simulated sleep.'

It had been an outrageous and brave attack by Gladstone in the face of ferocious hostility. He had confronted head-on the baying pack of Tory backbenchers to deliver a stinging rebuke to the chancellor. Finally, at four in the morning, a division was taken. The government, supported only by its own MPs, was defeated. 'There was an immense crowd,' wrote Macaulay. 'A deafening cheer when Hayter [the opposition teller] took the right hand of the row of tellers; and a still louder cheer when the numbers were read – 305 to 286.'

The Derby government had been humiliated. Resignation seemed inevitable. Yet all the talk in the lobby was not on the fall of the government, but the dramatic, hostile engagement between Disraeli and Gladstone. Few could believe what they had just witnessed although most understood there and then what it meant.

The Times the following morning captured the moment. 'Like two of Sir Walter Scott's champions, these redoubtable antagonists gathered up all their force for the final struggle, and encountered each other in mid-career,' it announced. 'How, rather equal than like, each side viewed the struggle of their chosen athletes, as if to prognosticate from the war of words the fortunes of two parties so nicely balanced and marshalled in apparently equal array.'

The enemies had engaged.

6

The Chancellor's Old Clothes

Carlton Club, 20 December 1852,
Four Days After the Budget Debate

William Gladstone was alone, comfortably ensconced in the newspaper room of this elegant Tory club. It had been an enjoyable evening. He had dined with two of his closest friends, Sidney Herbert and the Duke of Newcastle. In such intimate company Gladstone had been able to gloat over the events of a few nights earlier. What thrill in politics exceeded that of 'smashing an antagonist across the House of Commons'. And not just any antagonist, but Benjamin Disraeli, instigator of the downfall of Sir Robert Peel. In 1846, Peel had endured humiliating defeat after a savage attack. Now Disraeli had been given a taste of his own bitter medicine. The Derby government had collapsed. Disraeli was out. The Peelite Lord Aberdeen had formed a government the previous day, with Gladstone headed for the Exchequer. Things could hardly have been better.

Except that Gladstone was restless. 'My poor brain was strung very high and has not yet quite got back to calm,' he told his wife Catherine. He had retired to the Carlton for a nightcap to settle himself before returning home. Settled in the newspaper room he began to relax. Without warning the door burst open. There, standing in the doorway, was a pack of two-dozen Conservative MPs. They had been eating and, more pertinently, drinking in one of the private dining rooms. Informed that Gladstone was in the club, this angry mob had hunted him down. Now they abused him. Hurling furious insults, they moved to throw him out of the window, the better to help him on his way to the (Liberal) Reform Club. 'They being heated with wine and the

73

late excitements spoke to him roughly, so that he left the place, fearing insult or actual ill usage,' recorded Lord Stanley, who was elsewhere in the clubhouse. Having fled from the room, Gladstone regained his composure. Certainly he was not about to be bullied into leaving the Carlton. He sought out a sympathetic face, George Forester, who, although a member of the Derby administration, was 'kind and reasonable in a detailed conversation I had with him'. After a suitable period, Gladstone left with his dignity just about intact. Even so, he wrote in his diary on returning home, it had been a night in which 'I found myself in a lion's den'.

Gladstone had been ebullient about 'being able to screw Disraeli up to the mark', and was having difficulty hiding it. 'I've never gone through so exciting a passage of parliamentary life,' he told Catherine. The whole episode had been 'like a fox chase'. Yet the question being asked in political circles was why Gladstone's attack on Disraeli had been so vehement. No one doubted that he felt strongly about the financial measures, with his opposition to differentiated income tax well known, yet he had made no effort to intervene during the debate. Instead, Gladstone had waited, like a mugger, to catch the chancellor by surprise just before the division. In fact, he had even thought 'on the whole' that Disraeli's speech 'was grand: I think the most powerful I ever heard from him'. During the debate he had been riveted by the chancellor, whose 'superlative acting and brilliant oratory from time to time absorbed me and made me quite *forget* that I had to follow him'.

Most in the corridors of Westminster were convinced that Gladstone's rough treatment of Disraeli had been personal. After all, the battering had been a gratuitous act of premeditated parliamentary violence. Everyone had a pet theory as to why it had happened. The attack was petty revenge for the fall of Peel. Blatant anti-Semitism had driven Gladstone. Reunification of the Conservative party was impossible until he had destroyed Disraeli. Perhaps the most plausible reason came from Stanley. He recognised that for Gladstone to assail Disraeli in the way that he did implied the apparently contradictory emotions of contempt and esteem. Gladstone was a political heavyweight who would only condescend to throw his best punches at those who fought in his class. 'Gladstone is reported to have said of Disraeli "No words can express my hatred of that man, or my admiration of his genius",' recorded Stanley. 'These words are probably not genuine: the sentiment they embody, however, is so.' Attacking Disraeli, Stanley appreciated, had been the act of a man who recognised in the chancellor a dangerous yet worthy rival.

There were, perhaps, more intimate reasons for Gladstone's behaviour than Stanley was less likely to guess. The prime minister's son had observed that when Gladstone moved to speak after Disraeli, 'he rose choked with passion, for which he could find no vent in words'. Doubtless he would have been surprised, even if he had heard the rumours, that this fervour was but one symptom of the emotional and sexual crisis through which Gladstone was passing. The weeks leading up to the budget debate had been fraught. He spent many hours wandering the streets looking for acquaintances, old and new. Diary entries illustrate that temptation had run close to intolerable. 'Tonight I saw a most beautiful unnamed girl of 18,' he recorded in Italian, a sure sign of agony. 'I accompanied her to her house, where we lingered over a talk.' Attraction, and the punishment that went with it, was even worse with his regular temptress, Elizabeth Collins. 'Tea with E. Collins and remained till 11 nearly,' read one November diary entry, followed by the pitiful mark to indicate a self-scourging. In the days after his great confrontation with Disraeli, Gladstone was back on the streets. 'I had a conv[ersation] and was guilty of weakness that should be recorded here,' he noted, 'nor can I say mere weakness.'

It is hardly surprising that Gladstone, flushed with political success while dogged by personal remorse, was at a loss as to understand the emotions that coursed through him. 'The year which closes on me closes in one spiritual respect darkly,' he wrote on his birthday, 29 December. 'I have made no progress against the besetting sin often mentioned: and I have often too failed in the courage such as it is needed for self-discipline. Yet I trust my ultimate aim has not been wholly corrupt: and in some other matters my life might seem less unhopeful.'

'Never complain and never explain.' That was the lesson Disraeli had learnt from Lord Lyndhurst at the dinner in 1835 he attended with Gladstone. On 20 December 1852, as leader of the House, he came to the Commons to put that dictum into practice. Rising to announce the government's resignation, Disraeli was spruce in manner and dress. Sir William Fraser noted his 'exceptional air of gaiety'. Disraeli benignly offered MPs his 'grateful thanks for the indulgent, and I may even say the generous, manner in which on both sides I have been supported in attempting to conduct the business of this House'. He hoped that any ill will generated by the passions of heated debate would be quickly forgotten. 'The kind opinion of the members of this House, whatever may be their political opinions, and wherever I may sit,' he told them smoothly, 'will always be to me a most cherished possession, one which I shall always covet and highly appreciate.'

It was an elegant performance that drew praise from across the House. 'Nothing could be better in temper, feeling and judgement than Disraeli's farewell,' Gladstone reported to his wife. Lord John Russell complimented Disraeli on his fortitude and skill. Sir Charles Wood looked forward to renewing cordial relations. Even Sir James Graham grudgingly conceded that he had always admired Disraeli's talents.

Not everyone was able to match Disraeli's poise. In the House of Lords, the prime minister, Lord Derby, delivered a sour resignation speech, which denounced the incoming government in language that even his son found embarrassing. In the Commons, Charles Sibthorp, a Tory backbencher, accused the members opposite of hypocrisy towards Disraeli. 'I have heard that you may knock a man down, and then step forward with courtesy to give him a plaster,' he scornfully observed. 'I neither quite subscribe to the knocking down nor have I any faith in the sincerity of those who offer the plaster.' The new government was nothing more than 'a phalanx of conspirators' armed with 'man-traps and spring-guns'.

Away from the House, Disraeli kept under wraps any resentment he felt at his brutal despatch from office. Even Treasury mandarins, whom many Tories MPs blamed for giving him the wrong figures, were generously praised. He had been popular with his officials. 'I feel grateful for uniform cordiality and courtesy I have experienced from you,' wrote the permanent secretary, Sir Charles Trevelyan, 'and I shall always recollect with pleasure and bear testimony to the direct and obvious regard you have had for public interests in all my intercourse with you.'

Even Disraeli's private correspondence over Christmas and the New Year was free of rancour. Letters to friends make only light reference to the budget debate. His political antennae remained acute, but his preoccupation was the present not the past. The new government would be 'brief, and its end ignominious'. The Tory party, he confidently predicted, would not long be out of office.

For all this poise, Disraeli understood the unspoken third injunction of 'never complain and never explain': move immediately to attack.

★

The alliance that defeated the Derby administration had quickly formed a coalition government under George Gordon, 4th Earl of Aberdeen. He was the first Scottish prime minister since Lord Bute in 1763, and had been the acknowledged leader of the Peelites since the death of Sir Robert in 1850. The life of this clever and handsome sixty-eight-year-old had been dominated by personal loss and suffering. Both his parents died before he was eleven, and his grandfather, the 3rd earl, took no interest in him. His bereavements continued when, aged only twenty-eight, his beloved wife died. She left him with three daughters, all of whom died before reaching twenty-one. Although he wore mourning for his first wife all his life, he married again; this second wife died before he was fifty, followed the next year by their fifteen-year-old daughter. In the face of this escalating tribulation, it was hardly surprising that Aberdeen became an increasingly reclusive character. He liked nothing better than to retreat to Haddo, his Scottish castle, to dwell on his misfortunes. 'I have had enough of the world,' he explained to a friend, 'and would willingly have as little to do with it as is decent.'

This would have mattered less had he not been brilliant. He had been a classmate of Lord Palmerston at Harrow, but offered the mirror image of Pam's belligerent style on the world stage. As foreign minister under Peel, Aberdeen's shrewd and conciliatory diplomacy had produced a relationship with France that turned out to be happier than at almost any other time in the nineteenth century.

Aberdeen's move to No. 10, whatever disdain he professed for office, showed him to be a ruthless political operator. The Whigs and Liberals in the Commons outnumbered the Peelites by ten to one. Yet Aberdeen not only outmanoeuvred Lord John Russell for the premiership, he also secured six out of the thirteen cabinet positions for his own supporters. Gladstone, unsurprisingly, replaced Disraeli at the Treasury. Such a move inevitably entrenched the rivalry with his predecessor.

Gladstone's attack on Disraeli had been vituperative and personal, yet somehow he still expected it to be received as an essentially political act. Getting roughed up in the Carlton Club might have given him some idea of the ill feeling he had provoked, but Disraeli's own graceful performance doubtless reassured him.

'I am very sorry it fell to me to say it,' Gladstone wrote to Catherine. 'God knows I had no wish to give him pain, and really with my deep sense of his gifts, I would only pray they might be well used.'

Whatever Gladstone's sense of Disraeli's gifts, he had never really hidden his deep personal dislike of the man. Until this moment, things had been different for Disraeli. Only a few months before the budget debate, although he and Gladstone often crossed swords in the House, Disraeli felt able to say of him that 'he is the only one of the Peelites between whom and myself there was some inkling of sympathy'. When his young friend Lord Henry Lennox cast his vote at Oxford for Gladstone, and was condemned for it, Disraeli told him to 'utterly disregard what [is] said about your Gladstone vote. I am very glad you gave it.'

All this changed in the early hours of 17 December 1852. Never again would Disraeli think of Gladstone as anything but a personal enemy.

As if to formalise their rivalry, Gladstone and Disraeli now embarked on a bitter correspondence that was to be their lengthiest written exchange. Bizarrely the subject was the furniture in 12 (now No. 11) Downing Street, and the official robe of the Chancellor of the Exchequer.

On the furniture, Gladstone was completely in the wrong. By tradition a new chancellor would take over the furniture at No. 11 at a valuation arranged by his predecessor. Disraeli had been in the job less than a year. He suggested that 'for so trifling an amount' Gladstone simply give in turn the sum he himself had paid earlier that year to Sir Charles Wood. Instead Gladstone refused to pay. Under a new scheme, the Office of Public Works would run the chancellor's house, and so Disraeli should make application to them. Disraeli was furious, and suggested Gladstone consult Sir Charles Wood, 'who is a man of the world'. Gladstone refused to budge. 'I am afraid I did not make it sufficiently clear in my last letter that there was no longer any question as to the furniture to be settled between an outgoing and incoming Chancellor of the Exchequer.' Gladstone never did pay the money.

Disraeli's revenge was far more symbolic. The official robe of office was (like the furniture) handed down from chancellor to chancellor. The current robe had been worn by Pitt the Younger, a hero to Gladstone, and by his great patron, Sir Robert Peel.

During Gladstone's rebuke of Disraeli on 17 December, he had self-consciously wrapped around himself the fiscal mantle of Pitt; now he wanted the real thing. 'I adverted at the close of my letter to the Official Robe, but the allusion to it has perhaps escaped your attention,' Gladstone foolishly added to the note in which he had just refused to pay for the furniture. Disraeli in his reply never even mentioned it. The robe went back to Hughenden where it remains to this day.

During the course of this correspondence, which lasted a month, the venomous relationship between the two antagonists was formalised. Disraeli had signed off his first letter with the polite salutation that he had 'the honour to remain, Dear Sir, your obedient servant'. When Gladstone refused to pay up, Disraeli moved from writing in the first to the third person. 'Mr Disraeli regrets very much, that he is obliged to say that Mr Gladstone's letter . . . is not satisfactory,' he wrote. The coldness implied by the switch was immediately understood.

'Mr W. E. Gladstone has read with regret and pain the note which he received last night from Mr Disraeli,' came back the reply. 'He has endeavoured in this correspondence to observe towards Mr Disraeli the courtesy which was his due, and he is not aware of having said or done anything to justify the tone Mr Disraeli has thought proper to adopt . . . It is unpleasant to Mr W. E. Gladstone to address Mr Disraeli without the usual terms of courtesy; but he abstains from them only because he perceives that they would be unwelcome.'

The correspondence came to an immediate end. Gladstone never advanced Disraeli the money; Gladstone did not get Pitt's robe. By such trivialities were political hostility and personal detestation advanced. Who now could doubt that these two rivals loathed each other?

Chapel Royal, St James's Palace

William Gladstone had come to the royal chapel at St James's on the morning of 17 April to make his Holy Communion. Walking through the park beforehand, his mind had been taken up with 'figures'. Tomorrow he would present his first budget to the House. It was bound to be a controversial occasion. The Tories would be gunning for him after the humiliation of Disraeli the previous year. Even his own government colleagues were uneasy about Gladstone's plans and projections. If things got rough, he must have wondered, would the cabinet abandon him?

With his mind in this frenzied condition, Gladstone found it diffi-cult to concentrate on the service. Until the Psalms. As he sat listening to the sixteenth verse of psalm eighty-six, he suddenly felt over-whelmed by the presence of the Divine. 'That verse of the Psalms was as it were given me,' he wrote afterwards. 'O turn thee then unto me, and have mercy upon me: give Thy strength unto Thy servant, and help the son of Thine handmaid.' These visitations came only rarely – perhaps two or three times before in his life – at 'occasions of very sharp pressure or trial'. That morning, confronting the greatest test of his political life, the 'great storehouse' of the Psalms had 'come home' to him 'as if borne on angel's wings'. He might well be 'wholly unworthy of these consolations': but he was also inspired and fortified by them.

Gladstone's sense of doing God's work was central to his perform-ance as chancellor, but so was his sense of theatre. Huge expectations had been generated by the style and tone of his intervention against Disraeli. His would not be a budget in the conventionally accepted sense. Gladstone would adopt a new Evangelical tone, in which good finance was projected not just as a question of national wealth, but also as integral to the country's spiritual health. At last, Gladstone had found a grand statement to replace *State and Church* as his identifiable political creed.

The financial plan was as innovative and controversial as that of Disraeli only a few months earlier. Disraeli's great novelty had been the proposal for differentiated income tax. The long-term objective of Gladstone's statement was to make opposition to differentiation a first principle of financial orthodoxy and in this he was successful because the principle remained in force for the next forty years. Like Peel before him, Gladstone was determined to avoid taxation becoming a source of conflict between the classes, whether industrialists versus landowners or rich versus poor. Beyond this, by extending income tax until 1860 he laid out a programme for fiscal government that would allow long-term planning to replace short-termism. There was also a Peelite efficiency about the specifics of his proposals: 123 items were exempted from tariffs, and a further 133 others had tariffs reduced.

Gladstone had presented his proposals to a frankly astonished cabinet on 9 April. The Duke of Argyll recalled how Gladstone had entered carrying a battered leather case. His cabinet colleagues sat in a circle round him, while Gladstone balanced the case on his knee. He then spoke from memory and without pause for three hours. 'The order was perfect in its lucidity,' Argyll recalled, 'and the sentences as fault-less as they were absolutely unhesitating. Never for a moment did he overrun himself on any point, or require to hark back in order to recover some forgotten or omitted matter. It was like the flow of some crystal stream – passing sometimes through narrows, and elsewhere spreading itself over the broadest channels, but everywhere glancing with light, full of lively movement. Not one of us could think for a moment of interrupting him, even to ask a question.' Throughout his presentation Gladstone showed scant emotion, 'except just a little of a satisfied smile'. His sign of nerves was the occasional playing with the feather of his quill pen.

When his colleagues recovered their composure, a week of fevered argument followed in which half of them tried to talk him out of the most controversial measure in the budget: the extension of income tax. Gladstone's dilemma had been a straightforward one: everybody hated income tax, but there was little chance of maintaining prudent finance without it. His solution was to renew the tax for seven years and extend it to Ireland, but with a promise that it would expire by law in 1860. This allowed him to maintain the principle of the tax as a temporary expedient while including it in financial planning for the next seven years.

Even after fifteen hours of argument and debate, the cabinet failed to unite around Gladstone. Charles Wood and James Graham, who had taken the lead in condemning Disraeli, were now equally hostile to Gladstone. Even his close friend, Sidney Herbert, voted against him. The prime minister, Lord Aberdeen, took Gladstone to one side during the discussions to warn him: 'You must take care your proposals are not unpopular.' When he finally secured a bare majority in cabinet to proceed, it was at best a reluctant assent.

A chancellor, Gladstone later advised, should 'keep his own counsel and let the cabinet as a whole not know his plans till his mind was made up in the main, and the time close at hand'. The 1853 budget was the first time he had put this into action. Even so it was a high-risk strategy for a new chancellor. Despite the religious experience at St James's, Gladstone was a bundle of nervous energy before presenting the budget to the Commons. 'It was said that for three nights before this display, he was unable to sleep from excitement,' wrote Lord Stanley. It was an anticipation shared by most MPs as they gathered in the House on 18 April.

Gladstone moved towards the despatch box to address a packed chamber at a quarter to five. Opposite, he noted, 'Disraeli was on the watch'. Gladstone resolved that the occasion called 'for more than the ordinary degree of confidence: one that it would be almost hopeless to attempt with less – with an ex-finance minister who is also Leader of the Opposition, and who unlike other leaders of opposition stimulates and spurs faction instead of endeavouring to keep it within bounds.' Disraeli, for his part, lounged with feigned disinterest, displaying nothing more than a mordant smile. Before the debate, however, he had spared no effort in marshalling his forces. 'If our men are true, we must win, and triumphantly,' he supposed. 'Every sinew must be strained.'

For the next four and three-quarter hours Disraeli watched in muted horror as Gladstone transfigured himself into the economic conscience of the nation, and inextricably linked good finance with moral purpose. 'The first principles of taxation,' he declared, were 'the first principles on which men are united in a civilized society.' To appreciate fully the tax on income, 'you must consider what it has done for you, in times of national peril and emergency; you must consider what . . . it may do for you again, if it please God that those times shall return'.

Gladstone claimed as authority the inheritance of Pitt and Peel. Disraeli may have denied him their actual chancellor's robe, but could do nothing to stop Gladstone wrapping himself tightly in their legacy. Pitt – 'that great man, possessed with this great idea' – had been the first to recognise income tax as a 'colossal engine of finance' during the Napoleonic Wars. Income tax had been 'the defence, and the salvation of the country' in a time of 'havoc, war and bloodshed'. Peel had reintroduced the tax in 1843 as an instrument of 'effective reform of your commercial and fiscal system', which was the basis of Britain's current prosperity. 'We may look back upon it with some satisfaction,' he declaimed, 'and may console ourselves for the annoyances it may have entailed by the recollection, that it has been the means of achieving a great good immediately to England, and ultimately to mankind.'

Income tax was 'an engine of gigantic power for great national purposes'. Gladstone urged MPs to address the issue with earnestness. 'One thing I hope this House will never do,' he lectured, 'and that is nibble at this great public question.'

'You must be bold, you must be intelligible, you must be decisive,' Gladstone demanded.

The House agreed. When Gladstone sat down after almost five hours of powerful, confident oratory it was to a boisterous reception of cheering and waving of order papers. Contemporaries agreed immediately that they had witnessed one of the greatest parliamentary speeches in living memory, surpassing that of Disraeli the previous December. Lord Aberdeen thought 'the display of power was wonderful'. Lord John Russell drew parallels with 'Mr Pitt, in the days of glory'.

Prince Albert, after reading an account of the debate, wrote to Gladstone, '[I] should certainly have cheered had I a seat in the House.' Even Lord Stanley thought it 'an extraordinary effort of rhetorical skill'. It was Charles Greville who recognised the real significance of what Gladstone had achieved. The budget, he wrote in his diary, 'has raised Gladstone to a great political elevation, and what is of far greater consequence than the measure itself, has given the Country assurance of a *man* equal to great political necessities and fit to lead parties and direct Governments.'

Disraeli knew it. Immediately after Gladstone's speech 'the general feeling on our side was opposed to any attempt at a contest'. He was able to chip away at the edges of the budget, and had some success in undermining, to the tune of around £25 million, a conversion operation intended to reduce the national debt. On the important measures of the budget, and Gladstone's new status as a commanding chancellor, he made no impact whatsoever. 'I am voiceless,' he wrote to Lord Derby a week later. He meant it literally, but it might just as well have been figurative.

By early May, with the budget and the future of the coalition government secure, Disraeli slumped into depression. Dining alone with him, Stanley found Disraeli bored with politics, and talking of a return to literature. 'He talked of retiring from affairs, of writing an epic poem, and a life of Christ from the national point of view.'

'Mere talk, but characteristic,' Stanley concluded. Gladstone's triumph, following on from his annihilation of the 1852 budget, had raised the important question: was Disraeli a rival worthy of the name?

7

The Handshake

Leicester Square, London, 11 May 1853

William Gladstone was on his way home after a late night visit to the opera. He had spent the day at the House of Commons before going on to a performance of Donizetti's *Lucrezia Borgia*. Now, in the early hours of that morning, he decided to take a stroll around his usual haunts before returning to the chancellor's residence in Downing Street. There were many prostitutes about, and Gladstone quickly fell into conversation with one in Panton Street. She was not one of his 'regulars'. First she tried to entice him, then simply to get money from him.

As the two chatted, Gladstone was suddenly aware of a man at his side. He was young, with a Scottish accent. He immediately announced himself to be a supporter, but that he was shocked to find Gladstone consorting with prostitutes. If Gladstone did not immediately promise to find him a job in government service, the man continued, he would expose him to the *Morning Herald* as a whoremonger.

Gladstone was appalled. He angrily denounced the man, an unemployed Scot called Wilson, in the strongest terms. Grabbing the girl by the arm, he marched her off towards her lodgings in Soho. Wilson followed. His threats became louder and more vociferous. After leaving the woman in King Street, Gladstone moved off quickly, but could not shake Wilson. The situation was becoming embarrassing.

So often in politics it is not the indiscretion but its cover-up that harms a reputation. Gladstone understood this. After warning Wilson a final time, Gladstone searched for a policeman. Finally he came across PC Joy in Sackville Street. The pair were taken to Vine Street police station, where the abject Wilson, now in tears, was booked. Two days later a magistrate sent him for trial at the Old Bailey for blackmail, following a personal deposition by Gladstone.

'These talkings of mine are certainly not within the rules of worldly prudence,' he wrote on returning home from the police station. 'I am not sure that Christian prudence sanctions them for such a one as me: but my aim and intention did not warrant the charge wh[ich] doubtless has been sent to teach me wisdom and which I therefore welcome.' In order to try and find another outlet for his restless energy, that very morning Gladstone took up riding again in Hyde Park. He maintained the habit for two years, but the visits to the streets around Soho were quickly resumed.

Wilson's trial, which took place the following month, brought Gladstone a great deal of unwelcome publicity. He sat silently throughout the proceedings, but had to endure a performance by his own counsel that did as much damage as good. On prostitutes, the hapless barrister referred to his client's 'benevolence, and particularly in reference to this unfortunate class' as being 'well known to all who had the honour of his society'. Those who did not have the honour of his society, however, were simply astonished at the revelations.

Wilson was sentenced to twelve months hard labour (although Gladstone quickly persuaded the home secretary, Palmerston, to let him off after just two months). Yet the public airing of the chancellor's nocturnal habits came close to a major scandal. The incident 'created for the moment great surprise, curiosity, and interest', observed Charles Greville. 'It is a very strange affair, and has not yet been satisfactorily explained.' Even Gladstone had to admit there was 'a *prima facie* case against me'.

Perhaps even more embarrassing than the snide whispers were the efforts of those trying to help. After the initial incident was reported in *The Times*, a flurry of correspondents wrote to the Letters Page to defend Gladstone. Of these the most damaging was one from 'J.S.' of the Temple. He recounted how the previous year he had seen two prostitutes rescued from the clutches of an elderly man by another passer-by. The second man had given the women money and put them in a cab. Furthermore, J.S. knew that this Good Samaritan had been none other than Gladstone, who had subsequently become a 'kind and disinterested' friend to these unfortunate women. This incident reflected 'the highest honour upon Mr Gladstone', J.S. informed readers. He was happy to put this story into the public domain 'to show how Mr Gladstone acted in an analogous case with which I am acquainted, and to suggest, as a fair inference from that, that his motives were equally pure and honourable in the case now reported'.

From this time onwards, Gladstone's reputation would be subject to wounding attacks, such as that of Lord Clarendon to the Duchess of Manchester on 'our Jesuit' out and about on his 'benevolent nocturnal rambles'. Despite a certain malicious amusement in society circles, however, Gladstone's standing as a public man remained relatively unaffected by those night-time habits. Greville remarked that early interest had 'almost entirely passed away already, not having been taken up politically, and there being a general disposition to believe his story and to give him credit for having no improper motive or purpose'. Extraordinarily Gladstone's enemies did not try to ensnare him further. Gladstone's diary for the last week of June, immediately following the trial, records seven 'rescue' missions to prostitutes. 'Not all right with me,' he recorded forlornly after a meeting with his long-time temptress, Elizabeth Collins. Yet no further stories appeared in the papers. No reporters or grasping blackmailers seemed to be following him. While Gladstone's behaviour cried out for exposure, even his enemies held back from destroying him.

Greville thought that it was 'creditable in these days of political rancour and bitterness that no malignant attempt has been made to vilify him by his opponents or by the hostile part of the press'.

This was all the more surprising, because the most virulent anti-government newspaper, the *Press*, was under the direct control of one who might have been expected to choose this moment to exact revenge.

After losing office in 1852, Disraeli had been particularly concerned at how little support the Conservative government had been given in the newspapers. *The Times*, with its dominant circulation of forty thousand, was hostile to the party, although not to Disraeli personally. Of the other influential papers, none was sympathetic to the kind of progressive Conservatism espoused by Disraeli. The Peelites had the *Morning Chronicle*. The *Globe* supported Palmerston. The *Telegraph* and *Daily News* backed the Liberals. Those papers that were broadly conservative in outlook either were, like the *Standard*, supportive of Palmerston, or, like the *Morning Herald*, so vehemently reactionary as to be more hindrance than help.

In May 1853, Disraeli and his wealthy friends, including Stanley, set up a weekly journal, published on Saturdays, called the *Press*. It was both a newspaper and a review. Disraeli contributed to most of the early editions, writing many of the leading articles. This was clandestine, although most people guessed that he was writing for the paper. To put readers off the scent, Disraeli often criticised himself. The editor was instructed to destroy all copy. In fact, many even attributed articles to his pen that were written by others. Disraeli was widely believed to have written the letters 'to the Whigs, by Manilius', although in reality these were the work of his friend Bulwer Lytton.

The paper was contemptuous towards the coalition and its principal. 'His temper, naturally morose, has become licentiously peevish,' Disraeli lampooned the prime minister. 'Crossed in his Cabinet, he insults the House of Lords, and plagues the most eminent of his colleagues with the crabbed malice of a maundering witch.' Who could doubt, he asked, that Lord Aberdeen was only 'qualified to be the Minister of a second-rate German state'.

Gladstone, the 'Hannibal of the Exchequer', came in for hostile criticism, much of it sarcastic in tone. Gladstone, wrote Manilius, 'styled himself "a Conservative", pathetically expressing his regret for the rupture of ancient ties and his hope for some future reunion. Amiable regret! Honourable hope! Reminding us of those inhabitants of the South Sea Islands who never devour their enemies – that would be paying them too great a compliment: they eat up only their own friends and relations, with an appetite proportioned to the love that they bear to them.'

Yet for all this invective against Gladstone, much of it deeply personal, there was no attempt to exploit the chancellor's difficulties at the Old Bailey. A clue to explaining why Disraeli might have declined to hit such an easy target came just days before Gladstone encountered Mr Wilson from Scotland. 'Why is the country governed neither by the Liberal nor by the Conservative party?' Disraeli (anonymously) asked his readers. The reason, he suggested, was obvious: 'From personal and petty causes only. The Chancellor of the Exchequer, professing high Conservative opinions, will not, from personal feeling, combine with the leader of the Conservative party in the House of Commons.'

Disraeli did not want to add to that 'personal feeling'. This was not because he wanted Gladstone's friendship. He continued to loathe him. But he still believed that the best hope of a strong Conservative government, with himself featuring prominently, had to include

Gladstone. He thought the coalition would not last a year. They were, after all, just 'a motley crew of statesmen' who survived by 'veiling their mutual aversion with sinister frankness and affected cordiality'.

In fact, they would hang on for almost two years. Disraeli had to wait until 1855 for another bid for power.

House of Lords, 1 February 1855

Lord Aberdeen reclined on the crimson front bench, a study in brooding melancholy. Only days before his government had fallen. Now he had to decide how to play his exit. His dark mood could hardly have been in more contrast to the opulence of his surroundings. The Lords chamber was the masterpiece of the new Houses of Parliament. The ribbed wooden ceiling shimmered with gilded carvings, pierced inscriptions and painted panels. More colours came from the magnificent stained-glass windows and brass railings. At the heart of the chamber was the stunning throne and canopy, based on the fourteenth-century Coronation Chair in Westminster Abbey. Everything here exuded power, reverence and wealth. This was not a place in which failure, even noble failure, sat easily.

Observing the scene from the bar of the House was a stern, soberly dressed figure, whose lank, black hair gave him a baleful, ecclesiastical air. William Gladstone looked deeply concerned about what Aberdeen might say. Only hours before the two men had walked to Parliament together. Gladstone had begged Aberdeen to play it safe in his speech, 'entreating him not to say anything that would make it impracticable for him to resume the Govt'. Aberdeen's coalition might have collapsed, but the frantic attempts by others to form an alternative administration were by no means sure to succeed. Hold your fire, Gladstone told him, and 'it might make it quite practicable for Lord Aberdeen's Government to continue in office with such changes, under him, as might appear desirable'.

Aberdeen was 'the man in public life of all others whom I have *loved*', but Gladstone's appreciation of the man gave him every reason to think the bruising experience as premier would send the morose earl scuttling back to Haddo, leaving the Peelites abandoned and leaderless. Aberdeen's political misfortune, like that of Asquith sixty years later, had been to find his masterly peacetime leadership skills unequal to the task of fighting a war.

The Crimean War had begun in February 1854, yet another chapter in the Eastern Question saga that would dominate nineteenth-century European politics, not least for Gladstone and Disraeli. In 1852, the newly revitalised France, under the leadership of Emperor Napoleon III, had battered Turkey into ceding control of the Holy Places in Bethlehem and Jerusalem. This had infuriated the Russians, who recognised it as an attempt to upset the balance of power in the Near East. The following year, they invaded the Turkish province of Romania. After Turkey retaliated with a declaration of war in October, Russia destroyed the Turkish fleet, and looked set for a full-scale invasion. To stop this major Russian advance into Europe, Britain and France declared that they would support Turkey, if necessary by arms.

Public enthusiasm for the war had been intense, with much discussion of taming the vicious Russian bear. That zeal and expectation quickly turned to disenchantment. Britain and France took most of 1854 to make up their minds where to attack. The eventual autumn offensive was inconclusive, not withstanding the audacious charge of the Light Brigade at Balaklava. By the end of the year, despatches by William Russell, the first modern war reporter, in *The Times* called attention to military incompetence and the sufferings of ordinary soldiers. Popular opinion had turned on Aberdeen, who seemed incapable of ideas or vigour. Lord John Russell resigned from the cabinet in protest in early January 1855, and was followed by Gladstone's friend Newcastle. On 29 January, the government was thrashed in the House of Commons on a Radical motion to establish a committee of inquiry into the conduct of the war. This was the end for the Aberdeen coalition. 'The problem for the nation is no small one,' Gladstone had written the following day.

Watching Aberdeen in the House of Lords, Gladstone reflected that the immediate problem was who would lead the new government. There were at least five candidates for the premiership: Aberdeen himself, Derby, Lord Lansdowne, Russell and Palmerston. Each would have to put together a reasonably broad coalition; none could govern without Gladstone. His greatest hope was that Aberdeen might somehow emerge at the head of a new coalition.

Relief swept over Gladstone as he listened to Aberdeen's temperate speech. 'His words in the H of L,' he noted afterwards, 'by no means closed up the future.' Gladstone moved to leave as soon as Aberdeen returned to his seat. What confronted him sent a sudden flash of emotion through his nervous system. There standing in the shadows by the exit was Disraeli, looking on malevolently. Their eyes met, while all others looked on fascinated. Then something quite unexpected happened. 'Put out my hand which was very kindly accepted,' recorded Gladstone. No sooner had the two men shaken than the Westminster rumour mill buzzed into action. Surely, observers conjectured, this unlikely exchange of pleasantries between hostile rivals could mean only one thing: that Gladstone and Disraeli were about to join each other in cabinet.

Only the previous day the Queen had invited Lord Derby to form an administration. Derby had always displayed a certain aristocratic diffidence about power, but at no time was that impassiveness more apparent than now. Instead of simply kissing hands there and then, Derby asked the Queen if he might take a day or so to sound out potential cabinet members. This was a wartime situation, he explained, which called for a government of all the talents. Viscount Palmerston, in particular, with his widespread support in the country, had to be brought on board. And so did Gladstone.

The day had been one of bitter weather. As Lord Derby's carriage struggled through a blizzard, the horses slipping and skating on the icy Mall, news of his mission raced ahead to Westminster and St James's. 'I found the clubs crowded,' reported his son, Lord Stanley, in the thick of the intrigue and gossip. What he found was a great deal of hostility, particularly about Gladstone. He reported back to Derby, who knew that including Gladstone had an 'imminent risk of great disaster, for such is the intensity of feeling among the best of my supporters against him'.

Those 'supporters against him' did not include Disraeli. Most Conservatives believed that it would be impossible to accommodate Disraeli, Gladstone and Palmerston in cabinet together. Disraeli would have to forgo the leadership of the House to Palmerston. Surely he could not also give the Exchequer to his arch-rival. While Derby had been with the Queen, Tory MPs were already predicting failure on this question alone. Lord Henry Lennox told Stanley that 'the project of fusion had fallen through: that Gladstone insisted on retaining the Exchequer, which Disraeli could not with honour or consistency surrender, as they had been so directly and personally opposed on questions of finance: that both parties meant to [and] would stand firm, and he could see no possibility of a compromise'. Disraeli, in fact, had already compromised, telling Derby that he was 'sanguine' about giving way to Gladstone. It was a personal risk worth taking if it prised the Peelites away from the Whigs and back into the Conservative fold.

Derby had seen Palmerston at home straight from the Palace to offer him the leadership of the House. He also informed Palmerston that Gladstone and his Peelite colleague, Sidney Herbert, would both be offered seats in cabinet. It had seemed to go well, with Derby leaving in confident mood. 'Lord Palmerston,' Disraeli boldly reported later that afternoon, 'has agreed to act under him on certain conditions (as regards his colleagues) difficult to comply with, but I think not insuperable.' This was a crucial underestimation of Palmerston's own designs on the premiership. By nine o'clock that evening, the viscount had written to Derby declining to serve under him.

Three hours after Palmerston's letter arrived at Derby's, another came. Gladstone, too, was refusing to serve, but the tone of the letter was less definite than that of Palmerston. Gladstone had been much concerned that he should not be seen to return to the Conservative party as an individual. If he were to join the cabinet, it could only be en bloc with his fellow Peelites, Sidney Herbert and James Graham. Gladstone had been appalled at the treatment of Aberdeen by the Whigs, particularly Russell. He was distrustful of Palmerston. Events of recent days, he recalled later, had 'produced in me a political reaction favourable to Conservative reunion, provided that reunion were a reunion of a body with a body: for I never at any time contemplated replacing myself as an individual in the Conservative ranks'.

Gladstone in private was clear about why he would not return alone to the party. 'A strong sentiment of revulsion from Disraeli personally, a sentiment quite distinct from that of dislike, was alone sufficient to deter me absolutely from a merely personal and separate reunion,' he explained. He expected Derby to make him another offer, which would satisfy his conscience by including Graham. When it did not come, he was thunderstruck. There was 'no separate offer to the Peelites,' Gladstone wrote years later. Instead Derby no sooner received Gladstone's answer than he wrote to the Queen to inform her that he had been unable to form a government. 'I think that Lord Derby's error in not forming an administration was palpable and even gross,' recalled Gladstone. There had never been 'so fine an opportunity as this' to reunite the party; 'but he missed it'.

Gladstone thought his belief that Derby had acted in error was also 'the opinion of Disraeli'. He was right. Derby wrote to the Queen without even consulting his second-in-command. When he called at Grosvenor Gate the next morning, the letter already on its way to Windsor, Disraeli was appalled. 'Our chief has again bolted!' he fumed afterwards. He disconsolately fought his way through the bad weather, as foul as his temper, to the Commons. There he met Stanley. 'He appeared in low spirits,' observed Derby's son. Lord Malmesbury later found Disraeli 'in a state of disgust beyond all control; he told me he had spoken his mind to Lord Derby, and told him some very disagreeable truths'.

It was in this mood that Disraeli had slunk into the House of Lords to hear Derby and Aberdeen explain themselves. There ahead of him was Gladstone. The proffered hand had been a surprise, but he had accepted it. Today had been that most rare of occasions: a day when the two men had been in agreement. They might have worked together, if not happily then to mutual advantage. Each had taken significant steps to moderate their public hostility. Both blamed Derby for the current situation, which suited neither of them. All in all, it had been a most unsatisfactory twenty-four hours.

Westminster in the next few days stumbled into a Dickensian farce. Only two years earlier, the author of *Bleak House* had caustically taken apart the state of politics. 'England has been in a dreadful state for some weeks,' he wrote. 'Lord Coodle would go out. Sir Thomas Doodle wouldn't come in, and there being nobody in Great Britain (to speak of) except Coodle and Doodle, there has been no government. [. . .] Still England has been some weeks in the dismal strait of having no pilot (as was well observed by Sir Leicester Dedlock) to weather the storm; and the marvellous part of the matter is, that England has not appeared to care very much about it.'

On this occasion, however, England seemed to care very much who should 'come in', and it was certainly none of the Doodles or Coodles that were currently on offer. The people's choice was Lord Palmerston. 'Whatever the ignorant public might think,' Derby told the Queen, 'Lord Palmerston [is] totally unfit for the task.' Not only was he 'very deaf as well as very blind', it was 'evident that his day had gone by'. Politicians of all sides spent the next few days exploring every avenue to avoid the inevitable formation of a Palmerston ministry. After Derby's failure, the amiable Lord Lansdowne tried to put together a coalition of Whigs and Peelites. Gladstone refused to serve on the grounds that such an administration should be led by Aberdeen.

Lansdowne withdrew. Next up popped Lord John Russell. His rank disloyalty to Aberdeen weeks earlier was cause enough for the Peelites to scupper his hopes. Russell was so nervous when he saw Gladstone that 'his hat was shaking in his hand'.

Finally, on the 4 February 1855, Palmerston came to see Gladstone to tell him that there was 'no other government in view'. He wanted Gladstone to join him, but would kiss hands anyway. After an initial refusal, Aberdeen intervened to insist that there must be Peelites in the cabinet in order to fight for his legacy. 'We were like the light cavalry at Balaklava,' lamented Gladstone before accepting; 'we saw our doom'.

Both Gladstone and Disraeli believed Palmerston would be a disastrous prime minister. Disraeli in the past had shown a soft spot for Palmerston. He was another adventurer in politics who, like Disraeli, was out of kilter with the overserious Peel or Gladstone. He would later return to this admiration, but for the moment, at the height of his disappointment, he was splenetic. 'He is really an impostor,' Disraeli spat contemptuously, 'utterly exhausted, and, at very best, ginger beer and not champagne, and now an old painted Pantaloon, very deaf, very blind, and with false teeth, which would fall out of his mouth when speaking, if he did not hesitate and halt so in his talk.' It was not a generous portrait. A Palmerston government, he believed, would not last long. 'He is a name, which the country resolves to associate with energy, wisdom, and eloquence, and will until he has tried and failed.'

But Disraeli believed the real failure was Lord Derby's. There had been an opportunity to reunite the Conservative party in a strong government. That chance had been cast aside, not least because Derby's appetite for power was so wanting. 'We were afraid and incompetent,' he wrote morosely to his wife. Such a magnificent opportunity might not come again. 'Disraeli complained to me bitterly that we had lost our opportunity,' recorded Stanley, 'he saw no prospect for the future; this failure was final.'

Gladstone was scarcely any happier. Even on entering the government, he complained that 'P. is not fit for the duties of the office of Prime Minister'. This lack of enthusiasm for the new first minister went beyond concerns about his health. Gladstone had a similar protean dislike of Palmerston to that which poisoned his relationship with Disraeli. He detested the new prime minister's loose morals, bombastic nature and obvious enjoyment of life. Worse, Palmerston proclaimed that he was the heir to George Canning, a title to which Gladstone himself aspired. At least he could console himself, like Disraeli, that 'a Palmerston government, with Derby and J. Russell aloof, has no prospect of stability'.

They were both wrong. Palmerston turned out after all to be more champagne than ginger beer. He was set to dominate British politics for the next ten years while Gladstone and Disraeli, like new wines, were laid down for the future.

8

The Letters

Willliam Gladstone was at his desk in the North Room of his Welsh castle. Every available space around him was filled. The shelves of the library groaned under the weight of too many books in too small a space. China plates and alabaster busts were crammed on to the mantels and tables. With documents piled high on the desk, Gladstone's study was getting out of hand. If there was something he could not abide, it was disorder. Matters were being made worse by the removal of his father's books from the estate in Scotland to Hawarden. Five thousand extra volumes to catalogue and house. His thoughts drifted to extending the workroom and library. Soon this plan would become 'The Temple of Peace' – Gladstone's refuge for forty years and home to the 32,000 books that he would accumulate during his lifetime.

Thoughts of a bigger library were temporarily put to one side on the morning of 7 July 1855. Gladstone had spent the week at Hawarden working at his papers, or walking and riding in the grounds. He had simply grown tired of London and the House of Commons. The capital was too hot, Palmerston was dominant, and the Peelites in disarray about the Roebuck Report, which had humiliated Lord Aberdeen on the Crimean War. Palmerston's acquiescence in allowing this inquiry had led to Gladstone's resignation from the cabinet. On 8 February, five Peelites had been sworn in as cabinet ministers at Windsor; on 21 February, Gladstone, Graham and Herbert resigned while Lord Canning and the Duke of Argyll remained. The whole thing was a mess. The Peelites were disintegrating as a political force. Gladstone – having refused to serve under Derby, Lansdowne, Russell and now Palmerston – had created the impression of arrogance, a flaky character and a lack of integrity. By the summer it had all become too much. He retreated back to Wales into the welcoming embrace of his family, and the quiet of his library.

Not that this was a holiday. Later in life, Gladstone would write to one of his sons at Oxford to instruct him on the organisation of time. 'Establish a minimum number of hours in the day for study, say seven at present, and do not without reasonable cause let it be less, noting down against yourself the days of exception,' he wrote. 'There should also be a minimum number for the vacations, which at Oxford are extremely long.' This was an injunction to which the father himself happily conformed, each day recording his reading matter, correspondence and the hours spent working. His diary above all functioned as 'a short journal of principal employments in each day: most valuable as an account-book of the all-precious gift to Time'.

Those summer days at Hawarden gave Gladstone a chance to brood on a raft of recent personal and professional setbacks. Out of office, all his political bridges now apparently burnt, he was forced to recognise his declining status in public life. Added to this were the troubling sexual fantasies surrounding his 'rescue' work, which tormented and enthralled him. The death of his little daughter, Jessy, remained a source of painful grief. Sitting in the library on that hot July morning, his heart and head full of troubles, he began to devise a plan to regain equilibrium in his life. He had immersed himself in Westminster operations to the point of embittered frustration; perhaps a prolonged interval of study to work these disappointments out of his system would prove cathartic. 'Looked into my papers on Homer,' he recorded enthusiastically, 'and I am strongly tempted to undertake something.'

This was the first stage in a three-year project that would come to fruition in 1858 with the publication of a three-volume work, *Studies on Homer and the Homeric Age*. 'Mr Gladstone read Homer for fun,' Churchill would later remark, 'and it served him right.' Homer was a neglected writer in Victorian England, but Gladstone believed he made a profound and enduring contribution to European civilisation. 'The power derived from this source was to stand in subordinate conjunction to the Gospel,' he wrote, 'and to contribute its own share towards the training of mankind.' The Homeric Poems 'supplied materials for the intellectual and social portions of that European civilization, which derives its spiritual substance from the Christian faith'.

Lurking at the back of Gladstone's mind as he toiled on Homer were a number of demons to be exorcised. These included the 'betrayal' by Henry Manning and James Hope in converting to Rome. 'Worked much on arranging my letters,' he had written gloomily a few days after arriving home. 'In selecting Manning's through the long years of our intercourse I again go through that sad experience.' In many ways the sections on Greek religion in *Homer* can be read as straightforward anti-Roman Catholic polemic; in other ways they are an enraged lament for lost friendship.

There were other scores besides Manning and Hope for Gladstone to settle. In *Alroy* and *Tancred*, Disraeli had cited Judaism not just as the source of Christianity, but also the inspiration for modern culture. 'We hesitate not to say that there is no race . . . that so much delights, and fascinates, and elevates, and ennobles Europe, as the Jewish,' he had written in 1851, just four years before Gladstone began work on Homer. The Greeks, in contrast, were an exhausted, moribund race. The Jews were the inspiration for the creative, moral, intellectual and spiritual foundations of the modern world. Gladstone considered that Disraeli's conceptualisation of the Jews as 'the fountainhead' of civilisation was simply 'childish'. Central to *Studies on Homer and the Homeric Age* was a belittling of the Jews in the history of civilisation. They might have been God's chosen people, but they 'had no world-wide vocation committed to them; they lay ensconced in a country which was narrow and obscure . . . an unhonoured and undistinguished race, simply elected to be the receivers of the Divine Word'.

Disraeli's view on Gladstone's *Homer* is unrecorded. Those who did read it, however, were almost without exception hostile. Sir George Cornewall Lewis, Gladstone's successor as chancellor and a formidable classical scholar, told a friend that Gladstone's estimate of Homer as an exponent of religion was 'fundamentally wrong'.* Lord Tennyson, thought Gladstone's views on the subject to be 'hobby-horsical'. Lord Acton reported to his wife from Hawarden on 'a dreadful hour' listening to Gladstone expounding on Homer. Even John Morley, Gladstone's loyal amanuensis, conceded that the work on Homer was 'commonly judged fantastic'. Benjamin Jowett, the Regius Professor

---

*Sir George Cornewall Lewis was, however, about to suffer a crushing reverse. In 1857, he convinced the British Museum to purchase *The Fables of Fabrius*, which turned out to be fraudulent. As with Lord Dacre and the 'Hitler Diaries' more than a century later, Lewis's scholarly reputation never fully recovered.

of Greek at Oxford, summed it up best. When asked for his opinion of *Homer* he replied tersely: 'It's a mere nonsense.'

Homer obsessed Gladstone for three years, and he would return to it again as prime minister to bring out a popular edition entitled *Juventus Mundi* (1869). Drafting the original he withdrew from life at Westminster. He attended fewer debates, and often did not bother to speak even when present. Occasionally on issues about which he felt particularly strongly, such as divorce or finance, he would thunder back with a long speech. The pent-up frustration that this released often did further harm to his already tarnished reputation. On 20 February 1857, Gladstone stunned the House with a vitriolic, personal attack on Cornewall Lewis reminiscent of the assault on Disraeli in 1852. He accused him of introducing a 'reckless system of finance', and condemned his 'trifling with the House and . . . using us like children'. No wonder Lewis disliked his work on Homer. The Duke of Argyll observed that the speech had been 'very overstrained, and unfair in argument to the highest degree'. The diarist Charles Greville concluded simply, 'Everybody detests Gladstone.'

Even Gladstone recognised that Homeric studies appeared a better option. 'The House of Commons,' he wrote shortly after the budget debate, 'would sooner and more healthily return to a sense of its own dignity and of its proper functions, if let alone by a person who had so thoroughly worried both it and the country as myself.' So he left Palmerston and parliament to their own devices. Between 18 August 1857 and 16 February 1858 he was in London for just fourteen days. Abandoning his usual restlessness, he slept 153 out of 172 nights at Hawarden. His London house was put in mothballs. On returning to town in February he took modest lodgings near parliament. Gladstone had to all intents and purposes become the kind of disengaged country MP he had always despised.

Yet politics still came knocking. Just days after Gladstone returned to London the government unexpectedly fell. Less than a year earlier Palmerston had won a brilliant election victory on a patriotic agenda. Now he was hoist by his own petard. Felice Orsini, an Italian terrorist living in Birmingham, had attempted to assassinate Emperor Napoleon III in January. The French demanded that Britain crack down on anti-French fanatics. Palmerston, to everyone's astonishment, complied by introducing a Conspiracy to Murder Bill, which made it a crime to conspire in Britain to murder someone abroad. This was exactly the type of humiliating kowtowing to foreign pressure that Palmerston had been elected to resist. The Conservatives, who thought the bill unpatriotic, and the Radicals, who believed it breached civil rights, combined to defeat the government by nineteen votes: Palmerston was out.

Gladstone rose early the day after the government's resignation in order to attend Holy Communion at St James's in Piccadilly. 'From the sacred feast I went to Lord Aberdeen's,' he wrote in his diary. 'There Derby's letter reached me.'

This was a call back to the political fray.

While Gladstone had been enjoying the scholastic pleasures of self-imposed exile, Disraeli had been mired in the bitter frustrations of official opposition. He was physically and intellectually shattered. Already by 1856 the American consul in Liverpool, who had earned his post with a brilliant campaign biography of President Franklin Pierce, had offered a telling character sketch of a man close to burn out. 'By and by there came a rather tall, slender person, in a black frock [coat], buttoned up, and black pantaloons, taking long steps, but I thought rather feebly or listlessly,' he wrote after a visit to Westminster. 'His shoulders were round; or else he had a habitual stoop in them. He had a prominent nose, a thin face, and a sallow, very sallow complexion, and was a very unwholesome looking person; and had I seen him in America, I should have taken him for a hard-worked editor of a newspaper, weary and worn with night-work and want of exercise; shrivelled, and withered, before his time. It was Disraeli, and I never saw any other Englishman look in the least like him.' The writer was Nathaniel Hawthorne, author of *The Scarlet Letter*.

Now into his fifties, Disraeli had suddenly begun to find politics draining. His health had never been particularly robust, but the onset of middle age was taking its toll. He had begun to develop a marked, painful stoop, which ached when he sat in one place for too long. His weak lungs were susceptible to infection in the damp, foggy London winters. Jet-black locks now only retained their colour with the assistance of hair dye. To combat the onset of age, Disraeli and his wife would quietly slip off to the waters at Spa, Belgium. '[I] was so lethargically disposed the whole year, that many things escaped my wearied life,' he told Lady Londonderry in 1856. 'The suppressed gout, at which you laughed, at length, brought me here, where, after five weeks, I have found renovation in its bright fountains, and brown baths of iron waters.'

Concerns for the health of his wife, Mary Anne, matched those for his own. She was sixty-four in 1856 and beginning to feel her age. She was often ill, but always put 'my Dizzy's' wellbeing before her own. This poor health gave rise to all kinds of concerns. Not least of these was that, should Mary Anne die first, Disraeli would lose her considerable endowment and the house at Grosvenor Gate (in which she had only a lifetime interest). Financial worries added yet more anxiety to Disraeli's stressful life. He continued to carry a vast debt on which he struggled even to keep up the interest payments. Such was the level of this encumbrance that he was even prepared to conduct a twelve-year correspondence with a rich widow, Mrs Brydges Willyams from Torquay, who had promised to leave him her fortune on the condition that he wrote to her regularly. No wonder Disraeli felt himself in the grip of 'nervous debility'.

'I have not seen a newspaper, in any language, for more than a month, and I did not tell our own household where we were going, so that we have not received a single letter,' he wrote to his Torquay correspondent that summer from Spa. 'This complete breaking of the perpetual chain of public circumstances and the cares and troubles of business, has perhaps done me as much good, as the waters of Pouhon.'

Those 'cares and troubles' now seemed particularly heavy. During the Palmerston government, Disraeli lost the confidence and goodwill of his own MPs in the House of Commons. Matters were not helped by the lazy insouciance of their leader, Lord Derby, who had left the Conservatives at Westminster in disarray. The sybaritic earl had little appetite for power, let alone opposition. He rarely bothered to attend debates, ensconced himself at Knowsley, playing billiards and cards, shooting or planning trips to the races. 'As for our Chief we never see him,' Disraeli complained to Lady Londonderry.

Yet he was powerless to challenge him. Derby had once complacently told Prince Albert that 'Mr Disraeli knew that he [Derby] possessed the confidence of three hundred of his supporters whilst Mr Disraeli, if he separated himself from him, would very likely not carry five with him.' Disraeli had always survived because Derby, like most Tory MPs, put aside personal ambivalence in order to have his skill in the House. By the end of 1857, however, Conservatives were beginning to ask if Disraeli was a spent force. In the Commons, mutinous MPs regularly defied him to vote with the government. The chief whip, Sir William Jolliffe, instructed the whips to take soundings about whether Disraeli remained a viable leader in the Commons. 'All with whom I have spoken, without an exception, are angry, sulky, or otherwise dissatisfied,' reported back Thomas Taylor, a junior whip. Gossip around the corridors of Westminster already predicted that Lord Stanley, Derby's son, would soon pick up the mantle of Tory leader in the Commons (thus becoming heir to his father in every way). 'All the great persons I have known, even when what is called "ambitious" by courtesy, have been unequal to a grand game,' Disraeli lamented. 'This has been my fate and I have never felt it more keenly than at the present moment.'

Part of the problem was Disraeli's innovation. Rank-and-file Tories in the mid-century did more than most to justify the Conservatives' earlier reputation as the 'stupid party'. What they failed to grasp, or least appreciate, was Disraeli's original approach to opposition. He was perhaps the first political leader to demand that the foremost role of the opposition was to oppose. This may seem obvious now, but it was a novel approach in Victorian Britain. Even his most recent predecessors, Lord John Russell and Sir Robert Peel, had maintained a gentlemanly and statesmanlike detachment in the House, challenging legislation only if they really thought ill of it. Disraeli's view was that there would always be something to criticise. His job was to exploit any weakness, to make the life of the government as difficult as possible, to wear them down and win back power. This was highly unpopular with his own MPs, not least because it demanded that they attend the House more regularly. Foremost among the advice the whips had passed to Disraeli was the warning that 'however it may be adverse to his own inclinations to sit inactive on the front opposition bench, he has really not any choice left, but must if he cares for his own authority, and our continued existence, *bide his time*'.

Disraeli had ignored the advice. In doing so he was able to deliver the fatal blow to the Palmerston administration that enabled the Conservatives to return to power in 1858. It had been a brilliant assault during which Disraeli had first supported the government's Conspiracy to Murder Bill, before switching sides to kick them out. On the big occasion, he had once again shown himself the master of dramatic events. Discontent on the backbenches evaporated. Lord Derby went to the Palace to accept the invitation to form a government.

The letter was despatched to Gladstone.

At Lord Aberdeen's house on the morning of 21 February 1858 there was much discussion during breakfast about Derby's overture to

Gladstone. Meanwhile, as they deliberated, Lord Stanley was worrying about the prospects for the new government. There was a personal unease for him about joining a government not progressive enough for his tastes. These reservations were subservient to the matter of how the government might survive beyond the year, yet alone prosper. Gloomily he set down a list of reasons why a Derby government 'is not likely to stand'. It made depressing reading.

Among the reasons for predicted failure, two personalities stood out. Disappointment was inevitable 'because the character of Disraeli, who must lead the Commons, does not command general confidence, either in parliament or among the public,' wrote Stanley. 'If in difficulty, he would probably resort to desperate expedients rather than resign.' This from Disraeli's most loyal ally. Added to the loose cannon that was Disraeli, Stanley offered another problem of personality. 'For obvious reasons, it would be necessary to form a junction with Mr Gladstone and his friends: whose extreme unpopularity could only be a new source of weakness,' he calculated. Any hopes of successfully combining these two combustible personalities seemed 'hopeless'.

While Lord Stanley worried about how Gladstone and Disraeli would ever work together, another influential MP was making a determined bid to stop the alliance dead in its tracks. John Bright breakfasted that morning at the Reform Club. On his way to the club he had run into a confidant of Lord Derby in Park Lane who had gloatingly told him that finally they had recovered Gladstone and the Peelites. For years the Whigs and Radicals had fed off Conservative disunity. Now the Tories were on the brink of reconciliation, which would ensure their return as a political force. How ironic that Bright, who recently had engineered the fall of Palmerston, should have helped the Conservatives in such an astonishing way.

Bright had no special personal or political connection with Gladstone, so what he was about to do was not without risk. Yet if Gladstone were to join a Derby government, the potential reward seemed to justify the exposure. He composed a letter to Gladstone in which he set out reasons why a cabinet post should be declined. It was a brilliantly conceived note that combined principle, ambition and realistic politics. 'If you agree rather with the [Tory] men opposite than with those among whom you have been sitting, I have nothing to say,' Bright told him. But before he made the leap, Gladstone should understand that 'If you remain on our side of the House, you are with the majority, and no government can be formed without you.' Then came the real flattery. 'You have many friends [here], and some who would grieve much to see you leave them,' Bright gushed, 'and I know nothing that can prevent your being Prime Minister before you approach the age of every other member of the House who has or can have any claim to that high office'.

In the end, Bright's Park Lane gossip turned out to be wrong. He received a warm answer to his letter, reassuring him that Gladstone hoped never to be tempted by the allure of power for its own sake. The decision had not been a particularly difficult one. Gladstone the previous night had stayed up into the early hours with his friends Sydney Herbert and James Graham. Although they 'did not talk quite *through* the crisis', it was clear by the time they broke up that government was unlikely. Having slept on it, inclination became determination. 'The case though grave was not doubtful.' On leaving, he shared an emotional moment with Herbert, with both men declaring their 'fervent wish that in public life we might never part.'

For many the question was not if Gladstone would serve with his friends, but whether he might ever go into government with those he detested on both sides of the House. Few doubted that Gladstone had a visceral, personal dislike of both Palmerston and Disraeli. He had remained in government with Palmerston for a matter of weeks before private distaste made him quit. Three times now he had refused to work with Disraeli. He was, suggested the *Spectator*, on his way to becoming 'a mere Bedouin of parliament, a noble being full of spirit and power, but not to be tamed into the ordinary ways of civil life'. Disraeli put it more cruelly. Gladstone was 'a Simeon Stylites among the statesmen of his time'. Like the ascetic hermit on his pillar, William Gladstone seriously wanted to be alone, albeit with everyone watching.

A few short months later, Disraeli made a last attempt to coax Gladstone back to the Conservatives. The editor of *The Times*, John Delane, had told him that the government would 'do much better without Gladstone', but Disraeli knew better. Simple arithmetic made the point clearly enough for any observer. They were outnumbered by three to two. The Tories were only in office because their opponents were squabbling among themselves. More importantly, the new Conservative government had failed to win support from any senior figures outside its own ranks. As well as Gladstone, there were Palmerston, Russell, Cobden and Bright on the Commons benches opposite ready to torment the administration. On the government side only Disraeli and, to a lesser extent, Stanley came close to matching their political skill. The cabinet was of a higher quality than the 'Who? Who?' administration of 1852, but its authority remained just as fragile. The Tories, it seemed, were trapped in a cycle of office without power. To win back Gladstone would have had massive symbolic importance.

For a few months in 1858 the Derby government was sustained by the hostile rivalry between Palmerston and Russell, neither of whom wanted the other to be prime minister. Even a crisis that should have seen the government kicked out in May went unexploited. The president of the Board of Control for India, Lord Ellenborough, resigned after publication of his humiliating dressing down of the governor general, Charles Canning, about the settlement of the recently annexed Oudh. Motions of censure against the government were brought in both Houses. Disraeli prepared for the worst. 'I shall never forget that night,' he said later of the debate. 'I believed that we were smashed.' That the government survived, he gleefully told the Queen afterwards, was because 'the enemy suddenly fled in a manner the most ignominious. Never was such a rout! And never was a party in such a humiliating plight as was the great Whig coalition that was to have devoured Her Majesty's Government, as an ogre does a child.'

Disraeli demonstrated great courage and dash in the Ellenborough crisis, but even in triumph he recognised weakness. For all his skill, the government had only survived because the opposition was unable to agree. Now there was a vacancy in the cabinet. Derby and Disraeli resolved to fill it with Gladstone to give the Conservatives greater 'strength in the House of Commons'. On 22 May the home secretary, Spencer Walpole, was despatched to offer Gladstone a place in the cabinet either as president of the Board of Control or, facilitated by Lord Stanley, colonial secretary. Disraeli, as a gesture of goodwill, offered to relinquish the leadership of the Commons to Gladstone's ally, James Graham.

The offer at first seemed cursory, and Gladstone had little compunction about turning it down. Disraeli had offered to give up the lead in the House, but not the Treasury. The posts on offer were, in fact, relatively junior, although the idea of reshaping the administration of India had a certain appeal. Derby, significantly, had not as on previous occasions bothered to come in person to plead his case. Gladstone admitted that he 'thought it handsome on the part of Mr Disraeli' to waive the leadership, but the answer remained no. He must stand by his Peelite friends. 'I felt the personal misfortune and public inconvenience of being thrown out of party connection,' he told Walpole, 'but a man at the bottom of a well must not try to get out, however disagreeable his position, until a rope or a ladder is put down to him. In this case my clear opinion was that by joining the government I should shock the public sentiment and should make no essential, no important change in [your] position.'

Gladstone sent a memorandum of his conversation to Aberdeen and Graham. From Graham he got in return an unmistakable rebuke. Loyalty was an admirable quality, but the Peelite 'little band is broken up'. Aberdeen was too old to play the game. Newcastle 'stands aloof, awaiting his chance, which may place him at the head of affairs.' Cardwell was a stooge of Palmerston. Herbert had 'feelings' towards Disraeli that made reconciliation impossible. Graham himself, burnt out and ill, had no desire to return to the cut and thrust of office. 'I have now exhausted the short catalogue of your most intimate political friends,' he concluded brutally, 'and the result is, that you stand alone.'

Graham urged Gladstone to join the Derby administration 'with perfect honour'. Even the tricky question of Disraeli was surmount-able. 'I once thought and strongly expressed the opinion, that you could not without humiliation and dishonour accept a seat on the Treasury bench with D'Israeli for your leader,' he conceded. 'I am bound to say, that subsequent events have qualified this opinion.' Disraeli had offered an olive branch in his willingness to relinquish the leadership. Even if he remained there, 'side by side, you would soon virtually supersede him . . . and I feel certain that in the Commons pre-eminence will be yours'. The time was right for Gladstone to return to his natural party of allegiance before it was too late. 'Time is wearing away fast,' he urged. 'You have attained the utmost vigour of your understanding and of your powers.' Seize the day, Graham insisted: 'Without some risk no great advantage is ever gained.'

It was with these words in his mind that Gladstone considered another letter of 25 May. Perhaps it was the most extraordinary and unlikely communication of his political life. It is doubtful, in fact, that even US President James Buchanan, who that same year received from Queen Victoria the first ever transatlantic telegram (and assumed it was a hoax), was more surprised than Gladstone on opening his mail that day. For here was a letter from his arch-protagonist Disraeli. It contained a plea: join us.

Disraeli dispensed with the usual formalities of 'My dear Sir' and 'Your obedient servant'. He launched straight in without any salutation, and concluded with a simple 'B. Disraeli'. The third person hostility of his previous correspondence on the chancellor's robe had gone. In its place was a tone that was urgent, direct, and conciliatory.

> I think it of such paramount importance to the public interest, that you should assume at this time a commanding position in the administration of affairs, that I feel it a solemn duty to lay before you some facts, that you may not decide under a misapprehension.
>
> Our mutual relations have formed the greatest difficulty in accomplishing a result which I have always anxiously desired . . . For more than eight years, instead of thrusting myself into the foremost place, I have been, at all times, actively prepared to make every sacrifice of self for the public good, which I have ever thought identical with your accepting office in a Conservative Government.
>
> Don't you think the time has come when you might deign to be magnanimous? . . . I may be removed from the scene, or I may wish to be removed from the scene.
>
> Every man performs his office, and there is a Power, greater than ourselves, that disposes of all this.
>
> The conjuncture is very critical, and, if prudently yet boldly managed, may rally the country. To be inactive now is, on your part, a great responsibility. If you join Lord Derby's Cabinet, you will meet there some warm personal friends; all its members are your admirers. You may place me in neither category, but in that, I assure you, you have ever been sadly mistaken.

This theatrical, emotional letter, with its transparent references to the Almighty, had been pure Disraeli; the reply was authentic Gladstone.

> My Dear Sir – The letter you have been so kind as to address to me will enable me, I trust, to remove from your mind some impressions with which you will not be sorry to part . . . You consider that the relations between yourself and me have proved the main difficulty in the way of certain political arrangements. Will you allow me to assure you that I have never in my life taken a decision which turned upon those relations.
>
> You assure me that I have ever been mistaken in failing to place you among my friends or admirers. Again I pray you to let

me say that I have never known you penurious in admiration towards any one who had the slightest claim to it, and that at no period of my life, not even during the limited one when we were in sharp political conflict, have I either felt any enmity towards you, or believed that you felt any towards me.

At the present moment I am awaiting counsel [*with Aberdeen*] which at Lord Derby's wish I have sought. But the difficulties which he wishes me to find means of overcoming, are broader than you may have supposed. Were I at this time to join any government I could not do it in virtue of party connections. I must consider then what are the conditions which make harmonious and effective co-operation in cabinet possible – how largely old habits enter into them – what connections can be formed with public approval – and what change would be requisite in the constitution of the present government, in order to make any change worth a trial.

I state these points fearlessly and without reserve, for you have yourself well reminded me that there is a Power beyond us that disposes of what we are and do, and I find the limits of choice in public life to be very narrow. – I remain, etc.

Disraeli was disappointed, but not surprised. 'I wish [I] could have induced Gladstone to join Lord Derby's government when Lord Ellenborough resigned in 1858,' he later told Bishop Wilberforce. 'It was not my fault that he did not; I almost went on my knees to him.'

Disraeli had broken his own maxim in explaining himself to Gladstone. This was not a lapse he would make again.

9

Voyage of Discovery

Corfu Harbour, 24 November 1858

The Lord High Commissioner waited on the quayside in full dress uniform for the arrival of an old school friend. Behind him the General Officer of the British garrison stood easy, apprising the formal guard of honour awaiting inspection. Members of the military band worried about whether their instruments would stay in tune in the warm sunshine as they rattled off a jaunty medley.

Slowly, just after midday, the great warship *Terrible* edged carefully into the harbour. The commissioner, Sir John Young, understood only too well what emotions his guest must have been going through. The two men had been at Eton and Oxford together. To anyone who loved the classics – and which gentleman did not – this was a moment to be savoured. Corfu was the island of legend celebrated by Thucydides, Xenophon and Homer. It was here that Odysseus was washed ashore and awoken by the laughter of Princess Nausicaa. Jason and the Argonauts came here with the Golden Fleece. From these waters the Athenians had begun their expedition to Syracuse. In this harbour young Octavian had rallied his fleet before the Battle of Actium.

On board *Terrible* the newly appointed, specially named, Lord High Commissioner Extraordinary thrilled to the spectacle while drinking up the 'brilliant sun and mild air'. Corfu appeared to him, as it had to Homer, like 'a *mirage*'. The ship docked to a thunderous seventeen-cannon salute. As the commissioner came down the gangplank, the guard came to attention and the band struck up a tune. Sir John Young came forward to greet his friend warmly. The General Officer invited him to inspect the guard. The soldier moved off briskly, but then stopped in horror. The Commissioner Extraordinary had not moved. Instead he remained rooted to the spot with a cheerful, if slightly bemused, smile across his face. The General Officer awkwardly returned and invited the recent arrival to follow him.

William Gladstone, it seemed, had never inspected a guard of honour.

Gladstone may have been discomforted by military pageantry, but quite why he was in sunny Corfu in the first place was a question that perplexed and irritated his allies in London. 'His Homeric fancies prevailed, [. . . but he] must be damaged by it,' Lord Aberdeen told John Bright wearily. Gladstone was there to undertake an inquiry into the future of the Ionian Islands. Britain had been granted a protec-torate over this group of seven islands off the coast of Greece during the division of spoils at the 1815 Congress of Vienna, which had concluded the Napoleonic Wars; by the 1850s the islanders were agitating for union with Greece. There had been violent unrest and deaths, which encouraged the Derby government to commission a fact-finding exer-cise of several months to investigate conditions and make recommen-dations about the future. It was the kind of task that might ordinarily be undertaken by an assistant secretary in the Colonial Office. Instead the Conservative government managed to convince Gladstone to go.

Gladstone was frustrated with life at Westminster, and relished the chance to escape. The trip offered the potential for executive authority later down the line, which assuaged his current frustration at not actu-ally being able to get anything done in British politics. Moreover, the destination, with its Homeric connotations, chimed with his own intel-lectual hinterland. The weather would be congenial. He decided to take his wife, Catherine (who had recently lost her sister), and his daughter, Agnes – so the trip might also be something of a family holiday. Then there was the matter of his moral health to consider: Gladstone's night-time excursions had once again begun to take on a frenetic quality. Living with his wife and daughter on a small island in the Mediterranean would surely mean an inevitable curtailment to those activities.

Gladstone's diary entries for this Mediterranean adventure are more fulsome than was his usual custom. They show a genuine and pro-active enjoyment of his situation. The sense of stagnation, frustration and melancholy that had dominated his personal reflections for some time were now swept away. The journey to Corfu had turned into a 'Grand Tour' of some of Europe's great cities, with time spent in

Cologne, Berlin, Dresden, Prague and Vienna. The Gladstones spent much time buying fine china and looking at churches, being impressed most by the Dom in Berlin, and least by the cathedral in Cologne ('which now as ever disappoints me'). Perhaps the greatest treat of all was the magnificent journey from Vienna to Trieste by 'I suppose the most beautiful and wonderful railway in the world'.

Once in Corfu, Gladstone leapt enthusiastically into Homer's footsteps, visiting the sites of classical antiquity. On a visit to Athens, he was dumbfounded by the snow-dusted Acropolis. 'The view – the ruins – and the sculptures,' he wrote excitedly in his diary afterwards, 'are almost too much for one day.'

Gladstone may have been inspired by his Ionian adventure, but there was also more than an element of farce to this Odyssey. Even his admirers would later in his life compare the trip to the absurdities of a Gilbert and Sullivan opera. Whatever the Lord High Commissioner Extraordinary was, he certainly was not an 'apologetic statesman of a compromising kind'. On political matters in Corfu he acted ruthlessly, not least in the casual despatch of 'my old friend' Sir John Young. To replace Young, Gladstone proposed himself as the new High Commissioner with strengthened executive powers. Union with Greece, he reported back to London in late December, should be recognised as a long-term goal, but, first and foremost, he should reform British administration of the islands.

In London the colonial secretary read Gladstone's report with barely concealed delight. He despatched it immediately to Windsor with a note of whole-hearted government support. On 11 January 1859, he sent a jubilant telegram to Gladstone: 'The Queen accepts. Your commission is made out.'

The colonial secretary and author of that telegram was Sir Edward Bulwer Lytton, Disraeli's closest friend. It is hard to avoid the conclusion that Gladstone's Ionian adventure had been anything other than an elaborate setup.

Bulwer Lytton had entered Derby's Conservative administration as colonial secretary shortly after Gladstone turned down the post in May 1858. He stayed in government for eleven months and hated almost every minute of it. His health was poor (although not as poor as he often made out), his nerves were shredded, and the rough and tumble of the Commons compared feebly with the life of ease at his country retreat of Knebworth. Ministerial life had got off to a bad start when, obliged to seek re-election, he was abused by his estranged wife, Rosina, on the hustings. The infuriated Lytton had his wife committed in an attempt to silence her, but the gossip continued. Her doctors made matters worse by reporting once again that Rosina 'talked incessantly and vehemently, denouncing Sir Edward and Mr D'Israeli, accusing them of monstrous crimes'. She despatched letters to 'colleagues and friends' repeating the same claims. By the time Lytton actually took office he was already, according to the gleeful Rosina, 'as mad as Bedlam'. Six months in, and he was in such nervous disarray that he resigned in what Derby called a 'curiously pathological epistle'. In the end he was persuaded to stay only after an entreaty from Disraeli, who sardonically promised a public funeral if he died in office.

Lytton remained in the government because he had no desire to 'leave a shadow on that affectionate friendship which I trust to carry with me to the grave'. Both Disraeli and Lytton were men of temperamental, romantic natures, easily offended and susceptible to bouts of melancholia. Yet for all their occasional fallings out the two men remained lifelong friends; although Rosina Lytton's claims seem farfetched, Lytton was unquestionably Disraeli's closest friend of his own age. And in dreaming up Gladstone's Ionian escapade, there was more than a hint of a scam devised by comrades to twit an adversary. Despatching Gladstone to the Mediterranean would remove him from Westminster politics where he might create mischief for the government and offered the tantalising chance of humiliation. 'Now that we have got him down,' Disraeli crowed maliciously, 'let us keep him down.'

The plan was put into effect in the autumn of 1858 with a careful play to Gladstone's vanity. 'I have received some information privately which makes me believe that he would listen more favourably to such a proposal than you might imagine at the first blush,' Lytton had written cheerfully to Disraeli in September. 'The peculiar position of the man at present, his scholarly tastes and associations, the prospective fame of saving the freedom and reforming the constitution of a Greek people, might be so placed before him as to influence his choice; and at all events I think I could so put the proposal as to please and propitiate him.' Disraeli was delighted, but still could hardly believe it when Gladstone accepted. 'I was privy to the plot,' he told Lord Stanley, 'but never supposed it would result in anything but endless correspondence.'

Lytton's and Disraeli's brilliant conspiracy, delicately pitched to

Gladstone as a modern Odyssey, worked better than either man could possibly have hoped. When Gladstone proposed sacking Sir John Young and remaining in Corfu himself, Disraeli was beside himself. Lord Derby, however, almost ruined everything by hesitating to accept Gladstone's report. Disraeli immediately intervened to point out the obvious. 'I confine myself solely, in these rapid but deeply considered lines, to the expression of one of the strongest and clearest opinions that I ever entertained,' he told the prime minister frankly, 'that the general refusal of Gladstone's proposals would be to extricate him from a most difficult position, and to place him in a commanding one.'

Derby relented. When Gladstone's proposals became public they ignited a furious row. In London he was denounced both for his strategy and the arrogant way in which he had treated Young. This was 'one of those acts of eccentricity which tend so grievously to tarnish a brilliant reputation,' boomed the normally sympathetic *Times*, adding, 'after all the experience we have had, we have no right to be astonished at anything Mr Gladstone may do'. The reaction was scarcely less disparaging in Corfu, where the local assembly rejected his scheme point blank. Even poor Sidney Herbert, Gladstone's closest friend, was at the end of his tether. 'I cannot say how much I am annoyed with Gladstone,' he fumed. 'What an infernal position he has placed himself in! He really is not safe to go about out of Lord Aberdeen's room.'

Gossips immediately began to detect Disraeli's hand in events. Wags even suggested that he planned to install Gladstone as King of the Ionian Islands, which drew the earnest if troubled line from the heir apparent to Lytton, 'I hardly think it needful to assure you that I have never attached the smallest weight to any of the insinuations which it seems people have thought worth while to launch at some member or members of your government with respect to my mission.'

Even worse was to come for Gladstone. The full damaging extent of Disraeli's and Lytton's scheme only became clear to Gladstone in a letter that arrived by special steamer on 18 January. In becoming Lord High Commissioner he would not only have to resign his seat in parliament, but would, as an employee of the Crown, be ineligible to stand in the resulting by-election. 'This, I must confess, is a great blow,' he telegraphed immediately to Lytton in an uncharacteristic dropping of his guard. 'The difficulty and the detriment are serious.'

Gladstone had endured a tetchy relationship with his constituency, where his Anglo-Catholicism was viewed with a mixture of suspicion and contempt. Should he be removed from his University seat, it was unlikely that he would get back in. He grasped immediately that mischief-makers in parliament would move a petition for a by-election at the earliest opportunity. The obvious solution would be to resign immediately from his post in the Ionian Islands and return to Oxford to secure re-election. His dilemma was that the Queen, on appointing him, had commended his patriotic duty. How could he now withdraw without compromising his honour and reputation? To add to his woes, the telegraph station on Corfu chose this inopportune moment to break down. It was, wrote Arthur Gordon, Lord Aberdeen's son, who had accompanied Gladstone to Corfu, 'a political drama alternatively tragical and comical, not unmixed with occasional scenes of the broadest farce'.

Back in London, Gladstone's friends, however perplexed and angry they may have been, quickly moved to extricate him. Aberdeen used his court connections to ensure that no offence would be given to Her Majesty. Potential candidates for the vacant seat in Oxford were leant on heavily not to put their names forward. A new Lord High Commissioner, Sir Henry Storks, secretary for military correspondence at the war office and a friendly acquaintance of Gladstone, agreed to being hurriedly shipped out to Corfu. Gladstone resigned on 1 February; on 13 February he was (in his absence) re-elected unopposed at Oxford. It had been a narrow escape, although not without damage. Graham and Herbert feared that Gladstone had destroyed his career. Only Lord Aberdeen remained confident. 'Ah,' he warned them, '*but he is terrible on the rebound!*'

That seemed unlikely as Gladstone left Corfu on 19 February. The journey to Venice was miserable. Three days of wretched seasickness left him 'at the lowest depth'. Mournfully he wrote in his journal that only 'with the utmost effort could I get through my prayers'. There were moments on the remainder of the long journey home when his spirits rose, not least in Milan, 'which pleases more and more on each visit'. When not travelling, days were spent sightseeing with his wife and daughter. In the evenings he dismally wandered the streets alone looking for 'rescue' cases. ('Saw one,' he wrote impassively during a stopover in Turin.) During the languid train rides that brought him ever closer to London, he continued to brood with 'much rumination' over events of the recent months.

Gladstone finally reached London on the morning of 8 March after a 'rough passage' across the Channel. He went immediately to the

House of Commons to take the oath as the new member for Oxford University. From the House that evening he returned to the streets, where he 'saw R. Tull, Stapylton [prostitutes], and made other inquiries'. Two days later he 'saw L. Spur and R. Gray – new chapters! the latter should be looked after'. The threads of his old life had been easily picked up. He was back in the Commons, the usual round of friendships reactivated and the night-time walks continued. He had inveigled his way out of the Ionian misadventure with only minimal damage. Yet Gladstone could not help feeling that 'gratitude ought to overflow in me with shame'.

He had been made to look a fool in recent months, and pretty soon he knew who was to blame. Eton and Christ Church-educated Lord Carnarvon, who was under-secretary for the colonies, mischievously repeated to him Disraeli's remark, 'Now that we have got him down, let us keep him down.' Gladstone was apoplectic as the scales finally fell from his eyes. What had seemed obvious to others – that Disraeli and Lytton had duped him – finally became clear. After time in the doldrums, Gladstone's sense of purpose returned with an overwhelming objective. At dinner with the lawyer Robert Phillimore, a trusted friend since Oxford, Gladstone 'without any reserve' showed his hand.

He would have his revenge by 'dethroning Disraeli'.

Willis's Rooms, King St, St James's, London, 6 June 1859

The burble of excited chatter came suddenly to an end. More than two hundred and seventy faces turned expectantly to look at the door through which two elderly gentlemen had entered. Both moved slowly towards a raised dais. The older of the two, cheerful and pugnacious in demeanour, was first up the steps. Following behind was his considerably shorter companion who, though younger, was less fleet of foot. When he stumbled, the first man put out his hand to assist him up on to the platform. All those watching burst spontaneously into enthusiastic cheering. In that moment of comradely thoughtfulness the Liberal party was born. It was, wrote a later grandee of the party, '[the] nineteenth-century equivalent of Martin Luther nailing his notice to the church door in Wittenberg or of the embattled farmers by the rood bridge at Lexington firing "the shot heard around the world"'. For the first man was Lord Palmerston, and the second was his rival for the premiership, Lord John Russell.

Both men delivered rousing speeches in which they called for unity and promised each to serve under the other. Next up was the great Radical, John Bright, who offered his 'cordial support'. Then Sidney Herbert gave the proceedings a Peelite blessing by calling for 'a decided movement' to challenge the Conservative government. 'The entente cordiale seemed perfect,' wrote afterwards the new Radical MP for Tavistock, Sir John Trelawny. At the meeting's end, a motion was proposed that the united party should seize power through a vote of no confidence in Derby's administration. Amid raucous cheering and banging of chairs, the motion was carried. 'On the whole,' Herbert reported to his wife, 'it was very successful, no one objecting who was not expected to do so and others concurring who had not been reckoned on.'

This new party was at first sight a curious alliance. On the one hand there were the parliamentary Radicals. For much of the century they had led the charge against the outdated pre-industrial system, particularly 'land monopoly' – the special legal, financial and political privileges given to landowners – and the Church of England. Although they were a small cabal within the Commons, and even within this new political union, the Radicals provided much of the flavour and individuality of the Liberal message. Most of their leading figures, such as Bright and Richard Cobden, were rich businessmen who wanted to modernise the nation's political practices in line with its economic and trading base. They masked this capitalist purpose behind the egalitarian language of 'progress' and of promoting the interests of 'the people' against 'monopoly' and 'privilege'. Yet at heart, their politics came down to redefining the place of wealth-generating industrialists in a modern political society. 'They cannot endure,' summed up the constitutionalist Walter Bagehot, 'they ought not to endure, that a rich, able manufacturer should be a less man than a stupid small squire.'

The Whigs might have seemed strange bedfellows for these Radical capitalists. Their prominent families – the great houses of Russell, Cavendish and the rest – were, after all, England's most privileged landowners. Self-immolation by ending the 'land monopoly' was hardly likely to attract those for whom it had brought eight hundred years of supremacy. Yet other aspects did appeal. The Whigs revelled in their tradition as framers of the constitution – the idea of reinterpreting the principles of 1688 for a new industrial age appealed to many, not least to Russell (who had already done the trick once in 1832). This Whig commitment to constitutional improvement, married to an inclination to meddle ('what is, is wrong') and a detestation of the countryside, offered enough hope that the new alliance might prove a capable organ for progressive, metropolitan politics.

The first test came soon enough. Three days after the meeting at Willis's Rooms, the Marquis of Hartington, heir to the Duke of Devonshire and still only in his mid-twenties, took centre stage for the first time in the Commons to propose 'a want of confidence' in the government. At two in the morning on 11 June the House finally divided; Derby and the Tories lost, inevitably to be replaced by the first real Liberal administration. Out in Westminster Hall, the huge crowd that had gathered to hear the result let out a cheer so loud it could be heard in the Commons. Only months earlier, Gladstone had vowed to dethrone Disraeli. Now his great rival was out. Revenge had been taken. Or at least it would have seemed that way had Gladstone played even the slightest role in the downfall of his nemesis.

Gladstone was in town on 6 June, but had decided not to accompany his old friend Sidney Herbert to Willis's Rooms (despite previously expressing his 'fervent wish that in public life we might never part'). That failure was noted with disapproval, not least by Herbert's wife, who 'threatened' him immediately afterwards. During the 'want of confidence' debate in the Commons over the following three days, MPs on the Liberal side waited for Gladstone to make his contribution. As the debate went on rumours circulated that, contrary to his usual behaviour, Gladstone was not going to speak. Despite the fiery argument, he remained resolutely in his place. When the division was called, and he moved towards the lobbies, few doubted that he would vote to turn out the government. Most understood that this public identification with the new Liberal party represented the last rites on Gladstone as a Conservative. As they headed for the 'aye' lobby, nobody could blame the solemn member for Oxford University in not wanting to shout at a funeral.

Except that Gladstone did not follow them in. Instead he left the excited ranks of opposition MPs to fall in with the much quieter Tories trooping dejectedly into the 'no' lobby. As he passed through the doors, his name noted down by the teller, he would have seen Disraeli. Perhaps the two men looked at each other; maybe they carefully avoided each other's eye. Either way, Disraeli must have wondered exactly what game Gladstone was playing.

When Gladstone returned to the chamber he was met with a stream of abuse from fellow opposition MPs who roughly suggested that, as the Tories were about to occupy the bench where he was now sitting, he should stay exactly where he was. All this was temporarily put to one side when the tellers emerged to announce the result. But soon enough Gladstone's vote as much as the outcome was the hot topic in the clubs of St James's as dawn approached. 'Great principles are forgotten amidst personal squabbles,' reflected Trelawny in his journal.

The unified force represented by the Liberals had restored the two-party system to British politics that had been fractured since the repeal of the Corn Laws. Now, as W. S. Gilbert would later remark in the comic opera *Iolanthe*, 'every boy and every gal, that's born into the world alive, is either a little Liberal, or else a little Conservative!' Those who had been divided from their own party in the rancorous aftermath of the fall of Peel were now confronted with a clear choice if they hoped to continue in active politics: return to the fold, or join with the Liberals. Most MPs returning home in the early morning sunshine on 11 June believed that Gladstone's actions hours earlier signalled his shame-faced return to the ranks of the Conservatives.

Since returning from Corfu, Gladstone had played his cards extremely close to his chest. His determination to inflict humiliation on Disraeli apparently had not been helped by the behaviour of a Conservative administration that was determinedly Peelite in its commitment to fiscal rectitude and administrative reform. Despite being in office for just over a year, and without a majority in the Commons, the 1858–9 Conservative government could boast a record of moderate, progressive achievement. In 1858 they had introduced the Government of India Act, which transferred power from the East India Company to the state. This began a much needed process of comprehensive reform of British rule in India after the disastrous 'Indian Mutiny' of the previous year. (Disraeli, no doubt attracted by the exotic glamour of the posting, very briefly considered going to India as viceroy.) Other valuable measures included reform of Scottish universities and public health procedures. On Disraeli's personal initiative the government also supported an Oaths bill to allow unbaptised Jews to sit in the House of Commons.

The most spectacular attempt to implement 'Conservative progress' was the 1859 Reform Bill. It was a flawed measure, scathingly condemned by Bright for all its complicated 'fancy franchises', which gave the vote to, for example, university graduates, those with £60 in the bank, and others who earned at least £10 a year. In total the electorate would have been expanded by a fairly modest two hundred thousand.

Nevertheless, for all its faults, the bill showed that the Conservatives were willing to engage with what most sensed was the biggest domestic issue looming in British politics.

Administrative reform had been matched by Disraeli's thoroughly Peelite management of the nation's coffers. Following his savaging by Gladstone in 1852, Disraeli subsequently ensured that not so much as an order paper could be slipped between his own financial policy and that of Gladstone. In 1858 he used a healthy surplus to reduce income tax with an accompanying pledge that, as Gladstone had proposed back in 1853, it would abolished in 1860. The government fell before Disraeli presented his ambitious budget for 1859, but it would have included the free trade masterstroke of abolishing the duty on paper. The battles fought by Disraeli in cabinet to push through his measures were reminiscent of those fought by Gladstone in Aberdeen's government. All in all, commented Trelawny, the House was 'well satisfied with the apparent frankness and good sense of the Minister of finance'.

The government, in truth, had been broadly reformist in the practical, organic way that Gladstone admired. Although in many ways a canny, even devious, political operator, he was above all a gut-instinct politician. There had been his resignations, and many more threats of resignation, from governments on points of principle. Add to this the honourable loyalty first to Peel, and then to Aberdeen, that had kept him out of successive Conservative administrations, the last of which had been Gladstonian in mentality. Even his forays into scholarship – *State and Church* and *Homer* – had been published in the face of advice that his political reputation would be damaged. Gladstone was a man unable to act without self-justification accompanied by credible public rationalisation. In short, if he was going to abandon the Conservative party for the Liberals on a permanent basis, he needed in his own mind and on the national stage a cast-iron explanation for his actions.

For Gladstone the answer to the question 'why have you become a Liberal?' would be one word: Italy. On his journey back from Corfu, he had dined with Count Cavour, the prime minister of Piedmont. This turned out to be his own 'Willis's Rooms' moment of conversion. The Italian Question – namely, what position would Britain take on the inevitable war for Italian independence against the Austrian Hapsburg Empire – would quickly establish itself as one of the greatest and most contested ideological divides in nineteenth-century politics. This alone gave Gladstone a plausible reason to identify himself publicly with the pro-nationalist Liberal administration that took office in June

1859. When Palmerston invited him to join the government as chancellor, Gladstone could justify his acceptance by pointing to the prime minister's impeccable position on Italy. 'Never had I an easier question to determine than when I was asked to join the government,' Gladstone said; 'I can hardly now think how I could have looked any one in the face, had I refused my aid (such as it is) at such a time and under such circumstances.'

Never again would Gladstone be invited to, or consider, joining a Conservative administration. As the youngest of the government triumvirate that also included Palmerston and Russell, his eventual succession to the Liberal leadership would soon appear inevitable.

For the first time Gladstone and Disraeli genuinely found themselves separated by party.

'The great battle commences today,' wrote Disraeli, 'and we shall know whether we are mice or men.'

Budget Day, 1860

William Gladstone let out a thick barking cough at the despatch box. Lord Palmerston and Lord John Russell eyed each other uncertainly, wondering if the chancellor was up to the task he was about to begin. For several weeks he had suffered with bronchitis. The budget had already been cancelled once, leading *The Times* to mock that the most important political question of the day had become 'How is Mr Gladstone's throat?' In the week leading up to the speech, doctors had fussed at his bedside administering antimonial wine, James's decongestant powders, mustard plasters and huge sponges of boiling water applied to the chest. Even Gladstone wondered whether the budget statement might prove 'physically impossible'. He seized the large flask of wine and eggs beside him to pour a glassful. Gladstone drank it, cleared his throat and plunged into the debate. Four hours later, he sat down to loud cheers. 'This was the most arduous operation I ever had in Parliament,' he wrote on his return home that night.

Arduous it might have been, but that night of 10 February cemented Gladstone's reputation as the heir apparent to the premiership. Afterwards members swarmed around him as he glowed 'radiant with triumph'. Friends and admirers proclaimed him the foremost politician of his generation. 'How infinitely he excels the ordinary race of statesman!' exclaimed the euphoric John Bright. Prince Albert wrote that 'Gladstone is now the real leader in the House, and works with an energy and vigour almost incredible.' Even Gladstone's political opponents recognised the power of the moment. 'The speech,' said Disraeli's friend Bulwer Lytton, 'will remain among the monuments of English eloquence as long as the language lasts.'

Gladstone had succeeded through a mixture of intellectual rigour and chutzpah. The latter was required not least because 1860 was the year that the abolition of income tax promised in the 1853 budget was due to come into effect. The duties on tea and sugar were also expected to lapse. This would have left Gladstone with a huge deficit of almost £10 million. Instead he re-imposed income tax and the duties on tea and sugar, casually explaining that these measures would facilitate the wide-scale abolition of other duties and the overall simplification of the tariff system. In pursuit of this, he abolished duties on almost four hundred goods. Among other changes, he too would seek to abolish duty on paper, a proposal of great symbolic value in removing the last significant 'tax on knowledge'.

This was also a great free trade budget. 'It is a mistake to suppose that the best mode of giving benefit to the labouring classes is simply to operate on the articles consumed by them,' Gladstone had told the Commons. 'If you want to do them the *maximum* of good, you should rather operate on the articles which give them a *maximum* of employment.' This meant organising the economy around free trade to create more employment at higher wages. It was for this reason that Gladstone supported a commercial treaty with France, which reduced tariffs on goods between Britain and France, and set it alongside a wider policy removing almost all protective duties. The repeal of the Corn Laws in 1846 had signalled the adoption of free trade as an article of faith in British politics, but Britain did not become a free-trading nation overnight. Only with the budget of 1860 was Peel's vision completed, appropriately enough by his greatest apprentice.

Beyond the technicalities of the budget, explained happily by Gladstone in mind-bendingly precise detail, he had also offered some lofty oratory for the watching journalists. His budget, by creating stability, contentment and self-reliance, would 'scatter blessings among the people'. He was 'not endeavouring to do that for them which they ought to do for themselves; but enlarging their means without narrowing their freedom, . . . giving value to their labour, . . . appealing to their sense of responsibility, and . . . not impairing their sense of honourable self-dependence'. There was humour too when, glass of wine in hand, he recommended that tariffs on French wines should be reduced on health grounds.

Disraeli in reply rebuked Gladstone for his failure to deliver on the promise to abolish income tax. He maintained that the treaty with France would have a dire effect on trade with Spain, Portugal and Italy. Yet it was an uncharacteristically flat performance. Disraeli admitted that he was not 'at all anxious to reoccupy the place' where Gladstone now sat. He praised his rival's 'eager mind', and even mischievously suggested that his 'eminent position' would surely lead to a still higher office.

Gladstone's masterly budget had plunged Disraeli into an immediate fit of self-doubt. He had never been truly comfortable in economic debates. The painful memory of Gladstone's brutal attack during the 1852 budget debate remained. With the chancellor radiating such command, Disraeli seemed disinclined to launch a full-frontal attack in case he came off worse. His hesitancy seemed to ripple through the house, disheartening his own supporters. 'He betrays in the House of Commons a sort of consciousness of his inferiority to Gladstone,' wrote Charles Greville contemptuously, 'and of fear of encountering him in debate.'

The budget won a majority of 116, with many Conservatives staying away. Few would have disagreed with Greville that Gladstone 'is now *the* great man of the day'.

Gladstone's budget triumph could hardly have come at a worse time for Disraeli. Since the beginning of the year Conservative MPs had resumed talking about the need for a new leader in the Commons. During the middle of the budget debate, Sir James Ferguson, briefly not an MP, informed Disraeli of dissent in the ranks. 'I know, from authority I believe to be certain, that lately there was an imminent risk of a defection among those who act with you, so serious that the strong party you had in the House of Commons would not have been at your command,' he cautioned. Once again the dissent was rooted in Disraeli's determination that the role of the opposition was to make life as difficult as possible for a government. Ferguson had warned him that 'It would be in the last degree distasteful, not only to the great body of the Conservative party, but to most of your later colleagues, were you to attempt to turn out the present government, with a view to Lord Derby's administration again taking office.'

Faced with such defeatism and caution, Disraeli had quickly lost his touch on the budget. Knowing not whether he had come to bury Gladstone or praise him, Disraeli managed to do neither. 'Nothing could be more brilliant and complete than Gladstone's triumph,' wrote Greville, 'which did not seem to be a matter of much grief to many of the Conservative party, for I hear that however they may still act together on a great field-day, the hatred and distrust of Disraeli is greater than ever in the Conservative ranks.' Few in the House, whether members or observers, doubted that as much as a 'triumph' for Gladstone, the budget was 'a defeat of Disraeli'.

The full importance of this defeat became apparent weeks afterwards in a savage personal attack on Disraeli in the *Quarterly Review*. Disraeli was derided as a 'favourite of misfortune', who 'went forth blundering and to blunder', and had 'unrivalled powers of conducting his party into the ditch'. He had 'never led the Conservatives to victory as Sir Robert Peel had led them to victory. He had never procured the triumphant assertion of any Conservative principle, or shielded from imminent ruin any ancient institution.' Disraeli was instead a destroyer, a man whose 'tactics were so various, so flexible, so shameless' that he made government by any party 'an impossibility'. The Tories might only regain the nation's trust by removing him.

The article was anonymous, but there was no secret as to its author: Lord Robert Cecil (later Lord Salisbury) a future prime minister and one of Disraeli's own backbench MPs. 'I dislike and despise the man,' Cecil told his father, who had threatened not to pay any further election expenses unless he desisted from attacking Disraeli. 'I have merely put into print what all the county gentlemen were saying in private.'

What made the attack all the more galling was Cecil's accompanying paean of praise for Gladstone in the weekly *Saturday Review*. The chancellor had produced 'one of the finest combinations of reasoning and declamation that has ever been heard within the walls of the House of Commons'. Throughout 'the whole four hours of intricate argument neither the voice nor mind faltered for an instant'. This had been a master class in 'pure Gladstonianism – that terrible combination of relentless logic and dauntless imagination'.

Taken together, Lord Robert's articles in the *Quarterly Review* and *Saturday Review* were a devastating indictment of Disraeli's leadership. Gossip in the corridors of Westminster asked how long he might survive now that private grievances had been so publicly aired. Lord John Russell taunted Disraeli in the Commons, inquiring as to who exactly was now leader of the Conservatives. *The Times* joined the discussion with a leading article on Disraeli that read like a political obituary. 'Having uniformly to fight an uphill battle and to sustain a losing cause,' it opined, 'he has acquitted himself in a manner . . . to prove that he possesses talents which, under happier circumstances, might have made his Administration eminently creditable to himself and useful to his country.'

Disraeli felt – or at least showed – no personal animus towards Cecil and perhaps saw something of his younger self in the audaciousness of the attack. Encountering Cecil at Lord Salisbury's country estate, he threw his arm around him, declaring 'Ah, Robert, Robert, how glad I am to see you!' For all his bravado Disraeli understood that Cecil had brought the question of his leadership of the party to a crisis point. Rather than sit like a wounded dog in the corner, Disraeli moved to resolve the issue by offering his resignation. As a later Conservative leader would say, it was time to put up or shut up.

On 11 June Disraeli wrote to the senior Tory backbencher, Sir William Miles, who only days before had taken him aside to express concern at the level of dissent in the ranks. Disraeli's answer to this criticism was a masterpiece of self-justification, mock wounded pride and political gamesmanship. He reminded Miles he had taken on the leadership after the death of Lord George Bentinck at great financial sacrifice to restore the 'shattered remnants of the country party'. Personal pride had been set aside in the many attempts to bring the Peelites back into the fold, including offers 'of a flattering nature . . . made to Mr Gladstone'.

Disraeli had returned the Conservatives to office 'in order to save the party from political annihilation' despite the inevitability that those efforts must conclude in failure. This restored the fortunes of the party while leaving him 'to bear the brunt of disaster' when defeat came. Criticism and ridicule from political opponents was only to be expected, but from those on the same side this was intolerable behaviour.

The letter was a heartfelt if calculated rebuke to his party. 'So long as they were in distress, I have borne without a murmur the neglect, the desertion, the personal insults, that I have experienced,' he protested. 'But the Tories are no longer in distress – they have abundance of friends; and, with respect to the privacy of their feelings towards me, they chalk the walls in the market-place with my opprobrium.' And so to the knockout punch: 'I must resign a leadership which I unwillingly accepted, and to which it is my opinion that fourteen years of unqualified devotion have not reconciled the party.'

When Miles received the letter pandemonium ensued. He hurriedly rallied other senior Tories, such as Spencer Walpole, Joseph Henley and Lord Hotham, to whip dissenters into line. 'When the pinch comes, not withstanding their murmuring and cavil,' Miles shrewdly observed, '[they] come to the scratch like men'. The grandees were then able to assure Disraeli of the party's loyalty, to lard him with compliments and coax him to stay. Eventually, after much protestation and expressions of reluctance, Disraeli agreed to take back his letter. Even Robert Cecil was brought into line, writing in the next edition of the *Quarterly Review* that it had never been his intention to suggest a change of Conservative leadership in the Commons.

Gladstone, too, had obligingly played his part in Disraeli's rehabilitation. Tucked away in the letter to Miles was the boast that 'the finance of Mr Gladstone has blown up'. For in the months since delivering his budget, the chancellor had suffered a crushing reverse. Although an overwhelming majority had passed the budget as a whole, these changes still had to be debated in separate individual bills. On Paper Duties, this opened up dissent within the government and gave Disraeli an opportunity to exploit. It was an open secret that Palmerston opposed the measure. Disraeli in office had planned a similar measure, but now he rallied his own forces with a spirited defence of a reactionary position that would humiliate the loathsome chancellor without bringing down the government.

When the measure came before the Commons in early May, Disraeli launched a blistering assault. The Radical Trelawny described him 'attacking Gladstone with more vehemence and with *ad hominem* arguments – alleging rashness, inconsistency, intolerance and self contradictions'. When the vote was taken, the chancellor found that his majority of 116 had shrivelled to just nine. The question then became what the Lords would do with it. They certainly had the right to reject the bill, but for more than two hundred years the upper house had stayed its hand on financial matters. Radicals noisily proclaimed that a constitutional crisis would inevitably ensue if the bill were rejected. Palmerston, however, secretly went behind Gladstone's back to advise Lord Derby to throw out the bill. When the Queen asked for his opinion, he told her that Peers would 'perform a good public service' by voting against it. When the Lords did just that on 21 May, Lady Palmerston, watching from the gallery, rather gave the game away by conspicuously and enthusiastically joining the applause for what was, after all, a defeat for her husband's administration.

Gladstone was the real loser in the Lords defeat. With his tail between his legs, he left London for the country to reflect on 'these strange times and . . . our strangely constructed Cabinet'. By the following weekend, he thought 'my resignation *all but* settled'. Yet when he saw Palmerston four days later he was persuaded to stay. 'The *matter*,' he wrote of the interview, 'was first to warn me of the evils and hazards attending, for me, the operation of resigning, secondly to express his own strong sense of the obligation to persevere.'

So Gladstone remained, his reputation battered and spirits low. His friend Phillimore, by the end of the parliamentary session, found him 'physically weak, requires rest, air, and generous living'. In the clubs of St James's all the talk was of a diminished figure. At the Travellers' that summer Charles Villiers told Greville that Gladstone was 'very dejected and uneasy in his mind, and very gloomy in Cabinet'. To make matters worse, Gladstone had quietly resigned from the Carlton Club in March that year, leaving him to brood unhappily at Brooks's, where the Whigs openly despised him. He left London in low spirits in August for a family holiday at the Welsh seaside resort of Penmaenmawr, where the chilly waters seemed more welcoming than the unpleasantness of the Westminster hothouse.

The autumn of 1860 was a period of frustration for Gladstone. Away from London for all but a couple of weeks, and without any great intellectual project to occupy him, he quickly bored. The benefits of astringent sea-bathes soon dissipated when, just three days into his holiday, news reached him that his widowed brother-in-law, Henry Glynne, planned to marry the family governess. This had serious implications for the Gladstones. Should Glynne have a son, the boy would have claims on Hawarden (despite the estate having only been saved by Gladstone family money). 'It is startling and precipitate, and by no means what one would wish,' Gladstone recorded angrily in his diary.

Eventually poor Glynne would buckle under pressure from his overbearing brother-in-law to withdraw his hand. Gladstone paid off the jilted woman with £8000, which itself caused gossip that she had in fact been his lover. Although this was untrue, Gladstone was subject to the usual temptations during these stressful autumn months. Any time spent away from the family brought with it habitual late night visits to prostitutes. 'Saw Bennet' read the diary entry for 9 November. 'Really notable.' By the end of the year, Gladstone was again reflecting on 'my deep, deep, deep unworthiness'.

Low in spirits, wrestling with sexual temptation and with his political reputation in jeopardy, Gladstone finally pulled himself together in the early months of 1861. His plan was as brilliant as it was simple. Instead of presenting a budget of individual bills, he would offer all his financial proposals in one, unified bill. Henceforth this would give the House of Lords (but not the Commons) a straightforward choice between accepting and rejecting the budget as a whole.

This ingenious plan to reassert the primacy of the lower house in financial matters was presented to cabinet in one 'laborious and anxious day' on 11 April. For two hours he patiently explained his case to colleagues. Their immediate reaction was one of 'chaos!' The following day there was another 'very stiff' meeting in which 'we "broke up" in our sense and all but in another'. By the following day, through sheer force of argument and determination not to be shifted from his position, 'my plan as now framed was accepted, Lord Palmerston yielding gracefully'.

In private, however, the prime minister put his difficult younger colleague on notice that he would not protect him in the event of failure. 'I think it proper to record in writing the opinion which I have more than once expressed verbally in Cabinet in our discussion on these matters, namely that the financial arrangements of the country ought to have been framed upon a principle different from that on which your proposal has been founded,' he wrote to Gladstone on 14 April. 'The Cabinet at your recommendation have agreed to a course founded on different principles, and I have acquiesced in that course being proposed to parliament. But I think it right to say beforehand that, as far as I am concerned, I do not intend to make the fate of my administration depend upon the decision which Parliament may come to upon your proposal.'

The following day Gladstone introduced his budget in a three-hour statement in which he took a penny off income tax, further reduced the duty on wine, and, most controversially, repealed the paper tax. 'The figures rather made my head ache,' he wrote afterwards. 'It was the discharge of a long pent up excitement.'

Disraeli immediately sensed an opportunity. '[He] is in the highest spirits because the battle is to be fought by tactics and not brute force, and he thinks he is going to display great powers of generalship,' the up-and-coming Tory Sir Stafford Northcote wrote to his wife. Disraeli put all his efforts into marshalling the Tory forces. He wrote to MPs demanding their presence in the House for the crucial debates. 'I write to you with deep emotion, for I know how much is at stake,' he told them. Sir John Trelawny recorded that 'the Tories seem jubilant – and quite ready for office', but asked: 'Is the pear ripe?'

The night before the final division on 31 May no one was confident that the government would win. Lord Stanley, at a dinner given by the India tycoon Sir James Weir Hogg, found himself seated next to Mrs Gladstone. Her nerves were in shreds; she 'could think and speak of nothing but her husband and the division tomorrow: she seemed astonished at any of his measures being opposed, and almost intimated that she looked on such opposition as personal to him'. When the division came the budget scraped through by 196 to 181. 'One of the greatest nights on the whole of my recollection,' bragged the euphoric Gladstone.

Disraeli, in contrast, was apoplectic with rage. The government's majority had been reduced to just fifteen, but twenty of his own MPs had stayed away. In a blind fury he stormed away from the House. For four days he refused to return. All around Westminster, whispers grew more insistent that he had resigned the leadership in the Commons. There were angry scenes as Disraeli loyalists denounced the rebels. A number of his most vocal supporters, led by Sir Matthew White Ridley, wrote to Disraeli offering to put on a dinner at the Carlton Club as a 'testimony of the undiminished value they set upon [your] services to the Conservative party, and of their earnest and friendly feeling towards [you]'. Lord Derby sent his son round to beg Disraeli to play on. Although Stanley had been a waverer on the budget debate, he was close to Disraeli and could speak to him frankly. He found him in 'ill-humour', but managed to get out of him that he had 'no intention of resigning'. In the end, Disraeli agreed to resume his seat on the front bench. 'Politics is like war – roughish work,' he reflected ruefully to a colleague. 'We should not be over-sensitive. We have enough to do without imaginary grievances.' To his old friend in Torquay, Mrs Brydges Willyams, he was more forthright. 'In the very hour of victory,' he seethed, 'when the signal for the last charge was given, I had the mortification, great for a general indeed, to see a division of my own troops march from the field of contest.'

He would not have disputed John Trelawny's conclusion. 'The ascendancy of Gladstone is daily more conspicuous,' the Radical MP judged, while 'D'Israeli courted defeat, and won it.'

10

In the Arboretum

The Grounds of Hawarden

Striding purposefully through the woods of his castle, the Chancellor of the Exchequer was a sight both unnerving and perhaps a little comical. His face had a stern, purposeful look. He was wearing a filthy suit. The customary high-collared white shirt, now open at the neck, flapped untidily in the autumn breeze. On his head sat a tatty straw hat. His hand clasped a four-foot axe. When he reached his destination, off came the jacket; down went the braces. He marked his spot, lifted the heavy axe, and delivered the first, pulverising blow. Within minutes perspiration was dripping from his face and through the back of his shirt. His greying hair, matted with sweat, was wild and unkempt. For the next few hours, as he punished his body in concentrated physical exertion, the chancellor left behind the cares of the world. 'In chopping down a tree you have not time to think of anything excepting where your next stroke will fall,' he explained, 'The whole attention is centred upon the blows of the axe.'

Felling trees was a form of relaxation that Gladstone practised with zealous passion. In 1858 he had begun taking lessons in axemanship. By the time he became chancellor again in 1859, chopping down trees had already become his favourite leisure pursuit. During the long parliamentary recesses at Hawarden, he would venture into the woods on most afternoons with his son, Willy, to work up a sweat in attacking more trees. It was an interest that he would pursue well into his eighties, when (as he noted with characteristic precision in his diary) mere 'axe-work' replaced 'tree-felling'. Gladstone perhaps had more enthusiasm than real skill. One Christmas he almost blinded himself when a large splinter lodged in his eye. A few days later he almost killed another son, Harry, when 'a tree we were cutting fell with [him] in it'. Gladstone's suspect ability did not matter to his many admirers who saw in his woodland activities a rousing example of manly vitality and protean strength. Others were less impressed. 'The forest laments,' remarked Lord Randolph Churchill mordantly, 'in order that Mr Gladstone may perspire.'

William Gladstone and Benjamin Disraeli shared few interests outside politics, but one topic that grabbed their mutual attention was trees. Yet even here their instincts drove them in opposite directions. For while Gladstone enjoyed nothing better than cutting down trees, Disraeli's pleasures were more leisurely. 'I like to look at them,' Disraeli remarked in 1860. 'When I come to Hughenden I pass the first week in sauntering about my park and examining all the trees.' There was no visible perspiration on the lord of this manor as he wandered serenely through his grounds chatting to staff. On occasion he might lend a gentle hand in the planting of a tree to mark a notable visit to the house. At other times he was content to watch a master craftsman. 'To see Lovett, my head-woodman, fell a tree is a work of art,' Disraeli wrote in 1860. 'No bustle, no exertion, apparently not the slightest exercise of strength. He tickles it with the axe; and then it falls exactly where he desires it.'

Had he tried, Disraeli could hardly have delivered a more withering contrast to the clumsy efforts of his great rival. Even in the privacy of their country estates, Gladstone and Disraeli remained stubbornly incompatible.

Victorian statesmen enjoyed a civilised existence. Not overly concerned with being seen always at their desks, politicians organised their lives with time to recover their verve and peace of mind away from the Westminster hothouse. Each year the main business of the House of Commons was conducted in the first seven months. In August, MPs would disappear for the summer and autumn, occasionally returning in late November for a few weeks' business before Christmas. Then the cycle would begin again in earnest in the middle of January. The business of government during the long recess was generally conducted by post from landed estates around the country. Summits, endless committees, constituency surgeries and meetings with delegations were definitely not on the agenda – no wonder that every man of ambition wanted to be a member of the House of Commons.

For Gladstone, Hawarden was a genuine retreat. Although he did occasionally receive Westminster visitors, he never sought to make it one of the great 'political' houses to match Woburn or Chatsworth. Instead he spent his time engaged in thinking and exercising. Gladstone was in his fiftieth year by the time he returned to the Treasury in 1859. When he might reasonably have expected to be three-quarters of the way through his life, he was in fact determined about resisting the effects of time. 'Half a century! What do those little words enfold!' he wrote on his birthday. 'Yet there is in me a resistance to the passage of Time as if I could lay hands on it and stop it: as if youth were yet in me and life and youth were one.'

Gladstone was extremely fit for a man of fifty. At just over five foot ten inches in height, his weight was a mere eleven and a half stone. Mornings were spent at his desk in prodigious letter writing, but afternoons usually involved some kind of vigorous activity. If he was not chopping down trees, Gladstone was usually out walking. Each summer, on holiday at Penmaenmawr, Gladstone would habitually walk more than twenty miles a day in the mountains, usually having already started the day with an early morning sea-bathe. Gladstone preferred these bracing dips to those of its English rivals such as Brighton, where he found the water too warm. In 1859 he was still braving the punishing waters as late as October.

Flitting in and out of all this activity were Gladstone's seven surviving children – Willy, Stephen, Harry, Herbert, Agnes, Mary and Helen. Even when he was at Hawarden, their father was for much of the time a distant figure behind the closed door of his study. 'We grew to understand that he was much occupied and must not be disturbed,' the youngest boy, Herbert, later wrote. 'We were like little dogs who never resent exclusion but are overjoyed when they are allowed in.' Gladstone worked formidably hard, yet when he left the library was happy to spend time with his children. They often joined him on long walks in the grounds. Together the whole family would play 'cricket round the hat' on the lawn. The boys would help him chop down trees. As they grew older, six of the seven children found the attachment to Hawarden almost impossible to break. 'I am the only one of the seven with a separate home and life apart,' wrote Agnes in 1891. The others all married late, and continued to live at or near Hawarden. Life with Gladstone was intoxicating. 'So few people have lived their whole life,' observed Mary revealingly, 'with their father in the centre of history.'

Giving direction to life at Hawarden on a day-to-day basis was

Gladstone's wife, Catherine. 'How much might I say of her as a hero-woman,' he wrote in his diary after reading *Tannhäuser* on her birthday. Yet their relationship for many decades had been one of affection mixed with more than occasional frustration. What Catherine did not supply was excitement or refinement. For these qualities in the 1860s Gladstone had to look elsewhere.

In the summer after his fiftieth birthday Gladstone began one of the most significant relationships of his life. Harriet, Duchess of Sutherland, as the granddaughter of Georgiana, Duchess of Devonshire, followed in a magnificent tradition as a political hostess. Through blood and marriage, she was the epitome of illustrious, high-minded and well-connected Whiggery. She was a daughter of the Earl of Carlisle whose union linked the great families of the Howards and the Sutherlands. Her son-in-law was the Duke of Argyll. She was a personal friend of the Queen, serving regularly as Mistress of the Robes during Whig administrations. At Cliveden, her striking house on the Thames in Berkshire, or at Chiswick near London, Harriet hosted one of the most glamorous salons of the Victorian age.

By the time she fell in love with Gladstone she was in her mid-fifties and corpulent. His own taste was usually for younger, more beautiful women. Yet the duchess was clever, politically shrewd and well informed. She loved books and ideas in a way that Catherine did not. Most of all, her assessment of Gladstone's genius chimed with his own. For the next eight years until her death, Harriet organised a circle around him, which for the first time moved Gladstone into the Whig social scene.

The nature of Gladstone's relationship with the Duchess of Sutherland was open to conjecture, even though they maintained a certain propriety. Gladstone regularly included references to the duchess in his letters to Catherine, and, on occasion, they would even all stay together under the same roof. Yet most assumed that Gladstone and Harriet were involved. After the death of her husband in February 1861, Gladstone visited the dowager duchess alone with the frequency one might expect of a lover. In May he stayed at Cliveden for two weekends in succession, 'leaving Catherine which seems but selfish'. He was the only guest except her daughter and son-in-law, the Argylls. By early 1863 he was staying overnight on average twice a month, and visited more often during the day. Although Gladstone did not stop his rescue work among prostitutes during this period, he tellingly stopped the self-flagellation that had been a feature of his life since the 1840s.

'None will fill her place for me,' he would record later on hearing news of Harriet's death.

In fact, that turned out not to be the case.

Hughenden Manor

On retreat in the country, Benjamin Disraeli rarely did anything quickly. Pottering around the house, he liked nothing better than to 'saunter in the library, and survey the books'. There he would move between 'writing-tables, couches covered with yellow satin and profusely gilt, oak cabinets ornamented with caryatides, columns and entablatures of Dresden china'. In winter, he might sit gazing into the fire reflecting on 'Dreams! Dreams! Dreams!' The library was south-facing, so in fine weather he would throw open the windows or step on to the terrace to mull over problems of the day. An interconnecting door from the library led straight to Mary Anne's morning room. Together they would sit chatting while observing peacocks on the lawn and the fine view across to Wycombe with its elegant church tower. In the afternoons Disraeli loved to walk among his trees in the parkland. On the west side of the house, the ground fell away into a beech spinney that looked spectacular in the copper colours of autumn. From the rear of the house Disraeli could stroll through the 'German forest', planted with pines, laurels, and yew trees, to walk the generous rides, accompanied by Mrs Disraeli in pony and trap.

Disraeli took as much pleasure from Hughenden as Gladstone did in Hawarden. For both men their country houses were places where they could retreat from the demands of politics to a simpler life. Yet in many ways Disraeli's need was greater. By the time he arrived back in Buckinghamshire each autumn he was consistently exhausted. Although only five years older than Gladstone he enjoyed little of his great rival's healthy vitality. London winters in particular disagreed with his weak bronchial system. He was often disturbingly thin. His comment that 'I live solely on snipes' was witty but also close enough to the truth to give concern. Sallow skin, his pronounced stoop and lethargic deportment combined to give off an eerily death-like quality even by his mid-fifties. 'I believed D. was in reality a corpse; which occasionally came to life,' the otherwise admiring Sir William Fraser observed, adding 'that if he had ever been a human being, it must have been at a far distant period of the world's existence'.

His genuine sense of pleasure in arriving back at Hughenden at the end of a session is perhaps best captured in a scene from his novel *Endymion*: 'The woods were beginning to assume the first fair livery of autumn, when it is beautiful without decay,' he wrote. 'The lime and the larch had not yet dropped a golden leaf, and the burnished beeches flamed in the sun. Every now and then an occasional oak or elm rose, still as full of deep green foliage as if it were midsummer; while the dark verdure of the pines sprang up with effective contrast amid the gleaming and resplendent chestnuts.'

Disraeli recovered his sense of equilibrium by throwing himself into life as an English country gentleman. Since 1836 he had regularly attended the Quarter Sessions as a Justice of the Peace. He had been a deputy lieutenant of the county since 1845. The grounds of Hughenden would often be given over to great fetes for hundreds of his local constituents. He also enjoyed a fairly romanticised view of his staff on the estate. 'I like very much the society of woodmen,' he wrote in 1860. 'Their conversation is most interesting – quick and constant observation, and perfect knowledge . . . They live in the air, and Nature whispers to them many of her secrets.' That affection, however, did not prevent Disraeli from keeping their rents high in a vain attempt to pay off his prodigious debt.

The only aspect of English country life for which Disraeli showed no enthusiasm was huntin', shootin' and fishin'. To the amusement of his friends, and sneers of others, he would often dress not altogether convincingly in the clothes of a field sportsman. Yet the physicality of these pursuits was neither to his taste nor disposition. When visiting the great country houses of the landed gentry, he would usually absent himself to the library, or otherwise spend lazy mornings walking the grounds. For this reason his favourite place to visit was Lord Salisbury's Hatfield House, where he would be left alone and not even obliged to rise for breakfast.

Among the many pleasures of Hughenden for Disraeli was time spent with Mary Anne. He married her for money, but had quickly come to appreciate her many qualities as a wife. 'My own experience tells me,' Disraeli wrote to a young friend, 'that domestic happiness, far from being an obstacle to public life, is the best support of an honourable ambition.' Mary Anne dedicated her life to his comfort and wellbeing. She was a dozen years older than her husband, which enabled her to give the kind of motherly attention much needed by a man of Disraeli's nervous disposition. She ran the household with a parsimony that matched his extravagance (with breakfast notoriously accompanied by only one bread roll per guest). Mrs Disraeli kept the books, cut and dyed her husband's hair (even arranging his curl each morning), and chose his clothes. Disraeli's transition from dandy to dowdy owed much to Mary Anne's influence. 'Make the coat as if for a young man who stands upright!' she instructed Mr Jackson in Cork Street. 'No wonder the clothes don't fit him,' the miserable tailor grumbled to his other clients. Above all Mary Anne believed in Disraeli as a man of destiny. 'His whole soul is devoted to politics and ambition,' she wrote entirely without censure.

Her lack of education and modest social background led many in their circle to think Mrs Disraeli 'common'. Occasionally she would astound fellow guests at parties with outlandish remarks, such as telling ladies admiring a painting of a nude Greek god, 'You should see my Dizzy in the bath!' Yet for all her flightiness and occasional gaffes, Mary Anne could show steely resolve in protecting and nurturing her husband's genius. Often by the 1860s this meant downplaying her own increasingly poor health. Even when a clumsy footman shut her hand in the carriage door while accompanying Disraeli to the Commons for a vital debate, she would not tell her husband lest it put him off his stroke.

Unlike Gladstone, who persistently attracted rumours, there was very little gossip about Disraeli straying from the marital bed. Aside from his with Bulwer Lytton, the only friendship that attracted much attention was that with Lady Dorothy Nevill. Daughter of the Earl of Orford and a member of the Walpole family, she lived diagonally across from the Disraelis in Upper Grosvenor Street. Mary Anne was godmother to one of the Nevill children; she and 'Dolly' corresponded regularly when they were out of town. Twenty-one years younger than Disraeli, Dorothy Nevill was, according to him, 'without absolute beauty [yet] wild and bewitching'. During Mary Anne's increasing periods of illness in the 1860s and 1870s, Dorothy would often escort Disraeli to official functions. This inevitably gave rise to some low-grade speculation about the nature of the relationship. Enemies were quick to suggest that Ralph Nevill, Dorothy's third surviving son born in 1865, had a passing resemblance to Disraeli. Yet if this were the case, Ralph later gave no indication that Disraeli had been anything other than a celebrity childhood acquaintance. 'I well remember my mother telling me as a child to say "How-do-you-do" to him,' recalled Ralph of a visit to Grosvenor Gate. 'Dressed in a shabby old paletot, he sat looking at me as if I were a strange little animal, but with no unkindly expression on his inscrutable old face he shook me by the hand.' Difficult though Disraeli often was to read, especially for one so young, his bland reaction seems unlikely in a childless man when confronted by his own flesh and blood.

Throughout their marriage Disraeli did everything in his power to make Mary Anne happy. His letters are full of loving endearments. He cheerfully spent time with her, including those contented months at Hughenden when they were most often alone. 'She believed in me when men despised me,' he explained. When snide acquaintances tried to draw him into disloyalty he unfailingly responded devotedly.

'I saw you walking in the Park with Mrs Disraeli, Ben,' ventured "the rudest man in England", Bernal Osborne MP, 'and I can't for the life of me understand what sentiment she can possibly inspire you with.'

'A sentiment quite foreign to your nature, Bernal,' retorted Disraeli. 'Gratitude.'

The opportunity for a rare glimpse through the chink in the curtains to the private world of Disraeli's marriage came after a triumphant visit to Edinburgh in 1867. 'We were so delighted with our reception, Mrs Disraeli and I,' he told a friend, 'that after we got home we actually danced a jig (or was it a hornpipe?) in our bedroom.' This from a man who never smiled in public. Few would have doubted Mary Anne when she said that although he had married her for money 'Dizzy would have married me again for love'.

Perhaps it was his admiration of this sentiment that encouraged Gladstone towards a rare concession in judging Disraeli's character. Despite his poor relationship with her husband, Gladstone seemed genuinely to like Mary Anne and her unpretentious manner. During her frequent illnesses, he would call to inquire about her condition (having prudently first checked that Disraeli would be out). When she was recovering from a life-threatening illness in the autumn of 1867, Gladstone made a generous reference to her in the Queen's Speech debate, which uncharacteristically brought a tear to the 'much touched' Disraeli's eye. He even reported to the Queen that 'Mr Gladstone [was] very kind and considerate'.

Immediately afterwards Disraeli wrote to Gladstone. He did not try to hide their differences, but the tone, and that of the reply, made it one of the warmest exchanges between the two men.

'My wife had always a strong personal regard for you, and being of a vivid and original character, she could comprehend and value your great gifts and qualities,' wrote Disraeli.

'I have always been grateful for, and have sincerely reciprocated, Mrs Disraeli's regard,' Gladstone responded gracefully, 'and during the recent crisis I was naturally mindful of it, but, even if I had not had the honour and pleasure of knowing her, it would have been impossible not to sympathise with you at a moment when the fortitude necessary to bear the labours and trials of your station was subjected to a new burden of a character so crushing and peculiar.'

Gladstone's affection for Mary Anne ensured that at least a semblance of civility was maintained between the rivals.

St George's Chapel, Windsor, 1861

Bells tolled mournfully into the freezing December air. Minute guns fired. All was draped in black. Prince Albert's coffin, shrouded in a heavy embroidered pall, moved slowly in procession through the nave of the chapel towards a raised dais. Behind followed the chief mourners, all men as tradition prescribed, dressed in black morning coats. Prominent among them was the Prince of Wales, heir to the throne, visibly struggling to keep his emotions in check. Beside him was eleven-year-old Prince Arthur in floods of tears for his dead father. During the short funeral service, Dean Wellesley's voice faltered time and time again; the Garter King of Arms became so overwhelmed as he read out the Prince Consort's titles that he was inaudible. All around, the usually composed faces of the Establishment were flushed with emotion. One of the mourners, Lord Torrington, believed 'that more real sorrow was evinced at this funeral than at any that has taken place there for a vast number of years'. And all of this in front of the discreetly positioned reporters whose poignant accounts of the service would fill the next day's newspapers. To William Gladstone, who attended with the cabinet, it was 'a very solemn scene'.

The death of Albert brought a new relationship into the lives of Gladstone and Disraeli, which would have a profound influence on their rivalry. The widowed Queen had always been nervous and highly strung. After the death of her husband she plunged into depression. Only in her early forties, with a clutch of young children, the burden of state duties that the Consort had for twenty-one years done so much to carry almost immediately threatened to overwhelm her. Lord

Palmerston was not simply mouthing a platitude when he described the prince's fate as 'a matter of the most momentous national importance'. Even in his letter to the Queen immediately following Albert's death, the prime minister urged her to find the 'strength of mind and a sense of Duties commensurate with the position which you hold'. Instead she went into a period of conspicuous mourning that lasted another four decades. The memory of Albert took on a cult status as the authority to which, in a very real sense, all questions of dispute were referred. 'The thought, the *certain* feeling and belief,' wrote the Queen, 'that her adored Angel is *near* her, *loving* her, watching over her, praying for her and guiding her – is – next to the blessed Hope of that Eternal reunion – her only comfort in her overwhelming affliction.' It was an exact understanding of this sentiment that allowed Disraeli to trump Gladstone with increasing frequency in his relationship with the Queen during the next twenty years.

This was, ironically, a reversal of the actual relationship as it had stood during Albert's lifetime. Although Disraeli's rapport with the royal family had improved somewhat in the immediate years before the Consort's death, the connection remained an uneasy one. In 1852 Victoria had attempted to dissuade Lord Derby from appointing Disraeli to the Treasury. Derby had demurred, but when he went to see her later that year to resign, he was subjected to a lecture from the prince who expressed the view that Disraeli 'may become one of the most dangerous men in Europe'. Albert's view of Gladstone was entirely different. By the 1850s Gladstone had become a regular visitor at Osborne, the prince's Italianate villa on the Isle of Wight, where they would spend hours discussing art and social progress. Like Gladstone, Albert had shared a passion for administrative reform. Where the prince had tried to block Disraeli's rise to Chancellor of the Exchequer in 1852, it was his personal intervention with Lord Aberdeen that secured the post for Gladstone the following year.

Yet as the Queen, at turns hysterical and morose, plummeted into depression, Gladstone did not hesitate to express concern about her withdrawal from public life. As the second anniversary of Albert's death approached, Gladstone found himself in conversation with Victoria at Holyrood Palace, Edinburgh. She lamented how 'the one purpose of her life was gone' and hoped life might now be 'short'. For this Gladstone upbraided her. 'I told her that she would not give way, that duty would sustain her, . . . that her burden was altogether peculiar, but the honour was in proportion,' he wrote afterwards. Appalled, the Queen 'hustled me' out. 'Though I spoke abruptly enough, and did not find myself timid,' he concluded frustratedly, 'yet I could [not] manage it at all to my satisfaction.'

While Gladstone pursued an unwise strategy of speaking his mind, Disraeli's more febrile nature was able to coax the Queen in a more sympathetic way. Before Albert's death he had worried that 'the worst consequence possible is one, unluckily, not unlikely: that without being absolutely incapacitated for affairs, she may fall into a state of mind in which it will be difficult to do business with her, and impossible to anticipate what she will approve or disapprove'. From a fairly early stage he came to recognise that Albert remained the key to Victoria's heart and mind. Now, at audiences with the Queen, Disraeli rarely missed an opportunity to venerate Albert's memory while he flirted and flattered her. At suitable moments in parliament he would deliver fulsome speeches in honour of the prince, correctly anticipating that they would be well received at Osborne. Any previous wariness Victoria retained was quickly swept away on a wave of gratitude and affection. Soon she was telling courtiers that 'Mr Disraeli was the only person who appreciated the Prince'.

The Queen had a new favourite – and Disraeli had won a powerful new ally in his rivalry with Gladstone.

1862 Exhibition

The parliamentary delegation stood together gossiping in a close gaggle only occasionally bothering to glance at the exhibits that surrounded them. Throughout the hall were great shows of armaments – uneasy symbols of British military prowess following a below-par war in the Crimea – and more crassly commercial merchandise that would soon earn this showcase the unkind popular nickname 'the Palace of Puffs'. This was the follow-up to the Great Exhibition of 1851, now moved to a venue (later the Natural History Museum) just off Cromwell Road. The Queen had insisted that this new exhibition must still go ahead despite the death of Albert, but she did not bother to attend. With the energising patronage of the Prince Consort gone, and the Queen absent, this grand opening seemed flat and routine. 'This is not so fascinating a one as that you remember when you made me an assignation by the crystal [palace],' Disraeli afterwards wrote disappointedly to Mrs Brydges Willyams of Torquay.

That 1862 May Day outing had not been an easy one for Disraeli. While chatting in the parliamentary throng he had become only gradually aware of William Gladstone standing immediately behind him. The two men were so close their shoulders almost touched, but their backs remained unflinchingly turned against each other. Neither man seemed willing to make the first gesture. As more and more time passed, it became increasingly awkward for either to spin round so that they might speak to each other. Listening intently, all Disraeli heard was Gladstone chatting animatedly about Exhibition pottery, for which he was a competition judge. At the earliest opportunity, he veered away only to find that he had jumped from the political frying pan into the literary fire. There immediately in his path was that rare person of Disraeli's acquaintance: someone he detested more than Gladstone. William Makepeace Thackeray had written a vicious pastiche, 'Codlingsby', of Disraeli's novel *Coningsby* in 1847. The two men had not spoken since. Now, as their paths crossed, it was as if neither existed to the other. 'They saw each other,' observed the amused theatrical manager John Hollingshead, 'but showed no signs of recognition.' It had been a day of snubs for Disraeli.

Gladstone and Disraeli's mutual coldness ensured that even when they occasionally worked together their joint efforts were somehow fouled by bad luck. In the decade before his death, Prince Albert had planned the transformation of thirty acres of Kensington Gore into an imaginative cultural theme park of museums, colleges of art and music and scientific institutions. His last public function had been to open the newly completed Horticultural Gardens. Following his demise, the Queen was very keen that the scheme should continue in his memory. Gladstone, who had been an enthusiastic adviser to the prince on the scheme, eagerly promised Treasury support, including the purchase of the 1862 Exhibition site and building. Disraeli, with an eye on the Queen, readily offered opposition support. When the measure got to the floor of the House of Commons in the summer of 1863, both men discovered to their horror that what should have been a simple matter had turned into a major row. Questions were raised about the suitability of the building, which was generally considered ugly and impractical. Would it not be better just to buy the site, MPs asked reasonably, and put up a purpose-built museum rather than move into an unsuitable structure. Gladstone replied haughtily that it was not the business of MPs to decide these matters. Incensed by this remark, speaker after speaker rose to attack Gladstone and point out that if the chancellor did not want their opinion, neither would he get their votes nor the money.

Faced with a backbench revolt, Gladstone asked Disraeli to help rally numbers. Usually so assured in these arts, Disraeli now behaved with even less tact than Gladstone. He toured the tea room and bar, urging his own MPs to back the measure. Pointing conspiratorially to his pocket, he implied to each that he had a letter of support from the Queen herself – how could they turn their backs on the widowed monarch as she struggled to carry through her dead husband's great scheme? 'This had a disastrous effect,' laconically recalled the Tory grandee Lord Malmesbury. At the despatch box, Disraeli found himself in the disagreeable position of being jeered by MPs on both sides of the chamber. 'The House rose up en masse,' observed Malmesbury from the Gallery, 'and, after a scene of the utmost confusion and excitement, defeated the Government by more than two to one; Gladstone and Disraeli looking equally angry.' Disraeli usually took victory and defeat with the same passivity; a humiliating loss in the company of Gladstone, however, was more than enough to bring a flush of colour to his otherwise sallow cheek.

'Spoke on Exhibition Building,' wrote Gladstone blandly in his diary for that day. 'Defeat by much more than two to one.' While he would have recognised that working with the enemy, however unsuccessfully, was a rare event, Gladstone was also painfully aware that there were few trusted confidants left at Westminster with whom he could discuss such matters. During the first half of the 1860s Gladstone lost several of his closest friends. Shortly before Christmas 1860 Lord Aberdeen had died. Since the death of Sir Robert Peel, Aberdeen had taken over the role of father figure in Gladstone's life. Although often exasperated by his young colleague's flights of fancy, Aberdeen never lost sight of Gladstone's outstanding ability. His death removed an important stabilising influence. 'In the combination of profound feeling with a calm of mind equally profound, of thorough penetration with the largest charity, of the wisdom of the serpent with the harmlessness of the dove, in the total suppression and exclusion of self from his reckonings and actions,' he wrote to Aberdeen's son, 'in all this we may think him supreme'. He was Gladstone's last mentor.

Aberdeen's death six years beyond his 'three score years and ten' made his demise sad if not tragic. The loss the following summer of Gladstone's closest friend offered more troubling intimations on mortality. Sidney Herbert, 'that beautiful and sunny spirit', was only fifty when he died. Two days beforehand, Gladstone had deliberately gone to watch from a window opposite as Herbert returned home to Belgrave Square for the last time after a failed attempt to regain his health abroad. 'Alas it was a sore sight,' he wrote afterwards. When Robert Phillimore called on Gladstone the day after Herbert's passing he found him in a state of desolation. 'His eyes filled with tears all the time he spoke to me in a broken voice about his departed friend,' he recorded. Even five years later, Gladstone would tell of how 'it is difficult to speak of Herbert'. Instead he raged against time, writing for his 1861 birthday entry that 'the strangest, though not the worst, of all in me is a rebellion (I know not what else to call it) against growing old'.

Hard on the heels of the deaths of Aberdeen and Herbert came those of two more Peelites, James Graham and Charles Canning. The effect was to make the Peelites extinct as a political group, leaving Gladstone no tag other than 'Liberal'. The death of Herbert, despite the intense friendship, also removed a serious rival. The Whig grandee Lord Granville told Lord Derby that 'if Herbert had retained his health, he must have been Palmerston's successor, and even hinted that an arrangement to that effect had been made!'

Whether this might have been the start of a titanic political rivalry – Herbert and Disraeli – thus remains one of the 'what ifs' of history as another 'lost leader' bit the dust. With Palmerston approaching eighty and Russell about to turn seventy, Gladstone, despite the many reservations about his character, now seemed ideally placed to take up the mantle of leader-in-waiting of the Liberal party.

He moved into the wings stage left, eyeing his great rival stage right, both men waiting like eager understudies for the chance to move into the spotlight.

11

The People's William

Harry Clasper, a steamship named for the famous Tyne oarsman, moved slowly away from its moorings at Gateshead accompanied by a thunderous cacophony of gunfire and bells. On the quayside thousands of miners from the local pits of Durham and Northumberland cheered loudly, throwing their caps into the air. Young children were hoisted on to the shoulders of their fathers to get a better look. In front of the steamer scores of workers swam a muscular guard of honour. Behind followed twenty-five ships, clad in bright bunting, each sounding a high-pitched whistle in salute. As the flotilla made a dignified progress along the Tyne, thousands more men from chemical works, coal-staiths and shipyards lined the riverside for twenty-two miles to wave and cheer.

'Such a pomp I shall probably never again witness,' recorded William Gladstone, the man at the centre of all this attention. 'Circumstances have brought upon me what I do not in any way deserve . . . The spectacle was really one for [the artist] Turner, no else.'

Everywhere that Gladstone went on his five-day visit to the Northeast he found cheering crowds and packed halls. Gateshead, Newcastle, Middlesbrough and Sunderland all competed to give him the warmest, most rapturous welcome. Hundreds of working men crammed into town halls to hear him speak; thousands of others lined his routes. 'I ought to be thankful,' Gladstone noted, 'still more ought I to be ashamed.' Such was his exhilarated nervous state that 'giddiness came over me for a moment while I spoke in Sunderland, and I had to take hold of the table'. No wonder that as his train pulled out of

Middlesbrough station, accompanied by another ovation, Gladstone admitted that he was taking 'a reluctant goodbye'. For quite suddenly and unexpectedly Gladstone had become a celebrity – 'the People's William'.

The budgets of 1860 and 1861 had transformed William Gladstone into a hero of industrial workers. Slashing duties encouraged an immediate boom in popular consumption, which earned him the reputation as the champion of the people's breakfast table. Even more admired was the chancellor's defeat of the House of Lords on paper duties – 'don't tax knowledge' – that provided him with a new national constituency and grateful newspapers willing to promote him. Increasingly literate workers eagerly followed his speeches in the reports of the penny press. His couching of economic policy in moral tones, with an emphasis on prudence and balancing the books, chimed with the everyday reality of working families, who understood only too well the demands of prudent housekeeping. 'There is not a man who labours and sweats for his daily bread,' suggested John Bright, 'there is not a woman living in a cottage who strives to make her home happy for husband and children, to whom the words of the chancellor of the exchequer have not brought hope, and to whom his measures, which have been defended with an eloquence few can equal and with a logic none can contest, have not administered consolation.'

This was something of a shock, not least for Gladstone. It also offered an opportunity. He quickly recognised, as did others, that his great strength within the party lay in an ability to straddle different Liberal traditions. Gladstone offered comfort to the established order. He was, after all, an Eton and Oxford-educated high-churchman, a member of the landed gentry and (at this stage) a close confidant of the royal family. A background in trade gave him personal ties and credibility in the industrial heartlands. His modernising agenda at the Treasury had confirmed him as a man in touch with the commercial and manufacturing interests of the country. Now he was attracting huge demonstrations of support organised by the so-called 'plebeian radicals' – a mixture of industrial workers, tradesmen, craftsmen and small-factory owners. They warmed to Gladstone's moral politics and would encourage his self-conscious identification with 'the masses'.

The name 'William Gladstone' had suddenly become one to look for in the newspapers, elevating him to the kind of celebrity status matched only by that of the buccaneering prime minister Lord

Palmerston. For most of his career he had been an unpopular politician in the country at large. His great campaigning issues had hardly been likely to endear him to ordinary people. In recent years he had found himself against public opinion on concerns ranging from resisting an inquiry into the Crimean War, arguing for peace with Russia, denouncing panic on papal aggression and opposing a divorce bill.

This unpopular image was re-enforced by his reputation at Westminster. In the House of Commons, Gladstone was seen as a difficult, prickly character. He was a habitual resigner, even creating problems for those he admired such as Peel and Aberdeen. His preachy, arrogant manner had often infuriated fellow MPs. Even those who admired him, such as John Trelawny, found him aloof and cold. Trelawny observed from the backbenches Gladstone's 'fixed, stony, corpse-like countenance and an eye which seemed to be of glass'. At other times, the vehemence of his denunciations could be so personally offensive, such as that to Disraeli in the 1852 budget debate, as to make an enemy for life.

Above all, Gladstone was not a 'party man'. He had refused to bind the wounds of the Conservative party after the split during the Corn Laws debate. Now he sat as a well-placed but unloved member of a Liberal administration from which he always seemed on the brink of walking out. Following the deaths of Aberdeen, Graham and Herbert, the Peelite caucus of which he was a prime mover was no more. His sudden elevation among the labouring poor as the bringer of prosperity and cheap food – a man of the people – came just at a moment when Gladstone was dangerously isolated at Westminster.

Presented with the chance to create a new power base, Gladstone seized the mantle of 'the People's William' with alacrity.

To some extent, Gladstone's new role was one for which he, like so many of his background, had spent a lifetime in preparation. Whether the young William was to have been politician, priest, barrister or don, the ability to capture and command audiences, without any kind of microphone, was central to any success he could have. He might deliver a sermon from the pulpit of mighty cathedrals, address large crowds at the hustings, or argue his case from the benches of the House of Commons: in all these arenas, whatever his message, he had need of oratorical skill.

Arthur Godley, later Gladstone's private secretary, summed up his master's voice as rooted in 'admirable delivery, his command of words, and his grand voice'. The first of these two attributes came through a

Young Disraeli:
'I love fame.
I love reputation.'

Young Gladstone:
'the rising hope of those
stern and unbending Tories'

Sir Robert Peel

15th Earl of Derby

Lord John Russell

Lord Aberdeen's government, 1855
(Left to right: Wood, Graham, Molesworth, Gladstone, Argyll, Clarendon, Lansdowne,
Russell, Granville, Aberdeen, Cranworth, Palmerston, Grey, Herbert, and Newcastle)

Catherine Gladstone

Mary Anne Disraeli

'Like two of Sir Walter Scott's champions':
warring chancellors in the 1850s

The House of Commons

Disraeli with
Monty Corry: 'You must
be my impresario.'

Gladstone in 1861:
'The People's William'

Chancellor of the Exchequer, Gladstone (front row, near right), inspects the new Metropolitan Line – the world's first underground railway – on 24 May, 1862

The Hyde Park Riot, 23 July 1866: 'We are expecting to have all our heads broken tonight.'

The rivals as seen in the 1860s
by *Punch* (above) and the
London Sketchbook
(left and right)

blend of natural ability and the training drummed into him at Eton. The headmaster, Dr Keate, gave personal tuition in rhetoric, backed up by his favourite instrument of encouragement, the birch rod. (Keate notoriously once flogged more than eighty boys in a single day; his greatest regret at the end of his life was that he had not flogged far more.) Principal texts were Aristotle's *Rhetoric* and Hugh Blair's *Lectures on Rhetoric*. From Blair, boys learnt to develop a critical analysis of the spoken word, always with the stricture that command of grammar and vocabulary were not only essential to good writing, but also to 'eloquence, or public speaking'. This eloquence was not in reading a prepared text, but rather speaking extempore. By the 1860s Gladstone had total mastery in finding the right words while on his feet, aided by a prodigious memory to command facts and figures.

Later Gladstone would adapt Blair's advice into a brief set of suggestions of his own on public speaking: '1. Study plainness of language, always preferring the simpler word. 2. Shortness of sentences. 3. Distinctness of articulation. 4. Test and question your own arguments beforehand, not waiting for critic or opponent. 5. Seek a thorough digestion of, and familiarity with, your subject, and rely mainly on these to prompt the proper words. 6. Remember that if you are to sway an audience you must besides thinking out your matter, watch them all along.'

Added to Blair's lessons on rhetoric, young William had been trained in the visuals of public speaking, particularly posture and gesture. His key text was John Walker's *The Elements of Gesture*, which provided a practical guide for eager younger statesmen – a nineteenth-century version of *How to Make Friends and Influence People*. The speaker 'shall always keep the body in a graceful position, and shall so carry its motions at proper intervals, as to seem the subject operating upon the words, and not the speaker on the subject'. Specific instructions were then offered on the positioning of the head, legs, arms, wrists and hands, with explanations as to how changes of position 'if they keep time will be in tune as it were to each other, and to force and energy add harmony and variety'.

Instruction gave Gladstone proficiency from an early age in the art of public speaking, but this hardly made him unique among his contemporaries. Success on the platform required more than just a good training. What Gladstone discovered in 1862 was that he had an ability to move and inspire large audiences through sheer force of personality. To begin with, there was his voice: a resonant baritone, with variety of tone and marvellous projection. Gladstone had the kind of voice that demanded attention even when speaking on dull economic topics. Added to this was what John Morley, later his amanuensis, described as 'a falcon's eye with strange imperious flash' set in a large, imposing head that the Victorians believed suggested a big brain (such as Beethoven's). When combined with his mastery of language and gesture, a natural sense of authority and a certain easy confidence, it was clear that Gladstone possessed the elixir to become an 1860s celebrity.

If Gladstone was a great actor on the stage, then he was also a shrewd manager behind the scenes. From the beginning his visits to various provincial cities were carefully planned to extract the maximum advantage. The pattern, established early on, rarely changed. Visits usually lasted three or four days. Whatever his popular appeal, he would inevitably stay in lavish comfort at the house of a local aristocrat or wealthy magnate to escape the public eye.

The first day or so was spent inspecting factories and poor urban quarters. In the evening, Gladstone would be the guest of honour at large dinner parties for the rich and well connected, at which he would hold forth, or 'converse', on the great issues of the day. Then on the third evening came a grandstanding address at the biggest venue available, such as the Free Trade Hall in Manchester. Having brought events to fever pitch, Gladstone would conclude the visit with a triumphal civic event – perhaps a speech on the steps of the town hall, or a special service of thanksgiving at the cathedral – before boarding his train for a tumultuous send-off by cheering fans crowded on to the station platform. All in all, it was guaranteed to be quite a performance.

No wonder then that Benjamin Disraeli, observing from London, sourly noted that a new, not altogether agreeable, element had been injected into his rivalry with Gladstone. For while the chancellor was playing to packed houses, Disraeli lamented, 'I am an actor without an audience.'

Hughenden Manor, 13 October 1863

Disraeli sat brooding at his desk, telegram in hand, in the library of his Buckinghamshire country house. It was autumn, and parliament was in recess. He had spent more than six weeks away from London, recovering from the stresses and strains of leading the opposition in the Commons, enjoying these easy surroundings. The house had the previous winter been remodelled inside and out by his wife to lend even greater comfort. Mary Anne had carried out this Gothic refurbishment without telling her husband, so that when he arrived back for the 1863 Easter recess he had been greeted with this wonderful surprise. 'It is quite another place, and of far more pretension and effect,' he had written delightedly to Lady Dorothy Nevill, adding that his study in particular 'has quite lost the circulating-library look'.

For all the pleasure Hughenden afforded, Disraeli could not push aside darker thoughts that autumn. The telegram received that morning brought his suppressed gloom rushing to the surface. Lord Lyndhurst, Disraeli's early patron, had died, in his nineties. He had enjoyed a long life, two happy marriages, the company of many beautiful women and a career that had taken him to the pinnacle of the legal profession. All in all, not a bad lot, Disraeli might have reflected. Indeed, he immediately set down his thoughts on the great qualities of his mentor. 'He had a mind equally distinguished for its vigour and flexibility,' wrote Disraeli. He was 'indulgent, placable, free from prejudice and utterly devoid of vanity.' The measure of the man, Disraeli concluded, was that 'Lord Melbourne his great opponent and greatest admirer always addressed him in affection as the true aristocrat.'

This death prompted other morbid thoughts closer to home. Finishing his tribute to Lyndhurst, Disraeli jotted down on another piece of paper a truth that was disturbing him as he confronted his own bleak future: Lord Lyndhurst used to say, when a celebrity disappeared, 'No one is ever missed.' The first half of the 1860s were years of doldrums and regret for Disraeli. His reflection on Lyndhurst was one of many such notes made during these years. Thinking about his life and the people he had met, these personal observations would run to hundreds of pages. Disraeli was clearly preparing for the task of writing his memoirs, which in turn suggested he was readying himself for imminent retirement from public life.

Conservative party dissatisfaction with Disraeli had worn him down in the Commons, but there were personal losses too that contributed to his low spirits during these years. Disraeli's two closest confidantes outside his marriage died within a few years of each other. His sister Sarah, who adored him and was a weekly correspondent, had died at the turn of the decade. 'Poor Sa!' he would say later. 'We've lost our audience, we've lost our audience.' He had trusted her completely, often writing about his fears in a way that he kept from Mary Anne. Her death robbed him not just of a lifelong companion but a valuable outlet for his frustrations.

In 1863, just a few weeks after the death of Lyndhurst, another important correspondent died. Disraeli's relationship with Mrs Brydges Willyams had been an odd one, yet no one reading the letters spanning more than ten years could doubt that he wrote to her about politics in a way that would have been inconceivable had she been in society. After her death, the inner Disraeli, as revealed through his letters to this widowed benefactress, went silent for a decade until he began an astonishingly frank correspondence with the daughters of Lord Forester.

'I have lost a kind and faithful friend,' he wrote to Lord Derby of Mrs Brydges Willyams, 'but I have lost her in the fullness of years, and she has made me the heir to her not inconsiderable fortune.' That legacy of £30,000 enabled Disraeli to pay off a considerable part of the debts that had cast a shadow across his life for decades. This came on top of the generosity of another devotee, Andrew Montagu, a Yorkshire landowner, who bought up all Disraeli's debts, around £57,000, and charged him notional interest to significantly reduce his outgoings. Added to this was the government pension of £2000 he now received as a former chancellor. In total, Disraeli reckoned by the middle of the decade that his family income was £9000 per annum (of which half was Mary Anne's).

This relative financial comfort, after a lifetime in debt, added to Disraeli's contemplation of retirement. Sitting on the terrace at Hughenden, surrounded by his pink geraniums and blue African lilies, the temptation to quit political life for the leisurely existence of a country gentleman seemed more tempting than ever. He would turn sixty in 1864. The thought of leaving London, with its dirt and smog and noise was hugely enticing. There would be no more late-night sittings at the House, or whinging and difficult MPs to placate. The ceaseless, rancorous, dispiriting life that was the lot of Her Majesty's Leader of the Opposition would end.

Colleagues at Westminster now began to notice that Disraeli was fading. 'D. seems to me either growing old or in weak health,' lamented Stanley in February 1864. 'He has lost his former vivacity, and sleeps much in his seat.' Even the fires of political rivalry seemed to be going out. Among his personal reflections was a literary project to keep him amused during retirement. This would be an essay competition on 'the position of the Hebrew race in universal History, viewed with reference to their influence on Man'. Disraeli would put up the prize of £1000.

'The judges,' he wrote unexpectedly, 'perhaps to be Gladstone, Canon Stanley [of Christ Church, Oxford], and myself.'

Sheldonian Theatre, Oxford, 25 November 1864

For a man who had missed out on university, such an occasion could hardly fail to give surreptitious delight. Here, in Christopher Wren's glorious 'Roman' theatre, with its magnificent seventeenth-century painted ceiling, all eyes were upon him. The Bishop of Oxford, Samuel Wilberforce, was at the podium offering glowing words of welcome and tribute. The bishop, in inviting him to 'make us a great speech', had promised the attendance of 'the Senior University and the undergraduate and the pick of the county'. Now here they were: expectant, quizzical and grateful. All Oxford had turned out for Disraeli. All that is except the University's sitting Liberal MP. 'Stayed at home in evening with cough,' William Gladstone lamely recorded in his diary that day. Even basic good manners could not entice him to Oxford to be lectured to by Benjamin Disraeli on religion.

For Disraeli, on the other hand, the chance to discomfort Gladstone on his home turf had been too tempting to refuse. The religious debates at the university were no longer those of Newman and the Anglo-Catholics. Instead Oxford was dominated by the 'Broad Church' views of Benjamin Jowett and Arthur Stanley, and the fierce debate on evolution inspired by publication five years earlier of Darwin's *On the Origin of Species*. Broad churchmen and scientists tended to gravitate towards the Liberal party, which made them an obvious target for a sharp lash from Disraeli's tongue. He delivered it with typical epigrammatic flair. 'The question is this,' he told his Oxford audience: 'is Man an ape or angel? My Lord, I am on the side of the angels.'

Disraeli might have been in the doldrums in the early 1860s, but, as his visit to Oxford proved, he could still cause a sensation when the opportunity presented itself. When Gladstone proposed that income tax should be applied to charitable donations, Disraeli led the assault from the opposition benches that forced the chancellor to back down. The government's cack-handed response to the changing balance of power in Europe during the 1864 Schleswig-Holstein crisis prompted an attack that ran them close to resignation. Yet these forays were rare. For the most part, Disraeli was bound by Lord Derby's desire to keep the government in place for fear that the Conservatives would embarrass themselves in office. Opposition was easy enough for the gout-ridden Derby to accept: holed up for most of the year at Knowsley, drinking too much port, he had more interest in the fate of his racing stable than the party. This left his second-in-command to carry out a policy of drift that was profoundly uncongenial to his nature. 'The Tory party is only in its proper position when it represents popular principles,' Disraeli complained. 'Then it is truly irresistible.'

Voters seemed to agree. An election in the summer of 1865 returned the government with its majority intact. The ballot had, in effect, been a plebiscite on Palmerston. Despite the octogenarian prime minister's inept handling of the many international crises, which had left Britain's standing on the world stage at its lowest ebb of the century, his popular personality had been enough to carry the day. In 1859 the Conservatives had 287 MPs; now they had 290. The policy of treading water looked set to continue at the very least until Palmerston's death (the only way this formerly buccaneering personality seemed likely to leave office).

Election defeat plunged Disraeli into despondency. 'The leadership of hopeless opposition is a gloomy affair, and there is little distinction when your course is not associated with the possibility of future power,' he wrote glumly to Derby immediately afterwards. Now 'in the decline of life', Disraeli cleared the way for retirement. 'This course involves no sacrifice on my part,' he wrote simply. Perhaps his only consolation was a blow landed in Oxford, where Gladstone had sensationally lost his seat to Gathorne Hardy, a wealthy and fiery tempered Disraelian protégé. 'I am glad we helped him to such an euthanasia,' crowed the master afterwards.

Defeat was a bitter blow to Gladstone – 'A dear dream is dispelled,' he recorded – but it was hardly unexpected. He had been out of sympathy with his electorate for more than a decade and had often thought of finding a less querulous constituency. Yet as an Oxford man, he had felt honoured to represent the University in parliament. Rejection when it finally came was a palpable and genuine hurt.

Politics, however, went on. Defeat allowed Gladstone to take a step that had seemed inevitable since his great rallies had begun in 1862. Faced with the possibility of trouble at Oxford, he had taken the precaution of also entering his name on the ballot for South Lancashire. When it became clear that he would lose Oxford, he then hurtled to

Manchester to address an excited crowd of six thousand in the Free Trade Hall. 'They were in unbounded enthusiasm,' he recorded in great relief afterwards. He followed it with another monster rally in Liverpool that turned out to be 'if possible more enthusiastic than that at Manchester'.

And it was here, freed from the esoteric constraints of the University of Oxford, that Gladstone proclaimed himself the leader of the common man.

'At last my friends,' he thundered above the frenzied excitement of the crowd, 'I am come among you and I am coming among you unmuzzled.'

The People's William had spoken.

12

Cavemen

Brocket Hall, 18 October 1865

The door of the Billiard Room flew open. From inside came rushing a pretty young chambermaid in a state of wild panic. Running through the house calling for help, she tried hastily to rearrange her clothes. What happened next is anyone's guess. No doubt she found a senior member of the household staff who went back with her to the Billiard Room to assess the situation. What confronted them could hardly have been more obvious: sprawled across the green baize of the table was the lifeless body of an elderly gentleman in a state of considerable undress. Quick thinking was needed. The butler was immediately called, his duty to eradicate all evidence of the circumstances of this untimely demise. Together with the valet, he hurriedly reassembled his master's clothes and hauled the corpse upstairs to the bedchamber. From there these loyal servants proceeded quickly to the lady of the house to report the sad news: Lord Palmerston had died 'peacefully in bed', just two days short of his eighty-first birthday.

Whether or not this local gossip surrounding the death of the prime minister was true, it remained a fact that neither Brocket Hall nor Palmerston had been strangers to scandal. This beautiful 1760s house belonged to Lady Palmerston, who had inherited it from her brother, the statesman Lord Melbourne. It had been here, earlier in the century, that Melbourne's wife, Caroline, had famously tumbled from her horse on encountering the cortege of her lover Byron, never fully to recover her sensibility. Palmerston himself had enjoyed a louche reputation all his life. Even as prime minister he had recently been involved in a scandal when threatened with being named in court for having improper relations with a Mrs Cane. This prompted wags in the clubs of St James's to say of the septuagenarian Irish peer that, while she was certainly Cane, was he Able? The unusual circumstances of his death suggested that he was willing to the very end.

William Gladstone was at Clumber House in Nottinghamshire when he received the news hours after Lord Palmerston's death. He was already of a morbid disposition from clearing up the tangled estate of his dear friend the Duke of Newcastle. When the news from Brocket arrived, he went into shock. 'At $6^{1/2}$ a Telegram came announcing his death & made me giddy,' he recorded. But this giddiness did not prevent him moving immediately into a political frame of mind. Where previously he had reserved his own position, fussing and prevaricating when new administrations were formed, he now acted decisively. Aware that some of his more enthusiastic supporters would undoubtedly be touting his name for the succession, he wrote at once to Earl Russell (as Lord John Russell had become in 1861). In that letter he unambiguously proposed Russell as Palmerston's successor. 'I am quite willing to take my chance under your banner, in the exact capacity I now fill,' he wrote plainly, 'and I adopt the step, perhaps a little unusual, of saying so, because it may be convenient to you at a juncture when time is precious.'

It was a humane gesture. The elderly Whig had not held the premiership for thirteen years. Had Gladstone signalled ambitions of his own, he could at the very least have queered Russell's pitch. Instead his speedy and unequivocal support made the succession inevitable. Loyalty came with a reward. Russell, nowadays in the Lords, effectively named Gladstone as his own successor by inviting him to take the lead in the House of Commons. 'I suppose it must come to that,' Gladstone warily judged. Even devoted supporters had doubts as to his suitability. 'He is very great and noble,' wrote his friend, Richard Church (later Dean of St Paul's), 'but he is hated as much as, or more than, he is loved. He is fierce sometimes and wrathful and easily irritated; he wants knowledge of men and speaks rashly. And I look on with some trembling to see what will come of this his first attempt to lead the Commons and prove himself fit to lead England.'

Benjamin Disraeli, meanwhile, had been resting at Hughenden when the news came through of Palmerston's death. 'Mr Disraeli had a great regard for Lord Palmerston,' he wrote thoughtfully to the widow, 'and, although circumstances prevented them from acting politically together, there had subsisted between them, for twenty years, a feeling of mutual confidence, which often removed difficulties.' Although Disraeli had once raged against Palmerston's 'ginger beer' politics, he had enjoyed a genuine affection for old Pam. In the days following the prime minister's death, he sat down to pen some fond memories. How even at eighty, at a great feast, Palmerston could still answer the inquiry of his butler – 'Snipe, My Lord, or pheasant?' – with 'pheasant: thus completing his ninth dish of meat at that meal'. Then there was the last barbed witticism on Lord Granville, whose dairy farm had been wiped out by pestilence around the same time he had married a girl half his age. 'So, having lost his cows,' Palmerston remarked acidly to Disraeli, 'Granville has taken a heifer.' The most affectionate recollection was of Palmerston, after winning a vital debate in 1864, scrambling up the stairs to his wife in the Ladies' Gallery. 'What pluck – to mount those dreadful stairs at three o'clock in the morning and at eighty years of age!' Disraeli warmly recalled. 'It was a great moment!'

Having finished these admiring pen portraits, Disraeli set aside his reminiscences, and with them all thoughts of retirement from public life. 'He is in good health and excellent spirits,' wrote Stanley of Disraeli during a visit to Hughenden the day after Palmerston's death. 'It seems as if the prospect of renewed political life had excited him afresh, and that he had thrown off the lethargy which has been growing upon him for the last year or two.'

An era had passed away with the old premier. Politics had been on hold for too long. A great national debate on the most important issue of the day was about to begin. 'If Johnny [Russell] is the man, there will be a Reform Bill,' Disraeli predicted to Lord Lonsdale two days after Palmerston's death. 'I foresee tempestuous times, and great vicissitudes in public life.'

Politicians in Westminster for years had been circling around the question of reform of the vote. Most recognised that the quirky system established in 1832 needed revision. The five small towns of Honiton, Totnes, Marlborough, Wells and Knaresborough, for example, together enjoyed a population of less than 23,000 but returned as many members to parliament as the 1.5 million inhabitants of Liverpool, Manchester, Birmingham, Sheffield and Leeds. Then there was the delicate and emotive question of extending the franchise to industrial workers, but in a way that would see them represented without allowing them to 'swamp' the system.

Since 1849 no fewer than five Reform Bills had been introduced in parliament, with both parties having attempted the tricky task of reconstructing the political landscape to their own advantage. Of those five attempts, Earl Russell had introduced three. When the new parliament met for the first time in 1866, it seemed inevitable that he would in some way turn again to what had been the preoccupation of a lifetime.

Russell's reputation in history had been secured in 1832 as the man who steered the Great Reform Act through the House of Commons in the face of brutal Tory resistance. By the time he became prime minister for the second time in 1865, Russell had spent more than half a century in active politics. A difficult and contradictory character, he was both impressive and oddly brittle. He was a younger son of the 6th Duke of Bedford and believed profoundly in the superiority of a tight-knit group of fantastically rich Whig families, including the Dukes of Bedford, Devonshire, and Sutherland. Yet the Olympian attitude of this 'Whig of Whigs' was supplemented by nagging doubts about his own place within that aristocratic world. As a younger son he had very little of his own money. His father (and later his brother) gave him only a small allowance, no house of significance and insisted (even as prime minister) that he go down to Woburn Abbey in Bedfordshire to run through his expenses. If Russell left office, the dukes stopped paying his entertainment bills (an effective inducement to govern if ever there was one). Such was his level of indignity and humiliation that even the parsimonious Queen took pity, giving him in 1847 a grace-and-favour house, Pembroke Lodge in Richmond park, where he lived for the next thirty years.

Added to Russell's lack of money was a want of physical stature. Born two months premature in 1792, he remained painfully underweight throughout his life. His lack of stamina was most obvious in his sensitivity to heat, which often caused fainting fits. Just five foot four inches tall and weighing only eight stone, he was often cruelly caricatured by the popular press as a 'midget' or child. Even his friends often referred to him (although not to his face) as 'little Johnny'. This made him extremely touchy, often responding with vehement hostility to any perceived slight when self-deprecating charm might have served him better. In other circumstances the openness of his feelings could astonish even the most hard-boiled politicians. Stanley recorded in his diary how, after losing the 1854 Reform Bill, a 'deeply mortified' Russell 'burst into a hysterical fit of crying: a painful scene'. Many contemporaries at that stage had advised him to retire from active politics while his great reputation remained intact. But Russell had lingered on, spurred by an odd combination of self-doubt and the Whig sensibility that he was born to lead. His reputation had suffered, not least as a poor foreign secretary under Palmerston. Now his return to the premiership surely represented a last throw of the political dice. Few doubted that a successful Reform Act would crown Russell's illustrious career; most, however, thought him destined to go out with a whimper.

Not least of Russell's problems was a lack of interest in the country on the question of reform. For decades Radicals had been attempting to foment popular outrage at the lack of progress, but in truth most ordinary people remained blithely unconcerned. In April 1864 the foundation of John Bright's pressure group, the Reform Union, had given formal organisation to middle-class calls for household suffrage and the ballot. The Reform League followed the next year. All of this took place against a background of books and pamphlets by thinkers such as John Stuart Mill campaigning for an extension of the vote. Yet all told, popular opinion was just not interested. 'Certainly, as far as my constituents go,' wrote Gladstone at the beginning of 1866, 'there is no strong feeling for reform among them.'

Without this 'great tide of public opinion', Russell worried it would be impossible to drive a Reform Bill through parliament. 'He can't now resist bringing in a Bill but nobody professes to believe that he can carry one,' bragged *The Times*, no friend of Russell. The new prime minister tried to play for time by suggesting a royal commission to report on the whole question in a year or so. That this ploy failed was due entirely to his own party. Russell had to have a Radical in his government to keep extremists on his backbenches quiet. Gladstone refused point blank to accept John Bright, the obvious choice. So young W. E. Forster, a nonconformist from Bradford who had only been in the House four years, was made an under-secretary at the colonial office. His price: that the franchise question be addressed head on with the introduction of a Reform Bill.

'It [will] be a life and death question,' Russell ominously warned Gladstone.

The leader of the House introduced the principal measures of the new Reform Bill to the Commons on 12 March 1866. It was a modest scheme, reducing the property qualification for the vote to £7 rental value in the boroughs and £14 rental value in the counties. This would extend the franchise to an estimated four hundred thousand men, about half of them working class, in England and Wales (with Scotland and Ireland to follow afterwards in separate bills). It was estimated that this would shift the electorate from one in five to one in four of the adult male population.

As so often when anxious about presenting a case to parliament, Gladstone was ill on the day he introduced this latest Reform Bill. He had spent most of the day in bed with 'a stuffed head' before leaving for the Commons in mid-afternoon. 'But with God's help, I got through and all went as well as we could hope,' he wrote later. He asked the House to remember that 'the limbo of abortive creations was peopled with the skeletons of reform bills'. Sardonically he told members not to see this most recent bill as a 'Trojan horse approaching the walls of the sacred city, and filled with armed men, bent upon ruin, plunder, and conflagration'. Instead he asked, not entirely convincingly, that those 'whom we ask you to enfranchise ought rather to be welcomed as you would recruits to your army or children to your family'. Yet much of the speech was wrapped up in a plethora of dry and confusing statistics to show how the new bill might leave six middle- and upper-class voters for every four from the working class. No one could pay £7 rental every year on an income of less than twenty-six shillings a week, he argued, a sum which would make the vote 'unattainable by the peasantry or mere hand labourer'.

This had been a muted and curiously defeatist performance. Two years earlier, Gladstone, flushed with success as 'the People's William', had electrified the House with his bold assertion that 'every man who is not presumably incapacitated by some consideration of personal unfitness or of political danger, is morally entitled to come within the pale of the constitution'. In preparing the 1866 bill he had confidently predicted to cabinet colleagues that they would win the day despite 'some wry faces, some shrugging of the shoulders, and divers hairbreadth scrapes'. Now it seemed to MPs that the wry face and the shrugging of shoulders were Gladstone's. On becoming leader of the House, noted the foreign secretary Lord Clarendon, Gladstone 'had been warned by a personal friend (a woman: no man could do it) . . . to conciliate the House if possible'. The Dowager Duchess of Sutherland in offering this advice had apparently neutered Gladstone. Few doubted that he was on top of his brief, but gone were the characteristic passion and total commitment at the very moment they were direly needed.

When the unusually mild-mannered Gladstone sat down after introducing the bill, a fierce debate erupted. High Tories such as Lord

Cranborne (formerly Lord Robert Cecil) attacked the bill as democracy by the back door. From Gladstone's own benches, Robert Lowe led the Whig assault. Lowe was among the most extraordinary characters in the House. He was an albino, with extremely poor eyesight. Reading was a struggle, particularly in the murky gaslight of late night debates, so he undertook exceptional preparation to commit vast amounts of information to memory. At Winchester College he had initially been tormented, but the boy soon learnt that a quick mind and an acid tongue won admiration and a reputation for fearlessness. It was a technique that transferred effortlessly to the chamber of the House of Commons, where he was respected as a formidable, often cruel, debater.

Lowe's attack on the Reform Bill would become notorious. 'If you want venality, if you want drunkenness, and facility for being intimidated; or if, on the other hand, you want impulsive, unreflecting, and violent people, where do you look for them?' he demanded. 'Do you go to the top or the bottom? . . . The effect will manifestly be to add a large number of persons to our constituencies of the class from which if there is to be anything wrong going on we may naturally expect to find it.'

Ranged against Lowe and his supporters were John Bright and the Radicals. Bright was also a man of delicate health – during his campaign of opposition to the Crimean War he had suffered a complete nervous breakdown – and a brilliant parliamentary orator. Although he preferred to occupy the high ground in debate, Bright was every inch Lowe's equal in eviscerating political opponents. Now he launched an attack on Lowe, drawn from the biblical story of David, as a dweller in 'the political cave of Adullam' – the last refuge for 'everyone that was in distress and everyone that was discontented'. The term 'cave' instantly became a household word for a dissident group. Lowe's clique readily embraced the insult to become the 'Adullamites'. The Reform Bill automatically went through this first reading without a vote, but the lines for a vindictive and harshly personal war of attrition had already been drawn.

Throughout these opening skirmishes Benjamin Disraeli leered menacingly from the opposition front bench, but said nothing. In the lead up to the debate he had waited impassively to see how best to undermine the government. Lord Derby's gout, which left him persistently bedridden, gave Disraeli licence to follow his own instincts at Westminster. Only after viewing the disarray on the Liberal benches did he decide to oppose the Reform Bill. Bright's intemperate outburst had scandalised Whigs on the Liberal backbenches. Here then was an opportunity to work with them to smash Gladstone.

On 15 March, Disraeli sent Lord Stanley to negotiate with Robert Lowe. They agreed that a prominent Whig MP, Lord Grosvenor (later 1st Duke of Westminster), would propose a hostile notice of amendment. Stanley would second the motion, 'which I willingly undertook,' he wrote modestly, 'thinking that such expression of opinion might have weight with a certain number of people'. The next day, with the compact sealed, Disraeli told a bullish meeting of Tory MPs at Lord Salisbury's house that he intended to defeat the Reform Bill. Young Stafford Northcote, once Gladstone's private secretary but now a protégé of Disraeli, recorded how 'Dis. made a capital speech, reciting the history of the Reform Bills since 1852; throwing all the blame of the present agitation upon W. E. G[ladstone]'. The bill would be opposed, Disraeli told MPs, but they must trust him to decide tactics, which would shift from hour to hour. Stanley thought this 'one of the very best speeches I ever heard him make.'

'House adjourned for the Easter holidays,' wrote the eager Northcote. 'What will happen when we meet again?'

London–Liverpool Train

The powerful steam engine thundered through the English countryside belching sooty steam in its wake. Behind, in a first-class carriage, Gladstone sat quietly in a corner reading a theological study while gently juddering up and down to the rhythm of the train. The weather that spring was warm, so the window was open to keep the compartment ventilated, which allowed occasional bursts of thick smut to pour in. Spread between Gladstone and his wife was a picnic to keep hunger at bay during the six-hour journey. As the journey progressed, Gladstone's thoughts turned to the great speeches he would deliver in his constituency in the coming days. Parliament had given him a bloody nose the previous weeks. Now he would go above the heads of MPs and his own party to appeal to the masses for authority. Decided on his course, he went back to thinking about *Ecce Homo* by John Seeley: an arresting study on Christ as a roving, charismatic political leader.

Liverpool greeted Gladstone with the civic enthusiasm to which he was now accustomed. Returning again to the Amphitheatre on 6 April, he found an expectant crowd of thousands. 'I spoke again at length, and wholly on the Bill,' he wrote afterwards, to an audience 'full of enthusiasm.' It was a blazing performance. Where in the Commons Gladstone had been cautious in expression, now he raised the pitch of his oratory to a new demotic level. On the question of reform, he rallied eager listeners with a promise that the government had crossed a Rubicon, broken its bridges and burnt the boats. There was no turning back. He flayed the reputations of Robert Lowe, Lord Grosvenor and Lord Stanley – heir to the local 'King of Lancashire' – as anachronisms resisting the popular will. The people, not politicians, would decide reform. 'It is not in our power to secure the passing of the measure: that rests with you,' he shouted above the roar of his exhilarated audience.

Political society was scandalised by Gladstone's speech as reported in the next morning's *Times*. Radicals had long used popular rallies to agitate public opinion: but this was the Chancellor of the Exchequer and leader of the House of Commons chastising his own party, parliament and the aristocracy. The impropriety could hardly have been greater had he upbraided Stanley in front of the servants. Returning to the Commons chamber the next week, Gladstone walked into a torrent of abuse, not least from Robert Lowe. Despite the chancellor's blandishments to the contrary, he stormed, it was absurd to 'pretend that the influence of agitation was not resorted to' in a way that might 'develop into an influence of terrorism'. Was it right, he asked to much cheering and stamping, that the leader of the House should now present MPs with 'a languid *rechauffe* of the arguments of Liverpool; and thus the baked meats of the [Amphitheatre] did coldly furnish the tables of the House of Commons'.

Gladstone had gravely offended the propriety of the House. Watching quietly from the opposition front bench, Disraeli reflected once again on his rival's failure to grasp how to command affection. 'It [is] a great advantage to a leader of the House of Commons that he should be – not unable, but unwilling to speak,' he told Northcote. 'It is certainly a position in which silence is often golden.'

Reform Bill, Second Reading

Disraeli languidly resumed his seat on the opposition front bench, his face betraying little more than the hint of a smirk. Around him, MPs on both sides of the House were unusually quiet, subdued for a brief moment by a sense of expectancy. Six hundred and thirty-one of them, the largest number so far recorded, had squeezed into the chamber. Disraeli's final argument had been masterly in its understatement. Through more than a fortnight of parliamentary debate, Robert Lowe and the Adullamites had led the anti-democratic assault on the Reform Bill. That night of 27/28 April, Disraeli had taken great care to make his own arguments more measured than those of the 'Cave'. He had criticised the piecemeal nature of a bill that dealt with the vote without examining redistribution of seats. He defended the rights of the working classes to be represented, but argued for this to be done in a manner that reflected the 'English spirit' not an American one. You should represent opinion, not numbers, he told MPs; 'votes should be weighed not counted'.

For the current state of chaos, Disraeli blamed one man: the leader of the House, William Gladstone. The Whigs of old would not have attempted 'to reconstruct their famous institutions on the American model'. Even the youthful Gladstone would have understood this point, Disraeli taunted, reminding him of his fervent speech against the Great Reform Bill at the Oxford Union in 1831.

When Gladstone rose to reply, he was under intense pressure. 'Spoke from one to past 3 following D,' he noted afterwards. 'It was a toil much beyond my strength: but I seemed to be sustained and borne onwards I knew not how.' In fact, it was one of the great battling performances of his life and among the finest speeches ever made in parliament.

In defending the bill, he landed pulverising strikes on the 'depraved and crooked' Robert Lowe and his cave of malcontents. But his most withering, devastating personal attack was reserved for the man who had 'taunted me with the political errors of my boyhood'. This would be his most deadly assault on Disraeli since the 1852 budget debate.

'He, a Parliamentary champion of twenty years,' Gladstone chided, 'is so ignorant of the House of Commons, or so simple in the structure of his mind, that he positively thought he would obtain a Parliamentary advantage by exhibiting me to the public view for reprobation as an opponent of the Reform Bill of 1832.'

'What he has said is true,' Gladstone went on simply, but those youthful views had been expressed 'clearly, plainly, forcibly, in downright English, while the right hon. gentleman does not dare to tell the nation what it is that he really thinks, and is content to skulk under the shelter of the meaningless amendment which is proposed by the noble Lord [Grosvenor]'.

Having attacked Disraeli, Gladstone also sought to woo his own party, which had accepted him 'when I came among you an outcast'. He defended the reputation of Earl Russell. And he implored MPs on all sides of the House, in the words of Peel, to 'elevate your vision'.

At the end of a brave performance in which he had both thrust and parried, Gladstone offered only courageous defiance. 'You cannot fight against the future,' he declaimed. 'Time is on our side!'

MPs now thronged into the lobbies to vote before returning expectantly to the chamber to hear the result. 'The House was charged with electricity like a vast thunderclap,' wrote the journalist G. Barnett Smith, 'and now the spark was about to be supplied.' The tellers came to the floor of the House and announced that the government's majority had been slashed to just five. This provoked a 'wild, raging mad-brained shout from the floor and gallery such as has never been heard in the present House of Commons'. Gladstone rose to his feet, but could not be heard. He lifted his hands to ask for quiet, but this provoked only a shower of abuse. The euphoric Adullamites thronged deliriously around the uncharacteristically flushed Lowe. The Tories flung insults across the floor at ministers. Disraeli sat watching Gladstone malevolently, his face like that of a 'vivacious viper'. Finally, after a significant delay, Gladstone struggled to his feet to announce to a House suddenly fallen intimidatingly silent that the bill would go into its committee stage the following Monday.

'It was twilight, brightening into day, when we got out into the welcoming fresh air of New Palace Yard,' wrote Barnett Smith excitedly. 'It was a night long to be remembered. The House of Commons had listened to the grandest oration by the greatest orator of his age; and had then to ask itself how it happened that the Liberal party had been disunited, and a Liberal majority of sixty muddled away.'

The government had won a Pyrrhic victory. Only the manner of ultimate defeat was in doubt. At lunchtime that same Saturday, an unhappy cabinet gathered to discuss their options. Those on the left of the party wanted to call an election to win a mandate from the people for reform; the right simply wanted to resign. Spirited old Russell, however, was determined to fight on, gamely pointing out that the majority in the debate was five times that which he had won to pass the Great Reform Bill in 1832. Gladstone stood loyally by Russell, helping him to convince their reluctant and divided colleagues to persevere. Gladstone, however, gloomily admitted in private that 'we do not *know* our position, but shall learn it from day to day'.

Running a campaign of attrition on a day-to-day basis suited neither Gladstone's temperament nor ability. During the next weeks, Disraeli outmanoeuvred him on every flank. While the leader of the House hated the political dark arts involved in putting together a coalition of interests, the leader of the Opposition enjoyed little better. In the House, Disraeli was sweet (if mocking) reasonableness personified. 'We must help the government,' he sardonically told MPs. 'The right honourable gentleman must recross the Rubicon; we must rebuild his bridges and supply him with vessels.' Behind the scenes, Disraeli gleefully ran a campaign to harass and thwart the government at every turn.

The public face of opposition remained Robert Lowe. The two men were an unlikely team. Lowe told Northcote that he had 'no dislike of Disraeli, but a good deal of contempt for him'. Disraeli certainly had cause to dislike Lowe: his younger brother James had been Lowe's 'fag' at Winchester. 'No one knew what a bully was till he knew *him*,' Benjamin loyally observed. They dealt with each other mainly through Lord Elcho, the Adullamite's principal tactician, who appreciated Disraeli's strategic brain and courage. 'I cannot resist again expressing, in the midst of so much wavering, crookedness, and cowardice,' wrote Elcho enthusiastically during the heat of battle, grateful 'to find myself acting with a man of your frankness, straightforwardness, and resolution. Forgive me for saying this, for I really feel it.'

Together Disraeli and Elcho organised a war of attrition on the government. Amendments were put up at any opportunity. Their principal target was Gladstone himself. By the middle of May he was showing signs of breaking under the strain. He was working perhaps twenty hours each day. For the first time in his life he tried to snatch a little sleep on the front bench during debates. When the Adullamites cottoned on to this, they kept someone stationed behind him to kick and shake the bench so that he would wake. By 28 May, when the opposition succeeded in attaching an amendment to the Reform Bill on bribery, it had all become too much. A frazzled Gladstone wrote to Russell pleading for more help from cabinet colleagues. 'The Franchise bill alone I might have managed,' he told the prime minister in a burst of weary frustration, 'but to arrange, put into shape, to prepare for the Cabinet the multitude of points that arise upon the combined measure is physically as well as in every other way impossible for me.' Certainly his increasingly erratic personal behaviour was attracting gossip. 'Much talk of the situation,' wrote Stanley, 'and especially of Gladstone, whose extraordinary mental excitement is the general subject of comment.'

The broken chancellor was put out of his misery on 18 June. Disraeli and the Adullamites had agreed yet another amendment: this time to substitute rateable value for rental value, which would have dramatically cut the new working-class franchise in the boroughs. Few MPs understood the technicalities of the matter, but they all knew what was at stake. In the debate, Gladstone made a late plea for loyalty, even hinting at the last minute that the government might resign if it lost the vote. Disraeli said nothing. When the division came, the government was beaten by 304 to 315. Once again there were rowdy scenes. 'With the cheering of the adversary there was shouting, violent flourishing hats and other manifestations which I think novel and inappropriate,' recorded the disconsolate Gladstone. When MPs broke up, Disraeli and Derby retired to the Carlton Club, 'where we sat a short while drinking champagne and exchanging congratulations'.

Next day the cabinet voted to resign. The melancholy Russell, leaving public life after more than half a century, told Gladstone that he expected his successors to bring in 'a bill like ours' with 'some of Dizzy's elixir' stirred in.

'Finished in Downing Street. Left my keys behind me,' Gladstone recorded plaintively. 'Somehow it makes a void.'

13

Up The Greasy Pole

N o doubt the residents of this small Berkshire town had become quite blasé about the comings and goings each year, but those out and about that day must have experienced a slight frisson as the special train gave up its passengers. Climbing out of the compartments, dressed formally for an audience with the Queen, was the entire British cabinet. There was gout-ridden Lord Derby, about to become prime minister for the third time, struggling gamely towards the horse and carriage that would take him the short distance up to the castle. By his side was Benjamin Disraeli, pale and exotic, dressed in a heavy topcoat despite the muggy summer heat. Alongside them Tory grandees, including the Dukes of Montrose and Buckingham, mingled with the coming men of Conservative politics: Lord Cranborne, Gathorne Hardy and Stafford Northcote.

At the Castle, while they waited to be received, the weather quite unexpectedly broke. Lightning flashed across the sky. Thunder crashed. 'Some thought this a bad omen for us,' gloomily recorded Northcote, a pessimist by nature. Rain lashed the windows, and fell so heavily that the terrace soon flooded and water seeped into the room. Moving the cabinet quickly upstairs, the household staff inadvertently engineered a most unwelcome meeting. As the new ministers climbed the staircase, accompanied by a cacophonous natural soundtrack, the old cabinet taking its leave suddenly appeared before them. Handshakes and good wishes were coolly exchanged as the storm raged on. No doubt the conversation between Gladstone and Disraeli was terse. Disraeli, for once, seemed to be the more discomforted. 'Dis. had a bad omen of his own as we came down,' wrote Northcote. Thinking there was a seat for him, 'he sat down there, and found himself unexpectedly on the floor'.

It was not a propitious beginning for the new leader of the House of Commons and Chancellor of the Exchequer. Yet perhaps Disraeli was grateful still to be chief in the Commons. It had been a close-run thing. In the immediate aftermath of the Russell government breaking up, most MPs had assumed that the Tories would join the Adullamites in an anti-Reform coalition. Disraeli would later claim that his unwillingness to join forces with the Cave was due to his determination to face the Reform question head on. Of much more immediate concern had been the fact that his exclusion was a condition of Adullamite support. Egged on by the ultra-Tories, led by the Marquess of Bath who had long despised Disraeli as a Jewish upstart, the Cave had demanded that Stanley take up the lead in the Commons. They even suggested that his father Derby might also step aside for him. Only a combination of fancy footwork by Disraeli, Stanley's irresolute nature and Derby's revulsion at being dictated to by a mediocrity like Bath ensured that the much-expected coalition was stillborn. 'So much for Adullamite co-operation,' observed Derby icily.

The immediate question for the new government was what to do about reform. On 20 July Gladstone, now opposition leader in the Commons, prefaced a speech on foreign affairs with a taunt to Disraeli to pass the Liberal Reform Bill if he dared. Disraeli did not respond in the House, but the next day he began a letter to Derby that was 'the result of my reflections . . . on what Gladstone said yesterday'. His was a bold plan to take up the Reform Bill and pass it. 'You could carry this in the present House, and rapidly,' Disraeli advised Derby eagerly. 'It would prevent all agitation in the recess; it would cut the ground entirely from under Gladstone; and it would smash the Bath Cabal, for there would be no dangerous question ahead.'

By the time Derby, inevitably recuperating at Knowsley, received the letter a week later, events had taken a dramatic twist.

Hyde Park, 23 July 1866

It all began very politely. On this warm July day, twenty thousand cheerful, predominantly middle-class marchers strode purposefully up Park Lane towards Hyde Park. The atmosphere was good humoured and excited. Protests in favour of reform were two-a-penny, but the maladroit behaviour of the home secretary, Spencer Walpole, had given this particular march a certain importance. Without bothering to consult Derby or the cabinet, he had banned the marchers from gathering in Hyde Park. In response they changed their final destination to Trafalgar Square, but first would call at Hyde Park for the publicity value of being turned away.

Waiting for them at the entrance to the park was a police sergeant accompanied by a few constables. Leading the march was Edmond Beales, the Eton and Cambridge-educated president of the Reform League. He stepped forward to ask politely that the marchers be allowed into the park. The sergeant, equally civilly, replied that regrettably the Commissioner of Police had instructed that they should not be admitted. Each thanked the other for his courtesy. Beales then made to move away and take the protesters on to Trafalgar Square.

Events rapidly descended into chaos. Having led twenty thousand people to the gates of the park, Beales now had to turn them round. As the crowd began to push, tempers were quickly lost and fragile temperaments turned hysterical. When the mass of people began to push forward, those at the front were crushed against the gates and railings. These fixtures, more ornamental than defensive, were ripped out of the ground in a matter of seconds. Suddenly released, the multitude swarmed into the park, though taking particular care not to step into the colourful flowerbeds.

If the police reinforcements had been at the gates they would have seen that the intrusion was unavoidable. But these extra officers had been kept well back inside the park so as not to appear confrontational. What they saw looked liked a riot. They charged with truncheons on the trespassers. Most of the protesters fled, but a hard core remained to fight. In the ensuing battle a policeman was killed. By the time night fell, the police were forced to retreat. 'We are expecting to have all our heads broken tonight,' wrote an alarmed Northcote to his wife, 'as the mob are now trying it on in Hyde Park, and perhaps if they are defeated there, they will come on here.'

Northcote was not the only man at the House who was worried. Benjamin Disraeli was in a state of panic that night. His house at Grosvenor Gate overlooked the park. With Mary Anne at home, he immediately despatched his new secretary, Montagu Corry, to protect her. Sending an urgent despatch back to the Commons, Corry offered a vivid if reassuring account of events. 'No mob outside your house now,' he wrote breathlessly. 'The Inspector in charge at Grosvenor Gate tells me that while the crowd was at its worst here your house was never mentioned as obnoxious – though . . . others have come in for some threats.' As to Mary Anne, she faced events with her usual pluck. 'I really believe she sympathises with them,' wrote the bemused Corry. 'At any rate, I am glad to say she is not in the least alarmed.'

Events in the park rumbled on for a few days, but for the most part were reasonably well natured. Disraeli, concerns for his wife aside, maintained throughout the crisis a display of cool indifference. 'Public meetings are the recognized and indispensable organs of a free consti-tution,' he told the Queen. 'They are safety valves.' Yet his earlier letter to Derby on reform demonstrated a belief that the new government had to address the issue. The question of how was settled by Derby.

The riots had further divided the Liberal party as Radicals, Moderates and Adullamites squabbled over the rights and wrongs of reform. This offered a political advantage to the government to settle the question on their own terms. Derby later explained that he 'did not intend for a third time to be made a mere stop-gap'. On 16 September, the PM wrote to Disraeli to explain that he was 'coming reluctantly to the conclusion that we shall have to deal with the question of Reform'. Two weeks later he told him, 'The Queen spoke to me about it the other day – she said she was very anxious to see it settled.'

Everyone now expected the Conservatives to tackle the question of reform. It was therefore surprising that at this exact moment – 28 September 1866 – William Gladstone should have left for a holiday in Italy that would keep him away from London for a staggering four months.

Gladstone was at breaking point by the time he left with his wife for Italy. The previous months of disappointment had taken a heavy toll. After seven continuous years in office as chancellor, Gladstone was physically and emotionally exhausted. An unusually sheepish letter to the Liberal chief whip, Henry Brand, revealed Gladstone's desperation to escape. 'I think that I have said already in one way or other, all that I can usefully say, perhaps more than all,' he wrote wearily. 'So far as I am concerned, I now leave the wound of the Liberal party to the healing powers of nature.' To his brother, he went further. 'The truth is that after having from circumstances been so prominent during the Session it is well I should be in the shade for while now.' Robert Phillimore, Gladstone's loyal Oxford friend, understood this only too well: 'The journey to Italy [is] really a measure of self-defence, to escape the incessant persecution of correspondence, suggestions, and solicitations.'

Yet all told, it was a reckless act for a statesman whose reputation and leadership seemed to be on the line. The previous four months had been wretched for Gladstone. Much of the blame for the failure of the Reform Bill and collapse of the government had fallen squarely on his shoulders. Arrogance coupled with tactical ineptitude – always a dangerous combination for a politician – had led many in the Liberal party to question Gladstone's suitability for leadership. In the heady summer months of protest, his judgement had again been called into question. On 28 June a crowd of thousands had gathered outside his house in Carlton House Terrace to show their support for his attempts to pass a Reform Bill. Although Gladstone was out, his wife Catherine, who already had a taste for the public adulation that her husband attracted, appeared on the balcony to wave to the gathering below. This provoked widespread condemnation in the following morning's press, which accused (the absent) Gladstone of pandering to the masses. When a month later the Hyde Park riots excited national opinion, Gladstone, apparently having learnt his lesson, now offended all sides by saying very little. He took a morning ride through the park on 24 July – 'viewed the "field of battle"' – and privately criticised 'the folly that made it'. But he neither used his influence with the reform leaders to dampen popular discontent nor would he join with them to champion their cause. The result was that he appeared weak and irresolute.

With Russell on the verge of retirement from public life, Gladstone's position to succeed him, which until the previous months had seemed inevitable, was now in serious doubt. Gladstone's reputation had rested both on his competence and his authoritative presence. During the reform debates he had appeared to possess neither. Senior Liberals began to wonder if someone else might do the job better. That autumn Brand predicted that 'Granville will be the next prime minister'. Granville himself thought Sir George Grey was the man. Clarendon wanted anyone other than Gladstone who seemed to him close to a nervous breakdown. He gleefully reported to Russell, his brother-in-law, the bizarre story of Gladstone buying the entire contents of a toyshop, and Mrs Gladstone having to rush to the store to cancel the order. 'I have heard of her having had to do this several times within the last few months,' he wrote unkindly, 'a melancholy proof of his tendency and of what [those] who knew him well always told me would be his destiny if he lived long enough and gave himself no rest.

There were other more persistent signs of emotional turmoil. During the summer months of 1866, Gladstone underwent another sexual crisis that suggested his marriage might have been under genuine threat. There was the familiar trawling of the streets on long, hot summer days. During those weeks Gladstone became obsessed with one particular rescue case, L. St Clair, faithfully recording each meeting with an 'X' in his diary. 'Singing, luncheon, & some time after,' he wrote just the day before leaving for Italy, adding: 'I feel confident here.'

Catherine Gladstone could explain away her husband's fixation with prostitutes as well-intentioned charity work. His deepening relationship with Harriet Sutherland was more difficult to bear. Gladstone saw her frequently in London that summer. Several weekends were spent at her house in the country, including the weekend before departing from England. 'Left Cliveden at 11 with regret, even beyond the usual', he recorded mournfully afterwards. The effect of these two interests, summed up in one remarkable diary entry – 'The Duchess troubled. Saw one. X.' – was a profound dislocation from the intimacy of family and home. Throughout 1866 Gladstone did not make the journey to Hawarden even once. When he left for Italy in late September with his wife and daughters, it was a retreat to save his marriage.

As if to emphasise Gladstone's disturbed state of mind, as so often when under pressure, he immediately fell ill. During a stopover in Paris he was forced to keep to 'my bed all day (without reading, writing, or speaking)' while 'C read prayers for me'. It was not a happy beginning, but he recovered quickly, and by 11 October the family had arrived in Rome, where they would remain for the rest of the year. Cutting himself off from English politics was easier said than done. The Gladstones took elegant rooms overlooking the Spanish Steps, only to find that a former cabinet colleague, the Duke of Argyll, was soon to occupy the floor below. Lord Clarendon and Edward Cardwell were also in Rome. A day's journey away, Lord Russell was staying in Florence. When Russell asked Gladstone to visit him, he refused point blank, saying that too many people would be watching them. In reality, he simply did not want to talk politics. Lord Clarendon, who did not like Gladstone, left a vivid, gossipy description of this Roman holiday. 'Italian art, archaeology and literature are Gladstone's sole occupation,' he wrote to Hatfield House. 'Every morning at 8 he lectures his wife and daughters upon Dante and requires them to parse and give the root of every word. He runs about all day to shops, galleries and persons, and only last night told me that he hadn't time for the reading room, and had not seen an English paper for three or four days! . . . He is a curious man.'

In truth the trip did little to ease Gladstone's vexed spirit. 'We have had some discomforts,' he wrote disconsolately to Brand on Christmas Day. 'Our apartments twice on fire, a floor burnt through each time. Then I was laid down with a most severe influenza: very sore throat, a thing quite new to me. The Roman climate is as bad for me as can be.' Added to this was the pain of renewed acquaintance with Henry Manning, the recently appointed Archbishop of Westminster who was also resident that autumn in Rome, and whose conversion had thrown Gladstone into crisis in 1851.

Broken friendships, wet weather, dirty streets, politicians at every turn, and hour upon hour in the company of his unhappy wife: these all prevented Gladstone from regaining any sense of equilibrium. 'Incessantly and pressingly occupied,' he recorded despondently on New Year's Day 1867. Returning to London later that month, he picked up the threads of his old life within hours, which prompted the familiar diary entry: 'Saw L. S[t Clair] X.'

The Liberal party he returned to was in chaos. 'There seem to be no leaders, no plan, no union, no sympathy,' complained the MP David Dundas bitterly. 'Mr Gladstone, to be sure, has just arrived, but what he thinks or does, or is said to be thinking or doing, nobody seems to know.'

It was not a promising way for Gladstone to enter the biggest fight of his career. The only hope for his dwindling band of supporters was that this might be another of those occasions when Gladstone proved fearsome on the rebound.

Westminster, 14 February 1867

Torpor hung in the air of the House of Commons. Before the session had begun the previous week there had been much excitement about how the government would deal with the reform issue. The subsequent sense of anticlimax, as it became clear that Derby and Disraeli would kick for touch, had left MPs bored and irritable. The Conservative plan now seemed clear enough. A series of vague resolutions had been laid before the House for discussion. A Royal Commission on electoral reform would follow. Only when the Commission had reported would the government introduce legislation, probably in 1868. Thus the sprint for reform had become a leisurely stroll.

On his feet in the Commons chamber that afternoon was Lord Robert Montagu, a Tory backbencher and something of stroller himself on reform. He was a friend of Jonathan Peel (Robert's brother and one of a triumvirate of cabinet ministers reluctant to introduce a reform bill). Montagu now sought to press home an advantage. He asked Disraeli directly 'whether the Government will endeavour, as early as possible in this session, to bring in a [Reform] Bill?'. It was a loaded question, and one intended to force the leader of the House to say explicitly what most understood: that there would be no legislation on the question that year. When Disraeli stood to answer, he seemed uncharacteristically dithery. He began by talking hesitantly about 'the Bill which we might bring in'. Then he shifted to 'the Bill which we hope we may almost immediately introduce'. Finally, with more confidence, he moved to the assurance that 'not a moment will be unnecessarily lost' in introducing such a measure, because to do otherwise 'would be disgracefully trifling with the House'. Gradually aware that the ground had shifted, MPs stirred themselves. There was a great swelling up of noise as shocked whispers turned to shouts and cheers. A score of members jumped to their feet to intervene. Those on the opposition front bench huddled in towards Gladstone to confer.

Poor Montagu managed to get in first. 'The right hon. gentleman has misunderstood my Question,' he spluttered in a vain attempt to close Pandora's ballot box. Disraeli came to the despatch box again to spell out his policy in the clearest terms to an astonished House. 'I must repeat again, in the most distinct manner,' he said slowly, enunciating every syllable, 'that we brought forward these Resolutions as the basis of a Bill.'

As he resumed his seat on the Conservative front bench, Disraeli caught the looks of astonishment and anger on the faces of many of his colleagues. This had been a unilateral declaration: in the space of a few minutes, he had changed the course of government policy. Only Cranborne displayed no emotion, sitting characteristically 'with his eyes cast down upon the floor and his countenance overshadowed by his hat'. Away from curious eyes, however, he was vitriolic in his condemnation. 'He is firmly convinced now that Disraeli has played us false,' recorded the colonial secretary, Lord Carnavon, an old Oxford friend. 'That he is attempting to hustle us into his measure, that Lord Derby is in his hands and that the present form which the question has now assumed has been long planned by him. On comparing notes it certainly looks suspicious.'

The government had already committed itself to a debate on reform on 25 February. Following Disraeli's declaration to the House, the cabinet now had just eleven days to agree a policy and draft a bill. The internal arguments were ferocious. By the morning of the debate, no consensus had been reached, with Cranborne, Carnavon and Peel persistently threatening to resign. 'I could not look in the face those whom last year I urged to resist Mr Gladstone,' Cranborne told Derby. 'I am convinced that it will, if passed, be the ruin of the Conservative party.' At lunchtime that day the cabinet met in emergency session to thrash out the issue. The meeting, Derby told the Queen afterwards, was 'of a most unpleasant character'. Carnarvon recalled 'a very angry discussion'. Sir John Pakington thought it a 'distressing and unparalleled scene'. Throughout the meeting Disraeli sat 'white as a sheet'. Eventually, with only a few minutes remaining before Derby was due to address party MPs, the cabinet agreed limply to introduce a measure that was a pitiable imitation of the Liberal bill of the previous year, with £6 rating in the boroughs and £20 in the counties. All imaginative measures were dropped. When the last-gasp nature of this compromise got out, cynics immediately christened these proposals 'the ten-minute bill'.

'I am going down to the House,' Disraeli wrote to his wife immediately after cabinet. 'The ship floats; that is all.' When he rose to address the Commons just before five o'clock that afternoon the atmosphere was tense and expectant. MPs had crowded into every available space, with many spilling out from the stairs on to the floor. Eager peers and illustrious guests, including the Prince of Wales, were crammed into the galleries. In such an intense atmosphere, Disraeli took a passionless, businesslike approach to explaining that a bill would follow in due course. He spoke 'well, concisely, and clearly', recorded Stanley.

When Disraeli sat down, uproar ensued. Robert Lowe, architect of Gladstone's fall the previous year, led the charge. The government's attitude was one of 'Say what you like to us, only for God's sake, leave us in our places.' Let the fight on reform begin that night, he demanded. From the opposite flank, John Bright also insisted that the government immediately introduce 'a substantial and satisfactory Bill'. As the debate became increasingly fractious, so the cries of 'Bring in a Bill!' became louder and more insistent. It was, wrote Montagu Corry to Mrs Disraeli, an 'unexampled trial'.

If Disraeli might have had cause to limp disconsolately away from the debate, observers were surprised to find him curiously upbeat. Was this bravado, MPs asked, or just another cunning tactical ploy in a much grander campaign? Disraeli dined with Stanley that evening to plot the next move. Together they concluded that 'the resolutions have served their purpose, and may be dropped'. Each knew that, at that very moment, Tory backbenchers were meeting in the Carlton Club, anxious that the government should embark on a bolder policy. For twenty years they had been impotent. Minority governments, half-measures, always living on scraps and borrowed time: Tory MPs were tired of it, and now demanded a bold initiative to call their own. When they presented Disraeli with a signed letter urging just such a course, he embraced them. 'A greater instance of loyalty to colleagues has rarely been met with than Mr Disraeli displayed in his interview with me,' wrote S. R. Graves, their spokesman. Disraeli later told Derby, 'All I hear and observe, more and more convinces me that the bold line is the safer one, and, moreover, that it will be successful.'

Armed with the support of his backbenchers anxious to seize the day, Disraeli moved to marginalise Cranborne, Carnavon and Peel. He calculated that if the three rebels resigned they would find little support in the party. 'The loss of three able and honourable men is a great one,' wrote Lord Malmesbury to Derby the day before the cabinet showdown, 'but far greater would be the loss of reputation which a vacillating and subservient policy would inevitably bring upon us personally, and upon our party.' Even those on good terms with Cranborne thought that personal acrimony had warped his judgement. 'Clearly [he] will not long act with Disraeli,' wrote Gathorne Hardy in his diary. 'That is at the bottom of it.' Matters were brought to a head at an angry cabinet meeting on 2 March. Disraeli, firmly supported by Derby, pushed through his new proposals. Salisbury, Carnarvon and Peel resigned there and then.

'The Tory party is ruined,' lamented Derby, melodramatically slamming shut his red despatch box.

'Poor Tory party,' Disraeli added with a smirk.

Throughout all the disputes of February 1867, Gladstone had been disconcertingly quiet. 'Spoke after Disraeli on his extraordinary scheme and position,' he had recorded on 11 February. 'It was difficult in many ways.' Not least of those difficulties were the twin problems of second-guessing what Disraeli might do and trying to keep his own party in line. Initially he followed a policy of saying very little while waiting for Disraeli to show his colours. His utterances in the House were friendly and encouraging. He assured ministers that 'we are here embarked on a common cause'. When Lowe and Bright attacked Disraeli on 25 February, Gladstone took a moderate line, and again suggested, 'I am not taking the part of an opponent of the Government.'

This surprisingly consensual approach masked a fear about the upcoming debate. 'If you have to drive a man out of a wood you must yourself go into the wood to drive him,' he explained to the Liberal chief whip, Henry Brand. 'This is what I am afraid of.' For all his dubious skill as an axeman in the woods of Hawarden, somewhere lurking in Gladstone's subconscious was the fear that, when it came to stalking prey at Westminster, he was no match for the more fleet of foot Disraeli.

The Representation of the People Bill was introduced to a packed House of Commons on 18 March. Its basic provisions were clear enough: household suffrage in the boroughs for personal ratepayers who had lived in a property for at least two years;* dual votes for property; and so-called 'fancy franchises' for those with educational qualifications, those with £50 in the bank, or those who paid twenty shillings a year in direct taxation. It was estimated that these measures would enfranchise an additional four hundred thousand men.

The debate in the House that day was not so much about the intricacies of the Reform Bill – these would be taken care of during later readings of the legislation – but rather the reopening of serious hostilities between the rivals. Disraeli gave a dazzling performance that contrasted his own bill as a bulwark of the constitution with the complicated, flaky proposals introduced by Gladstone the previous year. His aim was not democracy, which 'I trust it will never be the fate of this country to live under', but rather to achieve a fair representation of society. 'Generally speaking,' he pronounced, 'I would say that, looking to what has occurred since the Reform Act of 1832 was passed – to the increase of population, the progress of industry, the spread of knowledge, and our ingenuity in the arts – we are of opinion that numbers, thoughts and feelings have since that time been created which it is desirable should be admitted within the circle of the constitution.' Disraeli concluded with a bipartisan call for cooperation. 'Act with us cordially and candidly, assist us to pass this measure,' he asked

---

* 'Personal' ratepayers made direct payment of their rates whereas 'compound' ratepayers made those payments through their landlord. Personal ratepayers by and large were wealthier.

MPs. 'We will not shrink from deferring to your suggestions so long as they are consistent with the main object of this Bill . . . Act with us, I say, cordially and candidly: you will find on our side complete reciprocity of feeling.' With all except Gladstone, he might have added.

Throughout Disraeli's speech the leader of the opposition had sat barely able to contain himself. On several occasions he had jumped to his feet to ask difficult technical questions. At other times he had fidgeted and fussed, manically writing down notes on sheaves of paper. This played into the hands of Disraeli, whose asides on Gladstone's angry demeanour – 'His manner is sometimes so very excited and so alarming that one might almost feel thankful that [we] are divided by a good broad piece of furniture' – drew noisy laughter from the House.

By the time Gladstone stood up to open for the opposition he was paroxysmal with rage. Flush-faced and tense, he began a brutal attack on Disraeli's proposals. The numbers were all wrong, the measures were inconsistent and ill conceived, it would lead to 'a war of the classes' and destroy equality before the law: all told, Gladstone declared, this Tory Reform Bill was an insult to the nation. In total he identified ten main defects, all of which were given detailed analysis in language that was uncompromising and often insulting. Through all of this Disraeli preserved his characteristic mask. Increasingly angry Tory backbenchers began throwing out abuse. Behind Gladstone, most Liberal MPs sat awkward and embarrassed at their leader's discordant tone. Their response came later in the debate, best expressed by the moderate J. A. Roebuck, who argued that the bill had to pass because 'the country [is] in a state of disquietude'.

The tone was set and the tactics laid bare for the coming fight: Disraeli was determined to pass a bill on any terms other than those of the leader of the opposition; Gladstone was determined to smash both the bill and its author.

'Gladstone,' summed up Lord Stanley apprehensively after the debate, '[is] for immediate war.'

Carlton House Terrace

William Gladstone stood halfway up the grand staircase of his St James's home delivering a stern rebuke. It had been going on for more than an hour. At the foot of the stairs Liberal members of parliament stood sullen, shifting their weight from foot to uncomfortable foot. The meeting at the leader's home had been called at short notice. Around seventy MPs had not shown up. Many of those who had attended now wished they had not bothered. Gladstone was scolding them from (literally) a great height on the need for discipline and loyalty. If the Liberals did not unite, he warned, Disraeli and the Conservatives would score a triumph. The Reform Bill had to be opposed vigorously by the party. As he spoke, Gladstone's face displayed that 'glare of contentious eagerness' and self-righteousness that irritated even his friends. And there were few at Carlton House Terrace that afternoon of 5 April who would have called themselves such.

When MPs finally escaped they complained bitterly among themselves about the indignity of the occasion. Once again Gladstone had 'monopolised the discussion'. Members 'had never even been asked to give [their opinions]'. He was a hectoring bully who treated members of parliament as naughty schoolboys in the headmaster's office. Gladstone had lost the confidence of his party the previous year on the question of reform; he seemed to have learnt nothing from that experience in how to coax and cajole MPs. 'I have never seen anything like it,' commented the former chancellor Charles Wood (now Lord Halifax), 'but the state of things this year enables me to understand what was very inexplicable in all I heard last year.'

Wood was not the only Liberal to be concerned. Two days after the meeting at Carlton House Terrace, a small group of MPs met at the Reform Club to discuss Gladstone's dictatorial manner. The next day, 8 April, they organised a meeting of more than fifty in the tea room of the House of Commons to plan how to confront Gladstone. The result was a delegation – the 'Tea Room Cave' – to the leader of the opposition 'to tell him that they could not support [his] instruction' for fear of being 'made to appear in the eyes of their constituents as having been opposed to . . . a bill which gave, ostensibly, that household suffrage which they had always advocated'. Gladstone was shocked by the force of the demonstration and had little choice other than to drop his full-frontal assault on the bill to maintain the semblance of party unity.

While Gladstone floundered, Disraeli did everything possible to increase his rival's discomfiture. In the early hours of 27 March he had delivered a brilliant speech on the bill, which had deftly exploited the differences between Gladstone, the Whigs and the Radicals. 'Pass the Bill,' he urged them, 'and then change the Ministry if you like!'

The journalist Edward Russell judged this 'the speech of the session', not just for 'its bold caricature of Mr Gladstone's cloud-compelling manner', but because 'the whole House seemed tickled too much ever seriously to fall out with Mr Disraeli on this subject again'. One Liberal backbencher recorded afterwards that 'it was the most wonderful piece of acting and the most extraordinary exhibition of talent I have ever heard. He pitched into everybody, he abandoned all his principles, and all through he delighted and amused the House.' To Gladstone's chagrin, MPs passed this second reading of the bill without even bothering to divide for a vote.

Disraeli's brilliant performance, welcoming interventions and suggestions from every source bar one, was followed up the next month by a number of adept manoeuvres. The budget contrived to keep the Liberal backbenches happy, and was in fact so Gladstonian that even the man himself could find no fault with it. Disraeli also connived with James Clay to instigate the Tea Room Cave against Gladstone. The two men had been close friends since meeting on the debauched tour of the Near East in 1831. Now they acted in tandem, to force Gladstone into retreat. 'Rumours rife that a large meeting of Liberals had thrown over Gladstone,' excitedly recorded Gathorne Hardy on 8 April. 'Gladstone lowering and gloomy, full of mortification, no doubt.' Even friends recognised that he had been humiliated. 'Entire collapse of Gladstone's attack on government [today],' wrote Robert Phillimore. 'Disraeli's insolent triumph.'

Gladstone had completely lost the confidence of the House. The *Spectator* quipped of his performance that the House was indifferent while Gladstone was earnest; the House was lax and he was strict; it was cynical about popular equality and he was enthusiastic; it was lazy about details, he revelled in the profoundest minutiae.

The *Spectator* might have added that he was Gladstone and not Disraeli. For as the Liberal grandee Lord Elgin observed, the melancholy intensity of the former had found its mirror image in the Mephistophelian nonchalance of the latter.

Matters came to a dramatic head in the early hours of 13 April when the House divided for the first time on the 1867 Reform Bill. The result would be in doubt right up to the last second.

Gladstone, having made a hasty retreat under pressure from the Tea Room Cave, had quickly returned to fight. He did not attack the bill outright, but laid down a series of cunning amendments on voter registration designed to reshape it in the image of his own efforts the previous year. Wording was vague to catch as many waverers as possible. Yet in that ambiguity, Gladstone left himself open to accusations that these new amendments were simply a ruse to bring down the government. He was also hampered by a rival amendment introduced by the MP for Oldham, J. T. Hibbert, that was supported by many of the Tea Room rebels. This split among the ranks of the Liberal party gave Disraeli his chance.

Everyone in Westminster understood that Disraeli was prepared to accept any changes to the bill provided they did not come from Gladstone. With Derby laid up again with gout, control of strategy and tactics passed completely into Disraeli's hands. He first ensured that a 'confidential' letter to his supporters found its way into *The Times*. This warned that if any amendment by Gladstone was passed, then the House would be dissolved and an election called. Then he made overtures to the Tea Room malcontents by promising to accept Hibbert's amendment if they would vote for the bill. When the cabinet heard about this unilateral action, a furious row broke out. Disraeli denied that any deal had been made. 'Stanley evidently thought this untrue,' observed Gathorne Hardy. Sharp words were exchanged, but Disraeli refused to have his hands tied before the debate. It was a high-risk strategy: win and he would be the man of the hour; lose and there would be calls for his head.

When Disraeli rose in the House that night to wind up the debate, he delivered a blistering, full-frontal and personal retort to Gladstone's 'declaration of war'.

'The right hon. gentleman is an opponent with whom any man may be proud to have to contend,' he began. 'I acknowledge the right hon. gentleman's position and talents – that he is perfectly justified in attacking the government; but do not let us misunderstand the motive or the conduct of the right hon. gentleman . . . It is a party attack.'

Disraeli then cut to the chase, making explicit that he would not accept any amendment from Gladstone. 'We are most anxious to co-operate with the House in bringing this question of Parliamentary Reform to a satisfactory settlement,' he explained, but added that when Gladstone 'comes forward suddenly with a counter-proposition to the main proposal of the government it is impossible for me to close my eyes to the nature of the movement; I must say to [him] that I cannot in any way agree to the propositions he has made.'

Gladstone was genuinely flabbergasted that the government would not take any amendment from him. His fellow MPs were not. Most agreed with Disraeli's characterisation of the leader of the opposition. They were weary of his games on reform and wanted a swift conclusion. Gladstone was not trying to improve the bill, but only to wreck it.

Goodwill towards Disraeli was heightened by a vicious racist attack by Alexander Beresford Hope, a Tory backbencher and owner of the *Saturday Review*. He concluded his bitter tirade by declaring, 'I for one, with my whole heart and conscience, will vote against the Asian mystery.' The House delighted in Disraeli's witty riposte to this man of Dutch descent that 'when he talks of Asian mysteries . . . there is a *Batavian grace* about his exhibition which takes the sting out of what he has said'.

It had been a bravura performance that won both votes and acclaim. As the bells of Big Ben struck two o'clock, the tellers announced the result of the vote: a defeat for Gladstone's amendment by a majority of twenty-two. The Conservative Reform Bill remained on track. Forty-five Liberals had deserted their party. Only five Tories, including Cranborne, had voted with Gladstone. When the numbers were read out, a great crowd gathered around Disraeli cheering, pushing in on him to shake hands and pat his back. Up in the Ladies' Gallery, Mrs Gladstone looked on 'white to the very lips'. When her husband returned home later that night, she found that he 'could hardly speak'. She had never seen him 'so knocked down'. When he dutifully wrote up his diary for the day his disappointment was simply expressed. 'Spoke in Reply: and voted in 289:310,' he recorded. 'A smash perhaps without example.'

As Gladstone had slunk off home, Disraeli was taken to the Carlton Club by his delirious supporters. When he got there, he found an excited crowd, which burst into spontaneous applause. Sir Matthew Ridley, amid great cheering, proposed a toast: 'Here's to the man who rode the race, who took the time, who kept the time, and who did the trick.' The celebrations went on until dawn, but Disraeli soon slipped out to go home. There he found Mary Anne waiting up for him with a bottle of champagne and a Fortnum & Mason's pie.

'Why my dear,' he told her contentedly at the end of a long, triumphant day, 'you are more like a mistress than a wife.'

The House of Commons broke for the Easter recess immediately after the vote, but for the next few days London remained electrified by the result. Everywhere the talk was of the great personal triumph of Disraeli over Gladstone. 'The most wonderful thing is the rise of Disraeli,' wrote that worldly prelate, Bishop Wilberforce. 'It is not the mere assertion of talent. He has been able to teach the House of Commons almost to ignore Gladstone, and at present lords it over him, and I am told, says that he will hold him down for twenty years.' Rear Admiral Octavius Duncombe wrote gleefully to Disraeli saying that 'you now have the whip hand of your . . . antagonist completely'. Even Gladstone's friends worried that Disraeli had completely hexed him. 'I met Gladstone at breakfast,' wrote a concerned Lord Houghton, 'he seems quite awed by the diabolical cleverness of Dizzy.'

Away from the capital, Monty Corry breathlessly reported on Easter Sunday from his aunt's house in Shrewsbury, Rowton Castle, that 'your name is in the mouth of every labourer, who without knowing what reform means, or caring, hears that Mr [Disraeli] has won a great victory . . . My private opinion is that my aunt's carpenter, who "heard say that Mr Disraeli laid Mr Gladstone on his back" thinks that you really knocked the godly man down.' It was a typically colourful review from Corry, who was already turning out to be a splendid private secretary. Disraeli had spotted him at a party in 1865 flirting with some attractive young women. 'I think you must be my impresario,' he had told him.

Disraeli characteristically had left London for Hughenden at the earliest opportunity, before returning to spend Easter at Windsor. The Queen was glowing in her praise, believing that 'Mr Disraeli is evidently the directing mind of the ministry, and that he is the person to whom any representation can now most effectively be made.' That representation, crisply expressed, was passed along by General Charles Grey, the Queen's private secretary. 'Her Majesty now desires me to express her earnest hope that you will avoid, as far as possible, the mistakes of the late Government,' he informed Disraeli, 'and should further amendments be carried against you, in a way to show that they are in accordance with the feeling of the House and of the country, that you will not refuse to accept them, and thus again postpone the settlement of this question, as Lord Russell did, the Queen thinks, so unnecessarily last year.' Buoyed by his success against Gladstone, Disraeli bullishly told Victoria that 'we ought to carry our Reform now in a canter'.

While Disraeli basked in royal approval, Gladstone slunk back to Hawarden to lick his wounds and consider his future. The whole thing, wrote Lord Dalhousie, was 'a nice mess'. Thoroughly trounced by Disraeli, Gladstone contemplated giving up the leadership of the Liberals in the Commons. Beginning a new volume of diaries on 1 May, he inscribed on the frontispiece a telling quotation from a memoir of the Prussian diplomat Baron Bunsen. 'My resolution is taken,' he wrote, 'I shall not again enter into public life, but devote the years yet remaining to me to reflection upon the great objects of eternal significance, to which from earliest youth I had consecrated my soul.' Apart from anything else, Gladstone was exhausted. He would listlessly complain to Harriet Sutherland that 'time tells on a man of my age and temperament; and my brain tells me that I want more rest and not less'. A few days with Harriet at Chiswick after Easter briefly steeled his resolve, but on 9 May, the first day back in the House, he was still complaining uncharacteristically of being 'much fatigued by heat and work'.

Debate on the Reform Bill meandered on for the next few weeks. Gladstone tried a change of tactics: where before he had led the charge against Disraeli, now he rarely spoke in debates, and instead coordinated amendments from the Liberal backbenches. This was too transparent for Disraeli, who maintained his first principles of accepting amendments from any source except the leader of the opposition (or his vassals), and winning votes at all costs. As the leader of a minority government Disraeli still had to muster the numbers in the House for each and every vote. For hour after hour, day after day, he endured tedious speeches from both sides on the minutiae of the franchise. His languid figure reclined elegantly on the government benches, his benign and encouraging face turned interestedly towards whichever droning backbencher was on his feet. More often than not the House was virtually empty. Disraeli spoke very little, but was always there: watchful, alert and ready with an answer to keep the bill on track. With the exception of his protégé, the new home secretary Gathorne Hardy, he rarely consulted members of cabinet. Decisions were usually made on the spur of the moment. If the government seemed likely to lose an amendment, he moved quickly to show that it would not be considered a matter of confidence. Disraeli remained courteous, helpful, always willing to indulge MPs, and to welcome all suggestions other than from the opposition front bench. To quite what extent, however, Gladstone had catastrophically failed to grasp.

Members' Dining Room, House of Commons, 17 May 1867

An unpleasant, sulphurous haze pervaded the air as a scattering of honourable members gossiped, drank and ate. The high temperatures that summer of 1867 had been unbearable. 'Lay awake great part of the night, from heat, which is extreme,' Lord Stanley had recorded in his journal. Dressed in heavy woollen frock coats, MPs perspired and scratched uncomfortably, often struggling for breath in the fetid atmosphere. From outside the malodorous stench of the River Thames wafted in through open windows. The disgusting odour of raw sewage heated by the powerful sun had made Westminster unbearable during those few weeks, even stinking out the enclosed environs of the Commons chamber. Many members had simply stayed away. At that very moment the clubs of Pall Mall and St James's were playing host to more MPs than the House.

Those who remained unhappily behind watched in desultory fashion as Gladstone came into the dining room. His face showed only disgust, whether from the unpleasant smell under his nose, or another political setback. He had come straight from speaking in the Commons chamber where he was suffering yet another indignity. He had had up his sleeve a cunning amendment to the Reform Bill by H. C. E. Childers, who had served under him at the Treasury in the previous Liberal government. Fortified by another of the 'monster rallies' in Hyde Park, Gladstone was making one last push to wrest the initiative on reform back from Disraeli. Yet once again his own party was thwarting him. A nonentity backbench solicitor, Grosvenor Hodgkinson, had put up his own clumsy amendment. This sought to get round the last remaining dispute of 'personal payment' of rates by abolishing compound payments altogether, which would have the effect of adding half a million voters to the electorate. It was a ridiculous motion, wasting the time of the House, and queering the pitch for Childers. Not wanting further to alienate Radicals on his own backbenches, Gladstone moments earlier had spoken blandly in favour of Hodgkinson's suggestion. Then he had left his place on the front bench, as Disraeli got to his feet to speak, not even bothering to wait for the reply.

No sooner had Gladstone taken his seat at the dinner table, than a sweaty messenger appeared at the door with a note. What it said Gladstone could hardly believe. Disraeli had accepted Hodgkinson's amendment. He rushed from the room, barking at those few of his supporters there to follow him back to the chamber. Scampering through the corridors at an inelegant canter, he shouted instructions to get MPs back to Westminster from dinner at the Reform Club.

Disraeli watched with malicious delight as his great rival careered back to his place on the front bench. But Gladstone was too late. Disraeli had accepted the amendment so quickly, and in a House virtually empty, that he had avoided a significant debate. By the time MPs dashed back to Westminster, the business of the House had moved on. 'To those at the clubs the electric wire soon sent the news, and at a hundred tables there were surprise . . . and consternation, the like of which has seldom been seen,' noted one amused observer afterwards. 'Many a snug dinner party was prematurely broken up . . . and by half past nine the House was full. As members rushed across the lobby, astonishment sat upon their faces [as they asked] is it true?'

Disraeli had accepted the amendment without approval of any kind from the cabinet. Even his lieutenant, Gathorne Hardy, was out of the House. He revealed his reasons for this stunning political coup to Hardy the next morning: 'I waited until the question was put, when, having resolved everything in my mind, I felt that the critical moment had arrived, and when, without in the slightest degree receding from our principle and position of a rating and residential franchise, we might take a step which would destroy the present agitation and extinguish Gladstone & Co.'

Disraeli was right: passage of the Second Reform Act was assured. At its final reading, the House did not even bother to divide for a vote. Gladstone was so downcast that he 'determined at the last moment not to take part in the debate for fear of doing mischief on our own side'. By the time the bill went to the House of Lords, Derby had recovered sufficiently from gout to steer through the measure with an imperiousness not seen since Wellington. By the end of the session, the Tories had enacted their first serious piece of legislation since the Repeal of the Corn Laws in 1846. After a generation in the wilderness, the Conservatives were restored as a serious party of power.

Thirty years later, William Gladstone would set down a memorandum on the Second Reform Bill that grudgingly recognised his own failings and the triumph of Disraeli. 'The governing idea of the man who directed the party seemed to be not so much to consider what ought to be proposed and carried as to make sure that whatever it was it should be proposed and carried by those in power,' he recorded. 'The bill on which the House of Commons eventually proceeded was a measure I should suppose without precedent or parallel, as on the other hand it was for the purpose of the hour, and as a government in a decided minority, an extraordinary piece of parliamentary success.'

Few would have disagreed at the time. Disraeli had thrashed Gladstone in a display of political skill that confounded his rivals and amazed even his friends.

A popular riddle of the day seemed to sum it up best:

Why is Gladstone like a telescope?

Because Disraeli can draw him out, look right through him, and shut him up.

Before the Second Reform Act was even signed into law, Gladstone departed on 10 August for a family holiday at Penmaenmawr. 'Found a happy party,' he recorded thankfully on arrival. 'We are nine; all together, and alone.' The previous year he had turned his back on the habitual escape to Wales; now after a humiliating session in parliament he returned once more to familiar pleasures and the reliable comforts of family. He stayed almost a month before returning at last for an extended residence at Hawarden. There was much to consider, not least a stern rebuke about his lamentable leadership skills from his old friend Sir Thomas Acland. 'There is an impression that you are absorbed in questions about Homer and the Greek world, about *Ecce Homo*, that you are not reading the newspapers or feeling the pulse of followers,' Acland wrote damningly, 'and beside that there is so little easy contact with small fry, as when Palmerston sat in the tea-room, and men were gratified by getting private speech with their leader.'

If Gladstone was bothered by the rebuke he did not confide it to his diary, yet the demons of the previous session needed exorcism. This came in an article for the *Edinburgh Review* about the Reform Act, but it was not done happily. 'Truly irksome toil,' he recorded despondently on 16 September. It was a half-hearted affair, attacking Disraeli's 'attempts alike despicable and ridiculous to claim originality and consistency in the very act of plagiarism and of tergiversation', and promising that 'Time' would be the 'vindicator and avenger' of the Liberal party.

While Gladstone skulked at Hawarden, Disraeli basked in the warm afterglow of his parliamentary triumph. Following recuperation at

Hughenden he made one of his rare forays to Scotland (where the Tories found their 'bitterest and most insulting foes'). There he addressed a great banquet of Tory grandees to set out in confident, ebullient terms what would soon become his defining creed of 'one-nation' Conservatism.

'In a progressive country change is constant,' he declared, 'and the great question is not whether you should resist change which is inevitable, but whether that change should be carried out in defer-ence to the manners, the customs, the laws and the traditions of a people, or whether it should be carried out in deference to abstract principles, and arbitrary and general doctrines. The one is a national system; the other is, to give it an epithet, a noble epithet – which it may perhaps deserve – a philosophic system . . . Now my Lords and Gentlemen, I have always considered that the Tory party was the national party of England . . . It is formed of all classes from the highest to the most homely, and it upholds a series of institutions that are in theory, and ought to be in practice, an embodiment of the national require-ments and the security of the national rights.'

To prove his point, Disraeli also addressed a workers' rally in Edinburgh. His métier was the House of Commons, with its rapier debate, witty asides and backstairs politicking. Yet when he put his mind to mass public speaking, which was not often, Disraeli demon-strated a common touch that even exceeded that of his rival.

'I have always looked on the interests of the labouring classes as essentially the most conservative interests of the country,' he told his huge audience. 'Be proud of the confidence which the constituted authorities of the country have reposed in you, by investing you with popular privileges; prove that you know the value of such privileges; and that you will exercise them to maintain the institutions of your country, to increase its power, its glory, and its fame.'

Edinburgh was a triumph for Disraeli, prompting that jig danced with Mrs Disraeli in their bedroom. Sir John Skelton (who would soon publish Disraeli's biography) was mesmerised by the couple. Mary Anne seemed to him like one of the witches in *Macbeth*. 'And the potent wizard himself, with his olive complexion and coal black eyes, and the mighty dome of his forehead (no Christian temple, be sure), is unlike any living creature one has met,' he wrote. 'The face is more like a mask than ever and the division between him and mere mortals more marked.' For all this ethereal strangeness, Skelton had few doubts about either Disraeli's patriotism or his destiny. 'England is the Israel of his imagination,' he observed shrewdly, 'and he will be the Imperial Minister before he dies.'

Given Disraeli's brilliant success as a popular speaker, and the evident rush of adrenalin it gave him, many wondered why he did not do it more often. The answer came quickly enough when the Disraelis got home. The trip to Scotland had been triumphant, but exhausting. Almost immediately afterwards, the seventy-five-year-old Mary Anne fell gravely ill. This could not have come at a worse time politically for Disraeli. The House was about to sit for a rare autumn session, occasioned by a crisis in Abyssinia. Lord Derby was again out of action with chronic gout. Disraeli had to turn to Stanley to undertake many of his official duties, telling him on 18 November that 'this has been a critical day in my wife's life'.

The next day Disraeli managed to get to the House for the Queen's Speech debate. It was on this occasion that Gladstone, as leader of the opposition, made his warm and affectionate reference to Mary Anne, prompting tears in Disraeli. A man whose face had appeared only weeks earlier to be 'more like a mask than ever' now had his bruised emotions on display for all to see. By the end of November, Disraeli's concern for his wife, coupled with the pressure of business in the House, overwhelmed him. On 30 November, after a late-night session, he collapsed in a cab on the way home. 'I could not get out,' he told Stanley, 'and the driver, I fancy, thought I was drunk.' It was almost a month before husband and wife both recovered. Each confined to bed in separate rooms, they were forced to communicate through scribbled love notes. 'I never felt worse or more desponding,' he told Mary Anne mournfully in one of them.

Disraeli's return to health in the New Year came just in time. Had he not recovered his vim by January his chance to fulfil the ambition of a lifetime might have slipped by. Lord Derby remained at Knowsley during the parliamentary recess crippled by pain. With so many decisions to be made about the forthcoming session, the prime minister's absence from London was increasingly a matter for concern. The cabinet did not meet. Important decisions were put on hold. 'I confess, if the Cabinet is postponed till Tuesday week and perhaps even later, I should tremble for consequences,' Disraeli told Stanley on 17 January. By the end of the month, Derby still had not returned to London. Such was his condition that doctors would not allow him to work. The rumour mill around Westminster began to speculate on an imminent resignation. By 11 February *The Times* was calling for a reconstruction of the government.

Two days later Derby wrote to Disraeli from Knowsley. 'Parliament sitting, and I still lying here, like a useless log!' he lamented. He knew that 'my attacks of illness would, at no distant period, incapacitate me for the discharge of my public duties'. Doctors had warned that to continue with the strain of office might cause 'a sudden and complete break-up'. Yet Derby could not quite bring himself to say that he would resign. He was still much younger than either Palmerston or Russell had been as premiers. So often he had seemed impervious to the attractions of high office. Now at the last his fingers let go of the reins of power only reluctantly. A week later he accepted the inevitable, writing again to Disraeli demanding that 'you will not shrink from the additional heavy responsibility'. Disraeli did not need to be asked twice. 'I will not shrink from the situation,' he told Derby, 'but do not underrate its gravity, and mainly count, when you are convalescent, on your guidance and support.' Derby immediately wrote to the Queen. In a break with protocol, he advised her (without having been asked) to send for Disraeli. 'He, and only he,' Derby told her, 'could command the cordial support, en masse, of his present colleagues.'

Gladstone learnt the news from Derby's son on 25 February. 'At one heard from Lord Stanley that his father has resigned, and that D. is at work upon a cabinet.' His thoughts on hearing this intelligence were unrecorded, but his actions speak for him. As so often, Gladstone for the next few days plunged into a frenzied stint of 'rescue work'.

While the troubled Gladstone wandered the backstreets off Piccadilly, Disraeli made his way to the Isle of Wight for a meeting with destiny. At Osborne House on 27 February 1867 the Queen invited him to form a government. 'All is sunshine here,' he recorded happily, 'moral and material.' The moment when he became prime minister was lovingly described in a letter home to Mary Anne. 'The Queen came into her closet with a very radiant face, holding out her hand, and saying, "You must kiss hands", which I did immediately, and very heartily falling on my knee,' he wrote. 'Then she sat down, which she never used to do, and only does to her First Minister, and talked over affairs for half an hour (I standing), so that I hardly had time to dress for dinner.'

The significance of the moment was not lost on the Queen. 'Mr Disraeli is prime minister!' she wrote to her daughter, the crown princess of Prussia. 'A proud thing for a Man "risen from the people" to have obtained!'

'Yes,' Disraeli would casually tell those who congratulated him, 'I have climbed to the top of the greasy pole.'

His real sense of elation mingled with awe came in an exchange with James Clay, his friend from all those years ago in the Near East.

'Well, Disraeli, when you and I travelled together, who would ever have thought that you would be Prime Minister.'

'Who indeed. But as we used to say in the East: God is great! And now he is greater than ever!'

14

Premier League

King Charles Street, 25 March 1868

Sleet and violent winds thrashed against the windows of the handsome reception rooms at the new Foreign Office. Guests outside, holding tightly to capes and hats, scurried from carriages to escape the atrociously unseasonable spring weather. This was not a night to be outdoors, but fashionable London had turned up to honour a new prime minister and to view the pristine building. Earlier that month, Benjamin Disraeli had asked his foreign secretary, Lord Stanley, if Mary Anne might use the (as yet unopened) Foreign Office for a party. The classical style of George Gilbert Scott's recently completed edifice hardly matched the prime minister's own Gothic taste, but at least it had grandeur. 'She can do nothing with Downing Street,' he wrote, 'it is so dingy and decaying.' So it was on this night that Mrs Disraeli hosted a splendid reception to mark her husband's rise to the premiership. And what a gathering it was. The Prince and Princess of Wales attended, which bestowed honour on the Disraelis and guaranteed that all society would follow. The wealthy, powerful, beautiful and famous glistered and glittered like characters from the pages of one of Disraeli's own silver fork novels. It was a sublime moment of triumph for the man 'risen from the people' to perhaps the most powerful office in the world.

Except that Disraeli felt wretched. Naturally he did his best to shine. 'Dizzy in his glory,' recorded Bishop Wilberforce afterwards, 'leading about the Princess of Wales; the Prince of Wales, Mrs Dizzy.' Yet the prelate could not help noticing that neither Mrs Disraeli –

'looking very ill and haggard' – nor the new prime minister seemed particularly to enjoy the occasion. It was not just that Dizzy looked rather sombre. Long gone were the days of youth when he would dress in all the colours of the rainbow, luxuriating in fine, sensual materials, with rings on every finger, ostentatious walking canes, and hair a flurry of tight dark tresses. Now he played the restrained statesman, soberly dressed, perhaps only a few last remaining curls hinting at a more flamboyant past. There was again on this occasion an apparent lack of effervescence. The smile seemed forced. The characteristic smirk was nowhere to be seen. 'The impenetrable man low,' concluded Wilberforce.

The man with the smirk that night was not the prime minister, but one who thought he might soon usurp him. William Gladstone had attended out of a sense of propriety and because he felt a genuine affection for Mary Anne. There had been a cool exchange of pleasantries with Disraeli. Now as he drank and mingled he could observe the first minister. Like all the political operators in attendance, he understood the reason for this display of obvious discomfort. Already the prime minister was floundering. Having been Disraeli's whipping boy the previous year, Gladstone was back in the ascendant. Only days earlier he had signalled his intention to destroy Disraeli's premiership in its infancy.

'[Gladstone's] teeth were set on edge,' wrote Gathorne Hardy, 'and he prepared to bite.'

Gladstone had been uncharacteristically vapid during the final parliamentary session of 1867. There had been the touching inquiries after the health of Mrs Disraeli that had so moved her husband. Scottish and Irish Reform Bills ambled through the legislative process without attracting any of the vitriol displayed in debates about their English counterpart. The previous summer's hostility, culminating in a bilious self-justification written for the *Edinburgh Review*, had apparently subsided. If not exactly sweetness and light, Gladstone was at least quieter. Yet there had remained that autumn a lingering sense of animosity towards him within his own party. Liberal MPs could accept that he was an arrogant man with a tendency to offend. This had always been balanced by his charismatic presence, commanding intellect and fiercesome ability in debate. His performance in the reform debates, in which Disraeli had outmanoeuvred him at every turn, raised the damaging question that the heir presumptive might actually be overrated. Even saintly John Henry Newman thought Gladstone 'too religious' to compete with Disraeli. The party under his leadership in the Commons was divided and ineffective. Gladstone complained that 'the H. of Commons is no better than a dead dog in ditch', little realising that many were saying something similar about him.

In the end, Earl Russell saved Gladstone. Reluctantly and slowly, he had concluded by Christmas that the time had come to pass the baton of Liberal leadership. By communicating this news to Gladstone a week before telling Lord Granville, the only plausible alternative, Russell settled the matter. He also gave Gladstone the means, or at least the subject, by which to reunite the party around his leadership: Ireland.

Russell had dashed off three pamphlets that would be his vale-dictory counterblast. In the first and most important of these, published in February 1868, he argued that the time had come to institute religious equality through the disestablishment of the Church of Ireland. Three-quarters of its revenue should be given to the endowment of the Roman Catholic Church and the remaining quarter divided between the Protestant churches. Ireland for Gladstone had been among a raft of issues, including the economy, education, the army, and the colonies in general, that he had identified the previous September as needing attention by any future Liberal government. Now the 'Fenian Outrages', which had included bombings, assassi-nation threats and the death of a policeman in Manchester, gave the issue a startling public profile. Gladstone therefore seized on Russell's call for disestablishment as a means to respond to public concern on Ireland in a way that might also unite the Liberals under his direc-tion. The party, after the calamitous divisions of the previous year, seemed ready to listen. After all, observed Lord Clarendon, Disraeli looked set for a long tenure as prime minister, 'for success is nowa-days the only divinity adored and he has all the Jews and all the press on his side'.

Just weeks after Russell's pamphlet appeared, Gladstone began a concerted campaign to sever the ties between the state and the Church of Ireland. The Liberal MP for Cork, John Maguire, made a speech in the House during a debate on Ireland in which he expressed 'fear and alarm . . . on the eve of a great struggle'. Shortly afterwards, on 16 March, Gladstone took up the theme in a searing attack on Disraeli's government. They had 'failed to realise in any degree the solemn fact that we have reached a crisis in the affairs and in the state of Ireland'.

So much needed to be done, but the most urgent task of all was to end the relationship between the state and the Church of Ireland. This would be 'a great and formidable operation', but not beyond 'the courage and statesmanship of the British legislature'.

Gladstone had been speaking for almost two hours by the time his intentions became clear. Midnight was approaching. The House, half-empty at the beginning, had quickly filled up as it became clear that 'something' was happening. Disraeli was unsurpassed in an ability to mask his feelings in debate. But MPs on both sides of the House that night noticed an unusual discomfort in the prime minister. As he rose to answer Gladstone, he took a large slug from a glass of brownish liquid. Only minutes into his speech, a whisper ran round the chamber that the prime minister was drunk. 'Disraeli ambiguous and his manner laboured,' wrote John Bright afterwards, 'giving the idea that he was the worse for the brandy and water he drank before he rose and during his speech.' From the Press Gallery, a *New York Tribune* reporter observed that Disraeli was 'blind drunk'. Sensing an opportunity, Gladstone mischievously popped up to inquire if the prime minister was toiling 'under the influence of [theatrical pause] a heated imagination'.

Drunk or not, Disraeli was clearly both shaken and stirred. He was never at his best in religious debates. It was a subject on which he had neither a mastery of detail nor an instinctive feel for nuance. That he had been ambushed made matters worse. Gladstone had inflicted a blow, which Disraeli recognised as such immediately. So often attack brought out the best in him, but his response on a subject that unnerved him was overblown and miscalculated. He hyperbolically condemned Gladstone for instigating a conspiracy between Anglo-Catholics and Roman Catholics to subvert established religion. This was 'a secret confederacy' that aimed 'to seize upon supreme authority,' he declared. 'They have their hand on the Realm of England.' Even 'the Crown' was in danger.

Gladstone's Irish salvo and Disraeli's botched reply electrified Westminster. 'There is great excitement about this Irish Church question, and Mr Gladstone has done immense mischief,' the Queen wrote to her daughter. 'The old religious feuds will return with great fury and bitterness.' Having sprung his trap, on 23 March Gladstone announced that he would bring three Irish Church resolutions before the House. But why this sudden haste on Ireland, asked a dim-witted friend of the Duke of Argyll? 'There really [is] no other way of getting Dizzy out of office,' came the blunt reply.

No wonder the prime minister looked so glum at his dazzling soirée two days later. He might even have been forgiven for wondering if Gladstone had timed the resolutions purposely to spoil the event. Either way, Disraeli was canny enough to know that Gladstone had him on the run.

Gladstone moved through the Westminster streets at a clip, his eager young companions trotting alongside. Behind them in the brightening dawn a crowd of excited well-wishers followed at a respectful distance. As he arrived back at Carlton House Terrace, Gladstone turned momentarily to take his leave before heading inside and straight to his study. He had enjoyed a triumph that April night. 'Spoke 1(½) hours after D. (who was tipsy) in winding up the Debate,' he wrote enthusiastically in his diary. 'Walked home with Harry & Herbert, a crowd at our tail. The divisions were wonderful.' Those votes, on the introduction of his Irish resolutions, had seen Disraeli and the government humiliated. The prime minister had again put on a mediocre display. Gladstone had shone. 'The counts are big,' he smugly reflected.

A first Gladstone government seemed assured. Although Disraeli had been able to put together an alliance to pass reform, he was still the leader of a minority government (the fate of all Conservative administrations since 1846). Only divisions between the Whigs and the Radicals had kept him in power. The Irish Church resolutions had reunited the Liberals and restored Gladstone's overall majority in the House. Disraeli surely would be compelled to resign in a matter of weeks, leaving the way clear for Gladstone to take possession of 10 Downing Street. That predicable Irish defeat for the government came in the early hours of 1 May. Gladstone celebrated with a call on a familiar rescue case, L. St Clair. The next morning he held a conclave of his closest advisers to prepare for government.

Except there was a problem. Had he but known it while writing that exultant April diary entry, the same day also saw the first signs of a festering discontent that would frustrate his immediate designs on the premiership. For Gladstone had seriously displeased the Queen. She visited Lord Derby on 3 April to express her outrage at Gladstone's behaviour. Derby reported to Disraeli that she spoke 'in the most unreserved terms of condemnation of Gladstone's motion and conduct'. She was particularly angry that Gladstone had given her no prior warning of his call for the Crown to relinquish its Church of Ireland land and revenue. Derby also reported to Disraeli that the

Queen had replied 'Quite right' when he told her of his view that the government should not resign if defeated. 'Really curious to know what *is* the course which it is supposed ought to have been taken in order to satisfy the principles of the Constitution, and the claims of personal loyalty and faith,' Gladstone complained irritably when he finally got wind of royal disapproval. No matter that the offence taken seemed unjust: an unhappy Queen now gladly assisted Disraeli in wresting the initiative away from Gladstone during the surprisingly prolonged lead up to their first head-to-head general election.

Having waited so long to be prime minister, Disraeli was eager not to relinquish the post in a matter of months. So he moved quickly to protect his position. He wrote to the Queen immediately after the crushing defeat on Gladstone's first Irish resolution on 1 May. He told her that 'under these circumstances the advice we would humbly offer Your Majesty is to dissolve this Parliament as soon as the public interests will permit', but added crucially 'that an earnest endeavour should be made by the Government that such appeal should be made to the new constituency'. The Queen, still angry with Gladstone and with no desire to have him back in government, readily concurred. At Osborne she refused Disraeli's token offer of resignation and urged him to carry on. Having connived with the Queen to remain in office, Disraeli dashed back to London ready to face a storm.

First he had to contend with his own cabinet. 'Disraeli has communicated with none of us, which is strange,' mused Gathorne Hardy. The Earl of Malmesbury was more forthright. 'The ministers are very angry with Disraeli for going to the Queen without a cabinet,' he reported. When their leader got back he engaged in a vigorous round of discussions to stop anyone resigning. Hardy was keen to go immediately, but stayed out of loyalty to the leader. 'A cabinet before Osborne would have altered everything,' he reflected wearily, 'but now?' On 4 May the full cabinet finally met together and, wrote Stanley, 'we all agreed to go on for the moment'.

That decision when announced provoked days of angry protest in the Commons. Gladstone – 'in a white heat,' said Hardy – accused Disraeli of discrepancies in advice to the Queen. John Bright went further by charging that the prime minister was poisoning the mind of the sovereign. In a bitter attack on Disraeli, he described him as 'at once pompous and servile' in relations with the monarch. Testimony as to what happened next conflicts. Either Disraeli, uncharacteristically, 'lost his temper and shook his fist at Bright'. Otherwise, and more typically, the Radical's claims were icily dismissed 'in the most gentlemanlike manner' by an invitation to produce evidence that Disraeli had dragged the Queen into party politics. Bright took the matter no further, but the unlikely twenty-year friendship that had endured between the two men came to an abrupt end.

Disraeli's resolve to hang on to office at all costs left Gladstone in a difficult position. Armed with a clear majority, he could simply carry a vote of no confidence in the government, which would trigger a general election. But Gladstone did not want an election, or at least did not want it immediately. The Liberal whips, Henry Brand and George Glyn, had advised him that the party was likely to win a bigger majority if the election took place using the new electoral register being drawn up under the terms of the 1867 Reform Act. This list, crucially, would not be available until the autumn. An election before November would have to take place using the old register. This left Gladstone with a dilemma: should he let Disraeli carry on and then fight him at the polls on more favourable terms, or otherwise kick him out immediately, but risk a tighter election result.

In the end, electoral expediency won out. 'I think we have got out of our danger, but it has been very ticklish,' Disraeli wrote to his wife on 14 May. While Gladstone was prepared to let Disraeli remain in office, he devised a straightforward method to undermine his exercise of power. Gladstone simply behaved as if he and not his great rival were prime minister. With a majority at his command, Gladstone steered all three resolutions through the House. Then he introduced and passed a bill on the Irish Church. The House of Lords swiftly rejected that bill, but even this worked to Gladstone's advantage by prompting a further display of his popularity with the newly enfranchised classes when protesters marching from Clerkenwell to Hyde Park stopped off at Carlton House Terrace to pay their respects to him on behalf of 'real working men'.

By the time the House of Commons was prorogued at the end of July in advance of the election, few doubted that it was the Liberal leader who had been the dominant force in parliament that year. All in all, recorded the despondent Hardy, it had been a 'miserable session' in which the Conservatives had endured nothing 'but retail humiliation'.

National Portrait Gallery

This was not an unpleasant way to spend a summer's afternoon, but as William Gladstone wandered from room to room he felt his spirits drop. It had been a fairly typical day. Correspondence in the morning, lunch with the new Duke of Newcastle, a visit to 'J. Turner', a favourite rescue case, and this quick trip to the gallery. These he hoped might compensate for a tedious dinner still to come with a 'mad' Mr Hubbards. Moving from portrait to portrait an uneasy feeling gradually overtook him. Here was Robert Peel, Gladstone's first and greatest mentor. Now Lord Aberdeen, who had guided him indulgently through those difficult middle years. Then Lord Palmerston, whom he had loathed and admired in equal measure. Looking from face to face, Gladstone finally recognised the source of his discomfort. 'Its two or three last rooms were indeed for me a meeting of the dead,' he wrote afterwards, 'I seemed to know every one.'

Death was on Gladstone's mind that day. Lunch with Newcastle had brought back painful feelings of loss for the previous duke, one of his two or three closest friends, who had died in despair four years earlier. His death, along with that of Sidney Herbert, had left Gladstone markedly friendless among his contemporaries. Now approaching his sixtieth year and braced for an apparently inevitable premiership, he increasingly sensed the march of time. 'I feel like a man under a burden under which he must fall and be crushed if he looks to the right or left, or fails from any cause to concentrate mind and muscle upon his progress step by step,' he wrote soon afterwards. 'This absorption, this constant "excess" is the fault of political life with its insatiable demands which do not leave the smallest stock of energy unexhausted and available for other purposes.' Disraeli, five years his senior, would soon put it more succinctly. 'Power!' he lamented, 'It came to me too late.'

The political landscape of Britain changed very little as a result of the 1868 general election. More constituencies were fought than ever before, but in most other regards the election was unexceptional. Around eighty seats remained under the direct control of landed aristocracy. In the cities of the north, factory owners continued to assert their influence. The elected members of parliament – mostly aristocrats, landed gentry, lawyers and sons of industry – looked and sounded just like their predecessors. Only around twenty seats changed hands. All in all the election of 1868 looked remarkably similar to that of 1865.

Except it did not feel that way. Disraeli's and Gladstone's sense of the passing of time was shared by so many of their generation. The 1868 election appeared to symbolise the shift from one world to another. The essayist Thomas Carlyle expressed that feeling more negatively than most. In *Shooting Niagara* he portrayed a civilisation plunging down the rapids. Taking the now inevitable 'Niagara leap of completed democracy' could only result in 'blockheadism, gullibility, bribability, amenability to beer and balderdash, by way of amending the woes we have had from our previous supplies of that bad article,' he protested. 'Certain it is, there is nothing but vulgarity in our People's expectation, resolutions or desires in this Epoch. It is all a peaceable mouldering or tumbling down from mere rottenness and decay.'

That reform had been a leap into the unknown, not least politically, seemed just about the only point of agreement as the two parties geared up for the election. George Glyn reported to Gladstone that 'all is new and changed and large and I fear I must say in some respects *dark*'. The Tory side was hardly any better off. Stanley recorded a long conversation with Disraeli in September on the forthcoming poll. 'D. says the elections are extremely difficult to speculate upon, the results will be unexpected in many places,' he wrote. 'He thinks the Conservatives ought to gain in England, and probably to hold their own in Ireland, but Scotland is their weak point.'

Even at the time, observers recognised that the personal rivalry between Disraeli and Gladstone would play a central role in the campaign. 'Confidence in Gladstone seems on the increase throughout the country,' wrote the Earl of Clarendon. 'On the other hand a demoralised nation admire the audacity, the tricks and the success of the Jew, and the fight between the two will be as personal on the hustings as it has been in parliament.'

Gladstone characterstically began the election season with illness brought on by nerves. 'An evil night from an attack of diarrhoea & sickness made this a *dies non* as to all outward work,' he lamented. 'I could not even read.' When the challenger recovered his equilibrium he launched into electioneering in a way that marked a new departure for a party leader. He demanded to be kept in touch with events on a daily basis, bombarding party managers with questions about progress in the constituencies. His principal innovation was the way in which he campaigned nationally. Although he hardly spoke outside his Lancashire constituency, he gave a raft of stirring addresses on an unprecedented level to galvanise opinion throughout the country. His aim was to 'raise the party standard'; in doing so he set both the tone and the pace of the Liberal campaign.

This meant, above all, the question of Ireland. In his last set-piece speech in Lancashire, the keen axeman ended with a great peroration in which he compared the Protestant ascendancy to the upas, a magnificent Javanese tree so poisonous that it destroys all life in its vicinity. 'There is the Church of Ireland, there is the land of Ireland, there is the education of Ireland; there are many subjects, all of which depend on one greater than them all; they are all so many branches from one trunk, and that trunk is the tree of what is called the Protestant ascendancy,' he declared. 'It is still there like a tall tree of noxious growth, lifting its head to heaven and darkening and poisoning the land so far as its shadow can extent; it is still there, Gentleman, and now at length the day has come when, as we hope, the axe has been laid at the root of that tree, and it nods and quivers from its root to its base. It wants, Gentleman, one stroke more, the stroke of these elections.'

By putting Ireland at the centre of the election campaign, Gladstone once again forced the prime minister to fight on territory that was not his own. Disraeli's principal election address – in effect the Conservative manifesto – was dominated by the Irish Question. Gladstone, he argued, had proposed 'a dissolution of the union between Church and State'. To that policy the Tories would offer 'uncompromising resistance [because] the connection of religion with the exercise of political authority is one of the main safeguards of the civilization of man'. In reality, as Stanley advised, two-thirds of Conservatives did want compromise, but Disraeli recognised that he could not afford to offend the other third who regarded the Church as untouchable. Ironically the place where his uneasy Protestant call to arms resonated most strongly was Lancashire. There the influence of Lord Derby, combined with intense anti-Irish and anti-Catholic sentiment, saw the Liberals routed. Among the losing candidates was one William Gladstone, who fortunately had taken the precaution of having his name added to the list of candidates in Greenwich, where he would be elected with a tidy majority.

On the eve of the poll, Disraeli attended the annual Lord Mayor's banquet at London's Guildhall, where he exuded wit and self-assurance. In particular he taunted Gladstone for his showy, personalised campaign style. 'I think I have read somewhere that it is the custom of undisciplined hosts on the eve of a great battle to anticipate and celebrate their triumph by horrid sounds and hideous yells, the sounding of cymbals, the beating of terrible drums, the shrieks and screams of barbaric horns,' he announced to peals of laughter and shouts of 'Gladstone'. 'But when the struggle comes, and the fight takes place, it is sometimes found that the victory is not to them, but to those who are calm and collected.' In private, however, Disraeli was less confident, telling Stafford Northcote on the first day of the protracted election that 'our shadows seem to grow very long'.

As the results slowly emerged it became clear that Disraeli's private fears were more accurate than his public bravado. By the 22 November, the Conservatives knew they had lost convincingly. 'Even taking the most favourable view . . . I cannot make out that Gladstone's majority will be less, and probably more, than a hundred,' wrote the Earl of Derby. He applauded Disraeli for the 'calm, temperate, and dignified' way in which he had conducted the campaign. This was 'a striking contrast to the balderdash and braggadocio in which Gladstone has been indulging on his stumping tour – and which, I am happy to say, has done him more harm than good'. They could not, however, ignore the obvious: 'the fate of the government . . . is, I apprehend, decided.' Derby, like almost everyone else, anticipated that Disraeli would quickly join him on the benches of the House of Lords as a safely retired prime minister and party leader.

When the final returns were all counted, the Conservatives' numbers in the House of Commons had fallen to 274 MPs, while the Liberals had risen to 384 MPs. When the smaller parties were taken into account, this gave Gladstone a majority of more than a hundred. Having lost the election, Disraeli now acted quickly and without precedent. The custom had been to wait for the first meeting of the new House before resigning. Instead Disraeli quickly signalled to the Queen that he would leave office immediately as the people had spoken. Victoria, disappointed as she was to lose him, approved of this exceptional but dignified exit. 'Nothing could have been more proper or manly than his way of taking what he admits to be a total defeat,' judged Grey, her private secretary.

If the manner of Disraeli's departure from office was unusual, his request for a peerage threw the court into paroxysms. The Queen would happily have elevated Disraeli to the Lords, but accepted his explanation that such an honour would be interpreted as retirement from public life. Awkwardness only set in when Disraeli asked whether the Queen might 'grant those honours to his wife which perhaps under ordinary circumstances your Majesty would have deigned to bestow upon him'. In case she missed the point, the departing prime minister requested that Mary Anne should be created Viscountess Beaconsfield (leaving him as plain Mr Disraeli).

'Very embarrassing!' Victoria exclaimed afterwards. Charles Grey summed up the dilemma as between 'the desire to do what would gratify Mr Disraeli, who certainly deserves it at your Majesty's hand, and yet not to expose him to the attacks, and even ridicule, which would surely follow the creation of Mrs Disraeli as a peeress in her own right'. In the end, said Grey, it was a decision in which the Queen should 'follow the dictates of your Majesty's own kind heart'. Eventually her fondness for Disraeli won through. 'The Queen can truly sympathize with his devotion to Mrs Disraeli, who in her turn is so deeply attached to him, and she hopes they may yet enjoy many years of happiness together,' Victoria wrote to him, alluding to her struggle to have Prince Albert named Prince Consort. 'Mr Disraeli, at your Majesty's feet,' came back the overjoyed reply.

The pleasure that the award gave at Grosvenor Gate need not even be imagined. The impecunious Miss Mary Anne Evans of Exeter was now Viscountess Beaconsfield, wife of the (just) prime minister. Letters to her husband, on paper ornamented with a coronet and the letter 'B', now ended with the flourish 'Your devoted Beaconsfield'. Furniture, book covers and even her wardrobe were embellished with that same 'B'. She insisted on the title being pronounced 'Beacon-' (to rhyme with deacon) rather than the more usual 'Beckonsfield'. Even self-assured Lord Rosebery said it would take more courage than he had to address Mary Anne by any other pronunciation.

Court fears about ridicule were misplaced. Typical of the reaction was that of the *Morning Post*, which wrote that Disraeli accepted 'the proffered coronet to place it on the brow of a wife to whose qualities he has borne public testimony, and to whose affectionate aid he has acknowledged himself indebted for much of his success in life'. Mary Anne, now in her late seventies and continually in poor health, had devoted her wealth and spirit to Disraeli, providing a haven of admiration, support and encouragement away from the vicissitudes of politics. To demonstrate in public his love and gratitude, Disraeli had risked both derision and his relationship with the Queen. A peerage for his beloved wife was indeed the most uxorious of gifts. Among those charmed by the gesture was Gladstone, who wrote to Disraeli asking him 'to present my best compliments on her coming patent to (I suppose I must still say, and never can use the name for the last time without regret) Mrs Disraeli'.

While Disraeli secured honours for his wife, Gladstone waited at Hawarden for the inevitable call. The government resigned on 1 December 1868. The Queen wrote immediately to the Liberal leader, not with the expected invitation to kiss hands, but to demand (as she had of Lord Derby in 1866) that he explain certain anticipated appointments. She particularly had in her sights Lord Clarendon, who referred to her as 'the missus'. ('He looked ill and worn,' Stanley would record when he finally handed over to Clarendon at the Foreign Office, 'and dwelt much on his own reluctance to take office again, which I should have believed, but for knowing the efforts which his family and friends have made to put him there'.) Gladstone's response to the telegram saying that the Queen's private secretary, Charles Grey, was on his way to Hawarden bearing the Queen's letter became legendary, helped by the evocative telling by Evelyn Ashley (formerly Palmerston's private secretary). Gladstone, in shirtsleeves, was chopping down a tree when the telegram arrived. 'Very significant,' he said obliquely after reading the message, and then returned his attention to the tree. 'I said nothing, but waited while the well-directed blows resounded in regular cadence,' recalled Ashley, who was holding the great man's coat. 'After a few minutes the blows ceased and Mr Gladstone, resting on the handle of his axe, looked up, and with deep earnestness in his voice, and great intensity in his face, exclaimed: "My mission is to pacify Ireland". He then resumed his task, and never said another word till the tree was down.'

In the privacy of his diary that evening, Gladstone wrote characteristically that 'the Lessons, as usual in times of crisis, supplied all my need. "The Lord shall give thee rest from thy sorrow, & from the hard bondage wherein thou wast made to serve . . . The whole earth is at rest, & is quiet: they break forth into singing." (Isaiah. 14).' More unusually, he added an excited coda: 'Much babblement: & saw divers.'

Grey arrived the following day. Gladstone made it clear that he would not give up Clarendon. 'If any other arrangement be made it will be ascribed directly to the Sovereign,' he warned. 'This would be a serious evil.' Having satisfied himself that Gladstone would not be moved, Grey telegraphed to his mistress. Early the next morning the two men set out from Hawarden to catch the London train. By the time they reached Chester station a reply had come from the Queen giving way. On arriving at Slough in mid-afternoon, they were told that Victoria was out on her daily carriage ride.

So Gladstone charmingly slipped away to nearby Eton, there to tell sixteen-year-old Harry that his father was about to become the Queen's first minister.

15

Die or Break Down

'Arrived at 10.45 in that very happy home,' wrote William Gladstone as he celebrated his fifty-ninth birthday. The Gladstones, most unusually, had spent Christmas in London to allow the new prime minister to conduct the arduous task of putting together a legislative programme. There were so many issues that demanded attention, including reform of the civil service and army, primary and university education, secret ballots, trade union law, and (most important to the prime minister) Ireland. For a few days Gladstone could step back from the constant flow of inquiries and demands to enjoy complete relaxation with the Lytteltons. Hagley Hall, with 350 acres of deer park and its own church, was like another home. Although Lady Lyttelton, Catherine Gladstone's sister, had been dead for more than a decade, the two families remained extremely close. William particularly valued his intimate friendship with the political yet unambitious Lyttelton. In these surroundings he stopped for the first time to contemplate the nature of his achievement. Constantly under so much pressure, it was often difficult to appreciate any real progress and achievement. After all, Gladstone wrote, 'Swimming for his life, a man does not see much of the country through which the river winds, and I probably know little of these years through which I busily work and live.' Yet under the guise of noting an interesting serendipity, Gladstone was able proudly to list a number of his greatest achievements. 'This month of December has been notable in my life,' he wrote:

1809. Born.
1827. Left Eton.
1831. [First] Classes at Oxford.
1832. Elected to Parliament.
1834. Took office: Lord of the Treasury.
1838. Work on Ch[urch] & State Published.
1846. Sec. of State.
1852. Chancellor. of Exr.
1868. First Lord [Prime Minister].'

So it was that Gladstone felt able to end his 1868 diary with the uncharacteristic, almost triumphant salutation: 'Farewell great year of opening . . . and welcome new year laden with promise and with care.'

While Gladstone basked in political power, Disraeli skulked. Visitors to Grosvenor Gate found the ex-prime minister willing to discuss anything but the state of the nation. 'Called on Disraeli, who talked little politics, and evidently thinks there is nothing to be done for the present,' recorded Lord Stanley on 7 February. A month later, Stanley found him still 'out of spirits, says he thinks the monarchy in danger . . . Nothing as to party prospects, which are obviously hopeless.'

Disraeli's emotional state was not simply down to political exhaustion. His health had been poor during the winter. He told Lord Henry Lennox that he had been 'feeling unwell all this year', adding that 'illness makes one selfish and disgusts one's friends'. Similarly, he complained to Stafford Northcote, 'I can't say much for myself – I have been to the seaside; but it has brought me no relief, and I still suffer, which is disheartening.' Added to concerns about his own health were serious worries about Mary Anne's increasing physical frailty. And as if the loss of office and illness were not enough to bring Disraeli low, his brother, James, had died over Christmas leaving an estate in chaos. All in all, Disraeli was at a low ebb, and might even have agreed with the *Dizzy's Lament* that was doing the rounds in Westminster: 'I never thought they'd turn me out, For well I knew my way about. So pity poor Benjamin Dizzy. Oh, if I could Bill Gladstone thump, I'd burst his nose, and kick his rump.' Certainly Bill Gladstone was amused enough to file the *Lament* among his papers.

Gladstone dominated the new parliament with an authority that had been long predicted, but which many in recent years had begun to doubt. Few could match Gladstone in command of detail and argument on matters of religion. On the principal question of the day, disestablishment of the Church of Ireland, Disraeli did not even try. He warned the Commons to fear the prime minister's zeal, but did not attempt to bother raising more than perfunctory opposition to the Irish Church Bill. Gathorne Hardy, the previous home secretary, complained of 'depressing work . . . [and] long dreary nights' of listless debate. Only Stafford Northcote, Gladstone's sometime secretary, managed to generate a certain interest by characterising disestablishment as a policy of 'robbery and bribery'. No one was surprised, however, when the bill was triumphantly carried with a sweeping majority of 114. 'In some other qualities of parliamentary statesmanship, as an orator, a debater, a tactician, he has rivals,' wrote one observer of Gladstone after the vote, 'but in the powers of embodying principles in legislative form and preserving unity of purpose through a multitude of confusing minutiae he has neither equal nor second among living statesman'.

Yet Gladstone's brittle nature and tactical ineptitude were always lurking. Argument on disestablishment only began to ferment once the bill was sent up to the Lords. This he disastrously mishandled. There an anti-Liberal majority proposed a series of amendments designed to postpone implementation and to win as much money as possible for the newly independent Church of Ireland. 'What will be the end?' wondered Hardy, as the Tories suddenly pepped up. 'Gladstone will not accept.' By the middle of July, the progress of the bill had developed into a full-scale crisis. 'The time grows more and more anxious,' Gladstone wrote on 12 July. When the Lords voted substantially against the government, the Tory Lord Carnavon asked, 'Is it like the first shot fired on Fort Sumter?' Certainly the effect on Gladstone was extreme. He fulminated against 'a great moral and political evil' and, on 20 July, petulantly threatened to withdraw the bill in its entirety. Cabinet members dashed to the prime minister's rooms in the Commons to plead with him to do nothing precipitate. Lord Kimberley found him 'obstinately bent on throwing up the bill at once'. Only the private intervention of the tactful Lord Granville calmed Gladstone. Even so, wrote Sir John Trelawny, 'he must I think succeed or resign'.

If anything was likely to shake Disraeli temporarily from his political slumber it was the sight of his nemesis losing his cool. Most recognised this immediately. 'Gladstone's own temper is visible and audible whenever he rises to speak,' reflected Lord Stanley. 'The mixture of anger and contempt in his voice is almost painful to witness. With all his splendid talent, and his great position, few men suffer more from the constitutional infirmity of an irritable nature: and this is a disease which hard mental work, anxiety, and the exercise of power, all tend to exacerbate. Disraeli is quite aware of the advantage which he possesses in his natural calmness: and takes every opportunity to make the contrast noticeable.'

As if to prove the point, Disraeli suddenly found renewed physical vitality as Gladstone fell ill. He told Stanley that he felt 'quite, quite myself'. To Lord Cairns, Disraeli confided that he had given up 'burgundy and champagne' in order to be fitter for the parliamentary battles ahead. Meanwhile, poor Gladstone, so often driven psychosomatically to his sickbed, collapsed – 'and no wonder,' quipped Trelawny. Leaving Granville to work out a deal in the Lords with Cairns on the Irish Church Bill, Gladstone stayed in bed or under a rug on his sofa. When the two peers agreed a compromise, which gave the government almost everything it wanted, the prime minister was forced to abandon his comfort blanket to recommend the deal to the Commons. His diary entries make it clear that nerves as much as illness were responsible for his physical weakness. 'Dr Clarke [his physician] came in the morning & made me up for the House whither I went 2–5 P.M. to propose concurrence in the Lords Amendments,' he wrote on 23 July. 'Up to the moment I felt very weak but this all vanished when I spoke, & while the debate lasted.'

A fortnight later parliament prorogued. It would not meet again until February 1870. 'Spent the morning in writing a paper on the meaning of the word ἀμύμων [blameless],' wrote Gladstone immediately afterwards, relieved both that the year was over and that his first major piece of legislation had at last passed. 'I have not done such a thing since taking office in Dec 1868.' Even this fleeting retreat into a life of the mind was redolent with meaning. Gladstone believed he was at that moment anything but blameless. The House of Commons, for all the trouble it brought, was at least a distraction from the emotional, and occasionally physical, flagellation to which he was so prone. In the absence of this parliamentary distraction, Gladstone was set to embark on perhaps the greatest emotional and sexual crisis of his life.

The 15th Earl of Derby listened with a mixture of amusement and astonishment as Lord Cairns revealed the extraordinary tale. The previous weeks had been difficult for Derby following the death of his father, the former prime minister. (The 14th Earl, caustic to the end, had replied when asked on his deathbed how he felt: 'bored to utter extinction'.) So

Stanley had become Derby, which brought with it rank, wealth and expectations. Most anticipated that within a few years he would follow Disraeli as leader of the Conservative party. His immediate frustrating responsibility was settling the estate, which 'burdens are almost more than I know how to clear off'. So it must have been with a certain relief that he listened agog on 11 December to Lord Cairns' gossip. 'Strange story of Gladstone frequenting the company of a Mrs Thistlethwayte,' he recorded that night. She was a reformed courtesan who had taken to religion, on which subject she now gave public lectures at London Polytechnic. 'This, with her beauty, is the attraction to G. and it is characteristic of him to be indifferent to scandal,' observed Derby shrewdly. Could it really be true what Cairns was saying, that the reckless Gladstone was about to spend the weekend with the Thistlethwaytes in Dorset? A few days later he had his answer. 'Malmesbury called,' he wrote in astonishment, 'and confirmed the story of Gladstone's going to visit the Thistlethwaytes! A strange world!'

Gladstone had set out from Waterloo railway station that weekend in the pouring rain, accompanied by Laura Thistlethwayte and the Liberal MP, Arthur Kinnaird, who provided respectable cover. Catherine Gladstone did not travel with them. Their destination was Boveridge in Dorset, country home of Laura's wealthy husband, Augustus Thistlethwayte. Behind him Gladstone left political society that was half-scandalised, half-titillated, not least because he had cancelled a cabinet meeting in order to travel to the Southwest. 'On Monday till evening I shall be out of town,' he had brazenly announced at the previous Friday's meeting. Cabinet was postponed until the following Tuesday. It was going to be another one of those significant Gladstonian Decembers.

Gladstone had first met Laura Thistlethwayte in 1864. Following her religious conversion she became a friend of both the Duke of Newcastle and Arthur Kinnaird. Inevitably she was introduced to Gladstone, but initially their relationship was one of sociable acquaintance. It was only when she sent him a draft of her autobiography that Gladstone began to take notice. We can only speculate on the contents of that now lost memoir of a reformed courtesan. What remains clear is that at the height of Irish Church crisis, his nerves shot through, Gladstone suddenly recognised in Mrs Thistlethwayte an awe-inspiring combination of physical beauty, religious sentimentality and barely repressed immorality. 'It is like a story from the Arabian Nights, with much added to it,' he breathlessly recorded after reading her tale. She was

Disraeli in 1875:
Prime minister and
best-selling author
of *Lothair*

With Queen
Victoria at
Osborne: 'Never
had I so kind
and devoted a
minister, and
very few such
devoted friends.'

Gladstone's government, 1870
(Left to right: Cardwell, Argyll,
Lowe, Hatherley, Kimberley,
Gladstone, Granville, Bruce, De Grey,
Clarendon, Fortescue, Hartington,
Childers, Bright, and Goschen)

Family life 'in the centre of history':
Gladstone with his granddaughter,
Dorothy Drew

Disraeli's inner cabinet, 1876: 'Turkish affairs have taken hold of Disraeli's mind and he can talk of nothing else.' (Left to right: Derby, Cairns, Northcote, Disraeli, Hardy, and Salisbury)

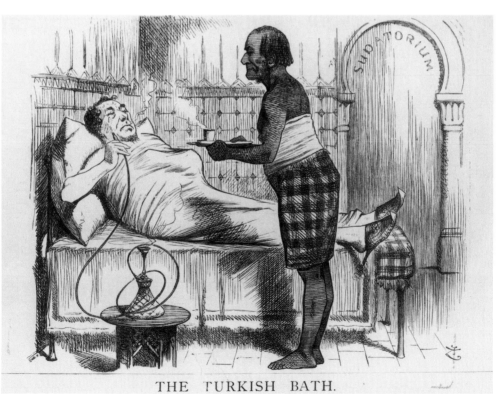

SUDATORIUM

THE TURKISH BATH.

Disraeli smokes a hookah as he contemplates the Eastern Question (October 1876)

'Der alte Jude, das is der Mann!': Disraeli at the Congress of Berlin, 1878

Hughenden Manor

The faithful gather at Hawarden
to hear Gladstone speak

'Finished England under
Lord Beaconsfield': Gladstone,
with Catherine at his side,
reaches out to supporters
from the balcony of
Lord Rosebery's house after
winning Midlothian in 1880

Hawarden Castle

'Catching each other's eye in artistic perpetuity': Gladstone (left, 1879)

and Disraeli (right, 1881) in matching portraits by Sir John Millais

'I am dead.
Dead, but in
Elysian fields':
Lord Beaconsfield

'The forest
laments in order
that Mr Gladstone
may perspire.'

clearly not a rescue case, but 'Mrs T.' shared with those in his diary the familiar culpatory 'X' denoting temptation. The death the previous autumn of Harriet, dowager Duchess of Sutherland, had left a significant emotional gap. Laura was no duchess, but she filled the breach. 'Friendships with women have contributed no small portion of my existence,' Gladstone told her revealingly. 'I know the meaning of the words "weakness is power": apparent weakness is real power.' By the autumn of 1869 the two were embarked on an affair.

From October onwards Gladstone's letters to Laura were addressed 'Dear Spirit'. He wore her gift of an engraved ring (which would eventually be placed in his coffin). Letters flowed back and forth to Hawarden on an almost daily basis – all sent in specially marked envelopes to sidestep private secretaries who otherwise opened everything. When they were both in London, Gladstone dropped in each day at Laura's house on Grosvenor Square for visits that lasted an hour or two. Often these calls were squeezed into a day's unremitting business. The afternoon of 10 November, for example, included individual meetings with the Chancellor of the Exchequer, the foreign secretary and the leader of the House of Lords, followed by a full cabinet until 4.45, and then 'Mrs Th. 5(¼)–7(¼)'. Sometimes these visits would provoke a burst of self-pitying remorse on Gladstone's part. 'Mrs Thistlethwayte: in great gravity of spirit,' he had recorded at the end of October. 'Duty and evil temptation are there before me, on the right & left. But I firmly believe in her words "holy" and "pure", & in her cleaving to God.' Yet for the most part he simply gave in to the inevitable: 'It is difficult to repel, nay to check or to dissuade, the attachment of a remarkable, a signal, soul, clad in a beautiful body.'

The relationship came to a head during the exhilarating visit to Dorset that had so astonished Lord Derby. Sunday, in particular, was a day of high emotion for Gladstone. Predictably it began with a visit to church, after which Laura took Gladstone for a long walk in the grounds. Later she 'came to my rooms afternoon & at night'. There she let down her beautiful hair. 'It is a robe,' gushed the premier, quoting Tennyson: 'So Godiva – "the rippled ringlets to the knee".'

The visit to Dorset would turn out to be the culmination of Gladstone's relationship with Laura Thistlethwayte. Ironically their relationship had restored equilibrium to his life following his nervous collapse the previous summer. With that renewed balance came a diminishing need for Laura. The letters would continue for several years, but with reduced ardour and frequency. At the end of 1869, however, Gladstone remained in thrall to her. In his traditional appraisal on his birthday, he recorded happily that 'my review this year includes as a prominent object LT: the extraordinary history, the confiding appeal, the singular avowal. It entails much upon me: and as I saw most clearly of all today, first to do what in me may lie towards building up a true domestic community of life and purpose there.'

Two days later he added to that assessment in a joyous diary entry that did not even bother with the customary reflection on his own unworthiness. 'At midnight listened to the bells which closed this for me notable year,' he wrote. 'Its private experience, in the case mentioned on Wednesday [Laura] has been scarcely less singular than its public. May both be ruled for good.'

In the great political houses of England many were asking if that 'private experience' was about to engulf Gladstone and his premiership. 'The Liberal party expect him either to die or break down,' recorded Lord Derby before travelling to stay with Disraeli at Hughenden. It was, he hoped, just the kind of news that might shake the Tory leader out of his renewed torpor.

Hughenden

Disraeli had always found it difficult to entice visitors to his country seat in Buckinghamshire. He might be leader of the Conservative party, and a former prime minister to boot, but he was also a parvenu who unnerved his aristocratic colleagues with his unusual ideas (not least in dress) about how a country gentleman lived and behaved. He abhorred country sports, was a poor rider and disliked traditional after-dinner entertainments. House parties at Hughenden were usually sedate affairs. The 14th Earl of Derby, even when Disraeli was his number two, had refused to stay (or even to have him up to Knowsley). The 15th Earl had been a regular visitor as 'Lord Stanley', but his first visit as Derby was an important occasion in Disraeli's life as a country squire. To the peer's chagrin, however, it was not much of a political occasion. 'Nothing passed between D. and myself as to current events,' he recorded dolefully afterwards. 'Our talk was almost entirely of the past and future, of literature, philosophy, history – everything rather than politics.' Except that Disraeli made it clear he was not resigning the leadership. Although he cared not 'if he never held office again' and 'the fatigue was considerable', Disraeli deflatingly told his erstwhile protégé that 'he saw no one in whose hands he could leave it, and that circumstance had decided him'.

When parliament had broken up that autumn, Disraeli had found himself with more free time than he had enjoyed for a decade. Not only did he have no government business to despatch, but such was the lie of the political land that his strategy for opposition was simply to do nothing. Gladstone had a commanding Commons majority implementing a programme for government that had successfully unified the disparate elements of the Liberal party. Disraeli's plan was clear if undemanding: in general keep quiet, make mischief where possible and wait for cracks to appear in the governing party. 'He is desponding, but looks forward to Gladstone becoming useless to the Radicals and a disruption,' wrote Gathorne Hardy after a visit to Hughenden. 'Gives two years or more.'

Sitting in patient quietude was not enough to keep Disraeli occupied. What neither Hardy nor Derby knew was that Disraeli was already embarked on a new project. Such was Disraeli's need for secrecy that he did not even confide in his private secretary. 'Montagu Corry,' he wrote afterwards, 'who possesses my entire confidence in political matters, who opens all my letters, and enters my cabinet and deals, as he likes, with all my papers in my absence, never knew anything about *Lothair* until he read the advertisement in the journals.' For Disraeli, sensationally, was writing another novel.

Lothair was nothing less than an extraordinary smash. Certainly it was an unprecedented business for a former prime minister to write a novel. But then Disraeli had been an extraordinary, unprecedented premier. *Lothair* was set during Disraeli's own ministry, although, in an uncharacteristic display of modesty, he played no part in his own narrative. Other well-known characters, however, did make appearances, although regrettably Gladstone was not one of them. The 'Bishop' was a barely disguised Samuel Wilberforce of Winchester, whom Disraeli had recently passed over for the London diocese. The ruthless 'Cardinal Grandison' was Gladstone's former ally, Henry Manning, Archbishop of Westminster. Wilberforce was furious about his character, telling a friend that 'my wrath against D. has burnt . . . so fiercely that it seems to have burnt up all the materials for burning and to be like an exhausted prairie fire – full of black stumps, burnt grass, and all abominations'. Manning was more sanguine, delighted at this enhancement of his reputation as a worldly Machiavellian prelate.

Lothair was a witty *tour d'horizon* of the state of contemporary

Europe and England's place within it. Disraeli was returning to a theme he had last expounded in *Lord George Bentinck* almost two decades earlier, namely the battle for European civilisation between the revolutionary secret societies ('which now cover Europe like networks') and the doctrines of religion ('the Semitic revelation'). The episode that had provided the starting point for this novel was the scandalous conversion to Roman Catholicism in 1868 of the fabulously rich 3rd Marquess of Bute. The hero of the novel, Lothair, bore a baleful resemblance to the youthful marquess as the forces of Catholicism and continental Nationalism battle between themselves and with Anglicanism for ownership of his soul, prestige and wealth. That struggle as Lothair experienced it was symbolised by the contest between Italian nationalists and Roman Catholicism for possession of Rome. The suggestible protagonist fell in love, first, with the feisty nationalist Theodora, then under the spell of the otherworldly Catholic Clare Arundel, before finally marrying the exquisite Lady Corisande. Thus continental marvels were rejected in favour of English aristocratic virtues of winsome beauty, common sense, Protestantism and gardening.

Along the way, Disraeli provided some of his wittiest moments in fiction (which Oscar Wilde claimed influenced his own epigrammatic style). 'Like sedentary men of extreme opinion, he was a social parasite,' Disraeli quipped of 'the Oxford Professor'. He observed that 'if every man were straightforward in his opinions, there would be no conversation. The fun of talk is to find out what a man really thinks, and then contrast it with the enormous lies he has been telling at dinner, and perhaps all his life.' To the book's many ironies was added one in reality in 1872. The Marquess of Bute was married at Brompton Oratory on 16 April. Archbishop Manning celebrated the nuptial mass and Disraeli acted as one of the witnesses.

When *Lothair* was published in the spring of 1870 it caused a sensation. 'If Mr Disraeli had given notice that on May 2 he would sing at the opera, dance on a tight-rope at the Crystal Palace, or preach a sermon at Mr Spurgeon's Tabernacle, popular surprise would not have been greater,' reported the *Saturday Review* on announcing the new work. Speculation was rampant as to what the book might be about and whom it would attack. 'There is immense and most malevolent curiosity about Disraeli's novel,' wrote Lord Houghton. 'His wisest friends think that it must be a mistake, and his enemies hope that it will be his ruin.'

Certainly there would be no financial ruin. Houghton and the novelist Anthony Trollope wagered on the size of Disraeli's advance, which Houghton put at £10,000. (Trollope rightly concluded that only Dickens was worth so much money.) Yet over the next six years Disraeli would easily make that amount from sales in Britain and America. Fashionable society and everyday readers alike clamoured to get hold of the novel. 'On Monday Mr Mudie's [bookshop] was I am told in a state of siege,' wrote the publisher, Thomas Longman, on the first day of sales. Matters were helped along by publication of an irate letter ('the stingless insults of a coward') from the historian Goldwin Smith, who had identified himself as the sedentary 'Oxford Professor'. Thereafter everyone who was anyone, and many more besides, had to read the book to see which other well-known characters might feature. International affairs too played their part. Just weeks after *Lothair* was published the Vatican proclaimed the dogma of papal infallibility; within months Italian nationalists had taken control of Rome.

The mixture of Disraeli's audacity in writing the book in the first place, its bitchy local gossip and sense of timeliness combined to make *Lothair* a runaway success. Such was the popularity of the novel that the name christened a new ship, a cologne, a song and a street. Baron Rothschild even named a filly after the English heroine, Corisande, which went on to win the Cesarewitch. At the Royal Academy banquet that year, at which Disraeli spoke on behalf of 'authors' while Gladstone spoke for 'politicians', Charles Dickens gave the response to the toast – 'Prosperity to the Interests of Literature'. The great novelist, who had only months to live, provoked a storm of laughter and applause, not least from Disraeli, when he lightly rebuked the former prime minister for his 'tardy return' to fiction after an absence of more than twenty years.

Whether Gladstone was pleased or not at being left out of the new novel, it is easy to imagine his irritation mingled with trepidation as he sat down to read 'a spice of *Lothair*' on 18 May 1870. 'Finished *Lothair*' was his bald comment after completing it a week later. This was in fact a case of life imitating, or at least half-imitating, art. On 14 May *Punch* had published a cartoon – 'Critics' – by John Tenniel (who famously illustrated *Alice's Adventures in Wonderland*). It showed a grumpy looking Gladstone reading *Lothair* while the scornful Disraeli flicked through the other's Homeric tome, *Juventus Mundi*, published the previous August. 'Hm! Flippant!' sniffs Gladstone. 'Ha! Prosy!' complains Disraeli. While it was undeniable that Gladstone read Disraeli's new novel, the Leader of Her Majesty's Opposition almost certainly did not bother with a work that even the prime minister thought 'unreadable'. And it would be more than a decade before Disraeli would settle down to pen a portrait in fiction of William Gladstone.

Lothair was a popular triumph for Disraeli, but its immediate predecessor, *Lord George Bentinck*, was of more relevance to the torpor of his current political life. 'There are few positions less inspiriting than that of the leader of a discomfited party,' he had written in that biography. Whereas in a closely contested parliament 'eager, anxious, excited, perhaps enthusiastic adherents' surround a leader only too ready to offer 'sympathy, appreciation, prompt counsel, profuse assistance'. But, continued Disraeli mordantly, 'he who in the parliamentary field watches over the fortunes of routed troops, must be prepared often to sit alone. Few care to share the labour which is doomed to be fruitless, and none are eager to diminish the responsibility of him whose course, however adroit, must necessarily be ineffectual. Nor can a man of sensibility in such a post easily obviate these discouragements.' The description was of Lord John Russell after the 1841 general election, but rereading in 1870 Disraeli recognised a dismal self-prophesy.

While Disraeli slumped disconsolately, Gladstone pressed on. Having negotiated the disestablishment of the Irish Church he turned to the more difficult question of land reform. Whereas on religious questions there was no one in the House of Commons with his command of detail and argument, on the subject of land reform Gladstone knew almost nothing. He had addressed this problem during the autumn of 1869 by throwing himself into 'three months of hectic consultation', which included a vast programme of reading and regular conclaves to discuss ideas or proposals for legislation. By the turn of the year few understood the question better, although comprehension did not make a solution easy to find. Conflicting interest groups, not least within his own party, pressed him towards their own resolutions. Radicals wanted the creation of a class of peasant farmers; Irish Catholic bishops demanded free sale, fair rents and fixity of tenure (the 'three Fs'); Whig landowners rejected both these claims to demand the protection of property rights.

During the many impassioned discussions that took place before the start of the 1870 session, there was much talk of an irreconcilable conflict between 'Irish ideas' – that disestablishment of the Irish Church should pay for the return of the land to the Irish people – and 'English' virtues of the inviolability of property rights and *laissez-faire*. Debate in cabinet was fierce with opinion ranging from the Radical Bright passing through all shades of moderate opinion in Kimberley, Granville and Cardwell to the implacable hostility of Clarendon, Argyll and Lowe (the latter announcing that he 'would rather give up everything than consent to put his hand in one man's pocket, and rob him for the benefit of another'). These divisions, predicted Disraeli, reflected fissures within the Liberal alliance that in time would destroy the government.

Gladstone's Landlord and Tenant Bill, which he wrote virtually unaided, papered over the cracks. The principles of free contract and *laissez-faire* were compromised, but the radicalism of these measures was skilfully camouflaged by an uncharacteristically hesitant use of language. The tone suggested a rather conservative premier who nevertheless wanted to do something to help deal with the muddle in Ireland. A visibly nervous prime minister introduced the bill in a three and a half hour speech on 15 February. He was frankly relieved that it was 'well received by the House at large'. The *Spectator* marvelled that 'No prime minister has ever attempted any task like it.'

For the next three and a half months Gladstone slogged away to push his land bill through each parliamentary stage. Most of the problems came from his own party, directed by Sir Roundell Palmer – a near contemporary at Oxford and among the most brilliant lawyers of his generation. Palmer had declined Gladstone's offer of the Lord Chancellorship in order to fight him on Ireland, which self-sacrifice added considerably to his political authority. At one point, he forced the government's majority down to just thirty-two, leaving the prime minister exhausted. 'Gladstone looked worn and fagged,' noted Robert Phillimore on 8 April. No wonder, then, that his relationship with Laura intensified again during this period. 'Visited Mrs Thistlethwayte after [House of Commons],' he recorded on the same day as Phillimore's diary entry. 'She is indeed an excepted person.' When she was unavailable he returned to the streets to find rescue cases. Whereas the previous year the tensions of the Irish Church debates had shredded Gladstone's nerves, in 1870 his ambiguous friendships provided sufficient escape to ensure that in parliament he never faltered as the bill became law. To this legislative success for Gladstone, Disraeli offered no opposition. The bill passed at each stage without the opposition even bothering to call for a vote.

'In doors and out of doors a disheartened opposition will be querulous and capricious,' Disraeli had written in *Bentinck*. As each parliamentary session succeeded the next, that sentiment increasingly came to grip the Conservatives benches. Apart from anything else, Disraeli looked ill and jaded, and sounded worse. Years of neglecting his teeth had left him in severe discomfort. New, badly fitting dentures made speech difficult. 'In the best part of [Disraeli's] speech and in the middle of a sentence his teeth fell out,' reported the Radical MP Lawrence on one occasion. 'He caught them with extraordinary rapidity in his right hand, turned round apparently to ask a question of his neighbour, put them in, and resumed his speech at the exact word where he had left off.' Such incidents were neither dignified nor inspiring for that sullen rank and file sitting behind him.

Disraeli might still rally himself and them for a big parliamentary occasion, particularly if Gladstone was in his sights. 'The premier was like a cat on hot bricks and presented a striking contrast to Disraeli,' noted one observer during a foreign policy debate in 1871. 'For Disraeli cuts up a minister with as much sang-froid as an anatomist cuts up a frog. Gladstone could hardly keep his seat. He fidgeted, took a quire of notes, sent for blue books and water, turned down corners, and "hear-heared" ironically or interrupted his assailant to make a denial of one of his statements, or to ask the page of a quotation so frequently that Disraeli had to protest once or twice by raising his eyebrows or shrugging his shoulders. And when Gladstone rose, you could see that every stroke of Disraeli's had gone home. He was in a white passion, and almost choked with words, frequently pausing to select the harshest to be found.'

Yet these successes were few and far between. As Conservative MPs prepared for the 1872 session, most were restlessly asking if their leader was up to the job. It did not help that Disraeli seemed apparently so detached that he was even cooperating with Gladstone about a matter on which most of his backbenchers would have preferred to attack the government. During the American Civil War, the South's *Alabama* had terrorised Unionist ships in the Atlantic. The ship had been built in Liverpool and, according to international law, should have been impounded. After the war, the United States demanded compensation. Gladstone agreed to settle the matter; Disraeli thought he was wrong, but believed it would be unpatriotic to say so. It was no comfort at all to the Tory leader that, when the matter was settled, Gladstone, with good grace, would tell the Queen of 'the signal prudence of Mr Disraeli during the anxious period of the controversy with the United States and the value of the example he had set'.

By early 1872, Tory MPs were mutinous. A youthful Cambridge student, Reginald Brett, best summed up their sentiments. Writing to his father, Lord Esher, solicitor general in the previous Conservative government, he shrewdly observed that 'Dizzy's speeches [are] brilliant enough', but that he would never 'frame a great opposition' because he failed to 'convince'. 'He is a critic, and a capital one of a bad government,' observed this precocious future MP, 'but not the counter-theorist who by dint of fact and perseverance can gain his end.' In other words, Disraeli was not Gladstone.

Burghley House, 1 February 1872

It had all the hallmarks of a political coup. A cluster of Conservative grandees had assembled near Stamford at the seat of Lord Exeter. (Throughout English history no intrigue had been complete without the presence of a Cecil.) Seven former cabinet members – Hardy, Northcote, Marlborough, Cairns, Ward Hunt, Pakington and Manners – were there to discuss the future of the party and more particularly its leadership. Hardy left a vivid description of events in his diary. It was Cairns who 'boldly broached the subject of Lord Derby's lead, and the importance of Disraeli knowing the general feeling'. The chief whip, Gerard Noel, piped up that 'from his own knowledge he could say that the name of Lord Derby as leader would affect 40 or 50 seats'. The mood on the backbenches was that 'Disraeli could not combine a new [government]' and that 'would it not be better that he should not try and fail?' Ranged against them were Stafford Northcote and Lord John Manners, who 'professed ignorance' to backbench discontent. And in the middle was Hardy, whose voice no doubt captured best the ambivalence of moderates in the party towards their leader. 'I expressed my view that D. has been loyal to his friends, and that personally I would not say that I preferred Lord D., but that it was idle to ignore general opinion,' he noted painfully. 'For my own part, I cannot but admit that Disraeli, as far as appears, has not the position in House and country to enable him to do what the others might.' When the likes of Hardy were considering the ruthless despatch of Disraeli into retirement, it was obvious that the political tide was turning.

But who, mused Hardy, 'could, or would undertake such a task as informing him?'

16

Volcanoes

St Paul's Cathedral, 27 February 1872

Benjamin Disraeli was too preoccupied to worry overmuch about the cheering crowds below. Instead he concentrated on his frail wife, Mary Anne, as she struggled gamely down the precipitous steps. They had just attended a service of thanksgiving for the return to health of the Prince of Wales, who had been dangerously ill with typhoid (the illness that had killed his father). All society was in attendance, not least because the Queen was using the occasion to mark her return to public life after the long period of mourning for Albert. When the pair reached the bottom of the stone steps, Disraeli offered a wan smile to those waving and clapping enthusiastically, before climbing arthritically into his carriage. They pulled away slowly in a long procession of coaches to make their sedate progress back to Hyde Park. Along the streets the waiting multitude craned forward to catch a glimpse of who was inside each carriage. Disraeli was instantly recognisable: the pale complexion, his dyed jet-black curls contrasting with his vast white coat. Only gradually did it dawn on the couple that the cheering was personal. 'Dizzy, Dizzy!' came shout after excited shout. 'An overpowering ovation: I should say "Triumph",' recorded one supporter. 'The cheers which greeted him from all classes convinced him that, for the day at least, a more popular man did not exist in England.'

Flushed with this affectionate public display, Disraeli dropped Mary Anne at Grosvenor Gate before heading to the Carlton Club. There a former MP, Sir William Fraser, observed him in the Morning Room talking to George Sclater-Booth, chairman of the parliamentary committee on public accounts. 'His face was as of one who looks into another world,' recorded Fraser. 'He seemed more like a statue than a human being: never before nor since have I seen anything approaching it.' Later that day Fraser contrived to bump into Sclater-Booth. What had they been talking about, he inquired. County business came the reply.

'I will tell you what he was thinking about,' Fraser told him: 'he was thinking that he will be prime minister again!'

Not the least pleasurable aspect for Disraeli of this public triumph was the impact it had on those in his own party agitating for a change of leadership. Even before this popular demonstration, he had already moved to quash any attempt to remove him. The plotters at Burghley had not included the Duke of Richmond, but the unfortunate Conservative leader in the House of Lords was the first to feel the hard leather of Disraeli's shoe on his backside. He rebuked Richmond for not keeping him informed about developments in the Lords, which, if continued, could only have 'injurious consequences to the cause which we are anxious to uphold'. This was unfair. 'After two years of apathy he [Disraeli] is beginning to wake up, and fancy all beside are asleep,' sympathised Lord Cairns when Richmond showed him the correspondence. 'I know how sincerely the Duke tried to keep up free intercourse with him in vain sometimes,' agreed Gathorne Hardy, 'so it is clear to me how unjust [Disraeli's] first letter was'. Nevertheless, few would have disagreed that the emergence from political hibernation of the leader of the Conservative party was both overdue and extremely welcome.

Disraeli's strategy of waiting for the Gladstone administration to run out of steam was beginning to look masterly. Observers at the St Paul's thanksgiving service could not help noticing that Disraeli's rapturous reception had been in marked contrast to that given to the prime minister. The Conservative leader had enjoyed cheers and waving. Gladstone met only stony silence, or even the occasional catcall. Whereas immediately afterwards Disraeli had headed to the Carlton Club to bask in this unexpected display of popularity, Gladstone had gone straight back to Carlton House Terrace for lunch alone.

Disraeli's popularity was in part a reaction to the success of *Lothair*, which had been a stunning bestseller, but there was more than a bit of politics involved as well. By early 1872 close observers sensed a marked decline in the fortunes of the government. Disraeli had predicted that fissures within the Liberal party would take time to reveal themselves. Moreover, he believed that Gladstone's prickly personality would be unable to ameliorate those tensions. The Whigs distrusted Gladstone on the principle of 'once a Tory, always a Tory'. The Radicals thought him tentative and too much in thrall to both Church and aristocracy. Only the middle-class Liberals, who had been in the ascendant since 1832 and admired their leader's moral and financial steadfastness, remained unambiguous supporters. Just days after the thanksgiving service, Robert Phillimore reported, 'Gladstone sees that the time is fast coming when he must sever himself from his extreme supporters.' The home secretary, Henry Bruce, accepted that 'he is vexed at the ingratitude of men for whom he has done such great things which would have been simply impossible without him, and would not be unwilling to leave them for a while to their own guidance, and his feeling is shared by many of the ministry'. There could be no doubt, concluded Bruce, that divisions within the party served only to 'encourage the discontented and envious, and animate the opposition'.

On this last point he was certainly right. When Richard Cross, the rising star of the Conservative party, dined with Lord Derby on 11 March, he confessed to being 'well pleased with the political situation: thinks a general election would reduce the majority against us by 50 at least, possibly more: wishes it could take place now'.

It was a sign of Disraeli's new determination to reassert his primacy that he should have agreed to a suggestion by the new party manager, John Eldon Gorst, to address large public meetings in Manchester and London in the spring of 1872. The former MP, a brilliant mathematician with a flair for electoral statistics, had been appointed in 1870 to establish Conservative Central Office and professionalise the party's electoral organisation. Gorst was as imaginative as he was unafraid to tread on toes. In particular, he breathed life into urban Conservative associations, recognising that it was newly enfranchised voters in the cities who had to be converted to the Tory cause if the party were to win back power.

Much of this was tedious work – drawing up lists of candidates and association chairmen, drafting rules for local associations, coordinating leaflets for distribution, records of voter registration, and so on – but it gave the Conservatives a new, ruthless edge (enabling perhaps for the first time talk of a party 'machine'). Tory grandees such as Derby and Cairns were by and large dismissive. But Disraeli took a keen interest in Gorst, who provided him with details about personalities, issues and party prospects in various constituencies. When the Tories won a by-election in Truro in 1871, Disraeli wrote to Gorst that the 'great victory' was 'entirely owing to your energy'.

So when Gorst told Disraeli that a personal visit to Manchester would help the party's cause in the north, he agreed. Reluctantly. Derby called a few days beforehand at Grosvenor Gate, where 'I found him very nervous, more so than I have known him to be on any occasion of late years: he said he did not like his visit to Manchester'. Disraeli's nerves were in part the result of concern about whether his feline oratorical style would stand up to the more robust demands of the monster meeting.

Throughout his parliamentary career, Disraeli's defining characteristics in speech had been scorn, mockery and sarcasm. Lord Curzon, a future foreign secretary, would record that Disraeli, even in his prime, 'was not an orator by nature or art', but was instead the master of 'the jewelled phrase, the exquisite epigram, the stinging sneer. He was like a conjurer on a platform, whose audience with open mouths awaited the next trick.' The success of his parliamentary speeches was inevitably judged on the number of these brilliant verbal tricks he was able to pull off. When the lines worked, they would reduce MPs on both sides of the House to helpless laughter. And they never worked better than when aimed at Gladstone. When recently the prime minister had momentarily lost the thread of his argument, stopping in mid-sentence, Disraeli had leant forward helpfully, saying: 'Your last word? "Revolution".' It was a classic Disraeli moment.

Sarcasm, so well suited to parliament, did not translate to mass meetings. 'Disraeli's peculiar powers do not lie in the direction of popular oratory,' suggested Derby. 'He wants a cultivated audience.' What worked at those large gatherings of ordinary voters was sincerity, an oratorical quality that Gladstone had in abundance. No wonder, then, that Derby, like Disraeli, admitted that he would be glad when 'this business is over'.

The Disraelis arrived in Manchester on Easter Monday to be greeted by a large crowd of well-wishers. Such was the apparent enthusiasm of the throng that for several minutes the slightly bemused couple were unable to disembark from the train. Waiting for them was a carriage, but the horses were quickly unbridled and replaced by a group of burly men who eagerly pulled the Disraelis along while the excited crowd breathlessly followed. The next day, an estimated thirty to forty thousand people turned up at the immense dance hall of Pomona Gardens to watch a parade of banners by hundreds of the region's Conservative Associations. This prepared the way for the main event that night: a public address in the Free Trade Hall. (It was spectacularly ironic that Disraeli, who in 1846 had split the Conservative party on the issue of Protection, was to give one of his most famous speeches in a hall named for Free Trade.)

When Disraeli arrived with Lord Derby – 'the King of Lancashire' – such was the extent of the crowd that for several minutes they were unable to get into the hall. 'The building was full, and the heat was oppressive,' recorded Derby afterwards. Estimates put the number present at around six thousand. Derby's was the most important of the speeches of welcome before the main event at 7.30 p.m. Disraeli spoke for almost three and a half hours, fortified astonishingly, noted H. C. Raikes, a local MP, by two bottles of white brandy. The watching Derby thought the speech 'fell flat' and was delivered 'in a weaker voice, not heard throughout the entire room'. There may have been an element of thwarted ambition in this observation. Derby, beforehand, had wondered whether he should attend given that his name was being spoken of as a probable successor to Disraeli. After Manchester, there would be no more talk of deposing the current leader. To make matters worse for Derby, he missed his train home. Others in the hall believed the night to be a popular triumph, none more so than Lady Beaconsfield. Afterwards she rushed into the arms of her husband, excitedly crying 'Oh, Dizzy, Dizzy! It is the greatest night of all. This pays for all!'

In fact, both Derby and Mary Anne were right. The address was overlong and dull in places. The first hour, in which Disraeli set out the case that 'the programme of the Conservative party is to maintain the constitution of the country', was more dry lecture than barnstorming for the party faithful. There were also intriguing hints about a new kind of social Conservatism aimed at poorer voters that would attract a great deal of attention in later years. 'The first consideration of a minister should be the health of the people,' declared Disraeli in an appealing combination of patriotism and social progressivism. 'A land may be covered with historic trophies, with museums of science and galleries of art, with universities and with libraries: the people may be civilised and ingenious; the country may be even famous in the annals and action of the world, but, gentleman, if the population every ten years decreases, and the stature of the race every ten years diminishes, the history of that country will soon be the history of the past.' To address this, he promised to legislate on 'pure air, pure water, the inspection of unhealthy habitations, [and] the adulteration of food'.

This was a key moment in the development of a new kind of Conservatism, but it was barely recognised as such in Manchester that night. What set the crowd alight was a brilliantly conceived attack on Gladstone and the government that would soon resonate throughout the country. The prime minister he attacked as a treacherous radical wolf in a moderate's clothing. A leader, Disraeli said, should 'speak with frankness and clearness to his countrymen'. Gladstone seemed unable to be clear about anything. 'Although the prime minister of England is always writing letters and making speeches,' Disraeli explained, 'he seems to me ever to send forth an "uncertain sound".' If Radicals called for the abolition of the monarchy, the House of Lords or the Church of England, Gladstone would slyly reveal his support with crafty nods and winks, saying it 'was no easy task, and that he must think once or twice, or even thrice before he could undertake it'.

As for Gladstone's administration, it was dismissed in a celebrated passage. The government had run out of energy and ideas. 'As I sat opposite the Treasury Bench the ministers reminded me of one those marine landscapes not very unusual on the coasts of South America,' he scornfully declared. 'You behold a range of exhausted volcanoes. Not a flame flickers on a single pallid crest. But the situation is still dangerous. There are occasional earthquakes and ever and anon the dark rumbling of the sea.' And dominating the range was Gladstone, who 'alternated between a menace and a sigh'.

Disraeli followed up his Manchester speech with another shorter and even better one in London in June. In searing heat at the Crystal Palace he addressed thousands of Conservatives drawn from the National Union, which included a good showing of working-class representatives. The speech was a blistering attack on the Liberal party, which 'is viewed by the country with disgust'. The government had ridiculed his Manchester speech as a 'policy of sewage', but, countered Disraeli in London, the 'elevation of the condition of the people' was a matter of life and death. 'It involves the state of the dwellings of the people, the moral consequences of which are not less considerable than the physical. It involves their enjoyment of some of the chief elements of nature – air, light and water. It involves the regulation of their industry, the inspection of their toil . . . the purity of their provisions, and it touches upon all the means by which you may wean them from habits of excess and brutality.'

The Conservative party would improve the condition of England;

it would also 'uphold the Empire'. Disraeli launched a direct attack on Liberal patriotism, asserting that 'if you look to the history of this country since the advent of Liberalism – forty years ago – you will find that there has been no effort so continuous, so subtle, supported by so much energy, and carried on with so much ability and acumen, as the attempts of Liberalism to effect the disintegration of the Empire of England'.

In his final peroration, Disraeli hit his stride in mass public oratory. He recommitted the party to preserving the monarchy, defending the empire and elevating the condition of the people. He warned that the time was coming when England would have to choose between 'national' (Conservative) or 'cosmopolitan' (Liberal) values. He demanded 'energy' and 'instinct' from his supporters. Then he issued a direct challenge to those in the hall. 'You must act as if everything depended on your individual efforts,' he entreated them. 'Act in this spirit, and you will succeed. You will maintain your country in its present position. But you will do more than that – you will deliver to your posterity a land of liberty, of prosperity, of power, and of glory.'

When the crowd rose as one, cheering and pushing excitedly towards the platform, it was a symbolic moment of transformation. The Conservatives had moved into the age of mass politics. And Disraeli had cemented his place as their leader.

'It is all well and good,' he said afterwards. 'I feel my position assured.'

'Dizzy was perfect,' Gladstone wrote to Lord Granville uncharacteristically. 'I understand he was much pleased with my having called to inquire after Lady Beaconsfield a few days ago. Perhaps this helped a little.' On the eve of the Whitsun recess, Gladstone and Disraeli both made statements about the *Alabama* negotiations with the United States. A consensual approach had effectively scotched opposition on this highly delicate process, and Gladstone, who was less assured on foreign affairs than economic ones, was grateful. And he was right that calling on Lady Beaconsfield had helped. For by the middle of 1872, it was clear to everyone, including the couple themselves, that Disraeli's wife was dying.

Mary Anne had been labouring with the effects of cancer for several years. To begin with neither husband nor wife referred to it, because each thought that the other did not know. Eventually the pain became too great to continue the charade. She had insisted on travelling to

Manchester in April, yet such was the strain of the occasion that she collapsed immediately afterwards. From then on it was common knowledge that she was fast fading. She tried to rally in the early summer to visit Buckingham Palace, but officials had to sneak her out of a side door when the heat and strain of standing became too much. She never appeared in public again. 'To see her every day weaker and weaker is heartrending,' Disraeli wrote to Corry. 'To witness the gradual death of one who has shared so long and so completely my life entirely unmans me.' For more than three decades they had barely spent a night apart.

They stayed at Grosvenor Gate while parliament sat throughout the oppressive summer months, which were relieved only by occasional carriage rides together out to the suburbs of Essex and Surrey. Disraeli could hardly wait for the end of the parliamentary year to get Mary Anne to Hughenden, away from prying eyes and the hubbub of the city. Then calamity loomed. The government's Ballot Bill, providing for voting in secrecy, was stuck in the House of Lords. Gladstone threatened a rare autumn parliamentary session if the Lords would not cave in, with an election to follow in November. Disraeli was frantic. The thought of staying in London was always unpalatable. In 1872 it was impossible. Leaving principle to one side he leant on Conservatives in the Lords to give way, thus averting the personal catastrophe of political drama coinciding with the last weeks of Mary Anne's life.

And so instead, in the autumn, Disraeli took his wife home to Hughenden to die. In the middle of November, he organised a last weekend party for her with guests including Lord John Manners, Lord Rosebery, Sir William Harcourt and Lord Ronald Gower. Mary Anne, noted Gower afterwards, was 'sadly altered in looks since London – death written in her face – but as usual gorgeously dressed'. Throughout the weekend, Disraeli was uxoriously attentive, and 'Mary Anne was constantly appealed to'. As the party left, she stood smiling with good cheer as she and Disraeli waved everyone off. All knew the truth, wrote Gower mournfully, that they 'would never again see poor old Lady Beaconsfield'.

It was her last social appearance. At the beginning of December, the eighty-year-old Mary Anne caught pneumonia. '*I am totally unable to meet the catastrophe,*' Disraeli wrote to his solicitor. The local rector called to inquire after her health (and soul). 'He told me to turn my thoughts to Jesus Christ, but I couldn't,' she said afterwards to Corry. 'You know *Dizzy* is my J.C.'

She died on Sunday 15 December with Disraeli at her side. Of the many tributes and condolences received, one came from Gladstone. He had truly liked Mary Anne, finding her sincere and unaffected in a way that her husband was not. He had been distressed early in 1872 to find her suddenly 'old'. During the last illness he had called often at Grosvenor Gate to inquire after her health. He was genuinely sad at her passing. So in writing to Disraeli (a letter he also copied out for himself) Gladstone mustered as much fellow feeling as he possibly could towards his rival.

'You and I were, as I believe, married in the same year,' he wrote. 'It has been permitted to both of us to enjoy a priceless boon through a third of a century. Spared myself the blow which has fallen on you, I can form some conception of what it must have been and must be. I do not presume to offer you the consolation, which you will seek from another and higher quarter. I offer only the assurance which all who know you, & all who knew Lady Beaconsfield, & especially those among them who like myself enjoyed for a length of time her marked though unmerited regard, may perhaps tender without impropriety; the assurance that in this trying hour they feel deeply for you and with you.'

Disraeli's reply was earnest, but displayed a slight bridling at Gladstone's awkward expression of his own good fortune in still having a wife. 'I am much touched by your kind words in my great sorrow,' he told the premier. 'I trust, I earnestly trust, that you may be spared a similar affliction. Marriage is the greatest earthly happiness, when founded on complete sympathy. That hallowed lot was mine, and for a moiety of my existence; and I know it is yours.'

Disraeli kept most of the letters of condolence on the death of his wife, but Gladstone's he threw away. Mary Anne's death marked the beginning of a transition in the rivalry from contempt and hostility to detestation and open, vitriolic hatred.

17

An Artful Dodge

The soberly dressed, stooped figure emerged watchfully from the front entrance of the hotel on George Street, just off Hanover Square. He rejected the offer to summon a carriage, following the advice of his doctor that he should walk as often as possible when the weather permitted. Heading towards Piccadilly he doubtless tried to keep his mind on matters political rather than personal. For Benjamin Disraeli, life was wretched. He remained in deep mourning for Mary Anne. Her death not only robbed him of her company, but also her house and annuity. Disraeli had been forced out of the elegant residence at Grosvenor Gate (which reverted to the family of Mary Anne's first husband), and he was poorer to the tune of £5000 a year. Only the combination of royalties from *Lothair* and the generosity of Andrew Montagu, who covered the income loss by reducing the interest on Disraeli's debt from 3 to 2 per cent, saved him from plunging back into the kind of liability that had blighted much of his early life.

Although a financial crisis was averted, there remained the pitiful nature of hotel life. 'My friends admire my rooms,' he told Corry. 'I cannot say I agree with them.' He was, he acknowledged dolefully, in 'a miserable state . . . for I have no home and when I tell my coachman to drive home I feel it is a mockery'. Matters were made worse by the fact that the affable Corry was away from London attending to his own dying father. All told, life for Disraeli was 'a cave of despair'.

Mary Anne, of course, had already predicted it. During an earlier illness, she had written him a 'last letter' commending him as 'a perfect husband', but with the instruction: 'Do not live alone.' At her funeral, observers wondered if Disraeli would ever return to London never mind to politics. He had trudged through the mud behind the coffin in lashing rain to the church. When her remains had been laid in the vault he stood bare-headed and alone for more than ten minutes just staring into her grave. Then he walked back up to the house in the downpour.

Disraeli had quickly realised that escape from 'the supreme sorrow of my life' would come in the hurly-burly of politics. Just weeks after Mary Anne's death, he instructed his closest supporters to scotch all rumours that his new status as a widower would coincide with a withdrawal from public life. Corry busily assured party grandees of 'Disraeli's continued interest in politics' and of 'his intention to be in his place in the beginning of the session'. In early January, Hardy and Cairns were summoned to Hughenden to discuss tactics for the coming year. 'We found him cheerful and pleasant, and though he looks worn, yet I do not know that he appears as haggard as he looked at times during the [previous] session,' Hardy judged. 'It is best that he should plunge into the thick of the strife at once.' Disraeli's first foray came in the Queen's Speech debate on 6 February 1873. 'Found him much relieved and cheerful,' reported Lord Derby immediately afterwards. 'He acknowledged to me that his nervousness had been so great that he did not think he could get through with it, but the plunge having been made, the rest was easy.'

In part, the claustrophobic nature of political life in London brought equilibrium – or at least busyness – to Disraeli's life at a difficult personal time. Nothing could be worse for a husband in mourning than the tyranny of spare time. It helped that most of the leading parliamentary figures on both sides lived in such close proximity, and were forever in and out of each other's houses. The topography of political London made them almost impossible to avoid. Most had addresses in St James's or Mayfair (making the loss of Grosvenor Gate a political as well as a personal misfortune for Disraeli). Mayfair in the 1870s counted among its residents, as well as Disraeli, Gathorne Hardy in Grosvenor Crescent, the up-and-coming Randolph Churchill in Berkeley Square and the Tory's 'new' man, W. H. Smith, in Grosvenor Place. On the other side of Piccadilly, in St James's, Salisbury lived in Arlington Street with Lord Zetland next door. Northcote was a couple of streets away in St James's Place. Beyond St James's Palace lay Carlton House Terrace from where Gladstone and Granville ran the Liberal government.

Much business was conducted in these private residences away from prying eyes at Westminster. It also avoided the risk of setting anything awkward down on paper. 'A single conversation is worth a dozen letters,' Disraeli explained to the Duke of Marlborough. This was invaluable for any party leader. Meetings with individuals, an inner circle, and even the shadow cabinet had often taken place at his house. This provided all the advantages of home territory. Lord Ashbourne, for example, would later recall being flummoxed at his first shadow cabinet meeting by Disraeli's 'drawing rooms, which appeared to be slightly perfumed'.

Living in a hotel had temporarily removed this benefit for Disraeli. He was now visitor not host. When politics left a few unattended hours, friends stepped in. Disraeli avoided set-piece dinner parties at which he was expected to 'perform'. Instead he preferred to be the only guest at other people's quiet family dinners. Or, as on this morning of 8 February, an unhurried breakfast with Lionel de Rothschild, the original 'Sidonia' in *Coningsby*. When he arrived at the vast Piccadilly mansion, his old friend met him looking shame-faced. There were other callers, who had somehow got wind that the Tory leader was coming. Disraeli's countenance drained of what little colour it had. He had expected a relaxed morning in 'a family circle'. Now he was on duty. His interest only perked up when he heard that those visitors were Charles Villiers, Bernal Osborne, Lord Cork and Lord Houghton: all Liberals. They had come, it was explained to Disraeli, to get his view on 'the bill'. This had been leaked to the editor of *The Times*, John Delane, who in turn had shown it to Rothschild (which rather undermined his tall tale that everyone else had come uninvited). Disraeli told them that 'he did not exactly think a crisis probable, but it might happen'. But the presence of these prominent Liberals clarified one point: his prediction back in 1868 that the government would eventually sink under the weight of its own internal contradictions was coming to pass.

Over breakfast there was much amusement about the most recent *Punch* cartoon. It showed Gladstone as a jockey hanging on for dear life to a horse named 'Liberal Majority' as together they careered towards a precarious jump labelled 'Irish University Bill'. Two other battered fences – 'Irish Church Bill' and 'Irish Land Bill' – had already been jumped. The caption above the cartoon asked the question on everyone's lips at that Piccadilly breakfast and beyond. 'Would he clear it?'

★

The Irish University Bill proposed the creation of a federal university to unite the Anglican foundation of Trinity College Dublin with John Henry Newman's Catholic University (later University College Dublin) and the various 'Godless' colleges established by Sir Robert Peel in 1845. The advantage to such a system, Gladstone thought, was that it preserved the denominational aspect of each college while providing Catholics (who were banned from attending Trinity by their own bishops) with a first-class education. The bill pleased few. On his own benches, MPs such as Henry Fawcett, professor of political economy at Cambridge, wanted a genuinely mixed education system without religious entrance tests to facilitate the liberalisation of Irish culture. Whigs, including the former prime minister Earl Russell, were concerned with safeguarding the future of Trinity College. Lord Hartington, chief secretary of Ireland, almost resigned from the government on the matter; the disapproving Duke of Argyll simply stayed away from cabinet meetings when the matter was under discussion. What neither of these groupings could understand was Gladstone's apparent infatuation with Irish Catholicism. Not that he got much thanks for it in Ireland. The Archbishop of Dublin, Cardinal Cullen, denounced the bill as the means by which Trinity would use its vast wealth 'as a bait to poor Catholics to desert their Denominational [Catholic] Tutors'. In an open pastoral letter, Cullen urged Irish MPs to vote against the bill.

As the critical debate approached in March 1873, Gladstone remained confident that once again he would manoeuvre another Irish reform through parliament. 'Overhead it is dark, and underfoot a chaos, but our course is perfectly clear and straight and as far as real criticism is concerned the Bill has stood it well,' he wrote to Earl Spencer, Irish lord lieutenant. 'The most serious danger & difficulty I see ahead is mutilation in the Lords, as I do not see how the Government could resign on it.' To concentrate Liberal minds further, Gladstone decided to make the debate a matter of confidence in the government. Thus to Lord Ripon, the lord president, he predicted that despite 'much coldness' on his own benches and 'discordant noises' on the other side of the House, 'it is not quite easy to see where or how the fatal blow is to be planted'. Others were less sanguine. On the same day that Gladstone wrote to Rippon, the Radical Trelawny recorded that the government 'seems to me to be in a very weak and sickly condition'.

Matters came to a head late at night on 11 March, the final day of the debate in the Commons. Disraeli rose at half past ten to deliver a personal attack on Gladstone that was at turns funny and wounding. 'The prime minister is no ordinary man,' he said at one point, which prompted shouts of approval from ministers. 'I am very glad,' Disraeli shot back, 'that my sincere compliment has obtained for the right honourable gentleman the only cheer which his party have conferred upon him during this discussion.' Earlier in the session Gladstone had ridiculed Disraeli's own attempts in 1868 to deal with the issue of Irish universities. 'The right honourable gentleman says I burnt my fingers on that occasion,' he smoothly reminded the House, before holding up his hands for all to see: 'I see no scars.' (Much hooting and laughter.) Then he moved in with an attack that seemed to capture a wider perception about the prime minister's zealotry. Staring directly at Gladstone, Disraeli landed blow after verbal blow: 'You have despoiled churches,' he alleged. 'You have threatened every corporation and endowment in the country. You have examined into everybody's affairs. You have criticized every profession and vexed every trade. No one is certain of his property, and nobody know what duties he may have to perform tomorrow.' Gladstone admitted to the Queen afterwards that it was an attack heard with 'wrapt attention'.

So often when under pressure in the House, not least from his own side, Gladstone would become hectoring and obtuse. But in the face of Disraeli's vituperative assault he responded with one of the most nuanced of his parliamentary speeches. At times he was even emollient, telling the House of his hope that 'I have not said anything that can offend'. He wanted only that all sides should think of the government that 'We, Sir, have done our best'. If MPs passed the bill, he concluded, 'you will by its means enable Irishmen to raise their country to a height in the sphere of human culture such as will be worthy of the genius of the people, and such as may, perhaps, emulate those oldest, and possibly best, traditions of her history upon which Ireland still so fondly dwells'.

When the prime minister sat down, it was to a thundering ovation from his own benches. 'Gladstone, with the house dead against him and his bill, made a wonderful speech – easy, almost playful, with passages of great power and eloquence, but with a graceful play,' wrote W. E. Forster, his cabinet colleague. Speaker Brand thought it 'a magnificent speech, generous, high-minded, and without a taint of bitterness, although he was sorely tried'.

Yet it was to no avail. When the division came, the government lost by three votes. It was a rejection, wrote Gladstone in his diary, 'which was believed to cause more surprise to the opposite side than it did to me'. On his own benches there was outrage and bemusement. 'This defeat is mainly the effect of bad judgement and mismanagement,' wrote Trelawny. 'The measure was not one on which the existence of a government ought to turn. Gladstone ought to have been surer of his ground before committing the party so far. And now – the Deluge?'

Cabinet Room, 13 March 1873

Forster looked on with barely concealed amazement. Members of the government had been discussing a way forward without reaching any conclusion. Almost thirty-six hours had passed since the defeat in the House of Commons, and still the cabinet seemed no closer to deciding what action to take. The previous day's meeting had broken up without resolution. Now the prime minister had finally given a firm lead, telling colleagues that he wanted to go to the Queen that very afternoon to resign. Around the cabinet table there was only relief that a decision – any decision – had been made at last. What happened next took everyone by surprise. Gladstone concluded the meeting 'playfully' with a good-humoured little speech. This was to be the last of some 150 meetings of the government. He wanted to offer his 'profound grati-tude' for what they had achieved together. 'And here,' wrote Forster afterwards, 'he completely broke down, and could say nothing . . . Tears came to my eyes and we were all touched.' Had they just witnessed the end of a magnificent political career? Certainly Gladstone thought it possible. Earlier in the day he had told Archbishop Manning that 'the future in politics hardly exists for me' (although he had quickly added the caveat 'unless . . . a special call may appear'.) In fact that recall – while hardly a special one – would come rather sooner than he imagined.

Just before three o'clock Gladstone made the short journey to Buckingham Palace to see the Queen. He explained simply that, after taking a day to consider the matter, cabinet had decided the 'safest and best course' was to resign. He suggested that she send for Disraeli. 'As for himself,' Victoria recorded afterwards, 'he wished to retire altogether for a time . . . [said] that he longed for rest, for the work and exer-tion for body and mind were beyond what human nature could bear.' Leaving the Palace at half past three, Gladstone went straight to the

Commons to make a brief announcement that he had offered his resignation to the Queen, who was sending for the leader of the opposition. By six o'clock he was back in Downing Street already looking forward to the first relaxation of his post-premiership: a visit to the studio of the artist John Everett Millais.

Gladstone had been at home barely fifty minutes when a message came that Colonel Henry Ponsonby, now private secretary to the Queen, wanted to see him urgently. 'Any news?' Gladstone asked when the court official was shown in. 'A great deal,' the colonel replied. Disraeli had refused to take office. The Queen was 'sending for you anew.'

For a moment Disraeli had wavered, but after meeting Gathorne Hardy (his most trusted lieutenant) they had agreed on 'the impracticability of office'. Certainly there were electoral advantages in declining. Disraeli had long been convinced that the Liberals would collapse and that the people would grow weary of reforming zeal. By 1873 these predictions were moving inexorably towards fulfilment. The lost confidence vote in the Commons had come not from particular Tory pressure, but through Liberals voting against their own government. In the country, the vox pop of approval given to Disraeli at St Paul's Cathedral in 1872 was backed up by the more solid fact that the Liberal party had lost six by-elections in 1871 and seven in 1872. Yet Disraeli believed that public alienation from the government still had some way to go. Taking office at this critical juncture, or even calling an immediate general election, would let Gladstone off the hook. Disraeli had endured enough minority administrations: he wanted office and power, not just office.

Disraeli had seen the Queen at six o'clock on 13 March, just as Gladstone was returning home. He found Victoria excited at the thought of having him back, and 'disappointed' when he told her 'that it would be useless to attempt to carry on the government with a minority in the House of Commons'. Throughout the audience the Queen did not even try to hide 'a repugnance to her present government', Disraeli told Hardy afterwards. 'So what is then to be done?' Victoria asked him. 'Mr Gladstone ought to remain in,' replied Disraeli firmly.

When Ponsonby related all this to Gladstone the latter immediately suspected Disraeli of a cunning political trick aimed personally at him. It was, he told Lord Granville, yet another instance of 'the artful dodger' at work. Accordingly he demanded of the Queen's private secretary that Disraeli should put his refusal to take office in writing.

Off scurried the peripatetic Ponsonby to see the Conservative leader at Edwards's Hotel. There he found Disraeli obliging but firm, telling the private secretary, 'I decline altogether to accept office.' There was an eighty-seat majority against him in the House. He would be prisoner to the Liberals. 'We did not defeat the government,' Disraeli explained. 'We threw out a stupid, blundering bill, which Gladstone, in his *tête montée* way, tried to make a vote of confidence. It was a foolish mistake of his.' As to the Queen's request that Disraeli put his refusal in writing, he readily agreed, saying, 'I can easily put down what is wanted.' He would surely have done so less cheerfully had he known that he was doing so at Gladstone's imperative.

Ponsonby left the hotel with a higher opinion of Disraeli than when he had gone in. He was by disposition a Whig, who greatly admired Gladstone. That evening he had found Disraeli 'over-civil' to begin with, 'but when he developed the reasons of his policy he rose and stood much more upright than I have ever seen him, spoke in a most frank and straightforward manner, and with a sharpness and decision which was different from his early words'. It had been a revelation, particularly having come straight from 10 Downing Street. 'He was far easier to speak to than Gladstone, who forces you into his groove,' he concluded, 'while Disraeli apparently follows yours.'

Disraeli's continued refusal to take office, now confirmed in writing, pitched Gladstone into a rage. 'I do not quite clearly *understand* it,' he told Ponsonby on 14 March before writing to the Queen questioning whether Disraeli had really refused office. The frustrated sovereign shot back immediately that 'Mr Disraeli's refusal to form a government is absolute.' Such was Gladstone's emotional state on receiving this reply that he rushed at once to see Mrs Thistlethwayte, marking the entry in his diary with the familiar 'X' to signify sin and remorse. Late that night, he sat down to prepare a memorandum of twelve pages for the Queen. (She later told the Duke of Richmond that it was less a letter and more 'a pamphlet'.) Gladstone admitted the next day to Ponsonby that the text might cause 'embarrassment' to the Queen. It marked the beginning of a vitriolic correspondence between Gladstone and Disraeli in which mutual enmity bristled behind the courtesies necessitated by the fact that the letters were all addressed to the Queen.

Gladstone's memorandum began by asking 'whether the proceedings which have taken place between Your Majesty and Mr Disraeli can as yet be regarded as complete'. He offered a 'recital of facts from the history of the last half-century' to demonstrate 'a very wide difference between the manner in which the call of Your Majesty has been met on this occasion by the leader of the opposition, and the manner which has been observed at every former juncture'. It was for this reason, he concluded, that he had to 'point out the difficulty in which he would find himself' should he ask his government colleagues to continue in office.

The exasperated Queen sent Gladstone's letter to Disraeli, who replied immediately in similarly excoriating terms. It was perverse that Gladstone should think that just because an opposition managed to overthrow a bill it must form a government. 'It amounts to this,' he wrote, 'that he tells the House of Commons "Unless you are prepared to put someone in my place, your duty is to do whatever I bid you". To no House of Commons has language of this kind ever been addressed: by no House of Commons would it be tolerated.' As to the personal nature of the premier's comments about his rival 'Mr Disraeli, for convenience, refrains from noticing'.

'After this the Queen *must* ask Mr Gladstone whether he will undertake to resume office,' Victoria wrote to the prime minister when forwarding Disraeli's letter. Except that Gladstone had escaped from London to rural Berkshire for a weekend at Cliveden. By ten o'clock on the morning of 16 March, the Queen's messenger tracked him down (arriving in the middle of a torrential rainstorm). Gladstone read Disraeli's letter, and wearily conceded that 'nothing more is to be expected in that quarter'. Within the hour he sent off a reply telling the Queen that with the greatest reluctance he would continue in office. Then he set about contacting senior colleagues with 'news of my having again taken to the harness'. Few disagreed with his assessment that the political equilibrium had been 'seriously unhinged by the shock' of recent events, or with his doubts about 'whether either the Administration or the Parliament can again be what they were'. After cabinet the following Tuesday, Lord Kimberley mordantly quipped that 'we looked like men who had been buried and dug up again'.

Disraeli was exultant about having successfully faced down Gladstone. The victory cemented his place at the head of his party and reinforced the wider opinion that his star was in the political ascendant. Lord Henry Lennox reported to Hardy (who in turn told Disraeli) a conversation at *The Times* with John Delane, who judged 'Disraeli had displayed the very highest qualities of rare statesmanship – he drew a contrast between our friend and Gladstone by no means to the advantage of the latter, whom he describes as quite incapable of the high qualities now shown by Disraeli, who, he considers, has established a substantial claim to the gratitude of his party and the admiration of his countrymen'.

This was a view confirmed in the House of Commons a few days later. 'Gladstone and D'Israeli made explanations on the late interregnum,' wrote John Trelawny.

'I think D'Israeli had the best of it.'

For the remainder of the 1873 session a blend of exhaustion, bad luck and poor judgement combined to create around Gladstone and his administration a growing sense of ineffectiveness and dislocation from the public mood. He cemented his reputation for arrogance by mishandling a series of legal and ecclesiastical appointments that would more usually have gone through on the nod. 'No manners, no temper, no conduct,' was Trelawny's scathing judgement when parliament prorogued. That July the administration had been embroiled in a scandal about the misallocation of public money to the telegraph service, which implicated numerous government ministers as far up as the chancellor, Robert Lowe. At least this gave Gladstone the excuse to reshuffle his fatigued cabinet, but this in turn led to more hullabaloo. For the vacant chancellorship, Gladstone decided the best candidate was in fact himself.

Whether it was a wise move for a man often on the verge of nervous collapse to take on the burdens of both the premiership and the chancellorship is one question. Perhaps it was weariness that led him to overlook another, more important politically. The convention of the day demanded (as it had for Gladstone in 1846) that every MP taking up public office must first resign his parliamentary seat to seek re-election. In the ordinary course of events those elections were typically uncontested. Gladstone, however, was no ordinary minister. Moreover, his Greenwich constituency was considered extremely unsafe for the Liberals. Because he was already in office, Gladstone had presumed that there would be no need to resign his seat in order to take up *additional* office. Some constitutional lawyers agreed with him, others did not. The argument would carry on into the New Year, and added to the sense of chaos and ineptitude that surrounded the government. 'Truly we go into the country with our tails between our legs,' wrote the colonial secretary, Lord Kimberley, as parliament broke up in August.

Gladstone reacted to the strain of all this in a familiar way: physical breakdown. His doctor had advised complete rest in March, but resuming power had made this an impossibility. The prime minister's friends and family began to worry that his poor health was no mere temporary setback. Robert Phillimore recorded Gladstone that summer looking 'very unwell, and much worn'. He was even walking 'with a stick'. And if the premier had needed any hint of creeping mortality it had been found the day before the crucial vote on the Irish Universities Bill. On 10 March, he had attended the funeral of 'my cousin & schoolfellow . . . who closed last week his sorely afflicted life'. It was like stepping on his own grave. The cousin's name was William Gladstone, and his year of birth, 1809, was the same as his illustrious namesake's.

There was also a feeling in London that Gladstone had become personally unlucky. No more was this true than in the unfortunate circumstances surrounding a more eminent death. After cabinet on 19 July, Gladstone had left for Holmbury to stay with Lord Edward Leveson-Gower. 'We were enjoying that beautiful spot, & expecting Granville with the Bishop of Winchester, when the Groom arrived with the message that the Bishop had had a bad fall,' wrote Gladstone afterwards. 'An hour & a half later Granville entered pale and sad: "It is all over." In an instant the thread of that very precious life was snapped. We were all in deep & silent grief.' The bishop in question was Samuel Wilberforce ('Soapy Sam'), perhaps the most celebrated clergyman in England. He had been riding to the house from Leatherhead railway station with the foreign secretary when he was thrown from his horse. The effect on Gladstone was immense. The next day he 'woke with a sad sense of a great void in the world'. He inspected the spot where the bishop had fallen and attended the inquest into his death. Just days afterwards he collapsed again 'under great heat, hard work, & perhaps depression of fever'. Throughout the rest of the summer there would be 'much discussion with Dr Clark' about the state of his health until he withdrew, exhausted, to Hawarden for the autumn.

No wonder, then, that he celebrated his birthday at the end of that year in gloomy fashion. Political capital was spent. Luck was in short supply. Mind and body were crushed.

'Sixty-four years complete today, what have they brought me?' he wrote glumly in his diary. 'A weaker heart, stiffened muscles, thin hairs.'

With Gladstone in visibly low spirits for much of 1873, Disraeli had finally decided to abandon his policy of allowing the Liberal administration to sink itself. Instead he went on the attack to keep up the pressure on the government even after parliament had broken up for the autumn. On 3 October he sent an open letter to Lord Grey de Wilton, the Conservative candidate at a by-election in Bath, which echoed his earlier searing attack on the government. 'For nearly five years the present ministers have harassed every trade, worried every profession, and assailed or menaced every class, institution, and species of property in the country,' he wrote scathingly. 'All this they call a policy, and seem quite proud of it; but the country has, I think, made up its mind to close this career of plundering and blundering.'

The Bath letter missed its target in the by-election itself as the Conservative candidate narrowly failed to win. Some Tories, such as Lord Derby, thought that the result was due to Disraeli's 'foolish and violent letter . . . which for both manner and matter was in very bad taste'. This missed the point. The letter encapsulated in one brilliant, pithy slogan – 'plundering and blundering' – the essential charge against the government on which Disraeli would eventually campaign throughout the country. And he was determined quickly to reinforce the point. Two years earlier he had been elected as Rector of Glasgow University. Mary Anne's poor health had prevented him from travelling to Scotland for his installation. Now he used that occasion in November to give a series of vigorous public speeches that would both keep up his attack on the government and warn off any in his own party, particularly Derby, who had thoughts of using the Bath letter against him.

'The fact is, the Conservative party can get rid of my services whenever they give me an intimation that they wish it,' Disraeli told Scottish Tories obligingly, although those who needed to hear could hardly have missed the underlying menace. As to the government, the time had come for Scotland to 'leave off . . . munching the remainder biscuit of an effete Liberalism'. It was a message greeted everywhere with 'loud huzzas' and thunderous ovations. 'Glasgow, without exaggeration,' he wrote happily afterwards, 'was the greatest reception ever offered to a public man: far beyond Lancashire even!'

Disraeli returned from Scotland exhausted. 'If there were a society to protect public men, as there is to protect donkeys, some interference would undoubtedly take place,' he told his friend Lord Barrington. Yet the trip had achieved its objectives of keeping pressure on the government while putting Derby's supporters back in their box. The Duke of Richmond told Corry that 'the mouths may now be shut of those who, "whenever Lord Derby goes about" . . . cry out "Here is the man!"'

For the next weeks the widower Disraeli moved restlessly from one country house to another, afraid of staying too long alone at home. His well-known dislike of hunting and shooting – 'the paraphernalia of pheasants' – left time for writing and thinking. On 19 December he held a political conclave at Gathorne Hardy's Hemsted Park estate (he could not face having everyone to Hughenden). There they discussed the assessment of John Eldon Gorst from central office that 'we were as well prepared for an election as we ever should be, and that for that reason the cabinet would put off dissolving as long as they could – some thought even till 1875'.

So it was that after Christmas Disraeli returned unhappily to London for a new session of parliament. He had the government on the run, but in all likelihood there would be at least another year before an election. The best he could hope for was a 'walk over the course'.

It was not a cheering thought as he returned to his gloomy rooms at Edwards's Hotel on 23 January.

'The foxes have holes and the birds of the air have nests,' he wrote glumly, 'but I – alas! alas!'

18

The Jewel Thief

Benjamin Disraeli's Bedroom,
Edwards's Hotel, 24 January 1874

The servant had already knocked once. This time he did so more insistently, but still there came no answer. As he pushed open the door, he could see clearly enough that his master was still soundly asleep. No doubt the exertions of the previous day's travelling had left him exhausted. And it was, after all, only the early hours of the morning. On a chair lay a flamboyant 'dressing gown of bright and many colours'. In a glass of water on the bedside locker was a set of dentures. And in the bed slept the masked leader of the opposition in a cap to protect his thinning curls. Whether when shaken awake he issued one of his famously dry epigrams or a harsh expletive, it soon became clear to him why he had been forced from his slumber. As the servant thrust that morning's *Times* towards him, Disraeli struggled to find his eyeglass. Squinting at the newspaper, he was amazed at what he read. There in print was a letter from the prime minister to the electors of Greenwich. It was an election address, which might have signified Gladstone's decision to resign his seat and fight a by-election on becoming chancellor once again. But this was no by-election address. This was the announcement of a general election.

'The great event found me abed on Saturday morning, and I at once saw the critical occasion,' Disraeli wrote afterwards. 'I saw the necessity of accepting the challenge of Gladstone, which of course he counted on my not being able to do so.'

Disraeli was right. Across London, Gladstone read the same papers that morning with smug contentment – 'well satisfied on the whole'

– before setting out for a typical day of political meetings and the temptations of rescue work ('Saw Birley X'). As he left Carlton House Terrace, he had a good idea of exactly what was going on at Edwards's Hotel.

'The enemy will be furious,' he gleefully told his son Herbert.

Disraeli may well have been 'taken by surprise', but he immediately sprang into action with the renewed vigour that had characterised his behaviour in the preceding nine months. He fired off telegrams to Lord Derby and Gathorne Hardy to join him in London to draft an immediate election reply to Gladstone.

Down at Hemsted, Gathorne Hardy was out shooting when the telegram arrived that 'hurried me off to town'. He had not bothered with the papers that morning, so read them on the train up to London. 'No one outside the Cabinet had even guessed it,' he wrote later, 'and the Liberal as well as the Conservative world was unprepared.' When Derby received his telegram, he was surprised, but delighted. 'To the Conservatives, I see no loss in this sudden summons: they are confident, well organized, and have been long preparing,' he wrote with that faint detachment of one who, on becoming an earl, would never again need to bother with elections. 'On the whole I incline to think Gladstone has made a mistake.' Yet he did not rush immediately to Disraeli, which signified the growing coolness in their relationship. By the time Derby did arrive in London, Disraeli complained, he was 'too late to assist with his counsel with my address'.

Disraeli, assisted by Lord Cairns and Hardy, did the bulk of the work. 'I have never had three days of such hard work in my life as the three last,' he wrote the following Tuesday. 'Writing, talking, seeing hundreds of people, encouraging the timid and enlightening the perplexed.' The most important issue had been to get an immediate response to Gladstone into Monday's papers. Gladstone's own address had covered more than three columns in *The Times*. 'I think his usual style is the worst I know of any public man,' Disraeli pronounced, 'and that it is marvellous how so consummate an orator should, the moment he takes the pen, be so involved, and cumbersome, and infelicitous in expression.' Disraeli's address in contrast was but a quarter of the length of Gladstone's. 'Where one is conscientiously argumentative,' said *The Times*, 'the other is brisk, curt and rapid.' The message was as straightforward as the means of expression. The Conservatives would seek to improve the condition of the people, but not through 'incessant and harassing legislation'. And they would protect the interests of Britain overseas. Disraeli's conclusion on the previous five years was that had 'there been a little more energy in our foreign policy, and a little less in our domestic legislation', the nation would be in much better health.

On Tuesday 26 January 1874 parliament was formally dissolved. The question on everyone's lips that day was why Gladstone had chosen to go to the country apparently in such haste. Most thought they knew the answer. 'Much . . . said about the Greenwich seat, which I believe influenced him,' Hardy wrote. The Clerk of the House of Commons, Sir Erskine May, who was a great admirer of Gladstone, expressed his shock and dismay more strongly. 'It is a coup d'état!' he declared. 'It would not have surprised me on the other side of the Channel, but here I may confess that I am astonished.'

This sense of the government having gone to the country to get the prime minister out of a tight spot put the Liberals into difficulties from the outset. Gladstone had opened the campaign by offering a huge bribe to the electorate: the abolition of income tax. Yet as Disraeli pointed out immediately this was something 'which the Conservative party [has] always favoured and which the Prime Minister and his friends have always opposed'. It was only a matter of days before Gladstone began to realise that he had fatally miscalculated. On 28 January he travelled to his own constituency of Greenwich, where he addressed five thousand of his supporters in driving rain. 'An enthusiastic meeting,' he recorded afterwards, before adding ominously, 'but the general prospects are far from clear.' Gladstone had somehow manoeuvred himself into an irreconcilable bind. The fact that he had little to offer the electorate besides a lame promise to do away with income tax made his administration seem stale and exhausted. Yet it was exactly the sense that he was prone to meddling and liked nothing more than to dream up bright ideas for their own sake that enabled Disraeli to attack him for harrying the people. Lord Kimberley understood this better than most. 'We had exhausted our programme, and quiet men asked what will Gladstone do next?' he complained. 'Will he not seek to recover his popularity by extreme radical measures? And it must be admitted that there was ground for this view.' As if trying to prompt fresh thinking, he immediately settled down on his return from Greenwich to read the speeches Disraeli had made in Glasgow the previous autumn.

The two contenders did not share a platform together or debate issues in public during the election. Instead they jousted from afar, with Disraeli landing the more powerful hits. In doing so he added to the rancorously personal nature of the debate, which lacked the usual veneer of civility. In Aylesbury on 31 January Disraeli delivered a febrile attack on his rival, conveyed with a storyteller's flair and no concern whatever for the conventions of political discourse.

'I read something the other day,' he began. 'A person entered a jeweller's shop and asked to look at a costly trinket that was before him, and when the respectable tradesman . . . handed him the trinket, the customer threw a quarter of an ounce of snuff into his eyes, and when the unfortunate tradesman had recovered his sight and his senses he found his customer had disappeared, and his trinket too.' Then Disraeli moved in for the obvious finale. 'And so it is that Mr Gladstone throws gold dust into the eyes of the people of England, and, before they clearly ascertain what it is like or worth, they find he has disappeared with a costly jewel as the price of his dextrous management.'

It was a witty, but shockingly personal attack. 'Perhaps too personal in reference to Gladstone,' wrote Derby afterwards, before adding 'but for this there was provocation.' Others were less understanding. 'We must reprobate . . . very strongly the personal bitterness and almost vituperation in which the speaker indulges,' rebuked *The Times*. 'It is going far beyond the bounds of gentleman-like controversy to compare Mr Gladstone to a jewel thief . . . This is in the style of a controversy which has long been banished from English political life.' It was forbidden no longer. Disraeli was ecstatic with the speech and the reaction to it. 'A complete success – to my content,' he enthused. 'And you know that as regards my own doing I am very rarely content.'

Gladstone made a feeble attempt to strike back two days later during a rally at New Cross. 'I have been sharply opposed to Mr Disraeli in political life for more than twenty years,' he began promisingly. 'But certain bounds and limits have been imposed on the character of the language which has been used between us. I do not wish to pass those limits; and if an example has been unfortunately set which I am sure he himself will regret, I for the moment undoubtedly will not follow him.' It was not what his supporters had wanted to hear. Even *The Times*, which had deprecated Disraeli's behaviour at Aylesbury, recognised that the prime minister had been pulverised. 'Mr Disraeli sparkles spontaneously with epigram,' it lamented, 'but Mr Gladstone's wit it must be confessed is somewhat elephantine.'

For the first time in modern politics the decision in front of the electorate had become a choice about individuals. 'The contest has been in an unusual degree a personal one,' concluded *The Times*, 'and it must have been perfectly well understood that the issue to be decided was whether the country should be in the hands of Mr Gladstone or Mr Disraeli.'

To many this seemed a simple case of life imitating art. Three years earlier, in 1871, Lewis Carroll had published his second 'Alice' story: *Through the Looking Glass and What Alice Found There*. The seventh chapter – The Lion and the Unicorn – had been widely interpreted as a subtle depiction of Gladstone and Disraeli. Illustrations by the great political cartoonist John Tenniel, which bore a resemblance to both men, only served to reinforce the metaphor. A breathless Alice encounters 'a great crowd, in the middle of which the Lion and the Unicorn were fighting'. Each wants 'the crown'. The unicorn runs the lion through with his horn. The lion chases the unicorn 'all round the town'. Everywhere there is a cacophony of noise that forces poor Alice to her knees, 'with her hands over her ears, vainly trying to shut out the dreadful uproar'.

Legend said theirs was a thousand-year battle in which there was never a winner. Politics, however, required a more decisive result.

'A wakeful night,' wrote Gladstone on election day, 'but I believe more from a little strong coffee drunk incautiously than from the polls: which I cannot help, & have done all in my power to mend.' He had every reason to be fretful. As returns began coming in from around the country, he quickly recognised that 'the general prospect was first indifferent, then bad'. Even in his own Greenwich multiseat constituency he only scraped through in second place, which was 'more like a defeat than a victory'. When all the votes were counted, it was clear that the administration had been routed. For the first time since 1841, the Conservative party had won an outright victory, with a healthy majority of more than fifty.

Few doubted that the election defeat signified a personal rejection of Gladstone. The Queen for one was convinced that the thrashing 'was greatly owing to his own unpopularity' and to the want of confidence people had in him'. Recalling that Palmerston had told her that Gladstone was 'a dangerous man', she launched into a tirade against him in a letter to her daughter Crown Princess Victoria. 'So very arrogant, tyrannical, and obstinate, with no knowledge of the world or human nature,' she wrote biliously, 'all this and much want of regard towards my feelings . . . led to make him a very dangerous and unsatisfactory premier.' The fact that the electorate had replaced him with Disraeli 'shows a healthy state of the country'.

Gladstone's first government had been among the most reform-minded of Victoria's reign, but it had yielded few political advantages for the man himself. Many of his grand schemes, such as the first Irish Land Act, had made an already difficult situation worse. Other legislation, including reform of the army, civil service and universities, had proved less effective than he had hoped. Controversial measures, such as the 1870 Education Act, had engendered lasting hostility, particularly in his own party. There had been successes – notably the introduction of the secret ballot – but, as so often in politics, those who had long been pressing for change faded away when it came to meting out praise (while opponents muttered threateningly about revenge). By its end the administration had simply come to look busy rather than effective. Disraeli's promise of a less meddlesome regime caught the popular mood. Gladstone judged that the defeat was 'the greatest expression of public disapprobation of a government which he ever remembered'. More likely, the country simply decided it was time for everyone to calm down.

The battered Gladstone petulantly resolved not to follow Disraeli's example in 1868 by resigning office immediately. To begin with there was the irritation that his rival had established the precedent. 'It is parliament, not the constituencies, that ought to dismiss the government, and the proper function of the House of Commons cannot be taken from it without diminishing somewhat its dignity and authority,' he huffily told Lord Granville, who was urging him to quit immediately. Besides matters of dignity and authority, Gladstone wanted to delay because he was furious at having to present a £5 million surplus to Disraeli. Surely he had a 'moral and honourable obligation to give effect if we can to the financial pledges rather than hand over the 5m to D,' he pleaded with Granville. 'I would give anything to abstract the 5m from Dizzy's manipulator,' replied Granville. 'But can it be done?' The answer was no, which only added to Gladstone's rage at defeat. His wife Catherine summed this up best in a letter to Herbert. 'Is it not disgusting,' she violently exclaimed, 'after all Papa's labour and patriotism and years of work to think of handing over his nest-egg to that Jew.'

Ultimately it was Victoria who forced Gladstone's hand. When she saw that he was determined to linger, the sovereign wrote in simple terms telling him to resign quickly. She deplored the 'disadvantage of three weeks delay, for the country', and clinched things by complaining that a hiatus would increase her own workload. Parliament would meet just as her recently married son arrived back in London. It would be too exhausting to host the wedding celebrations and oversee a change of government at the same time. 'People are apt to forget as she told Mr Gladstone the other day,' Victoria admonished, 'that the Queen is a *woman* – who has far more on her hands and far more to try mind and body than is good for any one of her sex and age.'

The letter pitched Gladstone into a state of nervous convulsion. 'To bed at 1:45,' he recorded, 'but lay 3 hours awake (rare for me) with an overwrought brain.' In the end there was no choice. The electorate had spoken and his closest advisers, including Granville, were urging him to resign. Now even the sovereign, treading on constitutional thin ice, was insisting that he go. So the following evening he went to Windsor to advise the Queen to send for Disraeli. Days later the last official to see Gladstone at Downing Street, Sir William Boxall of the National Gallery, detected in him a barely suppressed temper that was 'perfectly demoniacal'. Even the Queen found him 'very grave, and little disposed to talk'.

That mood was more than just a sulk. The furious Gladstone impulsively resolved to do 'something toward snapping the ties, and winding out of the coil'. So it was that on resigning as prime minister Gladstone flabbergasted everyone, including an astonished Lord Aberdare, with the 'startling announcement [that . . .] he would no longer retain the leadership of the liberal party'.

No. 2 Whitehall Gardens

In the space of a few short weeks, Disraeli had acquired two new houses. Montagu Corry had managed to secure from the Duchess of Northumberland an elegant residence just minutes from parliament. Frankly, it was a relief to 'live again like a gentleman'. As he settled into these comfortable private quarters, he busied himself with plans for taking possession of his other recently won accommodation at 10 Downing Street.

Disraeli went to see the Queen at Windsor on 18 February, when he was invited to form a government. No one seemed more delighted to see his return as prime minister. 'My dear mistress will be very happy to see you again and I know how careful and gentle you are about all that concerns her,' Lady Ely had written days beforehand from the court. 'I think you understand her so well, besides appreciating her noble fine qualities.' Certainly the Queen did not bother to conceal her excitement when she saw him that day. Afterwards she girlishly recorded how 'he repeatedly said whatever I wished should be done – whatever his difficulties might be!' At the end of the audience, Disraeli had gone down on one knee to kiss the royal hand with a flourish, and the theatrical declaration: 'I plight my troth to the kindest of Mistresses.'

For the next six years Victoria and Disraeli would exploit their closeness for mutual advantage. It was in many ways an attachment of courtly love. To those that the Queen did not like – including Gladstone – she could often seem rude, intimidating and arrogant. Yet those who won her favour – and of her prime ministers only Lord Melbourne, her first, would approach the intimacy Disraeli achieved – saw an altogether more charming side to the monarch. There is no doubt that she found Disraeli physically and personally attractive. Although to many his exotic looks, with the rouged cheeks and dyed black curls, appeared distinctly odd, to Victoria he appeared wonderfully, dangerously bohemian. She commissioned the society photographer Jabez Hughes to take a series of photographs of him. Two artists – Joachim von Angeli and John Millais – would be invited to paint his portrait (something Disraeli hated). When Millais showed his first attempt she made him paint it again, sending photographs to illustrate 'the peculiar expression about the corner of the mouth, suggesting a keen sense of humour, which contrasts with the extreme seriousness of the upper part of the face [which] prevents the whole expression being sad'. When Millais changed the portrait, she was delighted, praising him for catching 'the peculiar, intellectual and gentle expression of his face'.

Victoria looked forward to audiences with Disraeli, and took pains to ensure his comfort. By tradition, prime ministers would stand throughout, if for no other reason than it stopped them getting too comfortable and staying overlong. With Disraeli his comfort was paramount. Their meetings took place not in the grand public rooms, but most often in the privileged surroundings of Prince Albert's private study at Windsor. The Queen would bustle in, talk animatedly and laugh often and freely. The room had only one chair, but as soon as Victoria entered, a valet would bring in another small gold chair for the prime minister. Although the Queen was fanatical about fresh air, insisting on open windows all year round and daily walks, she relaxed her strictures for Disraeli. She would rebuke him if he insisted on attending when he had one of many chills. 'For fear of catching cold,' she wrote in one hurried note, 'the Queen will excuse your wearing pantaloons this evening.' Perhaps she was aware that her insistence on enjoying the outdoors taxed even Disraeli's loyalty. 'I was very ill and could scarcely get through it,' he complained to friends after enduring a chilly breakfast taken in a large tent pitched on the lawn at Osborne House.

Their meeting invariably went over the allotted time. Instead of boring the Queen with affairs of state, Disraeli engaged in 'the most animated, interesting and confidential gossip'. He would tease and flatter her, offering generous compliments and bitchy stories about those she disliked – in his own words, laying it on 'with a trowel'. So where Gladstone had tried to bully the Queen, Disraeli simply coaxed her. 'He had a way when we differed,' the Queen later told Lord Rosebery, 'of saying "Dear Madam" so persuasively, and putting his head on one side.' On occasion he could even treat audiences in the manner of a scampish nephew visiting an indulgent (albeit in this case younger) widowed aunt. At one meeting, when Disraeli was sched-uled to leave Windsor on a special train at 5.05 p.m., he leapt to his feet when the clock struck five and explained to the Queen that he had to leave. 'Run away! Run away!' she exclaimed. 'Instead of being dismissed,' he laughed with her the next time, 'I dismissed my Sovereign.' Only Disraeli could have got away with saying it.

Underlying all of this was Disraeli's tongue-in-cheek reverence for court life that both parties recognised and enjoyed. While others at court worried that a charlatan was taking in the Queen, her private secretary, Ponsonby, was shrewder. 'Disraeli,' he wrote, 'really has an admiration for splendour, for Duchesses with ropes of pearls, for rich-ness and gorgeousness, mixed I also think with a cynical sneer and a burlesque thought about them.'

As the relationship between Queen and premier developed, the irony became more elaborate and open. She became, like Edmund Spenser's Elizabeth I, the Faerie Queen. When she sent him flowers, they came, he wrote in thanks, as 'an offering from the fauns and dryads of the woods of Osborne: and camellias, blooming in the natural air, become your Majesty's Faery Isle'. Or was he in a dream state, receiving flowers from 'another monarch: Queen Titania, gathering flowers, with her Court, in a soft and sea-girt isle, and sending magic blossoms, which, they say, turn the heads of those who receive them'. No wonder Victoria was entranced.

The contrast with Gladstone could hardly have been more pronounced. Six years of the Liberal premier's seriousness had wearied and demoralised the Queen. His memoranda had been so convoluted that the Queen had insisted that secretaries prepare precis of them for her. At audiences, she complained, 'he speaks to me as if I were a public meeting'. Now with Disraeli she felt liberated.

'When I left the dining room after sitting next to Mr Gladstone I thought he was the cleverest man in England,' the Queen later told her granddaughter, Princess Marie-Louise, 'but after sitting next to Mr Disraeli I thought I was the cleverest woman in England.'

It was the basis of an intense and powerful friendship.

The Queen was not the only lady in London captivated by the widower Benjamin Disraeli. If power was an aphrodisiac then an un-attached prime minister could reasonably expect to be considered fair game. Interested parties included perhaps the richest woman in England, banking heiress Angela Burdett-Coutts. But the most predatory had been the dowager Countess of Cardigan (whose late husband had led – and then abandoned – the infamous charge of the Light Brigade during the Crimean War). She had been Cardigan's mistress before becoming his second wife, and was well practised in the art of seduction. She already had riches; now she wanted power. Throughout 1873 she had hunted Disraeli with determination, first by offering to act as his unpaid private secretary and, when required, a political hostess. It did not take long for her real intentions to become clear. She told him of the twelve proposals of marriage she had received since the death of her husband, all of which had been declined because she had been in love with him from afar. Shortly afterwards, she wrote proposing marriage. Disraeli's retort was dismissive. 'At present it would be better that we should not meet,' he replied curtly to this amorous sugges-tion. Afterwards she would claim that Disraeli had done the asking, although fortunately for his reputation he had kept her proposal letter. Perhaps less easy to bear was her damning verdict, widely reported, that he had bad breath.

Disraeli loved the company of women. He was never a 'clubby' person who, after the death of his wife, could have existed in the exclusively male world of the Carlton and the House of Commons. His great fortune by 1874 was to have fallen helplessly, but safely, in love with Selina, Countess of Bradford. The relationship could hardly have been more ideal. She was more than a decade younger than Disraeli, securely married, but with a husband more interested in horses than his wife. This left her free to concentrate her efforts on the almost seventy-year-old prime minister without the inconvenience of actually marrying him. It is unlikely that the friendship was ever consummated. Disraeli was used to this: Mary Anne had been much older than him, was often ill, and for much of their marriage the relationship had been platonic. Lady Bradford provided a perfect replacement, offering Disraeli an outlet for his enthusiasms, triumphs and disappointments. She also provided something very practical, fussing and petting him with small acts of thoughtfulness such as sending mittens to stave off the cold in the notoriously chilly Hughenden.

Between 1873 and 1881, Disraeli wrote an astonishing eleven hundred letters to Selina, and a further five hundred to her sister, Lady Chesterfield. 'Lady Bradford seems to know everything,' the Duke of Richmond grumbled to Lord Cairns. Rather as in the correspondence with Sarah Brydges Willyams, Disraeli opened up in these letters in a personal way that was closer in its confessional tone to a diary (although, typically, he needed an audience in order to bother composing them at all). The letters were all written on paper heavily edged in black in memory of Mary Anne. 'It is strange, but I always used to think the Queen persisting in these emblems of woe, indulged in a morbid sentiment,' Disraeli explained when Selina protested. 'When I have been on the point sometimes of terminating this emblem of my bereavement, the thought that there was no longer any being in the world to whom I was an object of concentrated feeling overcame me and the sign remained.' He continued to use the paper for the rest of his life (and also to wear a black mourning band on his hat).

Mary Anne was remembered, but there was little doubting that his affection and need for Selina was something exhilaratingly new. Often his letters were like those of a lovesick youth, dashed off in the middle of debates in the Commons or during a break in cabinet meetings. 'When you have the government of a country on your shoulders, to *love* a person, and to be *in love* with a person makes all the difference,' he explained in the autumn of 1874. 'In the first case, everything that distracts your mind from your great purpose, weakens and wearies you. In the second instance, the difficulty of seeing your beloved, or communicating with her, only animates and excites you. I have devised schemes of seeing, or writing to, you in the midst of stately councils, and the thought and memory of you, instead of being an obstacle, has been to me an inspiration.'

Throughout the next six years of Disraeli's premiership, Selina, alongside Monty Corry, would form that support team essential to keeping the prime minister going during success and failure.

'I live for Power and the Affections,' he told her shortly after becoming prime minister. He already had one; she provided him with the other.

19

The Other Guest

ooks, books, books. In the month Benjamin Disraeli returned to
power, Anthony Trollope began the monthly serialisation of a
new novel, *The Way We Live Now*. It was an embittered indictment of contemporary England, which this crusty old Whig saw as immoral
and degenerate. And along the way there were some sideswipes at the
new prime minister. The story centred on the rise and fall of a Jewish
anti-hero, Melmotte – 'a horrid, big rich scoundrel'. Supporters of the
fabulously wealthy financier hoped that he 'might become as it were a
Conservative tribune of the people – that he might be the realization of
that hitherto hazy mixture of Radicalism and old fogeyism, of which we
have lately heard from a political master'. Trollope reminded slower readers
that 'Melmotte was not the first vulgar man whom the Conservatives
had taken by the hand, and patted on the back, and told that he was a
god.' When the corrupt and depraved new MP was introduced to the
House of Commons, there was concern even among Tories about being
associated with such a wanton character. The fictional Disraeli, however,
embraced him. '"You had better let me accompany you," said the
Conservative leader, with something like chivalry in his heart. And so
Mr Melmotte was introduced to the House by the head of his party!'
The message could hardly have been clearer: Melmotte was a creature
of a new world fashioned by Disraeli. And it was a formation that was
insincere, dissolute and perverted.

Few, however, recognised this as 'the way we live now'. The novel
flopped. Reviewers savaged it and the public did not buy it. Disraeli
did not even trouble himself to read the book. Instead, on regaining

possession of 10 Downing Street, he turned not to Trollope, whose intense dislike he reciprocated, but to himself, or least a younger version of himself in *Coningsby*. Had he bothered to read Trollope he might have recognised the 'hazy mixture of Radicalism and old fogeyism'. Since 1846 the Tories had struggled without any kind of majority in the House of Commons. At last they had an unambiguous, popular mandate. What Disraeli wanted now was clarity. After hedging for so long in minority administrations, the time had come for a genuine Conservativism. 'What we want, sir,' says Harry Coningsby, 'is not to fashion new dukes and furbish up old baronies but to establish great principles which may maintain the realm and secure the happiness of the people.' To achieve this end, Disraeli had written three decades earlier, 'what the country requires is a sound Conservative Government'.

The prime minister was not the only one reading his youthful works in those politically charged months. In the week that Gladstone left Downing Street, he began reading his rival's 1820s novel, *Vivian Grey*. He had never bothered with it before, and that he chose to do so now, while contemplating retirement, suggested incomprehension at losing out to a man he detested. Perhaps by reading the young Disraeli, he hoped to find the key to understanding the older one. Like every other attempt to figure out his rival, reading *Vivian Grey* led only to frustration and disdain.

'Finished *Vivian Grey*,' he recorded in his diary that spring. 'The first quarter extremely clever, the rest trash.'

It might well have been his judgement on the man. Yet his days of duelling with Disraeli were apparently over. For that at least William Gladstone could be grateful.

Grillion's Club, 7 March 1874

Gladstone sat alone for breakfast that Saturday morning. While he deliberated on the classic morning dilemma for a Victorian gentleman – porridge or prunes – he sketched out on paper his reasons for withdrawal from political life. It was a succinct summary of his disillusionment with the political process and a frank consideration of his own failure:

    1. To engage now, is to engage for the term of opposition, & the succeeding term of Liberal Government. These two cannot

probably embrace less than a considerable term of years. (1830–41. 1841–52. 1866–74.). This is not consistent with my views for the close of my life.

2. Failure of 1866–8.

3. My views on the question of education in particular are I fear irreconcilable with those of a considerable portion of it. Into any interim contract I cannot enter.

4. In no case has the head of a govt. considerable in character & duration, on receiving what may be called an emphatic dismissal, become leader of opposition.

5. The condition of the Liberal party requires consideration.

   a. It has no present public cause upon which it is agreed.

   b. It has serious & conscientious divisions of opinion, which are also pressing, e.g. on Education.

   c. The habit of making a career by & upon constant active opposition to the bulk of the party, & its leaders, has acquired a dangerous predominance among a portion of its members. This habit is not checked by the action of the great majority, who do not indulge or approve it: & it has become dangerous to the credit & efficiency of the party.

Weeks earlier, most of those at a last cabinet meeting had believed Gladstone to be bluffing on relinquishing the party leadership. But nothing indicated his intent more than the decision to put his Carlton House Terrace home on the market without making any plans to buy another. It was inconceivable that a man who intended to take a leading role in political life could do so without a London residence (as Disraeli could testify having spent an unhappy year living in a hotel). No one understood this better than Catherine, who had been 'startled' when her husband suggested it (and more than a little anxious about having all that pent-up energy to contend with at Hawarden on an uninterrupted basis). 'Conversation with C. on the situation,' Gladstone wrote days before the Grillion's breakfast. 'She is sadly reluctant to my receding into the shade.' It would be only weeks before the house was sold and the Gladstones' possessions, including thousands of books, transferred to the country. And as if to make the point that Gladstone was determined to shake the dust of London politics from his feet, his diary that month even included a most unusual entry: 'A civil talk with Disraeli.'

Gladstone's breakfast musings were hardly surprising, for he knew that as he ate others were meeting at Lord Granville's in desperation to discuss how they might persuade him to stay on. 'We are in great straits about our leader,' wrote Lord Kimberley afterwards. This gathering of the previous cabinet agreed unanimously that Gladstone should 'earnestly' be asked to carry on as leader. 'In fact who else can lead?' Kimberley asked plaintively. Lowe was too unpopular. Forster was 'odious'. Hartington could not bring the left with him. Goschen was too weak. And as for the lily-livered Cardwell, he had 'run away to the Lords for fear he should be asked to take the lead'. The Liberals were in chaos, without a leader or a policy. A new session of parliament was only days away. Without Gladstone those at Lord Granville's that day feared the party might simply implode.

Two days later they all trooped over to Carlton House Terrace to entreat Gladstone to stay on. Journalists, who had got wind of what was happening, were hanging around outside to take a note of who was going in. Thus the entire ex-cabinet, led by the distinguished Granville, had to sneak in round the back so as not to add fuel to the fires of political gossip. Once inside, they were greeted by a sombre Gladstone. 'He seemed much depressed,' recorded one in attendance. When they asked Gladstone to stay on, he declined. They asked him again; he offered only reasons why he should not accept. Finally they begged him to continue as leader. Only then did he suggest his own terms. He would carry on as notional leader until the following year. Most of the work would need to be carried out by others. He would remain as a figurehead, contributing only in major debates. His intention to resign in 1875 would be announced immediately. All this was agreed to readily, and so, with Gladstone saying he would take 'a day or so' to think it over, out they trooped like children leaving the headmaster's office.

Once outside these members of the shadow cabinet gave vent to their frustration and anger. 'How foolish and undignified!' exploded Kimberley. 'To run away when beaten is natural, but the English people expect its leaders to [be] made of sterner stuff. For his own reputation if not for the sake of the party, G. should meet the House and the party as recognized opposition leader.' Instead of this, 'he wants to sulk'.

The sullen mood did not pass. When the House met on 19 March, Gladstone gave a muted, dejected performance that demonstrated to his own party and the government that he hardly wanted to be there at all. Disraeli was delighted. 'Gladstone made a queer dispiriting speech and in short told his party that the country had decided against them and that they were thoroughly beaten,' he gleefully reported to Lady Bradford.

It only added to the new prime minister's delicious satisfaction at trouncing his adversary. 'I begin to feel the reality of power,' he swaggered.

Disraeli might have been sensing his power, but he was also feeling his age and wondering if that elusive majority in the House of Commons had come to him too late. The business of government was exhausting. Throughout the spring and summer of 1874 it often seemed likely that he would simply buckle under the pressure. 'I hear also much talk as to Disraeli and his state of health,' wrote the foreign secretary, Lord Derby, in April. 'Many of his friends think he has lost his energy . . . and will not long bear the strain of parliamentary life.' The prime minister's list of complaints was long. His asthma was severe on damp days. He suffered frequent debilitating headaches. Acute gout made it difficult to walk without a stick, and forced him to wear velvet slippers during long parliamentary debates. Added to this was the exhaustion of interminable late-night sittings that left him worn out. 'It was past four when I got home and I could not sleep,' ran one typical letter to Selina. 'I have really only had two hours troubled and fitful slumber and literally cannot see out of my eyes.' On occasion the strain would become too much. 'Unceasing suffering' could make it 'physically impossible' to get to the Commons, obliging his loyal lieutenant Gathorne Hardy, the secretary for war, to stand in for him.

Despite his failing health and nervous exhaustion, Disraeli dominated parliament in 1874. 'Never did the peculiar genius of Disraeli shine more transcendently than during the past session,' wrote Henry Lucy of the *Daily News*. 'Not in the zenith of his popularity after the election of 1868 did Gladstone come near his great rival in personal hold upon the House of Commons.' The contrast in personal styles was the key to Disraeli's success. 'At the outset of his current premiership, Disraeli fixed upon a policy of polite consideration, to which he was the more drawn as certain members of the ministry he succeeded were notorious for the brusqueness of their manner, suggested Lucy. The addition of a bit of banter and of a dash of serio-comicality lent a spiciness to his speech which was always relished, and was never allowed to reach the proportion at which the mixture left an unpleasant taste upon the parliamentary palate.' The fact that Disraeli was often 'visibly tortured' while doing it only added to his authority.

Goodwill and the contrast with Gladstonian asperity got Disraeli off the hook during the first difficulty of his administration. He had come to power promising not to harry the people with ceaseless legislation. The initial draft of the Queen's Speech for the first session of parliament had proposed such a leisurely agenda that the cabinet had struggled to think of enough material to include. Reform to improve the 'condition of the people' would come later. For the time being Disraeli wanted a period of quiet and calm to give the country (and MPs) time to recover from the zealous activity of the previous administration. With so much time on the government's collective hands, the prime minister found himself with almost no excuse when the Queen began pressing him on the question of 'popery' in the Anglican Church.

Back in 1867, Lord Derby had initiated a royal commission to investigate ritualistic practices among Anglo-Catholics in the Church of England. By the time the commission reported, recommending legislation to tighten discipline, Gladstone was in office. A high churchman in charge of a party with a vocal nonconformist element, he immediately recognised a potential banana skin. So Gladstone did what any politician would do in similar circumstances: he welcomed the report, described the matter as 'urgent' and then quietly let it drop. In 1874, the Anglican bishops decided to press the matter by introducing their own bill in the House of Lords. The Queen was shrilly vocal in her support, but cabinet, particularly Lord Salisbury, advised Disraeli to leave the matter well alone. He may well have done so had it not been for an intervention from the leader of the opposition.

Gladstone had been skulking at Hawarden for much of the parliamentary session. But religious questions always grabbed his attention, and he came charging furiously back to London in July to denounce the bishop's Public Worship Regulation Bill. He had consistently opposed attempts by parliament to control religious practice, even when (as in the case of the 1857 Divorce Act) it left him open to the charge of hypocrisy. The corruption of religion through politics, however, was something 'against which, as Conservative or as Liberal, I can perhaps say I have striven all my life long'. When the bill came to the House of Commons Gladstone introduced six passionate resolutions on the nature of the Church of England and the absurdity of 'a bill to put down ritualism'. The reaction was violent and immediate, not least on the Liberal benches. 'Gladstone has created a complete breach between him and the Liberal party by his ill judged resolutions,' wrote the agitated Kimberley.

Disraeli had always lost his footing on religious questions, but now the opportunity to step up the pace was impossible to resist. He only had to look at the flushed, angry faces on the benches opposite to realise that Gladstone had infuriated his own party with his intemperate intervention. Urging the PM on from the sidelines was the Queen. 'What has become of the Protestant feeling of Englishmen?' she taunted him. Gladstone's behaviour was 'much to be regretted though it is not surprising'. But what of her beloved Disraeli? 'Pray show that you are in earnest and determined to pass this bill and not to be deterred by threats of delay.'

It was an admonishment that Disraeli did not need to hear twice. When debate on the bill resumed after the weekend, the prime minister put the weight of the government behind the measure, throwing in an assault on the leader of the opposition for good measure. Rather than denying Gladstone's claims, he tossed them back in his face. Of course the bill was conceived to 'put down ritualism'. There was nothing wrong with being a high churchman, but the time had come to regulate 'practices by a portion of the clergy, avowedly symbolic of doctrines which the same clergy are bound, in the most solemn manner, to refute and repudiate'. Roman Catholic doctrine and liturgy was a matter for Roman Catholics. In the Church of England there should be no 'mass in masquerade'.

The House erupted with cheering when Disraeli sat down. Across the despatch box Gladstone was downcast and sullen. When the bill passed this second reading without even the need for a formal vote, the Liberal leader bowed to the inevitable by withdrawing his resolutions.

'An immense triumph!' Disraeli wrote ecstatically. '*Gladstone ran away.*'

The Public Worship Bill passed in early August. Nothing confirmed Disraeli's ascendancy in the Commons more than trouncing Gladstone on his home turf of religion. Satisfyingly, there had even been an opportunity for a sideswipe at his most difficult cabinet colleague, the High Church 3rd Marquess of Salisbury (formerly Lord Cranborne), described by Disraeli with menacing humour as 'a great master of gibes and flouts and jeers'. (Almost a century later, another Tory prime minister, Harold Macmillan, would humiliate the 5th Marquess by saying just one word to him: 'Disraeli'.) That Salisbury took the blow – and that Disraeli was prepared to land it – provided further proof of the prime minister's mastery of his party.

That dominance continued to come at a price. Had Disraeli been subjected to the constant exertions of later political life he would have collapsed. As it was, even January to August was enough to drive him to the edge. And just when his physical reserves were running on empty, duty sent him north to endure the Spartan hospitality of the Queen at Balmoral (with its open windows and unlit fires). The cold played havoc with his gout and then incited an attack of bronchitis. 'This morning the Queen paid me a visit in my bedchamber. What do you think of that?' Disraeli wrote to Lady Bradford, before complaining of being trapped as 'a sort of prisoner of state' at the Queen's summer retreat. ('I am, in short, the man in the Iron Masque.')

The rest of the year would continue in the same wretched vein. As autumn turned to winter, Disraeli was unable to shake of the effects of gout and bronchitis. He was forced to cancel a visit to Ireland. (He would never go.) Instead, on the Queen's command, he spent Christmas in Bournemouth for 'the very salubrious air'. It was desolated: an out-of-season town beset with freezing temperatures, blustery winds whipping off the sea and snow underfoot, which made it almost impossible for a bronchial septuagenarian to get outside. To the Queen he reported 'a great success' at the resort she 'had deigned to recommend'. To friends he wrote: 'I detest the place.' He could hardly wait to get back to London in January for a new parliamentary session. Whatever the physical effects of the capital's fogs and smogs, it could hardly be worse than seaside boredom.

Among the many things that had kept the premier amused during the otherwise uncomfortable parliamentary recess was a major religious scandal involving an eminent peer who had been a member of Gladstone's cabinet. When Disraeli heard the news he did not even bother to conceal his delight. 'A great piece of social news!' he scribbled in a note to Lady Chesterfield from his rooms while staying with her at Bretby Park. 'A member of the late government, of high rank and great wealth, has gone over to the Holy Father! Who is it? No less a personage than the Marquess of Ripon KG!!!'

Disraeli predicted that Gladstone would be dismayed by the news. In fact it unleashed a burst of written activity at Hawarden on the question of religion and patriotism that further convinced the Liberal leader – if he needed convincing at all – of the need to break with his party in order to campaign freely on the great issues of the day. Other Liberals scarcely disagreed. Lord Selborne complained that Gladstone could 'hardly be brought to interest himself at all in matters (even when they are really great matters) in which he is not carried away by some too strong attraction'. And on the latter, 'he does not sympathise with, or take counsel with' his party. 'This makes it hardly possible for him to be a Minister,' Selborne concluded wearily.

Gladstone remained the dominant Liberal in parliament and beyond, with no rivals to his reluctantly worn crown. Even though he could spectacularly misjudge the public mood, he retained that gossamer ability to define an issue in a way that caught public opinion. In this he remained unmatched by any other figure in public life. He had found himself on the wrong side of popular opinion during the debate on ritualism, but this was immediately forgiven and forgotten in the wake of his attack on Catholics for their lack of patriotism. In October 1874, he had included in an essay for *Contemporary Review* the assertion on Roman Catholicism that 'no one can become her convert without renouncing his moral and mental freedom and placing his civil loyalty and duty at the mercy of another'. This drew an immediate response from prominent Catholics, including Newman and Ripon, which in turn prompted Gladstone to develop his theme that conversion to Rome put civil allegiance in doubt. The resulting pamphlet, *The Vatican Decrees in their Bearing on Civil Allegiance*, was a huge popular success, selling more than seventy thousand copies in a month.

'On this my 65th birthday I find myself in lieu of the mental repose I had hoped engaged in a controversy, which cannot be mild, and which presses upon both mind & body,' Gladstone wrote on 29 December in his habitual annual reflection. In reality the storm had provided just the prompt he needed to give up the leadership. For Gladstone withdrawal from the Liberal front bench did not equate to a withdrawal from public life. Although he would be found more in his study than in the House of Commons, the runaway success of *The Vatican Decrees* demonstrated that this fact alone would hardly affect his ability to shape public debate.

In January 1875, as Disraeli was leaving Bournemouth, Gladstone returned to London to give up the leadership. He had been talked into staying the previous year, with disastrous results. Now he was resolute even though 'all are against me' giving up. The shadow cabinet met at Lord Granville's house on 14 January. 'I shall not continue to discharge the duties of leader of the Liberal Party,' he told them gravely. 'No one will remain under any tie or obligation to me.' Or, Gladstone might more pertinently have added, he to them. 'I seem to feel as one who has passed through a death, but emerged into a better life,' he wrote immediately afterwards.

For the rest of the parliamentary session, Gladstone went only inter-mittently to the House of Commons, where Lord Hartington (heir to the Duke of Devonshire) took up the leadership of the Liberals. When he did attend, it could be guaranteed to cause something of a stir. 'Mr Gladstone not only appeared but rushed into the debate,' an amused and vaguely approving Disraeli reported to the Queen in March. 'The new members trembled and fluttered like small birds when a hawk is in the air.'

Others, however, were less intimidated. Gladstone admitted that Catherine had been 'rather low as [to] what has happened'. After giving him six weeks to adjust, the indomitable Mrs Gladstone that month demanded to know exactly what he would be doing with his time. (Not getting under her feet being the presumable implication.) 'Conversation with C. on house matters,' wrote the beleaguered Gladstone. 'They involve more than would at first sight appear.' He had been chivvied 'to lay out before C. my views about the future & remaining section of my life'. What this amounted to was 'that, setting aside exceptional circumstances which would have to provide for themselves, my prospective work is not Parliamentary . . . But there is much to be done with the pen, all bearing much on high and sacred ends, for even Homeric study as I view of it [sic] is in this very sense of high importance.'

So it was to Homer that Gladstone returned, but surely in expec-tation that those 'exceptional circumstances' would inevitably present themselves.

Marlborough House, Pall Mall, 12 March 1875

It should have been an evening of pleasure for Disraeli. All London society shimmered at this annual grand ball in a magnificent building by Christopher Wren. The prime minister was in possession of the site he enjoyed most: at the centre of illustrious attention. Although other guests thought him 'amiable, brilliant and amused', he was in fact exhausted, bored and fed up. The effects of the London winter continued to trouble him. The pressure of governmental business was gradually taking its toll. Carousing past midnight was a strain for a man of seventy. He had ordered his carriage for quarter past one, but, with an hour still to go, he gave up and headed out to the lobby. There would be a cab, or else someone would inevitably welcome an opportunity to drop the prime minister home.

When he slipped out into the lobby it was empty of guests. He was helped into his cloak, but was told by the flustered doorman that there were no cabs. From behind came steps and the anticipated offer of a ride home. 'Had it not been for the courtesy of [that] guest who was also retiring, [I] should have had to wait in the hall more than an hour,' the prime minister wrote afterwards. It would have been no ordinary journey, for 'the guest was Gladstone!'. Only the sudden, unexpected arrival of a cab ('which I seized,' said Disraeli) saved both men from that purgatorial carriage ride. It would have been a rare and serendipitous moment alone together.

If the two had ventured out there is little doubt who would have felt he had the upper hand. Gladstone's retirement from front-line politics had convincingly reinforced Disraeli's sense of triumph over his adversary. 'Never was a party in such a position and though I never would confess it to anybody but yourself, never was a man in a prouder position than myself,' he boasted to Selina days after the change in Liberal leadership. 'It never happened before and is not likely to happen again. Only those who are acquainted with the malignity of Gladstone through a rivalship of five and twenty years can understand this.'

Disraeli scored another palpable strike against his great opponent that year. In November he sensationally purchased Suez Canal shares for Britain. It was a spectacular *coup de théâtre*. When the canal opened in 1869, Britain had declined to take up its share option. This turned out to have been a huge mistake, not least when it became apparent that the canal would be the principal trading and communication route with India. Unexpectedly in the middle of November 1875, the playboy Khedive of Egypt, Ismail Pasha, put his shares up for sale in order to pay off his exorbitant debt. He began negotiations with two French banks, but Disraeli's financier friend, Lionel de Rothschild, got wind of the deal. The prime minister at once recognised an unmissable opportunity. 'The thing must be done,' he told the Queen. Cabinet, particularly the increasingly difficult Derby, was initially reluctant, but Disraeli hustled the deal through. Rather than go to the sclerotic Bank of

England to raise the capital, he simply asked Rothschild to put up the money. (This Rothschild did at extreme personal risk: although he took a commission on the loan, he could not know in advance whether the PM would get approval from parliament.) On 24 November, less than ten days after first being tipped off, Disraeli exultantly told the Queen: 'It is settled: you have it, Madam!' To Selina, he wrote: 'we have had all the gamblers, capitalists, financiers of the world, organised and platooned in bands of plunderers, arrayed against us, and secret emissaries in every corner of the world, and have baffled them all.'

Disraeli correctly judged that 'the whole country will be with me'. Public opinion swung enthusiastically behind the purchase, rightly viewing it as an audacious statement on Britain's place in the world. The deal would bring rich rewards. A future foreign secretary, Lord Clarendon, summed up the advantages of the deal as 'the overland communication with India . . . the progress of civilization and the development of the commercial resources of the East'. The canal would soon become the basis of Britain's command of the oceans. French influence in the region was undermined. It would be vital to the trade and security of India. In short, another foreign secretary Lord Curzon would write in 1909, the Suez Canal was 'the determining influence of every considerable movement in British power to the east and south of the Mediterranean'.

Gladstone would later have reason to curse Disraeli for Britain's increased role in Egypt. In 1875, however, his humiliation was confined to another Commons defeat. He denounced the transaction as flashy and vulgar, predicting that it would lead to further imperial expansion in the region. He was right about the implications (although he surely could not have foreseen that he himself would be the principal instigator of that expansion in the 1880s). His opposition to the deal in 1875, however, counted for nothing. The purchase of the Suez Canal shares passed through the House in triumph.

Kudos from the Suez feat encouraged Disraeli to risk a more controversial measure in the next parliamentary session. 'There is to be a war to the knife when the Houses meet,' he predicted in January 1876. Disraeli knew what was in store, understood that to a certain extent he was instigating a quarrel by calculated discourtesy, and fully anticipated that Gladstone would 'rush into the arena'. Yet in spite of continued poor health, Disraeli hardly seemed able to stop himself from a deliberate act of provocation.

The previous year the Queen had received her royal cousin Tsar

Alexander II in London. She always remained predisposed to slights, and was irked throughout the visit that the Tsar, as an emperor, outranked her, a mere Queen. And doubtless, when she thought about it, another potential mortification struck her too: that if her daughter, Vicky, became German empress, she too would outrank her mother. That would be a humiliation too far. So she cajoled Disraeli to find a way to address the problem. The result was a Royal Titles Bill that would see Victoria proclaimed Empress of India – *Regina et Imperatrix*.

Such was Victoria's excitement at the prospect of taking on an imperial title that she finally consented, after much pestering by Disraeli, to open the 1876 session of parliament in person. This was such a rare event that the increasingly infirm Disraeli was almost trampled underfoot as eager MPs dashed from the Commons to the Lords on 8 February to get a decent viewing position. The Queen's Speech was traditionally heard in silence, but the Royal Titles Bill when announced nevertheless drew gasps. 'It has been the custom for many years when any proposal was to be made to parliament, affecting the Queen personally, for the Government to communicate with the leaders of the opposition,' complained Lord Kimberley. 'This was not done by Disraeli.' The Liberals were appalled at the prime minister's discourtesy. They also objected to the Queen's imperial pretensions. 'It is said that the Queen is foolish enough to wish for the title of Empress, in order that her family may be put on an equality with the Continental Imperial Highnesses!' spat the contemptuous Kimberley. His scorn was shared by Gladstone who pronounced the whole matter 'a piece of tomfoolery'.

When matters came to a head in March and April, Disraeli's prediction that the bill would bring Gladstone charging back into the ring proved well founded. In the end it saved the prime minister. Lord Hartington had sought to find a way forward through conciliation, but his predecessor's blundering contribution would split his own party. 'Mr Gladstone who was brimful, took the reins in his own hands,' wrote the relieved Disraeli afterwards, but then 'fled . . . and left his party in a ditch'. Gladstone's intervention, and an even more intemperate one from Robert Lowe, supplied just the necessary momentum for Disraeli to pass a bill that was, said Lord Derby, 'universally disliked, and with some reason'. Throughout the debates, the PM noted, Gladstone had been consumed by 'his white rages' and kept 'glancing looks at me which would have annihilated any man who had not a good majority and a determination to use it'.

The unpopular Royal Titles Act, however, shattered Disraeli's authority in the House of Commons. The journalist Henry Lucy began to worry that this grand figure of British life would end his political career in embarrassment and ignominy. 'It would be a sad ending to a brilliant career to see Disraeli openly discredited in the assembly of which he has for thirty years been a chief ornament,' lamented Lucy. 'Of late, in increasing measure, he is losing his airy grace of manner, just sufficiently spiced with audacity, and his felicitousness of phrase, always admirably spiced with personality. When these are gone, the House, looking at what is left, finds that it is not much and is not at all desirable.'

Often the prime minister was so ill that he appeared at debates 'in a condition almost unrecognizable'. The decline was not just physical. Disraeli had lost his touch. His jokes were no longer funny. He regularly and uncharacteristically lost his cool in the House. His speeches rambled and his grasp of detail was scant. He even began to talk of retirement, while highly placed rivals for the premiership began to manoeuvre for position. 'Disraeli complains of over-fatigue . . . and seems to wish to throw it all up,' wrote the eager Lord Derby in May. 'If he does, it is on the cards that the succession will fall to me.'

And as the prime minister deteriorated, Gladstone remained at Hawarden in brooding semi-retirement. He would, said Disraeli, occasionally 'come down like the dragon of Wantley breathing fire and fury'. For the most part, however, Gladstone remained out of the fray. And by staying away, he seems inadvertently to have wounded his detested rival more severely than when meeting him head on to trade blow for blow.

For Disraeli, without his nemesis, had no dialectical sparring partner in the House of Commons to bring out the best in him.

20

A Clash of Civilisations

House of Commons, 11 August 1876

The 1876 session of parliament was coming to a dramatic conclusion. That month had been among the hottest on record. The House was unpleasantly malodorous and claustrophobic. A number of members had slunk away early to the more tranquil environment of their country retreats. Disraeli was not one of them. In fact he rarely missed debates. Whether as prime minister or leader of the opposition it had always been a point of principle to be in his seat on the front bench. 'Unless you are always there, how can you lead the House of Commons?' he would say, 'How can you feel their pulse? How can you know the men?' However obtuse or tedious the business in hand, or however ill he felt, Disraeli remained in his position, and insisted that his cabinet ministers did the same. For all the affection he retained for Gathorne Hardy, Disraeli could never quite take him seriously as a potential successor because each night he left the Commons in order to dine with his wife.

Disraeli this night was winding up for the government in a foreign affairs debate. He had just been subjected to an insolent attack from an admired opponent, Sir William Harcourt, which he was now rebutting in typically biting fashion. At the end came a final patriotic proclamation. 'What our duty is at this critical moment is to maintain the Empire of England,' he declared robustly, before resuming his seat to ebullient cheers from the remaining Tory MPs ranged behind him.

Sitting on the other side of the House was the young Liberal MP Thomas Burt. Only elected two years earlier, he retained a sense of awe about the Commons and its great characters. He had come to politics through trade unionism, having started his adult life working down a mine. While most MPs scurried from the House anxious to get to Brooks's or the Carlton, he remained on the opposition benches quietly observing the prime minister. Something in Disraeli's countenance had caught Burt's attention and he was the only one to notice. The prime minister had risen from the front bench, but instead of moving left as usual to the exit behind the Speaker's Chair, he had instead gone off to the right. Stopping alone at the bar of the House, he turned, and for a full minute stood motionless as he surveyed the wonderful neo-Gothic chamber. Then slowly retracing his steps past the despatch box and the government benches to the Speaker's Chair, Disraeli quietly slipped out of view. Thomas Burt had been his final Commons spectator. Disraeli would never sit in the House again. The following day it was announced that he had been created Earl of Beaconsfield.

Even at the time there was a recognition that Disraeli's elevation had brought down the curtain on one of the greatest – and surely the most extraordinary – Commons careers. He would remain as prime minister, but would lead from the House of Lords ('the dullest assembly in the world,' Lord Salisbury warned him). The cockpit of the Commons had been the epicentre of his political life, and both he and his fellow members lamented his passing. Harcourt, who had 'little thought' that Disraeli's riposte to him would be 'your last speech in a place where your fame will always live,' generously captured something of the vivacity that Disraeli had brought to the political cut and thrust. 'Henceforth the game will be like a chessboard when the Queen is gone – a petty struggle of pawns,' he affectionately judged. Others seemed too shell-shocked to take in the news. 'Small groups are dotted about here and there talking with bated breath, as though there were a coffin within the precincts of the House,' wrote Disraeli's young admirer Viscount Barrington of the scene at Westminster on the morning of the announcement. 'I am dead,' Disraeli quipped semi-seriously, 'Dead, but in the Elysian fields.'

Since his sensational attacks on Sir Robert Peel in the 1840s, Disraeli had been a dominant force in the House of Commons. Widely abused outside Westminster, the *Quarterly Review* had shrewdly observed as early as 1854, 'in the House it is rare for anyone but Mr Gladstone to meddle with him'. Whatever the contrasting merits of these two great rivals, most agreed that Disraeli had the upper hand within the

Commons chamber. The Whig George Russell, who as the son of a sergeant-at-arms saw many of the greats of the Commons in action, later recalled that 'one figure appeared to me to tower head and shoulders above the rest, and that was the leader of the Conservative party, the ridiculed and preposterous "Dizzy". His mastery of the House, on both sides, seemed absolute. Compared to him Gladstone played a secondary and ambiguous part.' The difference, he thought, was 'between genius and talent'.

Given that command of the House of Commons represented perhaps Disraeli's single greatest advantage in his decades-long rivalry with Gladstone, it is surprising that he was prepared to give it up. No doubt it helped that Gladstone himself seemed to have withdrawn from Westminster life. Disraeli did not think this represented anything but a temporary hiatus. 'Now mark, all this retirement from the leadership by Gladstone is a mere sham,' the Duchess of Manchester had warned him that summer. 'The moment he sees an opportunity he will come to the front.' Disraeli hardly needed telling (although he thought it significant enough to report to Selina Bradford). The reality was that if Disraeli were to remain in office his health simply would not allow him to do so from the Commons. Throughout 1876 he had been beset by illness after illness. 'I sat through the debate in great suffering . . . and went home very late and rather hopeless' ran a typical complaint to Selina that year. 'If I could have stayed at home, I should have been all right. But that is impossible.' The stark alternative laid before Disraeli that summer − by his doctors, political heavyweights such as Derby and Salisbury, his friends, and the Queen (who was terrified that he would resign) − was go to the Lords or else risk physical collapse.

In the end he accepted the inevitable. But in doing so he surrendered the field to Gladstone, who at the very moment that Disraeli chose to leave the Commons was at home in Wales preparing his most vicious assault on the prime minister and what he would quickly term 'Beaconsfieldism'.

'Cabinet at 12' had written Lord Derby on 24 May. 'Turkish affairs again: they are no doubt urgent and important, but not to the degree of superseding all other business. They have however taken hold of Disraeli's mind and he can talk of nothing else.' For much of the early part of the year Disraeli had been seriously minded to retire gracefully from political life. By May, however, events in Eastern Europe had persuaded him otherwise. Perhaps even at this stage Disraeli realised that this was the issue that would define him – and his rivalry with Gladstone.

The Eastern Question – who would fill the vacuum left by the crumbling Turkish Empire – engaged the minds of European statesmen throughout the second half of the nineteenth century and all the way through to (at least) the First World War. By 1876, some of the great powers had already been to war (in the Crimea in 1854) over the question; only the indecisiveness of Austria and Germany about which way to jump prevented the conflict from becoming a full-scale European war. During the 1870s rebellions within the Turkish Empire in the Balkans had escalated. There had been a serious war scare in 1875 as the great powers squabbled about whether to support insurgents in Bosnia and Herzegovina. Only a reform programme devised by the Austrian foreign minister, Count Andrassy, and accepted by the other powers (including Turkey), saved the day.

At the end of April 1876 a new wave of insurgency had broken out in Bulgaria, the most downtrodden of all Turkey's European possessions. From the outset it must have been obvious that the ramshackle band of rebels had no chance of success. Whereas the Bosnians the previous year had enjoyed enough resources to mount a serious challenge to Turkey, the Bulgars had no such advantages. Yet the cruelly intolerant nature of Turkish rule, which included random acts of extreme violence and financial corruption on a level that bled the country dry, made it worth the attempt.

It only took days for the Turks to crush the revolt, but it was the manner in which they did that provoked an international crisis. In London it was the liberal *Daily News*, famous for its overseas coverage, which broke the news of 'the Bulgarian atrocities'. Throughout the summer of 1876 it published a steady stream of revelations about the appalling nature of the slaughter in Bulgaria and the totally disproportionate nature of the Turkish response. Such was the shocking brutality shown by the fanatical Turkish irregulars – the murderous 'Bashibazuks' – that reports of the massacres and torture scandalised popular opinion throughout Britain.

Disraeli's initial reaction to the Bulgarian atrocities had been disastrously misjudged. When questioned in the House of Commons at the end of June, he had denounced the whole story as a set-up job by the hostile *Daily News*, whose 'object is to create a cry against the government'. Even in July, when forced to admit 'proceedings of an atrocious character in Bulgaria', he still claimed that the story had been exaggerated. 'Acts on both sides were equally terrible and atrocious,' he claimed. When asked about the reported ten thousand imprisoned and tortured, he unwisely retorted that 'oriental people seldom, I believe, resort to torture, but generally terminate their connection with culprits in a more expeditious manner'.

Disraeli's first encounter with Gladstone on the matter had come on 31 July. The latter denounced Turkish rule as 'a moral blight', eulogised the insurrection as 'the reflection of popular opinion', and called for a full inquiry into the atrocities. Disraeli replied angrily that there would be no official investigation in response to what was little more than 'coffee house babble'.

In his final speech in the House of Commons, Disraeli was forced to admit the massacre of twelve thousand Bulgarians, but contrasted this with earlier speculation of more than thirty thousand dead. Although a 'horrible event', he suggested, it could hardly be accurately described as 'the depopulation of a province' of almost four million inhabitants. Certainly it was not enough 'to justify us in talking in such a vein of Turkey' as in the present hostile debate. And so on to that final statement that his only duty at such critical moments was 'to maintain the Empire of England'.

It had been a bullish performance right to the end of the parliamentary session even in the face of incontrovertible evidence of an appalling massacre. But Disraeli knew that the issue had been 'very damaging' for the government.

'It is lucky for us,' he told Lord Derby, 'that the session is dying.'

'Preserved in the [Hawarden] Octagon is a large packet of notes on "Future Retribution",' wrote John Morley in the celebrated life of his friend Gladstone, 'and on them is the docket, "*From this I was called away to write on Bulgaria*". In the spring of 1876 the Turkish volcano had burst into flame.' It remains surely among the most evocative moments in any modern political biography.

Throughout August Gladstone held himself in reserve on Bulgaria allowing popular disgust to grow as ever more lurid updates came in. Crucial to this was a report to Washington by the highly respected American consul general in Constantinople, Eugene Schuyler, who had been despatched to see for himself. He catalogued an 'indiscriminate slaughter . . . a very large proportion of them women and children'. He recounted how the Bashibazuks had locked prisoners in local churches before setting fire to them. Women were often raped before they were murdered. And, crucially, he detailed the explicitly religious and ethnic nature of the violence. 'No Turkish women or children were killed in cold blood, no Mussulman [Muslim] women violated, no Mussulmans tortured, no purely Turkish village attacked or burnt, no mosque desecrated or destroyed.' Official Turkish denials of the events he dismissed as 'a tissue of falsehoods'. Critically, an American journalist, J. A. MacGahan, who worked for the *Daily News*, had accompanied Schuyler on his tour. Schuyler naturally gave him a copy of the report, which the newspaper immediately published.

A wave of public disgust swept through Britain as the full loathsomeness of events became apparent. By the end of the month, around five hundred public demonstrations had taken place. Lord Salisbury conceded that 'the country was roused'. Sir Charles Dilke expressed astonishment that 'foreign affairs had suddenly risen out of complete obscurity into a position in which they overshadowed all other things'. Even the Queen, who had escaped to Balmoral, was caught up in the agitation. 'More news of the horrors committed by the Turks,' she wrote on 23 August, 'which seem to be more and more verified, and are causing dreadful excitement and indignation in England, or indeed in Great Britain.'

What this 'excitement and indignation' lacked was a focus. At the end of that summer it got one. Among the leaders of popular agitation was a young Darlington journalist, W. T. Stead, who would later become perhaps the foremost parliamentary commentator of his generation. He pressed Gladstone to join the protest. 'It is still the cherished hope of the North Country that you may once more lead us to victory,' he wrote earnestly, 'and that hope has certainly not been weakened by recent occurrences abroad.' Gladstone was uncharacteristically hesitant about fuelling the unrest, not least because the leader of his own party in the Commons, Lord Hartington, had gone silent. By the end of August he could no longer hold his tongue. 'I really hope that on this Eastern matter the pot will be kept boiling,' he urged Granville, the party's leader in the House of Lords. 'Good ends can rarely be attained in politics without passion, and there is now, the first time for a good many years, a virtuous passion.' Then he added, almost as an afterthought: 'I am in half, perhaps a little more than half, a mind to write a pamphlet.'

That pamphlet – *The Bulgarian Horrors and the Question of the East* – was the single most influential work Gladstone ever wrote. It was composed in a burst of frenetic intellectual energy over four days at

Hawarden. As he wrote, Gladstone was in agonising spinal pain. 'Lumbago bad,' he complained on 29 August, 'aggravated by trying to walk and by writing, which (oddly) works the back.' Perhaps it was the pain that encouraged him to abandon his usual circumlocution in a direct and highly effective polemic.

On 3 September he sped to London on the mail train, arriving in a state of wild excitement at Lord Granville's door at five the next morning. After a further day in the British Library checking facts, he handed the manuscript to his publisher, John Murray, who rushed the work into print on 6 September. By the end of that month, Gladstone's *Bulgarian Horrors* had astonishingly sold more than two hundred thousand copies.

Its message was simple enough. 'Let the Turks now carry away their abuses in the only possible manner, namely by carrying off themselves,' he demanded. 'One and all, bag and baggage, shall I hope, clear out from the province they have desolated and profaned.'

Among the complimentary copies sent out hours before publication was one to the prime minister, Lord Beaconsfield. Disraeli was furious with what he read, even though Gladstone had stopped short (just) of accusing the government of knowingly covering up the true scale of the atrocities. 'Gladstone has had the impudence to send me his pamphlet, though he accuses me of several crimes,' he wrote angrily to Derby after reading it. 'The document is passionate and strong; vindictive and ill-written – that of course. Indeed, in that respect, of all the Bulgarian horrors, perhaps the greatest.' It was a put-down he happily repeated in public. In private, however, the fractious premier reluctantly conceded that the tract was 'not so ill-written as is his custom . . . so it is not so involved and obscure'. From Disraeli, that was as good as an endorsement.

Certainly the pamphlet was significant enough to bring him rushing uncharacteristically to London. 'It is raining cats and dogs here,' he complained unhappily to Selina. 'I hope it is at Greenwich, where G. is beginning to spout from his pamphlet.'

Blackheath

Disraeli would have been delighted. The rain was pouring down in south-east London as his antagonist prepared to deliver an oration. It was not a place that Gladstone loved in the way of his earlier constituencies. For all the supporters he had there, Greenwich was just too suburban for Gladstone's tastes, enjoying none of the high-brow élan of Oxford or the industrial vigour of South Lancashire. That day, as he looked out over the vast crowd below, ankle-deep in mud and huddled together against the lashing autumn rain, his spirits rose. More than ten thousand had gathered to hear him speak on the atrocities. The sense of dramatic expectation was palpable in their noisy, excited chatter.

Gladstone had been in a state of nervous exhilaration for the previous few days. As so often at moments of high tension he had sought release on the streets. Each night he could be found out hunting in Piccadilly to spend long hours in the company of prostitutes. 'In evening saw M. Phillips' ran a typical diary entry, with the familiar 'X' denoting temptation, the day after publication of *Bulgarian Horrors*. 'I might put down much,' he added elliptically. No doubt his suburban following on Blackheath would have been surprised had they known of these nocturnal proclivities, but instead that day all they got was the reassuring presence of Catherine Gladstone, who had arrived from Wales the previous night.

The rain continued to cascade down as Gladstone moved to the platform to speak. After a noisy burst of clapping and cheering, the gathering settled into an expectant hush. In a measured voice – Gladstone never harangued or even incited a crowd – he set out a case that struck a new tone not as a party man, but as a voice of the people. The agitation against the atrocities was not a partisan question, but rather the expression of national outrage. He recounted the journey he had taken down to London that week. As his carriage had clattered through the streets from Euston station, each house had looked eerily dark and hushed. 'But as I came through those long lines of streets,' he boomed, 'I felt it to be an inspiring and a noble thought that in every one of these houses there were intelligent human beings, my fellow countrymen, who when they woke would give many of their earliest thoughts, aye and some of their most energetic actions, to the terrors and suffering of Bulgaria.'

Yet what was to be done in this war on Turkish terror? After much discourse on the caveats and complexities of the situation, Gladstone offered solutions that were clear and breathtakingly populist. First, the most straightforward solution was that 'the Turkish authorities should walk out of the place'. If not, honour should go 'to the power, whatsoever its name, that first steps in to stop them'. Then, in cooperation, all the great powers should refrain from simply dividing the spoils of the Ottoman Empire between them, but rather should allow the inhabitants to rule themselves. Such a future was possible, because 'never have I known a great object so pressing in its urgency, upon which the Powers and the Peoples of Europe were so cordially united as upon this'. Through a coalition of the willing, tyranny might be vanquished and national self-determination prevail.

At the end of the speech that respectable suburban audience erupted into wild applause and shouting. 'The most enthusiastic by far that I ever saw,' Gladstone purred afterwards.

What gave him even more pleasure was a visit two days later to High Wycombe, just a few short miles from Hughenden. He was there to help the Liberals in the by-election for the parliamentary seat just vacated by Disraeli. 'The town gave me an enthusiastic reception, of course with relation to the present circumstances,' he glowed afterwards. It had been a deeply satisfying, triumphant week.

Disraeli had been at Hughenden when Gladstone spoke at High Wycombe, but there had been no invitation to dine or stay. It is possible that, had Mary Anne been alive, Gladstone would not have passed by so publicly without even a courtesy call, or that she might have prevailed on her husband to offer hospitality. After her death there was no ameliorating factor in their rivalry. On occasion Disraeli could be amusing about it. 'That is the most dangerous statesman in Europe,' he remarked to one of Gladstone's daughters at a reception to honour a foreign diplomat. 'Except, as your father would say, myself, or, as I should prefer to put it, your father.' Behind the gossamer façade of humour lay bitter contempt, which Disraeli found increasingly difficult to mask. Just weeks after the Blackheath speech, that antagonism triggered an outburst to Lord Derby. 'Posterity will do justice to that unprincipled maniac Gladstone – extraordinary mixture of envy, vindictiveness, hypocrisy and superstition – whether prime minister or leader of opposition – whether preaching, praying, speechifying or scribbling – never a gentleman.'

The truth was that Disraeli had miscalculated on the atrocities. He had taken early reports too lightly, failed to understand the extent of popular revulsion during the summer, and then allowed Gladstone to seize the initiative with a bestselling polemic. His tactic had been one of saying little, allowing Derby's diplomacy to do its work, while waiting for the agitation to blow itself out. 'Generally speaking, when the country goes mad, which it does every now and then,' he told Sir Stafford Northcote (the new leader of the Conservatives in the Commons) while Gladstone was speaking in High Wycombe, 'I think it best, that one should wait till every thing has been said and frequently in one direction, and then the country, tired of hearing the same thing over and over again begins to reflect, and opinion changes as quickly as it was formed.'

It was a disastrous ploy. Week after week Disraeli was denounced in newspapers and periodicals for his unresponsiveness to popular anxiety over an international crisis. 'The Sphinx is silent' ran one cartoon showing Disraeli's face on the famous Egyptian monument while below a crowd shouts 'speak, speak'. Another showed him as 'The Drowsy Pointsman', asleep outside the Eastern Line signal box as a clattering train of war approaches.

After Gladstone's impudent attack in his own backyard, Disraeli had to concede that a taciturn approach had failed. He therefore launched a ferocious attack on Gladstone in Aylesbury on 20 September. It went well beyond the norms of political discourse. 'He outrages the principle of patriotism, which is the soul of free communities,' Disraeli accused. 'Such conduct, if pursued by any man at this moment, ought to be indignantly reprobated by the people of England, for in the general havoc and ruin which it may bring about it may, I think, be fairly described as worse than any of those Bulgarian atrocities which now occupy attention.'

The Queen thought this attack 'masterly' and Lord Derby called it 'a very skilful ingenious speech'. Elsewhere the reaction was furious. Next morning *The Times* launched a bitter attack on Disraeli, accusing him of 'a negligence astonishing in so great a master of language'. He had issued 'one of the gravest charges ever made by one eminent English statesman against another'.

Although the Conservatives just scraped in at the Buckinghamshire by-election, the timing of Disraeli's speech could hardly have been worse. For on the day he made it, Walter Baring, who had been sent by the British embassy in Constantinople to investigate the atrocities, submitted his report (which appeared in the press almost immediately). It was less emotive than Schuyler's, but it confirmed twelve thousand dead, the religious nature of the slaughter and described in detail the gruesomeness of the brutal repression of a feeble insurrection. Ahmed Aga, said Baring, had set his Bashibazuks to 'slaughter them like sheep'. The scene of devastation was as the 'valley of the shadow of death'.

'No doubt [it] will be used largely for party purposes,' predicted Derby gloomily when he received his copy of the report. 'Gladstone is said to be possessed with the subject . . . He now threatens to return.'

It needed one more provocation from Disraeli. At the annual Lord Mayor's banquet in November, the prime minister laid out the government's strategy on the Eastern Question in the starkest terms: to maintain, by military means if necessary, the traditional British strategy of defending Turkey in order to prevent Russia expanding its sphere of influence. It was not something that he did without certain trepidation. 'He must speak on the great question, and every word he utters will be criticised throughout Europe,' Disraeli wrote in the third person that day to the Queen. He admitted it was a prospect that filled him with 'a sense of discomfort and nervousness'. The eminent guests at that night's feast would hardly have guessed. As Disraeli spoke, his warlike expressions of defiance drew astonished gasps. There was a sideswipe at Gladstone, of course, for the 'indignant burst of feeling' that had stirred up an already impassioned situation. But it was the threat of hostilities that shocked so many that night and at breakfast tables around the country the next morning. Russia was already threatening war with Turkey. Everyone had wondered how Britain would respond. Disraeli seemed to give them an answer. The drums of war were sounded.

'Although the policy of England is peace, there is no country so well prepared for war as our own,' Disraeli bullishly affirmed. 'If she enters into conflict in a righteous cause . . . if the contest is one which concerns her liberty, her independence, or her empire, her resources, I feel, are inexhaustible. She is not a country that, when she enters into a campaign, has to ask herself whether she can support a second or a third campaign. She enters into a campaign which she will not terminate till right is done.'

Reaction at one of those breakfast tables was particularly intense. 'The provocation offered by Disraeli at the Guildhall is almost incredible,' exploded Gladstone.

It was not a provocation he was prepared to ignore.

St James's Hall, 8 December 1876

Gladstone had travelled down from Hawarden especially to address those gathered excitedly in Piccadilly on 8 December. 'I came to the conclusion after much consideration that it was desirable for me to make a further utterance [although] it is anything but a pleasant task,' he implausibly told Granville beforehand. The apologetic tone was surely a response to Granville's subtle but unsuccessful attempts in the preceding weeks to calm Gladstone. Most senior Liberals were deeply distrustful of the agitation and Gladstone's part in it. Lord Kimberley despised it as 'violent and unreasoning'. Lord Spencer was 'amazed' that even 'men who I thought were staunch Liberals . . . are outspoken against Gladstone'. Before this St James's Hall meeting, Lord Hartington sent a message through Granville asking Gladstone not to attend. The rally was 'almost sure to get principally into the hands of men of extreme opinion,' he predicted, 'I am afraid that the tendency of anything of this kind is to drive our best men, or at events the Whigs, to the side of the government.'

At first sight the meeting seemed like a gathering of 'the great and the good' of Victorian society. The Duke of Westminster and Lord Shaftesbury presided. Those on the platform included bishops and prominent nonconformists, Anthony Trollope, thirty members of parliament, the designer William Morris, the author and artist John Ruskin and the historian William Lecky. Letters of support were read from Thomas Carlyle, Charles Darwin, Herbert Spencer and Robert Browning. 'We have never known any association for a political object which has obtained support over so large a part of the scale of English society,' commented *The Times* afterwards.

Gladstone's speech was the hit of the meeting. Unsurprisingly it consisted of a direct and unambiguous denunciation of Disraeli's Guildhall speech. 'No matter how the prime minister may finger the hilt of the sword,' Gladstone thundered, 'the nation will take care that it never leaves the scabbard!' He cleverly evoked the memory of the skilful and humane diplomacy in the Eastern Question of his (and Disraeli's) childhood hero, George Canning, who embodied the notion that 'the traditional policy of England was not complicity with guilty power but sympathy with suffering weakness'. Afterwards, in the company of Mrs Thistlethwayte at Claridges, Gladstone glowed with satisfaction. 'The meetings were great, notable, almost historical,' he boasted.

It was Hartington's, not Gladstone's, analysis that proved correct. Gladstone had been the star turn of the meeting, but the next day's newspapers were more concerned with the virulence of the other speakers, most notably the Liberal historian Edward Freeman. He had already outraged public opinion weeks earlier with his boast that 'I am sure we are a large enough part of the English people to make even the Jew [Disraeli] in his drunken insolence think twice before he goes to war in our teeth.' Now he accused the prime minister of wanting to declare war in order to defend the integrity and independence of Sodom. It was enough to prompt the Queen, not unsympathetic to the agitation, to ask if the legal authorities 'could be set at these men'.

Hartington scathingly dismissed the St James's Hall meeting as 'a failure' that had made most Liberal MPs 'rather more inclined than they were before to support the government'. Even more significantly, he recognised that the rally had damaged Gladstone politically (and therefore consolidated his own hold on the party). 'Gladstone might be supported in the country at a general election, though I doubt it,' Hartington told Granville, 'but I feel certain that the Whigs and moderate Liberals in the House are a good deal disgusted, and I am much afraid that, if he goes much further, nothing can prevent a break-up of the party.'

Gladstone would hardly have been surprised by Hartington's scathing assessment. 'When did the Upper Ten Thousand [i.e. the richest people in the country] ever lead the attack in the cause of humanity,' he complained petulantly. 'Their heads are always full of class interest and the main chance.'

What might have worried him more was a shift in popular opinion. This was symbolised by a new song that was gaining popularity in music halls up and down the country. 'We don't want to fight, but by Jingo if we do,' it ran, 'we've got the ships, we've got the men, we've got the money too!'

It was inspired by Disraeli's Guildhall speech.

21

Peace with Honour

High Wycombe Railway Station

L ord Beaconsfield stood serenely on the platform waiting for the
train to arrive on that fine sunny morning of 15 December
1877. That Saturday was special in many ways, not least because
it marked the anniversary of his beloved wife's death. How Mary Anne
would have revelled in the events about to take place. While Disraeli
chatted quietly to his secretary, Monty Corry, all around them an
excited burble grew to a crescendo of cheering as the train approached.
Small children ran alongside the railway line waving flags. The wives
of local dignitaries nervously adjusted their new hats. As the engine
eased into the station, a brass band struck up. The stationmaster leapt
forward to open the carriage door, and there before them – unmistakable, diminutive, smiling – was the Queen Empress. Disraeli bowed
low before introducing her to the local worthies. Perhaps a faint look
of unspoken amusement passed between them as the mayor launched
into a longwinded address of welcome. Then it was into an open
carriage and away for the short drive to Hughenden along roads
thronged with the inquisitive, proud citizenry of Buckinghamshire.

It was a remarkable event, redolent with meaning, not least because
the Queen had not visited one of her prime ministers at his country
home since her first: Lord Melbourne. Together they enjoyed a quiet
lunch. The Queen and her daughter, Princess Beatrice, each planted
a tree in the Italian garden. Afterwards there was time for tea, with
the Queen sitting on a chair with specially shortened legs, before the
royal party left at half past three. On her way out, Victoria's eye fell
on a statuette of Disraeli, which (as was her habit when visiting anyone)

she graciously consented to keep. 'The visit of Saturday a great success,' Disraeli told Selina Bradford afterwards. 'The Faery seemed to admire, and be interested in, everything, and has written to me a very pretty letter to that effect.'

Others were less impressed, not least Gladstone's friend Edward Freeman. He surpassed himself by describing the Queen as 'going ostentatiously to eat with Disraeli in his ghetto'. It was a virulent example of the anti-Semitism that the Eastern Question was bringing to the surface of political life. Gladstone kept his thoughts to himself on Victoria's Hughenden visit, but symbolically he spent that day reading a new biography of Prince Albert 'and made a beginning of a short article upon it'. They had been happier days when he, not Disraeli, had been a favourite at court.

Part of the reason for Victoria's visit was to stiffen Disraeli's resolve and to demonstrate royal support at a time of international crisis. She had 'strongly' advised him to keep his nerve on the Eastern Question and to 'bring things to an issue'. Only the previous week, the town of Plevna in Bulgaria had fallen to the Russians, a decisive moment in their war against Turkey. A Russian advance on Constantinople now seemed inevitable. Disraeli's ominous warnings of the previous year about the threat Russia posed to British interests in Egypt and India now more than ever seemed incredibly astute. He needed no prompting by the Queen. 'The country is asleep and I want to wake it,' he told her. In fact, the fall of Plevna did the job for him. The issue dominated the newspapers for weeks. A great wave of popular opinion rose up to counter the anti-Turkish sentiment that had held sway since the 'Bulgarian atrocities'. The new demand was that 'something' be done to counter Russian expansionism even if that involved sending British troops to war.

The upsurge of jingoism gave Disraeli a certain political leverage, not least over his own cabinet, which remained deeply suspicious about anything that might lead to war. He brushed aside their doubts to despatch the British fleet through the Dardanelles to warn the Russians off Constantinople. More controversially, he sent Indian troops to the Mediterranean. The foreign secretary, Lord Derby, and the colonial secretary, Lord Carnarvon, both resigned in protest (although the hapless Derby quickly returned on a technicality resulting from a mistranslated telegram about Russian intentions). On 31 January 1878 Russia and Turkey signed an armistice. The Sultan made a plea to Disraeli to save Constantinople. War between Britain and Russia seemed inevitable.

This was the beginning of the most vituperative phase of the Eastern Question in British politics. The country seemed divided as never before. Radicals organised meetings all over the country passing resolutions against war. Those in favour of war staged demonstrations at which the opposition was denounced for their lack of patriotism in not defending British interests. 'Everybody has taken sides,' wrote the manager of *The Times*, J. C. MacDonald, 'and there is a degree of heat and passion on the subject such as has not been developed for a very long time.'

And so it was no surprise that Gladstone should have chosen this moment of maximum tension to launch one of his most savage and explicit attacks on Disraeli.

On 28 January, Sir Stafford Northcote had asked the Commons for an extra £6 million to prepare the navy and army for war. Turkey was 'in danger of being dismembered,' he cautioned. Britain could not stand aside while its century-long policy of bolstering the Ottoman Empire was blown away. 'It may become the duty of England to watch over the action of Russia with regard to Constantinople,' he warned portentously, '[and] to use the force of England.'

The debate lasted five days, during which time the armistice was signed. Gladstone had spoken, but in a reasonably measured way. He had criticised the government's 'perfectly unreal' assessment of the international situation and then voted against the motion. Only ninety other Liberals joined him in the 'no' lobby as the government won a crushing victory.

It was a relatively tame performance, but it only needed to be: for on the third day of the debate, Gladstone had absented himself from the House to visit Oxford, where he had delivered a venomous assault on Disraeli. Nothing demonstrated more clearly his recognition of the importance of taking his argument away from Westminster to appeal over the heads of his own parliamentary leadership. And hereafter it would be impossible to doubt the highly personal nature of the battle. On the Eastern Question, Gladstone declared, 'when you speak of the Government, you mean Lord Beaconsfield, . . . for not one man in the Government has a tenth part of his tenacity of will and patient purpose'. In a rare flash of humour, he reminded his audience of the famous taunt of the Iron Duke's cabinet of ten men – 'one and a nought: the Duke of Wellington is the one and other nine the nought'.

Gladstone denounced Disraeli's policy as 'an act of war, a breach of European law'. It was for this reason, Gladstone declared in a sensational conclusion, that he played 'the part of an agitator. My purpose has been . . . to the best of my power, for the last eighteen months, day and night, week by week, month by month, to counterwork as well as I could, what I believe to be the purpose of Lord Beaconsfield.' Afterwards he wrote in his diary: 'I said what was meant to do a little good.'

Reaction to Gladstone's attack was a mixture of astonishment and outrage. The usually sympathetic *Times* observed that as 'the professed enemy of Lord Beaconsfield . . . [Mr Gladstone] will perhaps not be expected to judge affairs in the same way as other people'. Gathorne Hardy, Disraeli's closest adviser and leader of the 'war party' in cabinet, mockingly compared the speech to volcanic lava that 'poured forth in pent-up force'. R. A. Cross, usually the most mild mannered of politicians, condemned Gladstone for engendering 'a lying spirit abroad'.

As for Disraeli, he said little in public, but in private he confided his outrage to Selina. 'What an exposure!' he proclaimed. 'The mask has fallen and instead of a pious Christian, we find a vindictive fiend who confesses he has, for a year and a half, been dodging and manoeuvring against an individual – because he was a successful rival!' And then, in an indication that, like Gladstone, he was coming to appreciate the importance of taking the debate to the country, he added: 'There has been a monster open-air meeting at Wolverhampton and resolutions in favour of HM Government carried at Sheffield. The [London] City meeting an event!'

These gatherings showed how popular opinion was swinging decisively behind Disraeli. Because Gladstone had so publicly identified himself as the prime minister's enemy, the more aggressive elements among Disraeli's supporters began to focus on roughing him up. It began when Gladstone was confronted by taunting 'Jingoists' on his regular walks in Hyde Park. This was soon followed by attacks on his home. 'Between four and six, three parties of the populace arrived here the first with cheers, the two others hostile,' he reported on 24 February. 'Windows were broken & much hooting. The last detachment was only kept away by mounted police in line across the street both ways.' A week later he and Catherine were forced out of their home, taking refuge at a neighbour's house. When crowds began threatening that property too, they were whisked away in a carriage accompanied by mounted police outriders.

In addition to physical attacks, there were others on his character. A campaign of anonymous letters at this time fuelled rumours about his relations with prostitutes. One of his accusers claimed that Gladstone had requested her to strip, perch on his knee and tell him the story of her fall. Through this means, the nameless victim claimed, he had become aroused and had sex with her (followed immediately afterwards by prayers). 'There is strange work behind the curtain if one could but get at it,' Gladstone pondered darkly as the stones, literal and metaphorical, rained down on him.

Nor was Disraeli immune from criticism, in particular that he was too soft in not immediately declaring war on Russia. 'What are you waiting for, Lord Beaconsfield,' shouted one pro-war supporter at a banquet. 'At this moment for the potatoes, Madam,' the prime minister shot back smoothly. More worryingly, Disraeli was receiving wild letters from the Queen urging war, and talking threateningly of abdication.

By the spring it was clear that the momentum of events was moving decisively away from Gladstone and towards Disraeli. In March, the Russians forced on the Turks the punitive Treaty of San Stefano, which would have destroyed Turkey as a European presence. Disraeli responded by ordering the British fleet to Constantinople, calling up the reserve and sending seven thousand Indian troops to Malta. Derby again resigned, but, as his close friendship with the Russian ambassador in London was attracting mutterings of treason, the loss was minimal. He was replaced as foreign secretary by the more impressive Salisbury, who had by now developed a profound if businesslike respect for Disraeli. Faced with the prospect of war, Russia backed off, and agreed to attend a great power congress in Berlin that summer. 'This is a great triumph for England,' Disraeli proclaimed, 'and betokens, I rather think, still greater.'

Kaiserhof Hotel, 11 June 1878

Just after eight o'clock in the evening Disraeli and Monty Corry arrived exhausted at the Berlin hotel that would be their home for the next six weeks. The journey from England had taken a leisurely four days, but for a gouty, asthmatic seventy-three-year-old who disliked travel it had been an ordeal. Determined to put in the performance of a lifetime, Disraeli settled down to recover his vitality for the arduous task ahead. Barely had he settled into his rooms when a message arrived from his host, Prince Bismarck, asking to see him. Disraeli considered pleading tiredness, but thought better of it. Here was an early opportunity to catch up with the German chancellor – the man who had unified Germany and was the heir to Metternich as continental Europe's foremost diplomatist.

Disraeli was astonished on first seeing Bismarck. They had not met for sixteen years. 'But that space of time did not seem adequate to produce the startling change which Lord B. observed in the chancellor's appearance,' he reported in the first of a series of gossipy letters to the Queen from Berlin. 'A tall, pallid man, with a wasp like waist, was now represented by an extremely stout person with a ruddy countenance, on which he is now growing a silvery beard.' Crucially, reported Disraeli, Bismarck remained 'frank and unaffected as before'.

This central relationship of the Congress of Berlin would quickly develop into genuine mutual admiration, liking and respect. For years afterwards Bismarck would point to three pictures on the wall in his office. 'There hangs the portrait of my Sovereign, there on the right that of my wife,' he would tell visitors, 'and on the left, there, that of Lord Beaconsfield.' Indisputable synergy existed between the two statesmen. Both men were skilled in the art of *realpolitik*. Neither had time for what they considered the moral bleating of those espousing humanitarian causes or an ethical foreign policy. Each was cynical yet romantic. Both revelled in flamboyant gestures and lofty statements, concerning themselves with grand strategy while minions worked out the details.

One more question of judgement drew them together in fraternal solidarity: each detested Gladstone. At a 'recklessly frank' private dinner alone with Bismarck's family during the Congress, the two men laid into their liberal antagonist. Disraeli prophesied that Gladstone would die in a monastery or a madhouse. Bismarck countered that, after an inevitable political implosion, he might create a sensation by 'going over' to the Roman Catholic Church. If Gladstone were a widower, the prince ventured, the pope would even more sensationally make him a cardinal. Such was Disraeli's delight at this talk that he defied the strictures of his doctors to smoke and drink late into the night with Bismarck, thus providing, he told Selina, 'the last blow to my shattered constitution'.

From the outset Disraeli was the sensation of the Congress of Berlin. There was authentic fascination in watching a statesman whose rise and career, not least as a Jew, had been so extraordinary. There literally was no one like him in Berlin. He broke with convention by addressing the Congress in English. The British ambassador, Lord Odo

Russell, had suggested this to him on the grounds that 'they know that they have here in you the greatest master of English oratory, and are looking forward to your speech in English as the intellectual treat of their lives'. No doubt Disraeli's execrable French also had something to do with the suggestion. Disraeli would surely have been delighted that this marked the beginning of English supplanting French as the first language of international diplomacy.

Recognising Berlin as the defining moment of his career, the PM also found new reserves of energy and vigour. 'This is a wondrous scene,' he told Selina happily, 'life in its highest form.' Night after night he attended receptions, banquets and parties. Throughout each day there were exhausting meetings and negotiations in almost unbearable heat. Although Disraeli left most of the technical negotiation to Lord Salisbury, he attended almost every session and no one doubted that all the important decisions were taken by him. There was much poring over gigantic maps and throwing up of hands in mock despair. Disraeli's most theatrical brinkmanship came when the Russians tried to backtrack on an agreement about the partition of Bulgaria. Disraeli let it be known that he had summoned a special train so that he might return to London to prepare for war.* The Russians caved in. 'That old Jew really means business,' Bismarck purred admiringly.

The Treaty of Berlin was signed in the Radziwill Palace on Saturday 13 July 1878. In another break with tradition, the name of Britain's principal signatory was accompanied by the term 'prime minister' for the first time. Few doubted that the treaty was a humiliation for the Russians. Tsar Alexander II later spoke bitterly of the Congress as 'a European coalition against Russia' and her aim to turn the Near East into a sphere of influence. The Ottoman Empire, while diminished and mortified, had been propped up once more, with each of the great powers gaining territory for their troubles. Crucially for Britain, its principal objective was achieved: the Russian navy had been kept out of the Mediterranean. And in addition Disraeli had won a nice strategic prize – Cyprus – with its fine harbours and proximity to Egypt, Syria and the proposed Baghdad railway. Disraeli told Selina's sister, Lady Chesterfield, that it was 'a Treaty of Peace of which the country will not be ashamed, and which will secure the tranquillity for a long time

---

* Prime minister Harold Macmillan would repeat his hero's trick during his historic visit to Moscow in 1959.

of regions in which we are deeply interested'. Peace, in fact, until 1914. ('We have got as good a settlement as could fairly be expected – without bloodshed,' wrote Salisbury perspicaciously, 'but we have not settled the Eastern Question. That will not be done for another fifty years to come.')

The Congress of Berlin had been a triumph for Disraeli. Bismarck summed it up in a legendary assessment: '*Der alte Jude, das ist der Mann!*' No wonder the Queen should have written to Disraeli to report that 'high and low are delighted', before adding what surely must have completed their shared pleasure, 'excepting Mr Gladstone, who is frantic'.

Port of Dover

It was nothing if not a hero's welcome. The steamer docked alongside Admiralty Pier on the afternoon of 16 July. A huge crowd had gathered under extravagant bunting. When Disraeli and Salisbury appeared, the throng burst into applause and loud cheering while the band struck up 'Home, Sweet Home'. On the quayside Disraeli, with Salisbury beside him, proclaimed: 'We have brought a peace, and we trust we have brought a peace with honour, and I trust that will now be followed by the prosperity of the country.' Peace, honour, prosperity: it had more than a ring of an electioneering slogan about it. And the phrase 'Peace with honour' would go down in history, until Neville Chamberlain sullied it in 1938 by using it to describe his Munich agreement with Hitler.

Together the two men travelled to London on the boat train, where they were met at Charing Cross by an even larger crowd. The Marquess of Abergavenny had organised the formal reception, bedecking the station with flags, shields, arches, trophies and extravagant displays by the Queen's florist. For all the contrivance, there could be no doubting the genuinely excited nature of the popular demonstrations as Disraeli, resplendent in his familiar long white coat, stepped off the train. He insisted that Salisbury join him in the open carriage that would take them to Downing Street through streets jammed with cheering, union flag-waving crowds shouting 'Duke of Cyprus!'. *The Times* recorded the following day, 'The compact black mass of heads in one line hundreds deep impressed the imagination most.' On the steps of No. 10, they were greeted by Sir Henry Ponsonby, private secretary to the Queen, bearing flowers from a grateful monarch to her now tearful first minister. Both Disraeli and Salisbury made short speeches to the crowd, with the prime minister repeating his 'peace with honour' line. Then another band struck up 'Rule, Britannia!' as they went inside. When the crowd would not leave, they appeared at a Downing Street window to wave once more (Disraeli theatrically, the reserved Salisbury awkwardly). As the multitude slowly dispersed, Disraeli prepared to dash down to Osborne to receive the appreciation of the Queen in person. She would offer him the Order of the Garter, which he accepted on the condition that Salisbury should receive it too, and a dukedom, which, curiously, he declined.

In the midst of such a triumph, the proclaimed national champion chose this moment to answer his great rival's personal attack in Oxford at the beginning of the year. In the House of Lords at the end of July he condemned Gladstone for having 'indulged in criticisms complete with the most offensive epithets' such as calling him 'a dangerous devilish character'. Then, at a Knightsbridge banquet in his honour, Disraeli delivered a full-frontal onslaught on Gladstone that drew both gasps and cheers from his astonished audience. Gladstone had condemned the 'insane covenant' on Cyprus. 'Which do you believe most likely to enter an insane convention, a body of English gentlemen honoured by the favour of their sovereign and the confidence of their fellow-subjects, managing your affairs for five years, I hope with prudence, and not altogether without success,' he asked, ' or a sophistical rhetorician, inebriated with the exuberance of his own verbosity, and gifted with an egotistical imagination that can at all times command interminable and inconsistent series of arguments to malign an opponent and to glorify himself?'

Gladstone was incandescent on reading a report of the speech in *The Times.* He angrily fired off a rare letter to Disraeli demanding chapter and verse on when he had 'maligned' him or 'described you as a dangerous devilish character'. The prime minister replied coldly on 30 July, returning to the third person form of address that he had used during their 1852 spat about the chancellor's robe. He could not provide 'times and places' because this would 'involve a research over a period of two years and a half, during which Mr Gladstone, to use his own expressions at Oxford, has been counterworking "by day and by night, by week, and month by month" the purpose of Lord Beaconsfield'. But he was happy to provide some examples, so as not to appear 'wanting in becoming courtesy', including that it was 'Lord

Beaconsfield . . . by whom "the great name of England had been degraded and debased"'.

Gladstone rode the punch and that same day threw another of his own. In the Commons, he spoke for two and a half hours in an extended critique of Disraeli's foreign policy. Beforehand he had characteristically been unwell and unable to sleep properly. 'I was in body much below par,' he wrote afterwards, 'but put on the steam perforce.' His principal charge was that at Berlin, both Disraeli and Salisbury had betrayed the British diplomatic tradition. It was a clever attack in terms that might easily have come from Disraeli himself. 'I say, sir, that in the congress of the great powers, the voice of England has not been heard in unison with the institutions, the history and the character of England,' he charged. 'I do affirm that it was [Britain's] part to take the side of liberty; and I do also affirm that as a matter of fact they took the side of servitude.' His conclusion was stark: 'I think we have lost very greatly indeed the sympathy and respect of the nations of Europe . . . and consequently our moral position in the world!'

Few shared his conclusion. Both houses of parliament acclaimed the treaty. Lord Hartington's approach could hardly have been more different from that of Gladstone, offering what Disraeli described happily as 'a string of congratulatory regrets'. The thoroughbred Duke of Richmond presented Disraeli with an heirloom Garter badge (which he was now entitled to wear) as a mark of esteem. The Corporation of London gave him the freedom of the City. Even Cardinal Newman, for so long suspicious of the prime minister, professed his admiration. 'As to Disraeli's fireworks,' he told an astonished Lord Blachford, 'I confess I am much dazzled with it, and wish it well.' Throughout the country there was a brisk trade in commemorative mugs, jugs and plates, usually emblazoned with the words 'Peace and Honour'. In one of those great missed opportunities lamented by subsequent generations, the artist James McNeill Whistler asked, but was turned down, to paint Disraeli's portrait. 'We were the two artists together – recognizing each other at a glance. "If I sit to anyone, it will be to you, Mr Whistler" were Disraeli's last words as he left me at the gate,' Whistler bemoaned after their meeting, 'and then he sat to Millais!'

Nothing it seemed, could spoil Disraeli's sense of pleasure that summer. Or at least only one thing: a trip to see Gilbert and Sullivan's new musical smash, 'some nonsense, which everybody is going to see – Parasol or Pinafore'. His low expectations were not disappointed.

'Except at Wycombe Fair in my youth,' he told Selina disgustedly after-wards, 'I have never seen anything so bad as *Pinafore*.'

With everyone expecting Disraeli to call a general election soon to capitalise on his success at Berlin, it might have caused him a certain ironic amusement, had he not dozed off during the performance, that some of his most jingoistic supporters were already proclaiming his virtues in lusty Gilbertian fashion:

> For he is an Englishman,
> And he himself hath said it,
> And it's greatly to his credit,
> That he is an Englishman!

More satisfying to Disraeli was the verdict of the Queen's daughter, Crown Princess Victoria of Prussia, who told him that he should feel proud of 'realizing all the dreams of [his] life and castles not in the air'.

'Pretty good!' Disraeli judged, before departing for Hughenden and a much anticipated rest.

22

Midlothian

Wīlliam Gladstone sat in the 'Temple of Peace' on his birthday composing a journal entry in his familiar strong, right-slanting handwriting. Sleet hammered against the window-panes. The weather that winter had been of the bitterest kind. Gladstone had arrived from London just before Christmas in thick, freezing fog. Snow and ice had provided fun for the children skating on the pond, but Gladstone's favourite physical exercise – tree felling – had been frustratingly off limits.

'Sixty nine years of age!' he reflected. 'One year only from the limit of ordinary life prolonged to its natural goal!' In the past three years, instead of 'unbinding and detaching' himself from public affairs, they 'have immersed me almost more than at any former time'. This commitment had but one explanation: '[it] appears to me to carry the marks of the will of God.' His health had been 'so peculiarly sustained'. During his great public speeches, he had felt 'as it were upheld in an unusual manner'. Surely, he asked, 'was not all this for a purpose?'.

Gladstone's sensation of God's purpose for him was particularly acute in those freezing last days of 1878. He had before him a significant offer – one that appealed both to his vanity and sense of daring. If accepted, he understood only too well that it would put him at the eye of the political storm when the next general election came.

Despite the shows of affection that Greenwich Liberals had given him, not least during the Bulgarian agitation, Gladstone had never warmed to his south-east London constituency. The fact that in the last election he had come in second behind a Conservative drinks distiller ('more like a defeat than a victory') had wounded his pride. His Oxford University constituency had been difficult but glamorous. The seat in Lancashire had been urban and defiantly modern. Greenwich was none of those things. Having resolved not to contest the seat at the next election, he began to look around for a new and more congenial constituency. 'Under anything like ordinary circumstances my choice would have been, after having served already in 11 Parliaments . . . the least conspicuous and most tranquil seat which it might be within my option to obtain,' Gladstone reflected. Perhaps a seat like his first, at Newark, where a local nobleman still held sway, or else Leeds, which was a Liberal safe seat. 'But the circumstances of the present juncture are far from ordinary,' he went on in typical fashion. 'At no period of my public life have the issues awaiting the judgment of the nation been of such profound importance.' God's purpose for William Gladstone was never likely to be humdrum.

The offer before him was to contest the constituency of Edinburghshire, popularly known at Midlothian. It seemed, on the face of it, an unlikely place for Gladstone to attempt to reassert his authority over the Liberal party and the country, particularly when compared with Leeds, the other constituency under his consideration. While Leeds had almost fifty thousand electors, many of them industrial workers, Midlothian had only 3620 voters. Leeds was a seat that had benefited from the 1867 Reform Act, while Midlothian was a battle-ground for influence between two of the most powerful Scottish aristocratic families – the Duke of Buccleuch and the Earl of Rosebery – operating within the extremely restricted Scottish county franchise. In the end, Gladstone kept Leeds up his sleeve for his son Herbert, and committed himself to campaign in person for the Midlothian seat. What it offered was a sophisticated, metropolitan environment, steeped in the liberal intellectual tradition of the Scottish Enlightenment, that also had the potential for large crowds of working (albeit disenfranchised) men and women. The attractions of Beaconsfieldism had made little impact in Scotland outside Glasgow; that suggested potential for Gladstonianism.

The youthful Lord Rosebery – already much spoken of as a future prime minister – had been crucial to Gladstone's decision. He was fascinated by modern electioneering, particularly in the United States. In 1873 he had visited the Democratic National Convention in New York, which provided 'a great moral spectacle and a great political lesson'. It was an experience, he convinced Gladstone, which could be translated to Midlothian. Visual flamboyance and moral purpose would combine to create a new kind of demotic leader. British politics, quite literally, would have seen nothing like it.

Gladstone's satisfaction in having Rosebery as his campaign manager was enhanced by the fact that the earl had been a protégé of Disraeli since 1865. Rosebery's combination of flair, breeding, cynical wit and literary discernment was a perfect match for the Tory leader's tastes. Rosebery, more than forty years younger, had an appealing knack for flattery without obsequiousness. Meeting Disraeli at the 1875 St Leger at the Doncaster racecourse, he 'regretted that Phorphorus did not run (vide *Sybil*)'. 'You are my only literary friend!' exclaimed the delighted prime minister. Disraeli had hoped to convince him to join the Tories, but Rosebery's Whig family tradition made this unthinkable. Yet even during the height of the Bulgarian crisis, he sought him out, 'was very affectionate, calling me "dear child" and pressing my hand against his heart. He talked much about Mr Gladstone: "his character baffles me".' It was a judgement that Rosebery would soon come to share, but not before he had orchestrated Gladstone's most vehement and sustained attack on his great rival.

The nature of that contest – with its cheering fans, newspaper 'match' reports, codified rules, die-hard team allegiances and star players – shared something of the craze for organised sporting competition that was sweeping Victorian Britain. These events attracted huge crowds and generated passionate enthusiasm throughout the land. Important matches were organised to coincide with workers' time off. When Bank Holidays were instituted in 1871, a full sporting programme quickly established itself as a quintessential part of the leisure experience. The Football Association organised the inaugural FA Cup final in 1872. The first England–Scotland rugby international match had taken place the previous year. A tennis championship at Wimbledon began in 1877. England played Australia at cricket for the first time in 1876/77. Perhaps most appropriately of all, the Marquess of Queensberry had published his 'Rules for the Sport of Boxing' in 1867 – the year before Gladstone and Disraeli each became prime minister. Rule Six stated: 'No seconds or any other person to be allowed in the ring during the rounds.' Neither heavyweight in this political bout would have wanted it any other way.

It is unlikely that sport was much on Gladstone's mind when, on 30 January, he finally accepted the invitation to stand. Yet his statement to voters of Midlothian, reproduced in *The Times*, made it clear that the contest would need a result as conclusive as any FA Cup tie. 'The particular subjects before us, which separately are grave enough, all resolve themselves into one comprehensive question,' he declared, 'the question whether this is or is not the way in which the country wishes to be governed.'

John Bright was staying at Hawarden on the day that letter was sent. 'On a crisis he [Bright] said the entire Liberal party will require you to come forward,' Gladstone recorded. The new candidate for Midlothian had demurred, but understood well enough that he was on the threshold of 'a great shifting of events and parts'. Despite the enthusiasm generated by Disraeli's triumph at Berlin, Gladstone detected another change of mood in the country. 'The pot is beginning to boil,' he confidently predicted to Granville. Disraeli was heading for a 'great smash', perhaps more devastating than the humiliating one he himself had suffered in 1874.

'The terrible disaster has shaken me to the centre,' Disraeli complained to Selina's sister Lady Chesterfield on 13 February 1879, 'and what increases the grief is that I have not only to endure it, but to sustain others and to keep a bold front before an unscrupulous enemy.'

The 'unscrupulous enemy' was Gladstone. The 'terrible disaster' was perhaps Britain's most infamous military humiliation of modern times: the defeat at Isandhlwana by the Zulus. It was one of a number of calamities that were mounting up for Disraeli after the triumph of Berlin.

Shortly after returning from the Congress, Disraeli had briefly considered going to the polls to take advantage of his popularity. The matter was considered at a tense cabinet meeting on 10 August 1878, 'which lasted more than three hours – the longest I ever knew', but in the end the election was put on ice. It just seemed too undignified, and, with the parliament only four and a half years into a seven-year session, unnecessarily precipitate. It turned out to be a missed opportunity.

In 1879 three calamities befell Disraeli, none of which was particularly his fault. In South Africa, the overzealous high commissioner, Sir Bartle Frere, attempted to subdue the Zulus, which led to the mortifying defeat at Isandhlwana. This was followed later in the year by another overseas embarrassment, this time on the north-west frontier of India, when the British envoy in Kabul was brutally murdered. British power was quickly reasserted in both places, but each humiliation contributed to a sense that Disraeli's imperial policy was provoking unnecessary conflicts with questionable results. And to make matters worse, those battles were a drain on the Exchequer at a time when Britain could barely afford it. In addition to disconcerting reverses abroad, the world economy was entering a period of economic depression. Profits and employment were plummeting. The disastrous 1879 harvest was the worst of the century. The effects of a slump in trade and two costly wars contributed to an alarming growth in the government's budget deficit. Before an election this could hardly be met by taxation, which left only increased borrowing and a dip into the sinking fund. 'I think the agricultural bankruptcy must finish us,' Disraeli confided to Lady Bradford. All in all, he concluded at the end of the 1879 parliamentary session, 'we have had a terrible time of it.'

Not that he was going to let it show. In an audacious performance that autumn at the Lord Mayor's banquet in the Guildhall, Disraeli again raised the imperial banner on behalf of his party and government. 'They are men who are not ashamed of the Empire which their ancestors created, because I know that they are not ashamed of the noblest of human sentiments decried by philosophers – the sentiment of patriotism,' he defiantly proclaimed. 'One of the greatest of Romans, when asked what were his politics, replied, *Imperium et Libertas*. That would not make a bad programme for a British ministry. It is one from which Her Majesty's advisers do not shrink!'

It was a magnificent performance. 'You could not listen to a sentence without perceiving that he had a consummate knowledge of the art of speaking in public, and consummate cleverness in making the most of his knowledge,' wrote the admiring *New York Tribune* reporter George Smalley. 'What is genuine in the man is his intellect and his courage.' He was also aware of the personal cost to Disraeli. The PM had been dynamic, masterful and poised that evening. But Smalley had been waiting at the entrance when the great man arrived. He witnessed the supreme effort it took for Disraeli to marshal his strength. 'I could see him pull himself together and compose the muscles of his face till the desired expression was attained,' he recorded. 'A strange fire burned in his eyes. The jaw and lips were set fast . . . No man's face was more full of energy, no step firmer than his.' The image belied the unhealthy reality. 'The fogs and frosts of this harsh November have terribly knocked me down,' Disraeli complained to Selina.

It was a bad time to be in a poor physical state. In the Guildhall speech, Disraeli had caused 'much amusement' when he commented that he fully expected to have the honour of speaking at the following year's banquet. Everyone understood the sly dig. For Gladstone, in ferociously good health and brimming with visceral energy, had announced the opening of his campaign for the Midlothian seat. He had been suspiciously quiet throughout 1878. This was the beginning of his most sustained attack on 'Beaconsfieldism'.

'I have never gone through a more extraordinary day,' Gladstone wrote on 24 November 1879. And it had been a truly remarkable twelve hours. The Gladstones had left Liverpool station just before nine that morning on a special train to Edinburgh. At stops along the way, crowds had gathered to see the famous statesman, who thrilled each gathering with a rousing speech. The weather was biting cold – another fierce winter – but Gladstone stood in the open air, bare-headed, to harangue them on Disraeli's iniquities. At each stop the crowd was bigger than the last, as news sped down the telegraph that an 'event' was on its way.

The train finally pulled into Edinburgh shortly before five o'clock. Gladstone's sponsor at Midlothian, the mercurial Lord Rosebery, had organised an astonishing display of support. Every inch of the station was jammed with flag-waving, cheering supporters. Outside more crowds excitedly pushed forward to see Gladstone as he was driven through the streets in a torchlight procession. There were triumphal arches and glowing fairy lanterns. Celebratory fireworks exploded in the clear night air. 'The scene even to the West end of the City was extraordinary, both from the numbers and the enthusiasm,' Gladstone recorded happily on arriving at Rosebery's splendid Dalmeny House, seven miles west of the city. It had been a remarkable beginning to what would turn out to be an even more incredible fortnight.

Everywhere Gladstone went huge crowds followed. For one event in Glasgow where six thousand seats were available almost fifty thousand supporters applied for tickets. People travelled from all over Scotland to hear him speak. The biggest gathering was at Edinburgh's Waverley Market, where he addressed more than twenty thousand euphoric working men and women. 'People were continually handed out over heads who had fainted and were as if dead,' Gladstone noted afterwards. Those who endured heard him in hushed respect before cheering him to the skies (while Mrs Gladstone theatrically wiped her husband's brow with an enormous handkerchief). 'It has been the same story over and over again,' Gladstone's daughter Mary wrote halfway through the tour. 'All Scotland is panting for a look at him.'

Gladstone's message was a simple one, reiterated in a dozen different ways. The country would have a clear choice: Disraeli or Gladstone. 'The speeches were rallying battle cries, not sermons,' wrote John Morley, who was present in Glasgow, 'and everybody knew the great invisible antagonist with whom the orator before them was with all his might contending.' This was not just a question of rivalry, but of deep-rooted differences of principle and practice. Time and again Gladstone repeated that Beaconsfieldism was malignant in every aspect, not least foreign affairs and financial management. 'Indictment against the Government – abroad – everywhere!' he had scribbled in his speaking notes. On 25 November Gladstone denounced Disraeli for chasing 'false phantoms of glory'. Now it was time for 'every one of us [to] resolve in his inner conscience, before God and before man . . . that he will exempt himself from every participation in what he believes to be mischievous and ruinous misdeeds'. On 26 November he urged a wildly cheering audience not to let Disraeli's 'appeals to national pride blind you to the dictates of justice'. The next day he denounced the prime minister for violating every principle of morality by betraying the country and endangering world peace in wanton disregard of 'all the most fundamental interests of Christian society'. In Waverley Market he celebrated this 'festival of freedom', telling them: 'It is no light cause that brought together . . . this great ocean of life.' In Glasgow, where if anything he was received with even greater passion – 'an overpowering day' – he took office as rector of the university by pouring scorn on an aphorism of the previous incumbent. Disraeli had quipped 'nothing succeeds like success'. Gladstone begged to differ. 'Effort, gentlemen,' he declared, 'honest, manful, humble effort succeeds, by its reflected action upon character, especially in youth, better than success.' It did not stop the students giving him a thunderous reception.

At another Glasgow speech, Gladstone denounced Disraeli's global policy as 'pestilent' in every corner of the world. In Afghanistan he had driven 'mother and children forth from their homes to perish in the snow'. In southern Africa, he had slaughtered ten thousand Zulus 'for no other offence than their attempt to defend against your artillery with their naked bodies, their hearths and homes, their wives and families'. The prime minister was a disgrace, leading the people down a road 'which plunges into suffering, discredit, and dishonour'. Surely, he asked, it was better to take another path, one that 'leads a free and high-minded people towards the blessed ends of prosperity and justice, and of liberty and peace'. The reaction to this speech was so intense, Gladstone contentedly recorded, that 'the departure from Glasgow was *royal*'.

Every stage of the Midlothian tour was played out the next day across breakfast tables throughout Britain. All the serious newspapers carried extensive reports of the major speeches, adding their own written sketches that evoked the mood of the occasion. Most of England was under heavy snow, with many roads impassable, so reading reports from Edinburghshire provided, for many, welcome (if hardly light) relief. 'The event of the week has been Gladstone's Midlothian campaign,' wrote Lord Derby, shivering at Keston on 30 November. 'He has spoken a good-sized octavo volume, on a moderate computation, within five days: addressing enormous and enthusiastic audiences, and altogether making a deep impression not only on the local public, but throughout the country.'

The success of the Midlothian campaign exhilarated Gladstone. When he returned to Hawarden on 8 December, he immediately sat down to record in his diary the extent of his achievement, detailing exactly how many had heard him speak:

1879.
Mon. Nov. 24

1. Carlisle	500
2. Hawick	4,000
3. Galashiels	8,000

Tues. 25

4. Edinburgh Music Hall	2,500
5. Edinburgh City Hall	250

Wed. 26

6. Dalkeith Corn Exch.	3,500
7. Dalkeith Ladies & Committee	750

Thurs. 27

8. West Calder Assembly	3,500
9. Dalmeny, after dinner	50

Fri. 28

10. Dalmeny, Leith Address	50

Sat. 29
11. Edinburgh Corn Exchange   5,000
12. Edinburgh Waverley Market   20,000

Mon. Dec. 1
13. Inverkeithing Address   500
14. Dunfermline ditto   3,000
15. Perth, Freedom   1,500
16. Perth, Open Air, Addresses   4,000
17. Aberfeldie, Address   500

Tues. Dec. 2
18. Killin Address, Taymouth   50

Thurs. Dec. 4
19. Sir J. Watson's, after dinner   30

Fri. Dec. 5
20. Inaugural Address Glasgow   5,000
21. University Luncheon   150
22. St Andrew's Hall   6,500
23. City Hall   2,500

Sat. Dec. 6
24. Motherwell, Addresses   2,000
25. Hamilton Freedom (Dalziel)   100

Mon. Dec. 8
26. Carlisle, Station   1,000
27. Preston, Station   2,000
28. Wigan, outside ditto   6,000
29. Warrington, Station   1,000
30. Chester, Procession   3,000

     86,930

There were speeches running from six or eight minutes up to an hour & three quarters. There were some shorter addresses to crowds at stations, and acknowledgments of votes of thanks. Those above given occupied about 15½ hours.

No wonder, then, that Gladstone's niece, Lucy Cavendish, who was staying at Hawarden, should have recorded with amused affection in her diary that for the first time in her experience 'the Great Man' seemed to be 'a little *personally* elated'.

Gladstone's campaign had been followed with varying degrees of enthusiasm or disgust. Derby noted that his 'progress . . . has been more than royal'. The young Morley was galvanised by a 'campaign [that] had soul in it'. Gathorne Hardy (by now Lord Cranbrook) thought Gladstone 'disgracefully bitter'. Lord George Hamilton, whose brother was the Conservative candidate in Midlothian, denounced Gladstone as a 'man of high strung, nervous temperament [whose] verbosity [is] a positive danger'. The Queen complained that Gladstone's behaviour was nothing less than a 'series of violent, passionate invective against and abuse of Lord Beaconsfield'. One who agreed with her was Mary Ann Evans – the novelist George Eliot – who was 'disgusted with the venom of the Liberal speeches from Gladstone'.

Perhaps the only person who affected not to have paid the slightest regard to Gladstone's Midlothian visit was Lord Beaconsfield himself. 'I have not read a single line of all this row,' he contemptuously told Selina. 'What a waste of powder and shot! Because all this was planned on the wild assumption that Parliament was going to be dissolved.' To Cranbrook he again feigned indifference: 'It is certainly a relief that this drenching rhetoric has at length ceased – but I have never read a word of it.'

This insouciance was a mistake. He hesitated for almost two months before making an enfeebled attempt to strike back. He had convinced the Queen to add lustre to his agenda by opening parliament in person, but the spectacle only served to confirm the sense of a broken and vulnerable government. Disraeli was so ill that he was unable to take part in the ceremony. 'I am as shaky as a man can be, who has been shut up for two weeks,' he complained to Selina. He was not the only one. His government provided a litany of physical decrepitude. 'Salisbury is confined to his room at Hatfield and must do no work,' Disraeli grumbled. 'The lord chancellor [Earl Cairns] attacked by asthma for the first time was so frightened that he rushed to Bournemouth, where he found the fog blacker than here. The chancellor of the exchequer [Northcote] is in bed with influenza . . . Where John Manners's broken bones are I hardly know – but if there had been a cabinet today *six* would have been absent.' He dragged himself wearily back to the Lords to give a wretched performance during the Queen's Speech debate. 'What I did say, I said badly,' he admitted disconsolately, 'but when you have been shut up for more than a fortnight it is difficult to conceive how the nervous system is affected, when you re-enter the world.'

A glum cabinet agreed at the start of their next meeting that an immediate general election was out of the question. Under the electoral rules, the government had the maximum of a year to run. Their best option was to hold out for as long as possible – perhaps until the autumn – in the hope that something might turn up to re-energise them.

That 'something' happened much earlier than any of them could possibly have contemplated. In fact only minutes after cabinet had decided not to call an election, word came that the party had unexpectedly won a by-election in Southwark. Ministers were thunderstruck. This was a seat with a long Liberal tradition, which they should not have won. Disraeli banged his hand on the table in triumph, which uncharacteristic lack of restraint prompted a great burst of laughter. Fast on the heels of the telegram announcing the news came another (with accompanying Valentine gift) from the Queen. 'I am greatly rejoiced at the victory at Southwark,' she trilled. 'It shows what the feeling of the country is.' Back at Hawarden, Gladstone could only lament that 'Southwark is a disgrace as well as a defeat'.

Buoyed by such unexpected news, and sensing a favourable political wind, Disraeli seized the opportunity to call a snap election. It took all but his closest confidants by surprise. 'I hear that the scene in the Commons was absurd enough,' wrote Lord Derby on 8 March when the announcement was made. 'Forty or fifty members jumping from their seats at the same moment to rush to the telegraph office, which they besieged.'

Much of the excitement was due to the fact that most MPs had little or no idea about which party would triumph. 'Sober men on both sides acknowledge that the event is quite uncertain,' recorded the Whig Lord Kimberley. 'Sanguine men prophecy each according to his wishes and party. On the whole what seems least improbable is that there will be something like a tie: that is, the Tories will be no more than half the whole House.' Among those 'sober men' were the nominal leaders of the Liberal party. Lord Hartington told Sir Charles Dilke that he believed there was 'much doubt as to the prospects of the election'. Lord Granville confided to the pitiful Derby, who was on the verge of defecting to the Liberals, that 'all is uncertain'. Both men thought it might end up 'a tie'.

It was not a view shared by their troublesome former chief. Gladstone was certainly ready. 'Dissolution announced' was his bland diary entry on the day the election was called. His reading matter for the previous week suggested that he had already been expecting the unexpected from Disraeli. P. W. Clayden's caustic Liberal indictment, *England Under Lord Beaconsfield*, would be used extensively during this next phase of the Midlothian campaign. Gladstone also believed that the national campaign he had been running since 1876 – 'to counterwork the purpose of Lord Beaconsfield' – was on the verge of triumph. Disraeli, he believed, would be swept away on a tide of popular revulsion.

And God was with him. For this election would be won on 'what He knows to be the cause of Truth, Liberty, and Justice'.

Early in the battle, Lord Cranbrook ran into Disraeli leaving Westminster. The day was pleasant, so together they walked in the sunshine discussing Conservative estimates for the coming election. 'He was cheerful about our prospects,' Cranbrook wrote afterwards, 'but had his doubts . . . which surprised me. He often has the means of judging which others have not.' Either way, there was very little that each man could do. The rules prevented peers from electioneering, so for the first time in their political careers neither was in the thick of the action. In fact it was a strategic calamity, for the party's three most powerful hitters – Lords Beaconsfield, Cranbrook and Salisbury – were kept on the side-lines throughout the campaign. Sir Stafford Northcote, leader in the House of Commons, was a capable administrator, but he lacked both charisma and energy to rally the Conservatives nationwide.

Disraeli had come to power in 1874 on a programme of moderate social reform wedded to 'a little more energy in foreign affairs'. Few, not even Gladstone, would have doubted that their overseas policy had been 'a little' more animated. Even on domestic issues, Disraeli could claim to have delivered on his modest promise. Measures such as the Trades Union Acts, Artisans Dwellings Act, Sale of Food and Drink Act and Public Health Act had laid down benchmarks for the enhancement of national life, particularly in urban areas, and made funds available for their implementation (albeit at the discretion of local councils). These were not radical measures, but they did show that the Conservatives were engaging seriously with questions of how to improve the condition of the people.

Disraeli's only contribution to the campaign – an open letter to the Duke of Marlborough on 8 March – was a curiously lacklustre and poorly written defence of this record. To general incomprehension, much of the letter concentrated on Ireland. Most commentators recognised this as a clumsy attempt to rally anti-Irish sentiment in the crucial English marginal seats, particularly cities such as Manchester. Only at the end did Disraeli hit his stride. Like Gladstone, he declared the election to be a pivotal one. The British people had a straightforward decision to make about the direction of policy at home and abroad. 'Rarely in this century has there been an occasion more critical,' he declared. 'The power of England and the peace of Europe largely depend on the verdict of the country . . . May [the national voice] return to Westminster a parliament not unworthy of the power of England and resolved to maintain it!'

Disraeli retired to the country once serious campaigning began. Lord Salisbury put Hatfield House at his disposal (along with several cases of 1870 Château Margaux, 'because I mentioned once my detestation of hosts who give you an inferior claret at dinner'). So Disraeli surrendered himself to fate, the will of the people and the delights of Salisbury's wine cellar.

'Both sides have now placed their men and both are at the mercy of the Ballot, which baffles estimates,' he wrote evenly to Lady Chesterfield. 'The seed is sown and we must await the harvest.'

While Disraeli waited quietly at Hatfield, Gladstone was on the charge. He left London for Scotland on 16 March to resume his Midlothian campaign. It became the event of the election.

As the train waited that morning at King's Cross station, thousands gathered excitedly on the platform to cheer Gladstone off. It was a scene repeated again and again on the long journey to Edinburgh. At Grantham a crowd of more than two thousand greeted him. At York, it was six thousand. The scene in Newcastle was so chaotic that no one could even estimate the numbers. Gladstone gave a little speech at every place the train stopped. Each was heard in respectful silence and followed by a great ovation. When he finally arrived in Edinburgh, 'the wonderful scene of November was exactly renewed'.

For the next fortnight Gladstone made another frenetic campaigning tour around Scotland, demanding everywhere that voters deliver the verdict 'Guilty!' against Disraeli. These speeches were not aimed just at the three and a half thousand voters of Edinburghshire: this was a message to the national audience by the self-proclaimed champion of the people. 'I am sorry to say we cannot reckon on the aristocracy!' he proclaimed in West Calder on 2 April. (So much for Lords Granville and Hartington, not to mention his host, Lord Rosebery.) 'We cannot reckon upon the wealth of the country, nor upon the rank of the country . . . We must set them down among our most determined foes! But gentlemen, above all these, and behind all these, there is the nation itself. And this great trial is now proceeding before the nation!'

The speech in West Calder was his last of the campaign. 'And so ends the second series of the speeches in which I have hammered with all my little might at the fabric of the present Tory power,' Gladstone wrote in his diary that evening.

Voting had already begun.

The thrust of the result did not take long. At Hatfield that same night Disraeli sat up with Monty Corry, who was by now virtually a surrogate son. Corry would later recall that the prime minister was unruffled, almost serene, as news filtered through. It quickly became apparent that the Conservatives were going down to a crushing defeat. At seventy-five, Disraeli well understood that this was the end. He was surrendering power for the last time. He even seemed to welcome it. The physical strain of government had become almost unbearable. Lord Barrington soon reported that the chief 'was not sorry to have some rest, and pass the spring and summer in the woods of Hughenden, which he had never been able to do, and longed for'. His only apparent irritation was the certain knowledge that in the next few weeks those looking for honours would pester him. 'It is the last and least glorious exercise of power,' he told Selina in disgust, 'and will be followed, which is the only compensation, by utter neglect and isolation.'

Once the election result became clear – Liberals 347, Conservatives 240 and Irish nationalists 65 – Disraeli, in fact, seemed to have only one source of genuine bitterness. 'Lord B. spoke very strongly against Gladstone,' wrote Barrington, 'and said his conduct in "chucking up the sponge" as Leader, and spouting all over the country, like an irresponsible demagogue, was wholly inexcusable in a man who was a statesman.'

In addition to creating peers and baronets in those last weeks of power, Disraeli set about making life as difficult as possible for his great adversary. As Lord Derby shrewdly observed, 'hatred of Gladstone will make him fight on to the last'.

George Street, Edinburgh

Gladstone looked from his window on to the scene below. Outside more than fifteen thousand people had congregated to cheer his success. When the new MP emerged on to the balcony he was given a rapturous reception. Earlier that evening of 5 April, his electoral agent, Mr Reid, who prided himself on personally knowing every single elector (and their voting intentions), had called to announce the result: Gladstone 1579, Lord Dalkeith 1368. 'You will see that your two great series of speeches may have changed six votes since the estimate I gave you before you set foot in the constituency,' Reid pompously reminded him. 'Quite satisfactory,' replied Gladstone coolly. In reality, he was electrified by events. 'Wonderful, and nothing less, has been the disposing guiding hand of God in all this matter,' he wrote breathlessly in his diary. And in an entry loaded with double meaning, Gladstone added with relish: 'Finished *England Under Lord B.*'

Gladstone returned to Hawarden the next day, where he stayed for the next twelve days. His state of euphoria barely subsided. 'All our heads are still in a whirl from the great events of the last fortnight, which have given joy, I am convinced, to the large majority of the civilized world,' he told the Duke of Argyll. Not the least of his delights was that he had achieved a personal victory over Disraeli. That the defeat of his arch-rival was likely to be permanent made it all the more remarkable. 'The downfall of Beaconsfieldism is like the vanishing of some vast magnificent castle in an Italian romance,' he wrote. 'It is too big, however, to be all taken in at once.'

Each day brought hundreds of letters. Many were simple congratulations. Others were increasingly frustrated inquiries from Gladstone's own party about his intentions. The election was seen nationally as Gladstone's victory. The public wanted him to lead. Even most politicians expected him to take first place in the new government. 'All parties wish it for various reasons,' judged Derby. 'The radicals, sincerely and simply, for they consider G. as their leader; the Conservatives because they think his nomination will frighten the Whigs, and divide the party; the Whigs (not all but a majority) because, danger for danger, they think it is better that G. should feel the responsibility and be put under the restraints of office than that he should exercise a nearly absolute power over the parliamentary majority, and so over the cabinet, without having any account to give, or any colleagues to consult.'

The difficulty was that Hartington and Granville, despite being given little or no credit for the election victory, remained the nominal leaders of the winning party. The question, then, of who would be prime minister would remain frustratingly unclear for much of the rest of April 1880. Five days after Gladstone's victory at Midlothian, Lord Wolverton arrived at Hawarden as an emissary from the party leadership to test the waters. The question, tentatively put, was whether or not Gladstone would serve under either Hartington or Granville. 'I am stunned,' Gladstone recorded in his diary.

He was less blunt directly to Wolverton, but his meaning could hardly have been clearer. 'My labours as an Individual cannot set me up as a Pretender,' he explained. 'If they [Hartington and Granville] should on surveying their position see fit to apply to me, there is only one form and ground of application, so far as I see, which could be seriously entertained by me.' Certainly Gladstone would come out of retirement: but only if asked to become prime minister.

So it was that when, on 19 April, Gladstone finally took the train to London, his fate remained unclear.

'I vaguely feel that this journey is a plunge, out of an atmosphere of peace into an element of disturbance,' he wrote during the early hours. 'May He who has of late so wonderfully guided, guide me still in the critical days about to come.'

23

Falconet

Victoria's private secretary, Henry Ponsonby, hovered outside the rooms of the holidaying Queen in a state of anxious delight. In his hand was a telegram from the prime minister, Benjamin Disraeli, reporting that the government had lost the general election. Ponsonby by now despised the 'oriental' Disraeli – 'He is not one of us' – and would be glad to see the back of him. The prime minister's ceaseless flattery had constantly undermined his own influence at court. More than once he had suffered the indignity of the Queen sending Lady Ely to tell him, 'She wants you to like him.' Now Disraeli would get his comeuppance. To add to Ponsonby's satisfaction, there was also a tantalising prospect that William Gladstone, with whom he enjoyed excellent relations, might return to the premiership. Only one aspect of this new situation was disagreeable to the private secretary: he had to deliver the news to the Queen.

Her reaction was one of predictable fury and hysteria. 'Some of the language used,' Ponsonby said afterwards, was unrepeatable. Most of her anger was directed at Gladstone. She screamed that she would 'sooner abdicate than send for or have any communication with that half-mad firebrand who would soon ruin everything and be a dictator.' He would never, ever, be prime minister again. 'Others may submit to his democratic rule,' she howled, '*but not the Queen.*' As to Disraeli, her sense of loss was immediate and overwhelming. 'The grief to her of having to part with the kindest and most devoted as well as one of the wisest ministers the Queen has ever had is not to be told,' she protested. Writing immediately to him, she adopted the first person to pour out her disappointment and anger. 'I am shocked and ashamed at what has happened,' she wrote bitterly. And she knew whom to blame. It was 'Mr Gladstone, who has done so much mischief'.

When Victoria saw Disraeli on her return to England a week later, she 'thought him very low'. He officially offered his resignation on 20 April. It prompted another outburst from the Queen. 'What can be more cruel than for a female sovereign no longer young, severely tried – without a husband or any *one* person on whose help (when her valued minister leaves her) she can securely rest – to have to take those people who have done all they could to vilify and weaken her government?' she complained. '*Can* she have confidence in them?'

Perhaps to cheer them both up, Victoria launched a further tirade against the object of their mutual loathing. 'It [is] impossible for me to send for Mr Gladstone,' she fumed. His attacks had been a 'most unjust and shameful persecution'. Surely, she pleaded, it was impossible that 'he be my minister under such circumstances?'.

The answer they both wanted was 'no'. Disraeli was at least able to delay the inevitable by resorting to the important technicality that Hartington, not Gladstone, was the official leader of the Liberal party. 'Even if your Majesty wished Mr Gladstone to be chief,' Disraeli advised, 'the constitutional course would still be to send for an acknowledged leader of the opposition.' He told her to send for Hartington, who at that stage was actively trying to form an administration. 'The Queen has sent for Hartington, a foolish step,' wrote Lord Kimberley when the news broke. 'Evidently she has been advised to do this by Beaconsfield who has taken advantage of her dislike of Gladstone to endeavour to sow discord in the Liberal party.'

Lord Hartington had been in many ways an exemplary leader of the opposition. His view, similar to that of Disraeli after the defeat of 1868, had been that a government needed time for its contradictions to become apparent. The Conservatives in the mid-1870s, he understood, had had the wind behind them. By waiting for more blustery weather, Hartington had helped deliver a stunning success at the polls in 1880. He had cleverly united the Liberal party around a brisk programme of reform that appealed both to the landed and the middle classes. His difficulty was that his own low-key approach had contrasted with Gladstone's flamboyant Midlothian campaign, which had won both headlines and plaudits. Now, at the crucial moment, it was enough to cause him fatally to hesitate.

'Harty-Tarty' was a man who displayed no emotion in public and little more in private. He appeared to others both remote and self-contained. Certainly he did not care for social niceties or putting others at their ease. This meant that, like Peel, he was respected rather than loved by his party. Having just won an electoral victory he might have expected grateful supporters to clamour around him. Instead they offered only lukewarm encouragement tinged with faint embarrassment. Yet if Hartington had pressed the point, his claim was incontestable. Few would have guessed that in the end lack of confidence undid this apparently cold and aloof aristocrat. He simply lacked the stomach to fight Gladstone for the premiership. It was a weakness that the new MP for Midlothian exploited ruthlessly, despatching the luckless Hartington with contemptuous brutality.

Shortly after Disraeli's resignation, Hartington arrived at Windsor at three in the afternoon to tell the Queen the unwelcome news that no Liberal government could be formed without Gladstone – and that Gladstone would only join such an administration as first minister. Therefore he had to advise that she send for Gladstone. 'There is one great difficulty,' the Queen replied sourly. 'I cannot give Mr Gladstone my confidence. His violence and bitterness have been such, the way in which he has, in times of great anxiety, rendered my task and that of the Government so difficult, and the alarm abroad at his name being so great it would be impossible for me to have the full confidence in him I should wish, were he to form a government.' The laconic Hartington, aristocratically contemptuous of the Queen, admitted that Gladstone's behaviour had been 'unfortunate', but repeated that there could be no government without him. Then go and ask him outright to serve under you, the Queen demanded. Wearily, Hartington consented, but warned 'it will be of little use'.

Hartington saw Gladstone at seven. It was not a comfortable meeting. He asked explicitly if the former prime minister would serve under him. First Gladstone rebuked him. It was to Lord Granville, not Hartington, that he had 'resigned my trust' as leader of the party. The Queen should have invited Granville rather than Hartington to form a government. (Gladstone thus conveniently chose to forget that the party had elected Hartington leader on 3 February 1875.) As to the question of serving under him, Gladstone's answer was a blunt no. And in addition came a characteristically lengthy and brutal warning. While it would be his 'duty' even from the backbenches to give them 'all the support in my power', they should understand that 'promises of this kind [stand] on slippery ground, and must always be understood with the limits which might be prescribed by conviction'. In other words, not only would he refuse to serve under anyone else, he would not hesitate to oppose a Liberal government if principle demanded it. Hartington, Gladstone recorded afterwards, 'received all this without comment'.

The following day, the defeated Hartington trudged back to Windsor. For all his unruffled demeanour, this was a bitter personal blow. Not long beforehand, the mask of unflappability had momentarily dropped in a letter to his father, the Duke of Devonshire, in which he had eagerly reported that 'it does look a very hopeful prospect for me'. Now the heat of Gladstone's ambition had evaporated that hope. He reported to the Queen that Gladstone had refused to serve under him, which meant there was not 'any chance' of forming an administration. As to Gladstone, he advised, 'whatever opinion [the Queen] might have formed of his conduct, undoubtedly a great portion of the public seemed not to view it in that light'. The *vox populi* had spoken: there was 'no alternative' but to send for Gladstone.

Early that evening of 23 April – St George's Day – Gladstone went to Windsor for a tense meeting with the Queen. 'May Omnipotent Providence guide, guard and sustain your Majesty at this trying moment!' had written Disraeli beforehand, stoking the Queen's indignation. Her aspirant prime minister was unusually edgy. 'Mr Gladstone looks very ill, very old and haggard and his voice feeble,' Victoria cabled back to Disraeli later. The Queen tetchily asked Gladstone if he was able to form a government. Gladstone 'humbly' said he could. After some brief discussion about cabinet appointments (including Gladstone's incredible decision once again to be his own Chancellor of the Exchequer), the conversation took a lurch into difficult territory.

Time and again the Queen pressed him for an apology on the Midlothian campaign. 'She said I must be frank with you Mr Gladstone, and must fairly say that there have been some expressions, I think she said some little things, which had caused her concern or pain,' the aspirant prime minister recorded. Refusing to take the bait, he replied that while he 'had undoubtedly used a mode of speech and language different in some degree from what I should have employed had I been the leader of a party or a candidate for office', now as premier he hoped the Queen 'would not find anything to disapprove in my general tone'. All his 'desire and effort would be to diminish her cares, in any case not to aggravate them'. The Queen received this with 'some good natured archness', icily warning that 'you will have to bear the consequences' if it turned out otherwise. 'It was probably some new instance of her special identification with Beaconsfieldism,' Gladstone mused later.

At the end of the interview, the new prime minister kissed hands with his reluctant sovereign. For both of them it had been an 'effort'. Yet it could not take away from Gladstone's sense of pleasure at his return.

'All things considered,' he wrote understatedly, 'I was much pleased.'

Disraeli left Downing Street for the last time on 25 April. For all the insouciance he showed to the world, he was exhausted and dejected by this final defeat. The previous few months had been a 'battle of Armageddon where I have had to receive and endure blow after blow'. Now all he wanted was a 'dose of solitude' by retreating to Hughenden to lick his wounds. 'I am a hermit,' he told the dismayed Queen.

Ensconced in Buckinghamshire, Disraeli began brooding on defeat. He received few visitors, and spent most of his days in his library or walking with Monty Corry. There was some consolation that he had finally been able to reward this most loyal secretary and confidant by seeing him elevated to 'Baron Rowton'. ('There has been nothing like it since Caligula created his horse a consul' was Gladstone's ungenerous response to the news.) After such a trouncing, Disraeli's mind turned naturally enough to concerns about his legacy. Had the electorate really turned against 'Beaconsfieldism', or was this just the pendulum of politics swinging inevitably from Conservative to Liberal, just as it had swung so emphatically the other way in 1874. For peace of mind, there could be only one answer. 'Whatever philosophers may say, there is such a thing as luck and fortune – and the reverse – and that it should have fallen to my lot to govern England for a series of years with decaying commerce and the soil stricken with sterility presents an issue which, I believe, no calculation could have foreseen or baffled,' he told Lord Lytton. 'The distress of this country is the cause and the sole cause of the fall for the government over which I presided.'

Having purged himself of blame, Disraeli with typical élan moved on to other things. He might well be 'in the sunset of life', but there was still an audience to be won back. For if politics had sent him off to the wings, there was always literature to bring him back centre stage. Throughout the 1870s Disraeli had been working on a new novel – *Endymion* – that evoked the political and social world of his youth. Much of it had been written during the heady few weeks after his return from Berlin, but the pressure of events had forced him to put it away. Now in retreat from politics, he set about finishing the last hundred pages.

If Disraeli had been looking for confirmation that his celebrity cache remained undimmed by electoral rejection, then the contract negotiations for the new novel surpassed his wildest expectations. During a rare visit to the House of Lords in early August, Corry excitedly passed a note to him on the front bench. 'There are things too big to impart in whispers!' it read. 'Longman has today offered *ten thousand pounds* for Endymion.' This was a sensational amount, thought to be the largest advance ever offered to any author. (Dickens had previously earned £9000 for *Dombey and Son*, George Eliot a similar sum for *Daniel Deronda*, while Anthony Trollope never went beyond £3600 for any novel.) The amount of money was important, for it would allow Disraeli to take his own London house rather than rely on the charity of friends. Norton Longman went down to Hughenden the following month to collect the final manuscript. He found Disraeli as twitchy as a first-time author, concerned about how the publisher would transport the bulky package. No problem.

'My Glad . . . ,' blurted out Longman, choking back the name just in time.

'My bag!'

The novel was rushed out in November. Mudie's ordered three thousand copies for its subscribers – 'unprecedented' Longman told Disraeli. The initial run was 7000, and 10,500 copies were in circulation by the beginning of December. Press interest was overwhelming, and mostly positive, with 110 notices from British and Irish publications alone. When the cheap edition came out in the New Year, Longman more than recouped his initial investment. Reaction in society was captured best by Lord Derby (who now, having jumped ship to the Liberals, had to buy his own copy of the book): 'It is like all he has written, clever, amusing, fantastic: rather a fairy tale than a picture of real life, so far as the story is concerned, but with its extravagances are mixed so many shrewd traits of character and ingenious phrases that the absurdity of the tale is forgotten.' All in all, concluded Derby generously, 'it is a remarkable production for a man of 75, after six years of a kind of labour which does not stimulate the imaginative faculty'.

Derby's new chief, Gladstone, noted in his diary for 16 January 1881 that he had read Alfred Austin's notice of the novel in the *Quarterly Review*. 'What he did at twenty-five [in *Vivian Grey*], he is doing at seventy-five, only doing it better,' Austin had written. Given that Gladstone had pronounced *Vivian Grey* 'trash', it is perhaps no surprise that he did not bother with *Endymion*.

Perhaps he might have paid more attention had he realised that Disraeli was already at work on a new novel, the anti-hero of which was one William Ewart Gladstone.

'We get on badly in Parliament,' complained the colonial secretary, Lord Kimberley, as early as July 1880. 'The symptoms point to a break up at an early date of both Govt. and Parliament.'

After the triumph of Midlothian, when Gladstone had established himself indisputably as the dominant figure both in parliament and the country, he had unexpectedly stumbled badly at the beginning of his second administration. Part of the problem was that he had come into power on a negative promise: to sweep aside Beaconsfieldism. Having done that so conclusively at the general election, it quickly became apparent that beyond this he had little or no legislative programme in mind. Certainly there would be a tightening of the fiscal belt and a symbolic foray back into the Eastern Question (securing some territorial concessions for Montenegro from Turkey). From the outset both Gladstone and his government seemed surprisingly out of focus, not least in struggling to control events in Ireland. ('Is not that state a warning and a judgment for our heavy sins as a nation,' he wrote despairingly at the end of the year.) It was symptomatic of a general malaise. In 1868, he had come into power declaring boldly that 'my mission is to pacify Ireland'. Now there appeared to be no obvious agenda for Ireland or anything else besides. Matters were not helped by underlying tensions in cabinet, led by a powerful trium-virate. Both Hartington and Granville felt unmanned by Gladstone's leadership takeover; the former brooded listlessly, waiting for revenge, while the latter hardly bothered to do any work. Added to this awkward pair was a new minister, the radical Joseph Chamberlain, who disliked Gladstone personally and had designs on his job. Unlike in 1868, this was not a harmonious cabinet.

This might have mattered less if there had not been such an effec-tive Disraelian force at work in the House of Commons. Official lead-ership of the Conservative party in the lower house remained with the lugubrious Sir Stafford Northcote. Back in the 1840s, he had been private secretary to Gladstone (then a Tory). Now in parliamentary exchanges across the despatch box, he never quite managed to shake that sense of deference to his former master. Younger members gossiped about how, when Northcote spoke, Gladstone would fix him with his gimlet eye, which in turn provoked the leader of the opposition to flush and lose all composure. Prominent among those MPs who ridiculed Northcote was the so-called Fourth Party, dominated by two rising Tory stars barely turned thirty: Lord Randolph Churchill (father of Winston) and Arthur Balfour (a future prime minister and the nephew of Lord Salisbury).

Just as Disraeli had destroyed Robert Peel in 1846 by ridicule and impertinence, so now he quietly encouraged these young pretenders to do the same to Gladstone. Officially he warned them not to humiliate poor Northcote – 'he represents the respectability of the party' – but in the next breath gave them licence to roam by observing, 'I wholly sympathise with you all, because I was never respectable myself.' He was undeniably flattered that the avowed aim of the Fourth Party was that 'Elijah's mantle' should fall on those who would carry forward his policies on imperial rule and social reform. In their youthful idealism and parliamentary guerrilla tactics, these advocates of Disraelian principles reminded the ageing statesman of nothing less than his Young England self. Most of all, he warmed to them because they despised Gladstone, whom they baited and drove into another nervous collapse.

Their opportunity came in the Bradlaugh affair, a dispute that would run on for five years. The newly elected Radical MP for Northampton, Charles Bradlaugh had written to the Speaker in advance of parliament meeting to ask if, as an atheist, he might affirm rather than swear the oath (in other words not invoke God as his witness). Instead of dealing quickly and firmly with the issue, Speaker Brand referred the matter to a select committee, which rejected the request. Bradlaugh then agreed to swear, but when he tried to do so, other members objected on the grounds that it would be a self-proclaimed false oath. Chaos then ensued.

Bradlaugh represented much of what Gladstone detested: he was an atheist, a supporter of contraception and a vocal republican. Yet Gladstone thought that the man's right to sit as a duly elected MP was incontestable. 'I find my own scruples and objections stubborn,' he told Erskine May, that great parliamentary authority, on 19 June when challenged on the matter. So in the debates that followed, in which MPs voted repeatedly against admitting Bradlaugh, Gladstone bravely spoke up for him. This gave the Fourth Party its chance. The sight of Gladstone on his feet defending atheism, birth control and republicanism provided an unmissable opportunity to ridicule him from a position on the moral high ground. At one point in a debate, the charismatic Churchill theatrically produced a pamphlet by Bradlaugh, threw it towards Gladstone, and then marched down to where it had fallen to trample it underfoot to the accompaniment of wild cheering. For Disraeli, watching from the gallery, to see Gladstone mortified in the name of morality and religion offered some measure of sweet revenge for the pious accusations of the Midlothian campaign.

Habitually for Gladstone, emotional distress manifested itself in increased 'rescue work' followed by inevitable breakdown. So it proved that summer of 1880. Embarrassed and frustrated by events in parliament, he caught pneumonia after a late-night outing in the middle of July, and was unable to return to the Commons until a few days before the session ended in early September. 'Such was the state of my nerves and muscular system,' he recorded, '[that I had been] shaking as a house is shaken by an earthquake.'

'O, 'tis a burden, Cromwell, 'tis a burden,' he wrote on the first page of a new diary volume that month, quoting Shakespeare's *Henry VIII*. 'Too heavy for a man that hopes for heaven.' The truth was that Gladstone, suddenly aged, was feeling the strain of office like never before. Disraeli had been ravaged by poor health for years. Gout, asthma, poor circulation, constant colds and influenza brought on by chill east winds: these and many other afflictions contributed to the impression of ethereal frailty that always surrounded the Tory leader. Now, abruptly, Gladstone had caught him up. He may have seemed more robust than Disraeli – everyone did – yet like him he had now unquestionably become an old man. His hair was white and tangled. Never a dandy even as a young man, he was now unkempt in dishevelled clothes. He was chronically short-sighted. Sleep was increasingly fitful. Lumbago came more frequently and with increased pain. He suffered recurrent bouts of diarrhoea. His teeth hurt. And perhaps most significantly of all, as the Queen had noticed that May, his sonorous voice was losing its clarity and force.

'More and more my own thought is concentrated on the desire to bring to an early close the long period of my contentious life,' he wrote over Christmas 1880. 'Without this nothing can really avail to give me the attitude which becomes old age.' This desire to be released from the burdens of office was not unfamiliar, yet on this occasion it was accompanied by a more telling indication that Gladstone had finally aged. 'C[atherine] went for a midnight service,' he noted. 'I felt too tired & too distracted.'

Disraeli was at Hughenden that Christmas compensating for his own ill health by enjoying the restorative powers of eviscerating Gladstone in prose. Throughout those autumn and winter months in Buckinghamshire, he had become increasingly obsessed with his enemy – now christened 'the Arch-Villain'. 'I see no chances of salvation unless he really goes mad,' Disraeli had written to Selina Bradford in November, 'but he is such a hypocrite, that I shall never believe that till he is in Bedlam.' Lord Ronald Gower had found him similarly contemptuous during a visit that month. On reading a letter from Gladstone in *The Times* thanking the public for their sympathy during a recent illness, Disraeli had exploded: 'Did you ever hear anything like that? It reminds one of the Pope blessing all the world from the balcony of St Peter's.' Behind the scorn was recognition that there would be no political vengeance. 'I don't give my mind at all to politics,' he told Selina dolefully, 'the A.V. has carried everything before him.' But that did not mean he would not give his mind to settling scores.

'I believe he is engaged in writing something, but this he didn't tell me,' recorded Gower after his visit to Hughenden. That something was a *roman-à-clef*, whose anti-hero – Joseph Toplady Falconet – was recognisably William Gladstone. The name was artfully chosen. 'Joseph' was taken from Joseph Surface, the scheming hypocrite in Sheridan's *The School for Scandal*. 'Toplady' was the hymnist of the 'Rock of Ages', which it was known Gladstone had Latinised in 1839. There must surely too have been some innuendo hinting at the late-night excursions that so amused and baffled Gladstone's contemporaries. The name 'Falconet' conjured up Gladstone's appearance, both in the hawk-like intensity of his eyes and the beaky shape of his face. ('The new members trembled and fluttered like small birds when a hawk is in the air', Disraeli had written of Gladstone to the Queen in 1875.)

Disraeli spared nothing in his portrait of the young Falconet as a clever yet unappealing character. It was his most sustained assessment of his great rival's make-up:

He was a grave boy, and scarcely ever known to smile, and this
. . . from a complete deficiency in the sense of humour, of which
he seemed quite debarred. His memory was vigorous, ready, and

retentive; but his chief peculiarity was his disputatious temper, and the flow of language which, even as a child, was ever at his command to express his arguments . . . Though of an eager and earnest temperament, his imagination was limited, and quite conscious of his powers, being indeed, somewhat arrogant and peremptory, aspired only to devote them to accomplishing those objects which, from his cradle, he had been taught were the greatest, and the only ones, which could or should occupy the energies of man. Firm in his faith in an age of dissolving creeds, he wished to believe that he was the man ordained to vindicate the sublime cause of religious truth.

No wonder then, Disraeli tells us, 'with all his abilities and acquirements, Joseph Toplady Falconet [MP], was essentially a prig, and among prigs there is a freemasonry which never fails. All the prigs spoke of him as of the coming man.'

With ten chapters of his new novel completed, Disraeli put the manuscript in the safe at Hughenden before setting out for London on the last day of 1880 to prepare for the Queen's Speech.

Disraeli had feared no political enemy but the weather had always been his most pitiless foe. The winter of 1880/81 was particularly vicious – 'a white world' – and gradually it would draw him into a fatal embrace. On the day he left High Wycombe railway station, the snow and chill wind were already taking their toll. When he arrived later that New Year's Eve at Alfred de Rothschild's house, he collapsed from exhaustion and cold, unable to breathe. On 15 January, he moved from the Rothschilds to 19 Curzon Street, a house taken using the money from *Endymion*, and not too far from the beloved Hyde Park home he had shared with Mary Anne. But it was the coldest day of the month. London shivered in enveloping freezing fog. The house would take weeks to warm through. 'The weather has completely upset me,' he told Lady Chesterfield at the end of the month, 'and I really cannot fight against it any more.'

After his autumnal hibernation, Disraeli seemed determined, despite the cold, to throw himself back into London life. Each day, he struggled to Westminster to attend debates in the Lords, or, more frustratingly, as a spectator from the Gallery of the Commons. He took with relish any opportunity to attack Gladstone. In the Queen's Speech debate, Disraeli denounced the prime minister for the stridently partisan nature of his politics. 'In every manner and on every occasion it was announced that a change of government meant a change in every part and portion of the government,' he lamented. 'That everything which had been concluded was to be repudiated; that everything consummated was to be reversed . . . Perpetual and complete reversal of all that had occurred was the order that was given.' Later in the session, he would return to a familiar theme, that Gladstone was selling out the British Empire. Disparaging the government's decision to evacuate Kandahar, he contributed the last of his many celebrated political aphorisms: 'The key of India is London.'

As well as politics, Disraeli also threw himself into a maelstrom of parties, dinners and receptions, drifting from one to the other as the star attraction — the guest that all hostesses clamoured to invite. Sometimes he would shine. At a Rothschild wedding, he delivered a brilliant toast in the presence of the Prince of Wales. The evening was greatly enhanced for him by his first sight of 'magical' electrical lighting, which illuminated the garden. On other occasions, he simply sat and watched the proceedings, enjoying his status as the main exhibit, letting others do the talking. Finding Stafford Northcote's wife in conversation with the wife of the Liberal MP George Goschen at one party, he squeezed in between them on the sofa and stayed there for the rest of the evening. 'I am blind and deaf,' he told them sadly. 'I am like the birds, alive all day but must rest early — I am dead at half-past ten.' Writing to her husband afterwards, Lucy Goschen lamented that Disraeli seemed 'very aged'.

It was on leaving one such party that the ill-omened weather finally embraced him. On 22 March, in driving frozen rain, he was 'caught for a minute by the deadly blast of the north-east wind laden with sleet'. By the next day, a chill had developed into bronchitis, accompanied, his doctor recorded, by 'distressing asthma, loss of appetite, fever, and congestion of the kidneys'. To begin with, it seemed that this was just another in a long line of attacks. Visitors found Disraeli in upbeat form, not least in his enmity towards Gladstone. To the young MP George Hamilton, he 'bitterly criticised the vanity' of his famous rival. Sir Charles Dilke was delighted to find him 'still the old Disraeli' and observed that 'his pleasant spitefulness about "Mr G." was not abated'. That judgement remained hostile to the end. 'It was easy to settle affairs with Palmerston because he was a man of the world, and was therefore governed by the principle of honour,' Disraeli told callers, 'but when you have to deal with an earnest man, severely religious and enthusiastic, every attempted arrangement ends in unintelligible correspondence and violated confidence.'

Yet Gladstone was among those many visitors who called to Curzon Street to ask after Disraeli's progress.

'Went up to enquire for Lord B.,' he recorded on 29 March. '[They] reported him better. May the Almighty be near his pillow.'

Although the two men did not meet, it was the last time that Gladstone and Disraeli would be under the same roof.

Lord Beaconsfield may well have remained the 'old Disraeli', but by April concerns were mounting as the patient showed no signs of recovery. Most worryingly of all, in private he seemed to have decided that this was the end. 'Dear friend, I shall never survive this attack,' he told his lawyer Philip Rose. 'I feel this is the last of it.' Two days later, when Rose visited Curzon Street, Disraeli told him again: 'I feel I am dying. Whatever the doctors may tell you, I do not believe I shall get well.' Around the same time, the Queen discovered that Disraeli's illness was potentially life threatening. She asked if she might visit him at Curzon Street. 'No it is better not,' he told his doctors. 'She would only ask me to take a message to Albert.' Instead Victoria despatched her own physicians to examine him, brushing aside their haughty objections about Disraeli's unorthodox use of a homeopathic doctor. Each day she sent flowers from Osborne to fill the house.

Monty Corry, who had been in Algiers with his invalid sister, rushed back to London. 'When one sees how weak he is and how little real nourishment he is taking, the words scarcely raise in one a hope,' he reported morosely to Selina on 10 April. 'He talks of death without a shade of fear.'

The agony by this time was intense. Breathing had become difficult, and the struggle to do so often brought on choking fits. His weakened kidneys gave intense pain. Although bedridden, he refused most of the various contraptions that were suggested to make him more comfortable. 'Take away that emblem of mortality!' he declared when the unfortunate doctor brought in a giant inflatable cushion for him to rest on. Great statesmen did not expire on air beds.

By Easter Sunday, 17 April, those in Disraeli's close circle began to prepare themselves for the end. Rose remembered that Disraeli always took communion at Hughenden parish church on that day each year, but doctors forbade it because the patient might interpret this as the last rites. Later there would be rumours that Disraeli was received into the Roman Catholic Church in his final days. Others would say that his last words were 'Shema Yisroel' – the great Jewish affirmation of faith. More likely he died without any formal rites of religion, although it might have amused him that according to Christian tradition his death within the octave of Easter would have seen his soul ascend straight to heaven.

On Easter Monday morning the doctors posted their daily bulletin. 'Lord Beaconsfield has been rather more restless and taken rather less nourishment,' it read. 'As a consequence there has been no material gain in strength.' In fact, by this time Disraeli was already in a coma. His last recorded words had been 'I had rather live, but I am not afraid to die.'

By the early hours of 19 April, the anniversary of Byron's death, Disraeli was in the closing stages of life. 'The last day and hours were distressing from his laboured breathing, but the last minutes and moments were very quiet and evidently quite painless,' wrote Corry. Barely a quarter of an hour before he passed away, there was one last attempt to rally. 'It touched us all deeply to see the dying statesman rise up in the bed and lean forward in the way he used to do when rising to reply in debate,' wrote his personal physician, Joseph Kidd. 'His lips moved, but no sound came out.' He fell back immediately on to his pillow, and made no further attempt to speak.

The last moment, when it came, was peaceful. 'He passed away without suffering, calmly as if in sleep, at 4.30am,' recorded Rose. 'The very end was strikingly dignified and fine,' said Corry, 'and as I looked on his dear face, just at the moment when his spirit left him, I thought that I had never seen him look so triumphant and full of victory.'

Minutes after Disraeli's passing, Monty Corry put grief to one side to fulfil his role as loyal private secretary. Telegrams were despatched to the Queen and the Prince of Wales to inform them of the news.

And a message was sent to Hawarden, where, as he was preparing for church, the prime minister received word that his greatest rival was dead. 'There is no more extraordinary man surviving him in England, perhaps none in Europe,' he wrote that day, before adding resignedly that 'the event will entail upon me one great difficulty: but God who sends all, sends this also.'

Even in death, Disraeli could still needle Gladstone.

Epilogue

In Memoriam

Seventeen Years Later, Westminster Abbey

Muffled bells tolled out their mournful lament for William Gladstone on that morning of Saturday 28 May 1898. The precincts of the Abbey were crammed with more than one hundred thousand public mourners waiting with 'intense and unexampled stillness' to pay their final respects to 'the People's William'. As Big Ben struck eleven o'clock, the funeral cortege left Westminster Hall, where the body had been lying in state. There was no gun carriage or military guard of honour. Instead the simple wooden coffin, made by carpenters in Flintshire, was taken in procession by an ordinary funeral car, pulled by two horses and attended by groomsmen from the Hawarden estate and boys from Eton.

When the procession reached the west door of the Abbey, the coffin was carried aloft by illustrious pallbearers: the Conservative prime minister, Lord Salisbury and his eventual successor, Arthur Balfour; for the Liberals, Lord Rosebery – Gladstone's ungrateful political heir – Sir William Harcourt and Lord Kimberley; Lord John Manners (now the Duke of Rutland), who had sat with Gladstone at his first constituency of Newark; and wealthy devotees, George Armitstead and Lord Rendel, who had supported Gladstone financially in his last years. And there, sensationally accompanying the coffin, were the heir to the throne and his son – the future kings Edward VII and George V – breaking all known protocol, and infuriating the Queen in the process.

Gladstone's final resting place was to be the Abbey's North Transept, popularly known as 'Statesman's Aisle'. Here the bodies of William Pitt, Charles James Fox and Palmerston were buried. Memorials had been

least of those who compared the qualities of both men and their
[fune]ral arrangements was the Queen. She had telegraphed Catherine
[Glad]stone immediately to express her condolences, but pointedly had
[refrai]ned from any comment on the departed. The contrast with her
[effus]ive 1881 tribute to Disraeli in the Court Circular was interpreted
[as an] obvious snub. Gladstone's supporters were furious. 'The unanimous
[verd]ict of all shades of opinion, political and social in this Empire,' thun-
[dere]d the *Daily Chronicle*, '[is that] every word applied by the Queen to
[Lord] Beaconsfield applies with at least equal force to Mr Gladstone.'
[She] sent another telegram of sympathy to Catherine on the day of the
[fune]ral, but still no tribute appeared in the Court Circular. Victoria after-
[war]ds told the prime minister, Salisbury, that she '*regrets* all the fuss made'
[over] Gladstone. She judged, moreover, that the family had made a 'great
[mis]take' in not holding the funeral at Hawarden. They should have
[foll]owed Disraeli's example of a 'village' funeral.

[T]he Queen was not alone in that thought. *Reynold's Newspaper*
[com]plained that the Abbey service was 'a cold, formal, official affair'.
[Ho]w much better it would have been at Hawarden, the Radical paper
[sug]gested, where the 'great multitudes of Mr Gladstone's devoted
[fol]lowers' might have paid their respects. The implicit suggestion was
[tha]t Disraeli's funeral had been better handled.

[G]ladstone's provincial death and metropolitan committal were the
[mi]rror image of Disraeli's London demise and country burial. Yet the
[G]ladstone family had drawn explicitly on Disraeli's example while
[or]ganising events. They never deviated from their desire for a great
[pu]blic funeral, but there were obvious attempts to capture something
[o]f the simple rustic quality of events at Hughenden. On 25 May
[G]ladstone's remains were removed from Hawarden to the nearby
[v]illage church. An unpretentious hand bier, preceded by clergy and
[c]hoir, bore the locally made coffin along the route. Large crowds of
[m]ourners watched it pass. The procession stopped at various points
[a]long the way to sing Gladstone's favourite hymns. A private communion
[s]ervice followed, but in the afternoon the church was opened to the
[p]ublic, who filed past the coffin in 'huge numbers' for more than six
[h]ours. The following day a special train conveyed the remains to London.
[I]t slowed at stations along the way, where vast, hushed crowds had
[g]athered to pay their final respects. Gladstone was to be accepted into
the Pantheon of great statesmen at Westminster Abbey, yet his family
had striven to demonstrate that even in death he remained, like Disraeli,
a man rooted in provincial England.

---

raised to Canning and Peel, both heroes to Gladstone. At the head of
the grave stood the grieving widow, Catherine, 'erect . . . with her
expression half dreaming and half wild, but triumphant'. She watched
as her husband's mortal remains were lowered into the earth, while
John Henry Newman's 'Praise to the Holiest in the Height' was sung.
Afterwards Catherine prayed on her knees beside the grave. Then she
stood to receive the condolences of the pallbearers. In another break
with tradition the Prince of Wales came to her to offer commiser-
ation, which he demonstrated very publicly by kissing the widow's
hand.

As the congregation thronged out of the Abbey afterwards to
Schubert's *Marche Solennelle* most seemed to agree that the straightforward service, with Mrs Gladstone at its heart, had been a fitting
tribute. But amid the reverential chatter – discussing the service, remi-
niscing about the deceased, and reflecting on his place in history –
there was also a quiet, oft-repeated sense of amazement tinged with
ironic amusement.

Gathorne Hardy – Lord Cranbrook – felt compelled to record this
immediately in his diary on returning home that afternoon: 'Just back
from the simple, solemn and impressive service over Gladstone's grave,'
he wrote in astonishment, 'at the foot of Disraeli's statue.'

Gladstone died having been prime minister four times. In the seventeen years without his great rival, however, Gladstone had failed to
recapture either the energy of his great government of 1868–74, or
the popular élan of the Midlothian campaign. In fact, he found himself
strangely ambushed by Disraeli's legacy and agenda. There were still
moments of triumph. The 1884 Reform Bill, agreed in consensus with
the Conservatives under Lord Salisbury, raised the combined proportion of men eligible to vote in the United Kingdom to around 60
per cent and for the first time gave the great cities the number of
MPs to which they were entitled according to population. Yet
Gladstone's determination to pass the bill was rooted in his quest to
undo the mortification of 1866/7, when Disraeli had so comprehen-
sively trounced him. And this Third Reform Act lacked the historic
sense of a defining moment that had accompanied the Second Reform
Act.

The snare of Beaconsfieldism was even greater in foreign affairs.
Gladstone having run so vehemently in 1880 as an opponent of Disraeli's
imperial adventures could hardly have expected that he himself would

become the kind of super-imperialist premier that his nemesis might even have admired. To general astonishment he initiated a full-scale military campaign in 1882 to conquer Egypt, which remained a *de facto* part of the British Empire until the 1950s. Yet Gladstone had little of Disraeli's instinctive feel for the daring and brinksmanship of imperial leadership. This led to humiliation when General Gordon – the epitome in the public mind of a Christian-Soldier, but in reality a maverick with a martyr complex – was defeated and killed at Khartoum. Gladstone had dithered on sending an expedition to rescue Gordon, first refusing to send any such force and then, too late, changing his mind. Outrage ensued, led by the Queen, whose apoplectic telegram on Gordon's death, purposely sent unencrypted, was leaked to the press. Gladstone, popularly by this time referred to as G.O.M. (Grand Old Man) now found those initials reversed to M.O.G. – Murderer of Gordon. The crisis typically made Gladstone physically ill, 'which has had so many forms, having at last taken the form of overaction of the bowels'.

Worse, if that was possible, quickly followed. Disraeli, on leaving office in 1880, had uttered in dark tones a single-word prophesy of the issue that would rip British politics apart: '*Ireland!*' Amidst the fallout surrounding Gordon's death – during which time the Conservatives formed a short-lived minority government – Gladstone set about fulfilling that prediction. Sometime in 1885 he decided to give Ireland a measure of self-government. He kept this decision to himself until the end of the year, when his son Herbert leaked it to the press (the infamous 'Hawarden kite'). His first Home Rule Bill in March 1886 was a momentous turning point in British politics. The Liberal party split in a manner similar to the Conservatives in 1846 on the Corn Laws. A general election in June, fought on the question of whether Home Rule was Rome Rule, initiated twenty years of Conservative political dominance. Those who left the Liberals on the question of Home Rule included grand Whigs such as Hartington and new-money millionaires such as George Goschen and Joseph Chamberlain. Thus Gladstone not only emulated his hero Peel in splitting his own party and destroying it as a political force for a generation, he also inadvertently helped make the Conservative party what Disraeli had always predicted it would become: a natural home for patriotism, tradition and wealth.

There would, however, be one last attempted hurrah for Gladstone. In 1892 he made an unexpected if brief return to the premiership at the astonishing age of eighty-one. Supported by more than eighty Irish

Nationalists, he temporarily breached uninterru to make a final attempt at Home Rule for Irel the measure through the Commons before it was On 1 March 1894 he informed cabinet of his in politics immediately, something he had been p January 1875. This was the 556th meeting of the chaired as prime minister. The last would be kno blubbering cabinet', but throughout it all Gladston and still. The emotion . . . did not gain on him that day he quietly left the Commons for the las one years since his first election as a Member House showed feeling,' he wrote in his diary that I made no outward sign.'

All that remained for Gladstone was 'the gradual lo sive snapping of the threads'. Loathing of Disraeli, among those severed ties. This detestation had onl his adversary's death. He may have protested to his s rivalry was 'something totally different from person long conversations with his biographer, John Morley, age raged against Disraeli's malignant influence Democracy [has] certainly not saved us from a distin standard of public life,' he judged: 'For all this deteri and one man alone is responsible – Disraeli.' Unque true that in '*parliamentary wit* Disraeli had never been this could not be allowed to mask the truth that hi been wholly depraved. 'He it was who sowed the s fumed. 'He is the grand corrupter!'

It was an opinion taken with him to that Westminst William Ewart Gladstone died on 19 May 1898 – As after several painful weeks battling cancer of the mout out in the Temple of Peace at Hawarden, dressed in s scarlet Oxford doctoral robes. Prominent among the down upon his remains was that of Disraeli. Gladstone's f tions were suitably ambiguous, asking for a burial that w simple unless they [his executors] shall consider that ther sive reasons to the contrary'. This left room for a public f honour), which was immediately offered by parliament by the family. Thereafter in the civic mind everything dr ison with the interment of Disraeli.

Gladstone's distinguished opponent remained a focus of attention at the burial in Statesman's Aisle that morning of 28 May. Disraeli's statue had been dedicated fifteen years earlier and had become a site of devotion for the faithful. The Primrose League had been established that same year by, among others, Lord Randolph Churchill, to continue Disraeli's conservative vision. Each year, on the anniversary of Disraeli's death, league members from around the country came to lay vast quantities of primroses – the same flower sent by the Queen for his coffin – at the base of the statue. No wonder those mourners at Gladstone's funeral should have wondered about a burial next to this place of Disraelian pilgrimage. 'Throughout the morning,' reported the *Times* correspondent, 'the eyes of many were constantly turned to the white statue of the Earl of Beaconsfield, startlingly distinct against its sombre background, a silent, and to the fanciful mind, a mournful witness of the interment of his great rival'.

The Times was hit not just by the irony of Gladstone's interment at the feet of his adversary. There remained the fundamental question of their different legacies. 'Beaconsfield left a policy, a school of admirers and something like a creed and a cult,' the newspaper suggested. 'Where are the Gladstonites? What policy did Mr Gladstone originate; what institutions which he erected stand stable; what saying which he, a master of speech, uttered is memorable; what divisions in the state did he terminate; what seed did he sow which is now surging to life; what page in his voluminous writings will be long read?' These were 'the tests' by which any great statesman must be judged, not least 'one who had for an almost unparalleled span of years the ear of a large number of our countrymen'. History, it warned, 'tells us to be mistrustful of the flying fame and crude exaggeration of the hour.'

This was a harsh verdict by a newspaper that since 1886 and Home Rule had counted Gladstone as an enemy. The editor of *The Times*, George Earle Buckle, would soon enough have his opportunity to establish the case for Disraeli as the greater man. Between 1914 and 1920 he would complete the final four volumes of the massive official life begun by William Monypenny. Buckle's accomplishment, wrote the elderly courtier Viscount Esher, was to '[reconstruct] for those who never knew Lord Beaconsfield that strange figure of a Jew of Aragon, which Disraeli loved to think he was, clothed in the robes of the most ancient order of Christian chivalry'. Among those who congratulated Buckle on his achievement was John Morley, whose biography of Gladstone had been published in 1903. 'We have each of us done his best to keep public life and public opinion on a wholesome and self-respecting level,' he concluded, 'and we have done our best to make the two great political rivals immortal.'

Lord Morley, for all his loyalty to Gladstone, understood that the legend of both men was somehow embedded in the synergy of their rivalry. Certainly young Winston Churchill had recognised this when, on his way to India after his first political speech in 1897, he sent an urgent request to his mother: 'I want Lord Beaconsfield's and Mr Gladstone's speeches!' Maybe others appreciated it too. In 1881, following Disraeli's death, the Dean of Westminster, Arthur Stanley, had proudly chosen the location in Statesman's Aisle for the statues of those he had dubbed the 'Great Twin Brothers' of public life. Each would stand across the aisle from the other in perpetual opposition. When the time came for a memorial to be raised to Gladstone, however, it was not placed on the spot chosen by the late dean. Rather the statue was sited next to Disraeli, on his left, where it remains to this day. For sure, Gladstone, his back half-turned, is giving his adversary the cold shoulder. Instead his hand stretches out in friendship towards Sir Robert Peel. Disraeli, meanwhile, stares off into the middle distance, as he had done for so many years in parliament, affecting not to notice the snub.

In the end these two Englishmen stand together not apart, memorialised as they lived: celebrated protagonists forever linked by history.

Notes

PROLOGUE: THE FUNERAL (pp. 1–7)

For an excellent analysis of the death and funeral of Disraeli, see John Wolfe, *Great Deaths: Grieving, Religion, and Nationhood in Victorian and Edwardian Britain* (2000), pp. 157–169. On Gladstone's reaction, see John Morley, *The Life of Gladstone* (2 vols, 1907 edn), II, p. 329; Roy Jenkins, *Gladstone* (1995), pp. 457–460; Richard Shannon, *Heroic Minister* (1999), pp. 273–8; Philip Magnus, *Gladstone* (1954), pp. 280–81, and H. C. G. Matthew, *Gladstone* (1997), pp. 536, 635–8. On Disraeli's funeral arrangements, see: W. F. Monypenny and G. E. Buckle, *The Life of Benjamin Disraeli* (2 vols, 1929 edn), II, pp. 1488–99; Stanley Weintraub, *Disraeli* (1993), pp. 625–6, 658–65, and Robert Blake, *Disraeli* (1966), pp. 749–56. On the relations of both men with Queen Victoria, see Philip Guedalla, *The Queen and Mr Gladstone* (2 vols, 1933), II, pp. 153–62, and Robert Blake's essay in Peter J. Jagger (ed.), *Gladstone* (1998), pp. 51–70.

Hawarden. 'It is a telling . . .', 'entail upon me . . .', and 'which will be regarded . . .': M. R. D. Foot and H. C. G. Matthew (eds), *The Gladstone Diaries, 1825–1896* (14 vols, 1968–94) [Henceforth: *Gladstone Diaries*], X, 19 April 81. 'I am in deep grief . . .' and 'Mr Gladstone would not . . .': Guedalla, *Queen and Mr Gladstone*, nos 773 and 774. 'I am not and never . . .': *Gladstone Diaries*, X, G. to Harry Gladstone, 21 April 81.
Curzon Street. 'Wishes to be laid . . .' and 'gloomy pomp . . .': Wolffe, *Great Deaths*, pp. 160–62.

Hughenden. 'Just a village . . .': Wolffe, *Great Deaths*, pp. 160–62 'Der alte Jude . . .' and 'I hardly dare trust . . .': Weintrub, *Disraeli*, pp. 598, 658. 'Was delayed for . . .': *The Times*, 27 April 81

Royal Academy. 'There is something . . .': *Gladstone Diaries*, X, G. to Harry Gladstone, 21 April 81. 'It is indeed . . .': *Gladstone Diaries*, X, footnote 1, 30 April 81. 'Made my speech . . .': *Gladstone Diaries*, X, 30 April 81. 'Twin brothers . . .': Weintrub, *Disraeli*, p. 663.

10 Downing Street. 'My very difficult . . .': *Gladstone Diaries*, X, 9 May 81. 'This latter . . .' and 'the difficult motion . . .': *Gladstone Diaries*, X, 5 May 81. 'Rush of first rate . . .': Bruce L. Klinzer (ed.), *The Gladstonian Turn of Mind* (1985), p. 104. 'I commit . . .': *Gladstone Diaries*, X, 9 May 81. Gladstone's tribute to Disraeli: *Hansard (Commons)*, 9 May 81. On Disraeli's political courage: Monypenny, *Disraeli*, II, p. 1496. 'Firm conviction . . .': *Hansard (Commons)*, 9 May 81. 'To express to him . . .': Guedalla, *Queen and Mr Gladstone*, no. 781. 'All went better . . .': *Gladstone Diaries*, X, 9 May 81. 'Great men . . .': Job 38: 9. Not well . . .': *Gladstone Diaries*, X, 17 May 81. 'Ever brooding . . .': *Gladstone Diaries*, X, G. to Harry Gladstone, 21 April 81. Jenkins, *Gladstone*, p. 459. Wolffe, in *Great Deaths* disputes the quotation (p. 162, n. 46.)

CHAPTER ONE: THE DINNER PARTY (pp. 11–22)

Accounts of the dinner party from John Morley, *The Life of Gladstone* (2 vols, 1907 ed.), I, p. 123; Roy Jenkins, *Gladstone* (1995), p. 60; Richard Shannon, *Heroic Minister* (1999), p. 60; Philip Magnus, *Gladstone* (1954), p. 21, W. F. Monypenny and G. E. Buckle, *The Life of Benjamin Disraeli* (2 vols., 1929 ed.), I, p. 281; Stanley Weintraub, *Disraeli* (1993), p. 157; Robert Blake, *Disraeli* (1966), p. 123; Peter J. Jagger (ed.), *Gladstone* (1998), p. 57, and M. R. D. Foot & H. C. G. Matthew (eds.), *The Gladstone Diaries, 1825–1896* (14 vols, 1968–94) II, 17 January 35; Dennis Lee, *Lord Lyndhurst* (1994), pp. 90–1; William Hutcheon (ed.), *Whigs and Whiggism: Political writings by Benjamin Disraeli* (1913), p. 3. The character description of Lyndhurst (John Singleton Copley II) is from Edgar Feuchtwanger, *Disraeli* (2000), pp. 18–21. Robert Blake cleverly assesses whether Gladstone or Disraeli would be the better dining companion in Jagger (ed.), *Gladstone*, pp. 59, 67. Unblemished character . . .': *Edinburgh Review*, April 1839, reprinted in Hugh Trevor-Roper, *Macaulay's Essays* (1963), p. 213. 'Never defend . . .' and 'rather dull . . .': Monypenny, *Disraeli*, I, p. 281.

Gladstone's Diary. The best introduction to Gladstone's early life, on which this section draws liberally, is found in Travis L. Crosby's imaginative psychological biography, *The Two Mr Gladstones* (1997). On Gladstone's family, see S. G. Checkland, *The Gladstones* (1971) and a useful summary by the same author: 'The Making of Mr Gladstone' in *Victorian Studies* 12 (1969), pp. 399–409. See also early chapters of the other main biographies: Eugenio F. Biagini, *Gladstone* (2000); John Morley, *The Life of Gladstone* (2 vols., 1907 ed.); Roy Jenkins, *Gladstone* (1995); Richard Shannon, *Heroic Minister* (1999); Philip Magnus, *Gladstone* (1954), and H. C. G. Matthew, *Gladstone* (1997). 'My birthday . . .': *Gladstone Diaries*, II, 29 December 34. 'The work . . .', 'To the destruction . . .': Crosby, *Two Mr Gladstones*, p. 20. 'Stunning . . .', 'I think . . .': *Gladstone Diaries*, I, 8 July 32. John Brooke & Mary Sorensen, *The Prime Ministers' Papers: W. E. Gladstone*, I, (1971), p. 53. 'Excessively . . .': Crosby, *Two Mr Gladstones*, p. 23. 'This is a . . .': *Gladstone Diaries*, II, 17 December 34.

Contarini Fleming. The central text on the young Disraeli is Charles Richmond & Paul Smith (eds.), *The Self-Fashioning of Disraeli, 1818–1851* (1998). This includes an excellent introduction by Paul Smith, along with insightful essays on Disraeli's nervous breakdown and the emergence of his Jewishness. Disraeli's early life is covered in all the major biographies, including those by Robert Blake, Stanley Weintraub, André Maurois (1927), Sarah Bradford (1982), Monypenny and Buckle, and Edgar Feuchtwanger. See also the excellent essay: Jonathan Parry, 'Disraeli, Benjamin, earl of Beaconsfield (1804–1881)', *Oxford Dictionary of National Biography* (2004). The first chapter in Paul Smith's *Disraeli* (1996) is particularly instructive. Detailed analysis is found in Jane Ridley, *The Young Disraeli* (1995). Jewish influences in Disraeli's novels are discussed in Todd M. Endelman & Tony Kushner (eds.), *Disraeli's Jewishness* (2002), pp. 40–61. See also the first volume of M. G. Wiebe et al (ed.), *Benjamin Disraeli Letters* (1982–1997, 6 vols.), and Helen M. Swartz and Marvin Swartz (eds.), *Disraeli's Reminiscences* (1975). On Byron, see Benita Eisler, *Byron: Child of Passion, Fool of Fame* (1999). On Lytton, see Leslie Mitchell, *Bulwer Lytton: The Rise and Fall of a Victorian Man of Letters* (2003). William Kuhn in *The Politics of Pleasure* (2006) suggests that Disraeli was gay, a claim he bases on a reading of Disraeli's novels. This is, however, entirely speculative.

I tell you what . . .' : Disraeli, *Contarini Fleming* (1832); Monypenny and Buckle, *Disraeli*, I, p. 192. 'Trash': *Gladstone Diaries*, VIII, 20 February 74. 'I don't know . . .': Bradford, *Disraeli*, p. 10. 'With what horror . . .':

Disraeli, *Contarini Fleming* (1832); Monypenny, *Disraeli*, I, p. 88. 'Cold, dull world . . .': quoted in Jonathan Parry, 'Disraeli, Benjamin, earl of Beaconsfield (1804–1881)', *Oxford Dictionary of National Biography* (2004). 'Delight at being . . .': Feuchtwanger, *Disraeli*, p. 10. 'Thunderstruck . . .': Richmond & Smith (eds.), *Self-Fashioning of Disraeli*, p. 113. 'When it was crowded . . .', 'The people . . .': Richmond & Smith (eds.), *Self-Fashioning of Disraeli*, p. 79. Descriptions of Disraeli's dress: André Maurois, *Disraeli* (1937 edn.), pp. 29, 48, 61 & 77. 'Ersatz Byron': Richmond & Smith (eds.), *Self-Fashioning of Disraeli*, p. 79. 'Naughty house . . .', 'A facsimile . . .', 'Talked incessantly . . .', 'Two inhabitants . . .': Mitchell, *Lytton*, pp. 100–2. 'Very showy . . .', 'The Whigs . . .': Bradford, *Disraeli*, pp. 80–81; 'In a lisping . . .': Monypenny, *Disraeli*, p. 288; 'He has . . .' Blake, *Disraeli*, p. 125. 'We shall meet . . .': Maurois, *Disraeli*, p. 84. 'Greatly . . .': Monypenny, *Disraeli*, p. 297. Final sentence, with apologies to my friend Patrick Geoghegan of Trinity College, Dublin.

CHAPTER TWO: YOUNG ENGLISHMEN (pp. 23–39)

Palace of Westminster. The Commons were, in fact, sitting in the old House of Lords following the fire of 1834. Descriptions of Disraeli's maiden speech: W. F. Monypenny and G. E. Buckle, *The Life of Benjamin Disraeli* (2 vols., 1929 edn), I, pp. 399–412; Stanley Weintraub, *Disraeli* (1993), pp. 175–7; Robert Blake, *Disraeli* (1966), pp. 148–50. For the contrast between Whigs and Tories, I have drawn extensively on Leslie Mitchell, *The Whig World* (2005).

'D'Israeli made his . . .': Blake, *Disraeli*, p. 148. Maiden speech: Monypenny and Buckle, *Disraeli*, pp. 406–9. 'I wish . . .' Weintraub, *Disraeli*, p. 176. 'Be very quiet . . .': Blake, *Disraeli*, p. 150. 'Gladstone spoke very well': M. G. Wiebe et al (eds.). *Benjamin Disraeli Letters*, III (1993), no.715. 'A most brilliant . . .': *Disraeli Letters*, III, no.766. 'The world outside . . .': *Gladstone Diaries*, II, 28 April 38, footnote 1. 'Which returns . . .: *Gladstone Diaries*, I, 1 April 31. 'The barrier . . .': H. C. G. Matthew, *Gladstone* (1997), p. 49. 'Mama . . .': Roy Jenkins, *Gladstone* (1995), p. 44. 'I live . . .' & 'Active duty . . .': *Gladstone Diaries*, II, 4 June 38. 'I seek much . . .': Philip Magnus, *Gladstone* (1954), pp. 38–9. 'He really was . . .': Jenkins, *Gladstone*, p. 52. Catherine Gladstone; 'soft face . . .'; 'intent on one . . .': H. C. G. Matthew, 'Gladstone, Catherine (1812–1900)', *Oxford Dictionary of National Biography* (2004). 'The truth is . . .': *Gladstone Diaries*, II, 6 February 39. 'Blessed creature . . .': *Gladstone Diaries*, II, 8–9 June 39. 'A pretty little . . .': Paul Smith, *Disraeli* (1996), p. 36. 'I avow when . . .': *Disraeli Letters*, III, no.882. 'He is a genius': Monypenny and Buckle, *Disraeli*, I, 466.

On Peel, see: Travis L. Crosby, *Sir Robert Peel's Administration, 1841–1846* (1976); Robert Stewart, *The Foundation of the Conservative Party, 1830–1867* (1978); Robert Blake, *The Conservative Party from Peel to Thatcher* (1985, 2nd edn). The best biographies of Peel are by Norman Gash (1961, 1972, 2 vols), Eric J. Evans (1991), and T. A. Jenkins (1999). On Gladstone's relationship with Peel, see the excellent essay by Eric Evans in David Bebbington and Roger Swift (eds.), *Gladstone Centenary Essays* (2000), pp. 30–56. On Peel's wealth and his similarities with Gladstone, see the neat summary in W. D. Rubenstein, *Britain's Century* (1998), pp. 70–71, 146. 'But if the . . .': Blake, *The Conservative Party*, pp. 40–41. 'He had managed . . .': Blake, *Conservative Party*, p. 18. 'Rising hope . . .': Hugh Trevor-Roper (ed.), *Macaulay's Essays* (1965), p. 213. 'That young man . . .': Travis L. Crosby, *The Two Mr Gladstones* (1997), p. 29. Gladstone's meeting with Peel: *Gladstone Diaries*, III, 31 August 41; Morley, *Gladstone*, I, pp. 242–3. 'I have had . . .': *Disraeli Letters*, III, no.1186. 'My husband's political . . .': *Disraeli Letters*, III, no.1186, n.2. 'All is over': *Disraeli Letters*, III, no.1188.

On Lord Ripon: P. J. Jupp, 'Robinson, Frederick John, first Viscount Goderich and first Earl of Ripon (1782–1859)', *Oxford Dictionary of National Biography* (2004). 'Gladstone could do . . .': Bebbington and Swift, *Gladstone Centenary Essays*, p. 42. 'Natural and proper . . .': Bebbington and Swift, *Gladstone Centenary Essays*, p. 43. 'The negative character . . .': *Gladstone Diaries*, III, 5 February 42. 'The most palpable . . .': John Brooke and Mary Sorensen, *The Prime Ministers' Papers. W. E. Gladstone. I: Autobiographica* (1971), p. 125. 'I have to . . .': *Gladstone Diaries*, III, 13 May 43. 'Deliberate and even . . .': Shannon, *Heroic Minister*, p. 173. 'I really have . . .': Bebbington and Swift, *Gladstone Centenary Essays*, p. 46. 'I could not . . .' and 'Gladstone's career . . .': Morley, *Gladstone*, I, pp. 278–9

Disraeli's speech, 11 April 45: T. E. Kebbel (ed.), *Selected Speeches of the Earl of Beaconsfield* (1882), pp. 82–97. *Gladstone Diaries*, III, 11 April 45. On Young England, see the neat summary in Smith, *Disraeli*, pp. 57–8, and Mary S. Millar, *Disraeli's Disciple: the Scandalous Life of George Smythe* (2006); Jonathan Parry, 'Manners, John James Robert, seventh Duke of Rutland (1818–1906)', *Oxford Dictionary of National Biography* (2004). 'Chiefly of the . . .': *Disraeli Letters*, IV,

No.1229, 11 March 42. 'Mournful delusions': Shannon, *Heroic Minister*, p. 167. On Disraeli's trilogy, see the essay by Daniel R. Schwarz in Charles Richmond & Paul Smith (eds.), *The Self-Fashioning of Disraeli, 1818–1851* (1998), pp. 42–65. 'Origin and condition . . .' & 'order, decency . . .': Richmond & Smith (eds.), *The Self-Fashioning of Disraeli*, pp. 57, 59. 'An attempt . . .': *Coningsby*, bk II, ch. 5. 'The gentleman in Downing Street'. *Sybil*, bk VI, ch. 1. 'Chattering on subjects . . .': Weintraub, *Disraeli*, p. 242.

CHAPTER THREE: STRANGERS (pp. 40–49)

Disraeli provides his own entertaining account of the repeal of the Corn Laws in *Lord George Bentinck* (1851). The best scholarly work on repeal is Travis L. Crosby, *Sir Robert Peel's Administration, 1841–1846* (1976). A summary of his views is found in his later work, *The Two Mr Gladstones* (1997). See also the more recent study by Anna Gambles, *Protection and Politics: Conservative Economic Discourse, 1815–1852* (1999). W. D. Rubenstein, *Britain's Century* (London, 1998) provides a typically pithy review of events. On Gladstone's relationship with Peel, see David Bebbington and Roger Swift (eds), *Gladstone Centenary Essays*, (2000), pp. 30–56. Biographies of Peel include those by Norman Gash (1961, 1972, 2 vols), Eric J. Evans (1991), and T. A. Jenkins (1999). On the Conservative party, see Robert Stewart, *The Foundation of the Conservative Party, 1830–1867* (1978); Robert Blake, *The Conservative Party from Peel to Thatcher* (1985, 2nd edn).

Colonial Office. 'Something is in . . .': *Gladstone Diaries*, III, 6 December 45. 'I see constantly . . . ' : W.F. Monypenny and G. E. Buckle, *The Life of Benjamin Disraeli* (2 vols., 1929 edn), I, p. 747. Disraeli's speech: T. E. Kebbel (ed.), *Selected Speeches of the Earl of Beaconsfield* (1882), pp. 98–110. 'The skies are . . .' : *Gladstone Diaries*, III, 23 January 46. Gladstone's search for a constituency: Roy Jenkins, *Gladstone* (1995), pp. 82–4, and Richard Shannon, *Gladstone: Peel's Inheritor*, (1982), pp. 189–191. 'Peel was most . . .' : *Gladstone Diaries*, III, 22 December 45. 'Somewhere or other . . .' & 'should not have . . .' : Shannon, *Peel's Inheritor*, p. 190.

On Peel's reorganisation of the economic and financial system, see Boyd Hilton, 'Peel: a reappraisal' in *Historical Journal*, 22 (1979), 585–614. On 1840s Ireland: C. O'Grada, 'The Great Irish Famine', *UCD Centre for Economic Research, Papers*, No.97/12, (Dublin, 1997); Donal Kerr, *A Nation of Beggars? Priests, People, and Politics in Famine Ireland, 1846–1852* (1998); Peter Gray, *The Irish Famine* (1995). Summary of Protectionism: Gambles, *Protection and Politics*, pp. 21–2. Summary of repeal measures: Crosby, *Sir Robert Peel's Administration*, pp. 148–150.

'In the lobby . . .' : *Disraeli Letters*, III, no.747, 16 March 38. 'Evening party . . .' : *Gladstone Diaries*, III, 11 February 46. 'A most gracious . . .' : *Gladstone Diaries*, III, 31 March 46. 'What I cannot . . .' : K. T. Hoppen, *The Mid-Victorian Generation* (1998), p. 135.

Disraeli's speech on the third reading of the Corn Importation bill: Kebbel (ed.), *Selected Speeches of the Earl of Beaconsfield*, pp. 144–72. 'To unite his . . .', 'nothing of the . . .', and 'intimated to me . . .': Monypenny and Buckle, *Disraeli*, I, pp. 787–9. A. A. W. Ramsay in *Sir Robert Peel* (1928) suggests that Peel was too gentlemanly to produce the letter, but Blake disputes this. He also dismisses the claim in Monypenny and Buckle that Peel had lost the letter (Blake, *Disraeli*, p. 238). 'Insulted the honour . . .': Blake, *Disraeli*, p. 240. 'Shortest cabinet . . .' *Gladstone Diaries*, 26 June 46 (fn. 12). 'The Ministry . . .': *Disraeli Letters*, IV, No.1499. '"Dizzy"'s . . .' and 'quite as wonderful . . .': Morley, *Gladstone*, II, p. 705. 'In chaos': *Gladstone Diaries*, III, 7 July 46.

CHAPTER FOUR: THE GAME (pp. 50–62)

Summer Exhibition. On Gladstone and Disraeli's table talk, see Lord Blake's essay in Peter Jagger (ed.), *Gladstone* (1998), pp. 66–7. The most colourful description of Gladstone's nightlife is found in Roy Jenkins, *Gladstone* (1995), ch. 7. A discussion of Gladstone's diary entries on the subject is found in H. C. G. Matthew, *Gladstone, 1809–1898* (1997), ch. 4. Catherine Gladstone: H. C. G. Matthew, 'Gladstone, Catherine (1812–1900)', *Oxford Dictionary of National Biography* (2004).

'It is not . . .': A. Tilney Bassett (ed.), *Gladstone to his Wife* (1936), p. 82. 'R.A.s were . . .' and 'It went off . . .': *Disraeli Letters*, V, no. 2000. 'Dinner at the . . .': *Gladstone Diaries*, IV, 4 May 50. 'Never could command . . .': Helen M. Swartz and Marvin Swartz (ed.), *Disraeli's Reminiscences* (1975), p. 6. 'I did not go . . .': *Gladstone Diaries*, IV, 12 May 50. 'Long and shameful . . .': *Gladstone Diaries*, IV, 15 January 47. 'Channels' etc: *Gladstone Diaries*, III, 26 October 45. 'Some regular work . . .': Matthew, *Gladstone*, p. 90. 'Out at all . . .': *Gladstone Diaries*, IV, 19 July 48. 'Path of danger': *Gladstone Diaries*, IV, 31 April 51.

'Conversed indoors or . . .': *Gladstone Diaries*, IV, 20 January 54. 'The retrospect of . . .': *Gladstone Diaries*, IV, 29 December 1809. On Gladstone and Peel, see David Bebbington and Roger Swift (eds), *Gladstone Centenary Essays* (2000), pp. 29–56. 'Unable to speak . . .': John Vincent (ed.), *Diaries of Edward Henry Stanley, 15th Earl of Derby*, vol.1 (1978), p. 23. On Hope and Manning, see Richard Shannon, *Gladstone: Peel's Inheritor* (1982), pp. 234–7. 'Such terrible blows . . .': *Gladstone Diaries*, IV, 30 March 1851. 'Lovely beyond measure': *Gladstone Diaries*, IV, 1 July 52. 'I can no longer . . .': Lytton Strachey, *Eminent Victorians* (1918), p. 54. 'Strange, questionable . . .': *Gladstone Diaries*, IV, 23 July 51. 'Wrenched away . . .': *Gladstone Diaries*, IV, 19 August 51.

Hughenden. *Disraeli Letters*, V, no.1773. 'It will be . . .': Stanley Weintraub, *Disraeli* (1993), p. 279. 'The high game . . .': *Disraeli Letters*, V, no.1730. On financial discussions following Bentinck's death, see Robert Blake, *Disraeli* (1966), pp. 253–4.

'Disraeli was soon . . .': Blake, *Disraeli*, p. 248. On Derby ('Why is heaven . . .'; 'He made no . . .'): Angus Hawkins, 'Stanley, Edward George Geoffrey Smith, fourteenth earl of Derby (1799–1869)', *Oxford Dictionary of National Biography* (2004; online edn, May 2005); W. D. Rubenstein, *Britain's Century* (1998), pp. 102–3. On the scandal involving Disraeli and Lord Henry Stanley, see C. L. Cline, 'Disraeli and Peel's 1841 Cabinet' in *Journal of Modern History*, vol. 11 no.4 (December 1939), 509–12. Letter from Stanley to Disraeli, 21 December 48: W. F. Monypenny and G. E. Buckle, *The Life of Benjamin Disraeli* (2 vols, 1929 edn), I, pp. 937–40. 'I am Disraeli . . .': John Vincent (ed.) *Diaries of Edward Henry Stanley, 15th Earl of Derby*, vol. 1 (1978), p. 1.

On the state of the Tory party in the late 1840s, see Robert Blake, *The Conservative Party from Peel to Thatcher*, pp. 77–83. 'The lukewarmness . . .': Blake, *Conservative Party*, p. 78. 'The cabinet would . . .': *Disraeli Letters*, V, no.2069. 'He speculated . . .': Vincent, *Derby Diaries*, I, p. 24. 'He did not . . .': Blake, *Disraeli*, p. 287. 'Protection is . . .': Blake, *Disraeli*, p. 293. 'D. expressed his . . .': Vincent, *Derby Diaries*, I, pp. 46–7. Gladstone's meeting with Stanley: *Gladstone Diaries*, IV, 26 February 51.

CHAPTER FIVE: THUNDER AND LIGHTING (pp. 63–72)

House of Lords, February 1852. 'My Lord . . .': Elizabeth Longford, *Wellington: Pillar of State* (1972), p. 396. 'Who is he . . .': John Vincent,

Derby Diaries, I (1978), p. 72. Palmerston and 'extend as far . . .': David Steele, 'Temple, Henry John, third Viscount Palmerston (1784–1865)', *Oxford Dictionary of National Biography* (2004); also, Jasper Ridley, *Lord Palmerston* (1970), pp. 400–2; E. D. Steele, *Palmerston and Liberalism, 1855–1865* (1991). 'Promised forbearance . . .':Vincent, *Derby Diaries*, I, p. 72. 'we built up . . . :' *Disraeli Letters*, VI, no.2336.

The description of the new Houses of Parliament is taken from Richard Cavendish, 'State Opening of Parliament, November 1852' in *History Today* (November 2002); the parallel between Pugin and Disraeli is drawn by David Cannadine in *The Houses of Parliament: History, Art, Architecture* (2000), pp. 15–20.

The best discussion of the controversy surrounding Disraeli's 1852 Budget is found in Martin Daunton, *Trusting Leviathan: The Politics of Taxation in Britain, 1799–1914* (2001), pp. 91–97. See also P. R. Ghosh, 'Disraelian Conservatism: a financial approach' in *English Historical Review*, 99 (1984), 268–96, and H. C. G. Matthew, 'Disraeli, Gladstone, and the Politics of Mid-Victorian Budgets' in *Historical Journal*, 22 (1979), 615–43. On Wood: David Steele, 'Wood, Charles, first Viscount Halifax (1800–1885)', *Oxford Dictionary of National Biography* (2004). 'I fear we . . .': W. F. Monypenny and G. E. Buckle, *The Life of Benjamin Disraeli* (2 vols, 1929 edn), I, p. 1241. 'Not a gentleman':Vincent, *Derby Diaries*, I, p. 85. 'Jews make no . . .': (Sydney Herbert) Stanley Weintraub, *Disraeli* (1993), p. 321. 'No man knows . . .': Monypenny and Buckle, *Disraeli*, I, p. 1255 [changed to present tense]. 'A. Tilney Bassett (ed.), *Gladstone to his Wife* (1936), p. 92. 'Marvellous talent . . .': Bassett (ed.), *Gladstone to his Wife* pp. 80–82. 'I have a . . .': Bassett (ed.), *Gladstone to his Wife* p. 92.

Treasury Front Bench. The summary of Disraeli's budget is taken from Daunton, *Trusting Leviathan*, pp. 95–6. 'A daring bid . . .': John Brooke and Mary Sorensen (eds), *The Prime Ministers' Papers: W. E. Gladstone*, I, *Autobiographica* (1971), p. 76. Disraeli's Budget speech: *Commons Hansard*, 16 December 52; Monypenny and Buckle, *Disraeli*, I, pp. 1258–63; T. E. Kebble, *Selected Speeches of Beaconsfield*, I (1882), pp. 396–435. Gladstone's reply: *Commons Hansard*, 16 December 52; A. Tilney Bassett, *Gladstone's Speeches* (1916), pp. 155–181. See also,Vincent, *Derby Diaries*, I, pp. 89–90. Report by E. M. Whitty, quoted in T. A. Jenkins, *Disraeli and Victorian Conservatism* (1996), p. 44. Bright and Trevelyan: Weintraub, *Disraeli*, p. 323. 'Gladstone's look when . . .': Vincent, *Derby Diaries*, p. 90. 'Placing his eyeglass . . .': Christopher Silvester, *The Pimlico Companion to Parliament* (1996), p. 320. 'Spoke with great . . .':Vincent, *Derby Diaries*, p. 89. 'Dull': Monypenny and Buckle, *Disraeli*, I, p. 1264. 'There was an . . .': Monypenny and Buckle, *Disraeli*, I, p. 1264. 'Like two of . . .': Morley, *Gladstone*, I, p. 439.

CHAPTER SIX: THE CHANCELLOR'S OLD CLOTHES
(pp. 73–83)

Carlton Club. 'Smashing an antagonist . . .': Stanley Weintraub, *Disraeli* (1993), p. 325. 'My poor brain . . .': A. Tilney Bassett (ed.), *Gladstone to his Wife* (1936), pp. 94–5. 'They being heated . . .': John Vincent (ed.), *Derby Diaries*, I (1978), p. 92. 'I found myself . . .': *Gladstone Diaries*, IV, 20 December 52. 'Being able to . . .', 'fox-chase', 'my great object . . .', 'superlative acting . . .': Bassett, *Gladstone to his Wife*, pp. 93–5. 'Gladstone is reported . . .': Vincent, *Derby Diaries*, I, p. 91. 'Tonight I saw . . .': *Gladstone Diaries*, IV, 4 November 52. 'Tea with E. Collins . . .' *Gladstone Diaries*, IV, 19 November 52. 'I had a . . .': *Gladstone Diaries*, IV, 31 December 52. 'The year which . . .': *Gladstone Diaries*, IV, 29 December 52.

On Aberdeen: Muriel E. Chamberlain, 'Gordon, George Hamilton, fourth earl of Aberdeen (1784–1860)', *Oxford Dictionary of National Biography* (2004). 'An exceptional air . . .', 'grateful thanks . . .', 'I have heard . . .', 'I feel grateful . . .': W. F. Monypenny and G. E. Buckle, *The Life of Benjamin Disraeli* (2 vols, 1929 edn), I, pp. 1265–6. 'Nothing could . . .': Bassett (ed.), *Gladstone to his Wife,* p. 95. 'Brief, and . . .': *Disraeli Letters*, VI, no.2473. 'I am told . . .': Bassett (ed.), *Gladstone to his Wife*, p. 95. 'He is the . . .', 'Utterly disregard . . .': *Disraeli Letters*, VI, no. 2335. Correspondence between Gladstone and Disraeli about the Chancellor's robe: *Disraeli Letters*, VI, nos 2492 & 2500; also Monypenny and Buckle, *Disraeli*, I, pp. 1292–6.

On Gladstone as chancellor, see Richard Shannon, *Gladstone: Peel's Inheritor* (1982), pp. 264–273. The best general discussion on the question of income tax is by Roy Jenkins, a former chancellor himself, in *Gladstone* (1995), pp. 137–57. For a more academic discussion, see also Martin Daunton, *Trusting Leviathan; the Politics of Taxation in Britain, 1799–1914* (2001), pp. 91–108. On Gladstone's financial policy throughout the 1850s, see: Angus, B. Hawking, 'A forgotten crisis: Gladstone and the politics of finance during the 1850s' in *Victorian Studies* (26) 1983, pp. 287–320. 'That verse . . .', 'wholly unworthy': *Gladstone Diaries*, IV, 19 April 53. 'Great storehouse', 'come home', 'as if': Shannon, *Peel's*

Inheritor, p. 269. 'You must take . . .': Jenkins, *Gladstone*, p. 151. 'It was said . . .': Vincent, *Derby Diaries*, I, p. 106. 'The order was . . .', 'to keep his own . . .': Travis L. Crosby, *The Two Mr Gladstones* (1997), p. 76. The text of Gladstone's budget speech (with an excellent editorial note): A. Tilney Bassett, *Gladstone's Speeches* (1916), pp. 182–252. 'Disraeli was on . . .', 'seems to call . . .': John Brooke and Mary Sorensen, *The Prime Ministers' Papers, W. E. Gladstone*, III (1978), pp. 133, 144. 'If our men . . .': *Disraeli Letters*, VI, no. 2526. Reaction to the speech: Morley, *Gladstone*, I, pp. 469–70; 'extraordinary effort . . .', 'the general feeling . . .': Vincent, *Derby Diaries*, I, p. 106.

CHAPTER SEVEN: THE HANDSHAKE (pp. 84–94)

Leicester Square. The account of Gladstone and Wilson is from Richard Shannon, *Gladstone: Peel's Inheritor* (1982), pp. 273–5, and Roy Jenkins, *Gladstone* (1995), pp. 172–3. 'These talkings of . . .': *Gladstone Diaries*, IV, 10 May 53. 'Not all right . . .': *Gladstone Diaries*, IV, 23 June 53. All other quotations from Shannon, *Peel's Inheritor*, pp. 273–5.

Writings of 'Manilius' are collected in William Hutcheon (ed.), *Whigs and Whiggism: Political Writings by Benjamin Disraeli* (1913), pp. 436–69. 'His temper . . .', 'qualified to be . . .': *Press*, 11 June 53, 21 May 53. 'When our Hannibal . . .', 'Styled himself . . .': Hutcheon (ed.), *Whigs and Whiggism*, pp. 463, 454. 'Why is the . . .', 'A motley crew . . .' W. F. Monypenny and G. E. Buckle, *The Life of Benjamin Disraeli* (2 vols, 1929 edn), I, p. 1311.

House of Lords. Description of the chamber, Christine Riding and Jacqueline Riding (eds.), *The Houses of Parliament: History, Art, Architecture* (2000), p. 123. 'Entreating him . . .', 'It might make . . .': *Gladstone Diaries*, V, 1 February 55. Aberdeen's relationship with Gladstone is drawn from Jenkins, *Gladstone*, pp. 40–41. On the war, see Clive Ponting, *The Crimean War* (2004), H. W. V. Temperley, *England and the Near East: The Crimea* (1936); G. B. Henderson, *Crimean War Diplomacy, and Other Historical Essays* (1947). On the political implications, see Michael Bentley, *Politics without Democracy* (1996), pp. 102–4. 'The problem . . .': *Gladstone Diaries*, V, 30 January 55. 'His words . . .': *Gladstone Diaries*, V, 1 February 55.

On Derby's attempt to form an administration, see J. R. Jones, 'The Conservatives and Gladstone in 1855' in *English Historical Review*, 77 (1962), 96–8. 'I found the . . .', 'the project of . . .', 'sanguine': John

Vincent, *Derby Diaries*, I (1978), p. 131. 'Imminent risk of . . .': *English Historical Review*, 77 (1962), 97. 'Lord Palmerston . . .': *Disraeli Letters*, VI, no. 2727. Gladstone's recollections: John Brooke and Mary Sorensen, *The Prime Ministers' Papers: W. E. Gladstone*, I *Autobiographies* (1971), pp. 80–83. 'Our chief has . . .': *Disraeli Letters*, VI, no.2730. 'He appeared in . . .': Vincent, *Derby Diaries*, I, p. 131. 'State of disgust . . .': Monypenny and Buckle, *Disraeli*, p. 1381. 'England has been . . .': Charles Dickens, *Bleak House* (1853), ch. XL. 'Lord Palmerston is . . .': Monypenny and Buckle, *Disraeli, I*, p. 1376. 'His hat shaking . . .' *Gladstone Diaries*, V, 3 February 55. 'No other government . . .': Shannon, *Peel's Inheritor*, p. 303. 'The truth is . . .', 'we were like . . .', 'a Palmerston government . . .': John Brooke and Mary Sorensen, *The Prime Ministers' Papers: W. E.. Gladstone*, III (1978), pp. 166–7, 172. 'P is not . . .': *Gladstone Diaries*, V, 4 February 55. 'We were afraid . . .': *Disraeli Letters*, VI, no.2733. 'Disraeli complained to . . .': Vincent, *Derby Diaries*, I, p. 133. On Palmerston: E. D. Steele, *Palmerston and Liberalism, 1855–1865* (1991), James Chambers, *Palmerston: The People's Darling* (2005); David Steele, 'Temple, Henry John, third Viscount Palmerston (1784–1865)', *Oxford Dictionary of National Biography* (2004).

CHAPTER EIGHT: THE LETTERS (pp. 95–107)

Hawarden. On Gladstone's Homeric studies, see David Bebbington and Roger Swift (eds), *Gladstone Centenary Essays* (2000), pp. 58–74, and, especially on the contrast with the Old Testament, H. C. G. Matthew, *Gladstone, 1809–1898* (1997) pp. 152–7. 'Establish a minimum . . .': John Morley, *Life of Gladstone* (1905), I, p. 205. 'Worked much on . . .': *Gladstone Diaries*, V, 12 June 55. 'Looked into my . . .': *Gladstone Diaries*, V, 7 July 55. 'The power derived . . .': Matthew, *Gladstone*, p. 153. 'We hesitate not . . .': Todd M. Endelman & Tony Kushner, *Disraeli's Jewishness* (2002), p. 57. Criticism of Gladstone's 'Studies on Homer': Bebbington & Swift (eds), *Gladstone Centenary Essays*, p. 58. Sir George Cornewall Lewis: D. A. Smith, 'Lewis, Sir George Cornewall, second baronet (1806–1863)', *Oxford Dictionary of National Biography* (2004). 'Reckless system . . .', 'very overstrained . . .', 'everyone detests . . .': Travis L. Crosby, *The Two Mr Gladstones* (1997), p. 85. 'The House of Commons . . .': Morley, *Gladstone*, I, p. 567. For a full list of Gladstone's travels, see *Gladstone Diaries*, V, Endmatter: 'Where he was'. A neat summary, used here, is found in

Jenkins, *Gladstone*, p. 186. 'From the sacred . . .': *Gladstone Diaries*, V, 21 February 58.

'By and by . . .': Stanley Weintraub, *Disraeli* (1993), p. 347. 'I was so . . .': *Disraeli Letters*, VI, no.2863. 'Nervous debility': Robert Blake, *Disraeli* (1966), p. 367. 'All with whom . . .': T. A. Jenkins, *Disraeli and Victorian Conservatism* (1996), p. 52. Disraeli's approach to Opposition is from Blake, *Disraeli*, p. 355. 'His house is . . .': *Disraeli Letters*, VI, no.2669. 'Mr Disraeli knew . . .': Blake, *Disraeli*, p. 368.

'Reasons why a Ministry formed by Lord Derby is not likely to stand': John Vincent, *Derby Diaries*, I (1978), p. 155. 'If you agree . . .', etc: Morley, *Gladstone*, I, pp. 579–80. 'Like a Bedouin . . .', 'Simeon Stylites . . .': Morley, *Gladstone*, p. 583.

'Do much better . . .': W. F. Monypenny and G. E. Buckle, *The Life of Benjamin Disraeli* (2 vols, 1929 edn), I, p. 1518. 'I shall never . . .', 'the enemy . . .', 'strength in the . . .': Monypenny and Buckle, *Disraeli*, I, pp. 1547–9, 1556. 'Handsome on the . . .': John Brooke and Mary Sorensen, *The Prime Ministers' Papers: W. E.. Gladstone*, III (1978), pp. 221–4. Graham to Gladstone: Brooke and Sorensen, *W. E. Gladstone*, III (1978), pp. 225–7. 'I think it . . .': Monypenny and Buckle, *Disraeli*, I, pp. 1557–8. 'My Dear Sir . . .': Morley, *Gladstone*, I, p. 589.

CHAPTER NINE: VOYAGE OF DISCOVERY (pp. 108–127)

Corfu Harbour. Gladstone makes detailed diary entries on his travels. The evocation of Corfu on arrival is from Morley, *Life of Gladstone*, I (1905), pp. 602–3. 'His Homeric fancies . . .', 'my old friend': Richard Shannon, *Gladstone: Peel's Inheritor* (1982), pp. 366–8 ' Which now as . . .', 'by what I suppose . . .': *Gladstone Diaries*, V, 10 & 20 November 58. 'Apologetic statesman . . .': Gilbert and Sullivan, *The Mikado*, Act I. 'Gladstone's despatch to Bulwer Lytton: *Gladstone Diary*, V, 28 December 58. 'Talked incessantly . . .': Leslie Mitchell, *Bulwer Lytton* (2003), p. 101. 'Mad as Bedlam': Mitchell, *Bulwer Lytton* , p. 208 'Leave a shadow . . .', 'I have received . . .', 'I was privy . . .', 'I confine myself . . .' : W. F. Monypenny and G. E. Buckle, *The Life of Benjamin Disraeli* (2 vols, 1929 edn), I, pp. 1561–3. 'Now that we . . .' : Travis L. Crosby, *The Two Mr Gladstones* (1997), p. 90. 'One of those . . .' (*The Times*, 13 January 59), 'I cannot say . . .' : Shannon, *Peel's Inheritor*, p. 371. 'I hardly think . . .' : Morley, *Gladstone*, I, p. 613. 'This I must . . .' : Morley, *Gladstone*, I, p. 612. 'A political drama . . .' : Shannon, *Peel's Inheritor*,

p. 372. 'Ah, but he . . .' : Morley, *Gladstone*, p. 613.' At the lowest . . .'
: *Gladstone Diaries*, V, 21 February 59. 'The town pleases . . .' : *Gladstone Diaries*, V, 1 March 59. 'Saw one': *Gladstone Diaries*, V, 3 March 59.
'Much rumination': *Gladstone Diaries*, V, 5 March 59. 'Saw R. Tull . . .',
'saw L. Spur . . .', 'gratitude ought to . . .' : *Gladstone Diaries*, V, 8, 10,
13 March 59. Carnarvon: Crosby, *The Two Mr Gladstones*, p. 241.
'Without any reserve . . .' : Morley, *Gladstone*, I, p. 623.

Willis's Rooms. Description of the meeting of the Liberal party: *The Times*, 7 June 59. Summary of 'Liberalism': G. R. Searle, *The Liberal Party* (2001); also Jonathan Parry, *The Rise and Fall of Liberal Government in Victorian Britain* (1993), J. R. Vincent, *The Formation of the Liberal Party* (1976 edn), P. F. Clarke, *Lancashire and the New Liberalism* (1972) and E.F. Biagini, *Liberty, Retrenchment and Reform* (1992). 'The nineteenth-century . . .' : Jenkins, *Gladstone*, p. 204. 'The entente cordiale . . .' : T. A. Jenkins, *The Parliamentary Diaries of Sir John Trelawny* (1990), p. 81. 'On the whole . . .' : Lord Stanmore, *Sidney Herbert*, (1906), II, p. 158. 'Fervent wish . . .', 'threatened me', *Gladstone Diaries*, 21 February 58, 8 June 59. 'Great principles . . .' : Jenkins, *Trelawny Diaries*, p. 84. 'Every boy and . . .': *Iolanthe*, Act II. Summary of the 1858–9 Conservative administration is from T. A. Jenkins, *Disraeli and Victorian Conservatism* (1996), pp. 52–6. 'Well satisfied with . . .' : Jenkins, *Trelawny Diaries*, p. 60. 'Never had I . . .' : Morley, *Gladstone*, I, p. 627. 'The great battle . . .' : Monypenny and Buckle, *Disraeli*, I, p. 1633.

Budget Day 1860. The summary and analysis of Gladstone's 1860 budget comes directly from Martin Daunton, *Taxing Leviathan: the Politics of Taxation in Britain, 1799–1914* (2001), pp. 168–72. The full text of Gladstone's speech: A. Tilney Bassett, *Gladstone's Speeches* (1916), pp. 253–311. 'Physically impossible', 'this was the . . .' : *Gladstone Diaries*, 5 and 10 February 60. 'Radiant', 'Gladstone is now', 'the great man' : John Morley, *Gladstone* (1905), I, pp. 661–3. 'He betrays . . .': Monypenny and Buckle, *Disraeli*, II, p. 12. 'He is the . . .': Christopher Hibbert (ed.), *Greville's England* (1981), p. 279.

'I know from . . .': Monypenny and Buckle, *Disraeli*, II, pp. 18–19.
'Nothing could be . . .': Hibbert (ed.), *Greville's England*, p. 279. 'A favourite of . . .': Monypenny and Buckle, *Disraeli*, II, pp. 20–21. 'I dislike and . . .', 'throughout the whole . . .': Andrew Roberts, *Victorian Titan* (1999), pp. 75, 66. 'Ah Robert . . .': Robert Blake, *Disraeli* (1966), p. 427. Disraeli to Sir William Miles, 11 June 60: Monypenny and Buckle, *Disraeli*, II, pp. 23–5. 'When the pinch . . .': Monypenny and Buckle, *Disraeli*, II, p. 26. 'Attacking Gladstone with . . .': T. A. Jenkins,

The Parliamentary Diaries of Sir John Trelawny (1990), p. 121. On Palmerston and paper duties, see, Jasper Ridley, *Lord Palmerston* (1970), pp. 496–8. 'These strange time . . .', 'my resignation . . .': *Gladstone Diaries*, 26 May and 2 June 60.

'It is startling . . .' *Gladstone Diaries*, 3 September 60. 'Saw Bennet . . .': *Gladstone Diaries*, 9 November 60. 'My deep, deep . . .': *Gladstone Diaries*, 29 December 60. 'A laborious and . . .' etc.; *Gladstone Diaries*, 10–13 April 61. 'I think it . . .': Philip Guedalla (ed.), *Gladstone and Palmerston Correspondence* (1928), pp. 166–7, 'Now seem to . . .': John Vincent (ed.), *Derby Diaries*, I (1978), p. 170. 'Disraeli is in . . .': Monypenny and Buckle, *Disraeli*, II, pp. 30–31. 'The figures rather . . .': *Gladstone Diaries*, 15 April 61. 'The Tories seem . . .': Jenkins, *Trelawny Diaries*, p. 168. 'Could speak of . . .': Vincent, *Derby Diaries*, p. 171. 'I write to you . . .', 'testimony to . . .', 'politics is like . . .', 'in the very . . .': Monypenny and Buckle, *Disraeli*, II, pp. 33–6. 'One of the . . .', 'today's debate in . . .': *Gladstone Diaries*, 31 May, 7 June 61. Jenkins, *Trelawny Diaries*, p. 105.

CHAPTER TEN: IN THE ARBORETUM (pp. 128–141)

Grounds of Hawarden. 'In chopping down . . .': W. T. Stead, *Gladstone* (1898), p. 52. 'A tree we . . .': *Gladstone Diaries*, V, 27 December 67. Helen M. Swartz and Marvin Swartz, *Disraeli's Reminiscences* (1975), pp. 118, 130.

A full account of Gladstone's life at Hawarden in the 1860s is found in H. C. G Matthew, *Gladstone* (1997), pp. 150–69. See also Roy Jenkins, *Gladstone* (1995), pp. 172–85, Travis L. Crosby, *The Two Mr Gladstones* (1997), pp. 95–102. 'Half a century . . .': *Gladstone Diaries*, V, 29 December 59. 'We grew to . . .': Crosby, *Gladstone*, pp. 95–6. 'Cricket round the . . .': *Gladstone Diaries*, 4 September 67. 'I am the . . .', 'So few people . . .': Bruce L. Kinzer, *The Gladstonian Turn of Mind* (1985), pp. 97–8. On Gladstone's relationship with his daughters, see Kinzer, *The Gladstonian Turn of Mind*, pp. 97–121. Roy Jenkins provides an elegant character sketch of Catherine in *Gladstone*, pp. 54–8. 'How much might . . .': Matthew, *Gladstone*, p. 161. 'Oh William dear . . .': Jenkins, *Gladstone*, p. 55. On the Duchess of Sutherland, see Crosby, *Two Mr Gladstones*, pp. 99–101; Matthew, *Gladstone*, p. 159. 'Leaving Catherine which . . .': *Gladstone Diaries*, 18 May 61. On the frequency of Gladstone's visits to Cliveden and Chiswick, see *Gladstone Diaries*, V, VI, Endmatter: 'Where he was'. 'None will fill . . .': *Gladstone Diaries*, 28 October 68.

Descriptions of life at Hughenden, including the grounds and walks, are drawn from: W. F. Monypenny and G. E. Buckle, *The Life of Benjamin Disraeli* (2 vols, 1929 edn), I, pp. 970–77; National Trust, *Hughenden Manor* (1997). The account of Disraeli's private life is from Robert Blake, *Disraeli* (1966), pp. 409–424. For his relationship with Mary Anne, see Stanley Weintraub, *Disraeli* (1993), pp. 348–54. 'Saunter in the . . .': Swartz and Swartz, *Disraeli's Reminiscences*, p. 130. 'I live solely . . .', 'I believed D . . .': William Fraser, *Disraeli and his Day* (1891), pp. 325, 151. 'I like very much . . .': Swartz and Swartz, *Disraeli's Reminiscences*, pp. 117–18. 'My own experience . . .', 'Make the coat . . .', 'you should see . . .': Weintraub, *Disraeli*, pp. 349, 351. 'His whole soul . . .': Blake, *Disraeli*, p. 159. 'Without absolute beauty . . .': Swartz and Swartz, *Disraeli's Reminiscences*, p. 92. 'I well remember . . .': Weintraub, *Disraeli*, p. 428. 'She believed in . . .': André Maurois, *Disraeli* (1937 edn), p. 178. 'I saw you . . .', 'We were so . . .', Dizzy would have . . .': Weintraub, *Disraeli*, p. 354. The story of how Monty Corry became Disraeli's private secretary is from Blake, *Disraeli*, p. 418. 'Mr Gladstone . . .', 'My wife . . .': Monypenny and Buckle, *Disraeli*, II, pp. 304–5.

St George's Chapel Windsor. The description of Prince Albert's funeral is from John Wolffe, *Great Deaths: Grieving, Religion and Nationhood in Victorian and Edwardian Britain* (2000), pp. 205–6. 'A very solemn . . .': *Gladstone Diaries*, 23 December 61. 'May become the . . .': John Vincent, *Derby Diaries*, I (1978), p. 90. 'The one purpose . . .': Morley, *Gladstone*, I, pp. 737–8. 'The worst consequence . . .': Weintraub, *Disraeli*, p. 386. 'Mr Disraeli was . . .': Monypenny and Buckle, *Disraeli*, II, p. 119.

1862 Exhibition. On Prince Albert and the exhibition, see John McKenzie, *The Victorian Vision: Inventing New Britain* (2001), p. 43. The meeting at South Kensington is from Stanley Weintraub, *Disraeli* (1993), p. 394. 'This had a disastrous . . .': Monypenny and Buckle, *Disraeli* II, p. 129. 'Spoke on Exhibition . . .': *Gladstone Diaries*, VI, 2 July 63. 'In the combination . . .: Morley, *Gladstone* II, p. 823. 'Alas it was . . .': *Gladstone Diaries*, VI, 31 July 61. 'That beautiful and . . .', 'His eyes . . .', 'It is difficult . . .': Morley, *Gladstone* I, p. 722. 'If Herbert had . . .': Vincent, *Derby Diaries* I, p. 174. 'The strangest though . . .': *Gladstone Diaries*, VI, 29 December 61.

CHAPTER ELEVEN: 'THE PEOPLE'S WILLIAM' (pp. 142–151)

Tyneside. Description of Gladstone's trip to the Northeast: John Morley, *Life of Gladstone* (1905), I, pp. 711–13. Quotations from *Gladstone Diaries*, VI, 6–11 October 62. On 'the People's William', see Eugenio Biagini, *Gladstone* (2000), pp. 38–42, and Travis L. Crosby, *The Two Mr Gladstones* (1997), pp. 110–12. On Gladstone's oratorical style, see the excellent essay by Glynne Wickham in Peter J. Jagger (ed.), *Gladstone* (1998), pp. 1–32. 'There is not . . .': John Morley, *The Life of William Ewart Gladstone* (1905), I, p. 669. T. A. Jenkins, *Diaries of Sir John Trelawny* (1990), pp. 210–11. 'Get up your . . .', 'shall always keep . . .': Jagger (ed.), *Gladstone*, pp. 11–12. 'Study plainness of . . .': Morley, *Gladstone*, I, p. 192.

Hughenden. 'It is quite . . .': W. F. Monypenny and G. E. Buckle, *The Life of Benjamin Disraeli* (2 vols, 1929 edn), I, p. 978. 'He had a . . .', etc.: Helen M. Swartz and Marvin Swartz (eds), *Disraeli's Reminiscences* (1975), pp. 118–21. 'Poor Sa!': Robert Blake, *Disraeli* (1965) p. 425. Monypenny and Buckle, *Disraeli*, I, p. 1289. 'D. seems to me . . .': Vincent (ed.), *Derby Diaries*, I, p. 208.

Sheldonian. Disraeli's Oxford visit is described in Monypenny and Buckle, *Disraeli*, II, pp. 104–10. 'Stayed at home . . .': *Gladstone Diaries*, 25 November 64. Gathorne Hardy: Jonathan Parry, 'Hardy, Gathorne Gathorne, first earl of Cranbrook (1814–1906)', *Oxford Dictionary of National Biography* (2004). 'The Tory party . . .': Monypenny and Buckle, *Disraeli*, II, p. 114. 'The leadership . . .', 'I am glad . . .': Monypenny and Buckle, *Disraeli*, II, pp. 149–51. Gladstone's tour of South Lancashire: Morley, *Gladstone*, I, pp. 778–80.

CHAPTER TWELVE: CAVEMEN (pp. 152–164)

Brocket Hall. Generations of local gossip have claimed that Palmerston died in the arms of a chambermaid at Brocket Hall. However, this information is not included in E. D. Steele's *DNB* entry on Palmerston, which cites the cause of death as pneumonia: David Steele, 'Temple, Henry John, third Viscount Palmerston (1784–1865)', *Oxford Dictionary of National Biography* (2004). 'At 6 ½ a telegram . . .': *Gladstone Diaries*, 18 October 65. 'On the general . . .': John Morley, *Life of Gladstone* (1905), I, p. 785. 'He is great . . .': Morley, *Gladstone*, p. 789. 'Mr Disraeli had . . .': W. F. Monypenny and

G. E. Buckle, *The Life of Benjamin Disraeli* (2 vols, 1929 edn), II, p. 157. Palmerston's last joke, 'What pluck . . .': Helen M. Swartz and Marvin Swartz, *Disraeli's Reminiscences* (1975), pp. 124–5, 143. 'He is in . . .': John Vincent (ed.) *Derby Diaries*, I (1978), p. 237. 'If Johnny is the man': Monypenny and Buckle, *Disraeli*, II, p. 159.

Electoral statistics: K. T. Hoppen, *The Mid-Victorian Generation* (1998), p. 246. Character sketch of Russell: John Prest, 'Russell, John [formerly Lord John Russell], first Earl Russell (1792–1878)', *Oxford Dictionary of National Biography* (2004); Jonathan Parry, *The Rise and Fall of Liberal Government in Victorian Britain* (1993), pp. 132–5, and W. D. Rubenstein, *Britain's Century* (1998), pp. 87–8. See also, John Prest, *Lord John Russell* (1972). John Bright: Miles Taylor, 'Bright, John (1811–1889)', *Oxford Dictionary of National Biography* (2004). Summary of public opinion on reform: Ian Machin, *The Rise of Democracy in Britain* (2001), pp. 56–7. 'Burst into a . . .': Vincent (ed.) *Derby Diaries*, I, p. 124. 'He can't now . . .': Michael Bentley, *Politics Without Democracy* (1996, 2nd edition), p. 128. 'Certainly as far . . .': Morley, *Gladstone*, I, p. 832. 'It will be . . .': Richard Shannon, *Gladstone: Heroic Minister* (1999), p. 7. 'But with God's . . .' *Gladstone Diaries*, 12 March 66. 'Every man who . . .', Roy Jenkins, *Gladstone* (1995), p. 247. 'Wry faces . . .': Shannon, *Heroic Minister*, p. 12. 'The limbo of . . .': Morley, *Gladstone*, II, p. 834. 'Trojan horse . . .': Shannon, *Heroic Minister*, p. 13. 'had been warned . . .': Richard Shannon, *Gladstone: Peel's Inheritor* (1982), p. 554. Summary of the first reading: Monypenny and Buckle, *Disraeli*, II, p. 164. 'Unattainable by . . .': Hoppen, *Mid-Victorian Generation*, p. 247. Jonathan Parry, 'Lowe, Robert, Viscount Sherbrooke (1811–1892)', *Oxford Dictionary of National Biography* (2004). 'If you want venality . . .': *Commons Hansard*, 13 March 66. 'Cave of Adullam . . .': Blake, Disraeli, pp. 440–41. 'Dis made a . . .': Stafford Northcote, *Life, Letters, and Diaries* (1899 edn), p. 154. On Robert Lowe, see James Winter, *Robert Lowe* (1976).

London–Liverpool train. Gladstone was reading *Ecce Homo: A Critique by Presbyter Anglicans*. He had read Seeley's controversial *Ecce Homo* (1865) over the previous Christmas. Liverpool speech and Westminster reaction, and 'It is not . . .', 'a languid . . .': Shannon, *Heroic Minister*, pp. 17–18. 'A leader of the . . .': Northcote, *Diaries*, p. 156.

Reform Bill, Second Reading: 'votes should be . . .': Monypenny and Buckle, *Disraeli*, II, p. 167. 'To reconstruct their . . .', and summary of Gladstone's speech: Shannon, *Heroic Minister*, p. 19. Full text of Gladstone's speech: A. Tilney Bassett, *Gladstone's Speeches* (1916), pp. 342–379. 'Vivacious viper': T. A. Jenkins, *Trelawny Diaries* (1990), p.

204 (21 May 62). 'It was twilight . . .', etc.: Shannon, *Heroic Minister*, pp. 20–21. 'We do not . . .': *Gladstone Diaries*, 28 April 66. 'No dislike of . . .': Blake, *Disraeli*, p. 441. 'We must help . . .', 'I cannot resist . . .': Monypenny and Buckle, *Disraeli*, II, pp. 168, 171. 'The franchise bill . . .': Shannon, *Heroic Minister*, p. 23. 'Much talk of . . .': Vincent, *Derby Diaries*, I, p. 252. 'With the cheering . . .': *Gladstone Diaries*, 18 June 66. 'Where we sat . . .': Vincent, *Derby Diaries*, I, p. 253. 'A bill like . . .': Prest, *Lord John Russell*, p. 414. 'Finished in Downing . . .': *Gladstone Diaries*, 6 July 66.

CHAPTER THIRTEEN: UP THE GREASY POLE (pp. 165–189)

Windsor Castle. The classic accounts of the Second Reform Act remain, F. B. Smith, *The Making of the Second Reform Bill* (1966) and Maurice Cowling, *1867: Disraeli, Gladstone and Revolution* (1967). For a neat summary, see K. T. Hoppen, *The Mid-Victorian Generation* (1998), ch. 8. 'Some thought this . . .', 'Dis had a . . .', 'We are expecting . . .': Andrew Lang, *Life, Letters and Diaries of Sir Stafford Northcote* (1899 edn), p. 160. 'So much for . . .': James Winter, *Robert Lowe* (1976), p. 229. 'No mob outside . . .': W. F. Monypenny & G. E. Buckle, *The Life of Benjamin Disraeli* (2 vols, 1929 edn), II, p. 186. 'Did not intend . . .' etc: Smith, *Second Reform Bill*, pp. 134–5.

'One of my . . .', 'the journey to . . .': John Morley, *Life of Gladstone* (1905 edn), I, pp. 847–8. 'The truth is . . .': Travis L. Crosby, *The Two Mr Gladstones* (1997), p. 114. 'Viewed the field . . .': *Gladstone Diaries*, VI, 24 July 66. Granville will be . . .', etc.: Cowling, *1867*, pp. 121, 399. 'Singing, luncheon . . .': *Gladstone Diaries*, VI, 27 September 66. 'Left Cliveden with . . .': *Gladstone Diaries*, VI, 24 September 66. 'Duchess troubled . . .': *Gladstone Diaries*, VI, 25 July 66. 'My bed all . . .': *Gladstone Diaries*, VI, 28, 29 September 66. 'Italian art . . .': Herbert Maxwell (ed.), *Life and Letters of Fourth Earl of Clarendon* (1913), II, p. 328. 'We have had . . .': Morley, *Gladstone*, I, p. 851. 'Incessantly and . . .': *Gladstone Diaries*, VI, 1 January 67. 'Saw L . . .': *Gladstone Diaries*, VI, 29 January 67. 'There seem to . . .': Maxwell (ed.), *Clarendon Letters*, p. 330.

Westminster. 'Whether the government . . .', etc: Smith, *Second Reform Bill*, p. 149. 'With his hat . . .', 'He is firmly convinced . . .': Andrew Roberts, *Salisbury: Victorian Titan* (1999), pp. 88–9. 'But if I . . .', 'most unpleasant . . .', 'distressing and . . .', 'white as a . . .': Roberts, *Salisbury*, pp. 92–3. 'I am going . . .', and debate of 25

February 67: Monypenny and Buckle, *Disraeli*, II, p. 234ff. 'Well, concisely . . ', 'the resolutions . . ': John Vincent, *Derby Diaries*, I, (1978), p. 291. 'A greater . . ', 'All I hear . . ', 'The loss of . . ', 'clearly he will . . ': Monypenny and Buckle, *Disraeli*, II, pp. 237, 242, 245–6. 'The Tory party . . ': Smith, *Second Reform Bill*, p. 161.

'Spoke after . . ': *Gladstone Diaries*, 11 February 67. 'We are here . . ', 'I am not . . ': Richard Shannon: *Gladstone: Heroic Minister* (1999), p. 32. Disraeli's speech, 18 March 67: T. E. Kebbel (ed.), *Selected Speeches the Earl of Beaconsfield* (1882), I, pp. 544ff. The account of the debate is from Smith, *Second Reform Bill*, pp. 167–9. 'Gladstone is . . ': Vincent (ed.), *Derby Diaries*, I, p. 295.

Carlton House Terrace. 'glare of contentious eagerness', 'I have never . . ': Morley, *Gladstone*, I, pp. 862–3. 'always monopolised the . . ', 'had never even . . ': Shannon, *Heroic Minister*, p. 36. 'to tell him . . ': Cowling, *1867*, p. 196. 'Entire collapse of . . ': Morley, *Gladstone*, I, p. 866. 'We will not . . ': Monypenny and Buckle, *Disraeli*, II, pp. 265–6 'It was the . . ', 'speech of the session . . ': Smith, *Second Reform Bill*, p. 262. 'Rumours rife . . ': Monypenny and Buckle, *Disraeli*, II, p. 264. The *Spectator* & Elgin: Morley, *Gladstone*, I, p. 863. 'Stanley evidently . . ': Smith, *Second Reform Bill*, p. 180. Disraeli's speech, 12 April 67: Smith, *Second Reform Bill*, pp. 180–81; Monypenny and Buckle, *Disraeli*, II, pp. 265–6. 'I for one . . ': Alexander Ewald, *Earl of Beaconsfield and His Times*, II, p. 58. 'White to the very . . ', etc.: Philip Magnus, *Gladstone* (1954), p. 187. 'Spoke in . . ': *Gladstone Diaries*, VI, 12 April 67. 'The most wonderful . . ', 'I met Gladstone . . ': Morley, *Gladstone*, I, p. 864. 'You now have . . ': Smith, *Second Reform Bill*, p. 183. 'Your name is . . ', 'Her Majesty . . ', 'we ought to . . ': Monypenny and Buckle, *Disraeli*, II, pp. 268–72. 'Mr Disraeli is . . ': G. E. Buckle, *The Letters of Queen Victoria 1862–1878* (1926), I, pp. 424–5. 'A nice mess': Herbert Maxwell (ed.), *Life and Letters of Fourth Earl of Clarendon* (1913), II, p. 332. 'My resolution is taken . . ' *Gladstone Diaries*, VI, 1 May 67. 'Time tells . . ' Morley, *Gladstone*, I, p. 868. 'Much fatigued . . ': *Gladstone Diaries*, VI, 9 April 67. Corry: M. G. Wiebe, 'Corry, Montagu William Lowry, Baron Rowton (1838–1903)', *Oxford Dictionary of National Biography* (2004).

Members' Dining Room. 'Lay awake . . ': Vincent, *Derby Diaries*, I, p. 307. 'To those at . . ': Smith, *Second Reform Bill*, pp. 197–8. 'I waited until . . ': Monypenny and Buckle, *Disraeli*, II, p. 274. 'Determined at the . . ': *Gladstone Diaries*, VI, 15 July 67. 'The governing idea . . ': John Brooke and Mary Sorensen, *The Prime Ministers' Papers: W. E. Gladstone*, I (1970), p. 93.

'There is an impression . . .': Jenkins, *Gladstone*, p. 274. 'A bonfire of
. . .': *Gladstone Diaries*, 6 September 67. 'Attempts alike . . .': Shannon,
Heroic Minister, p. 44. 'Bitterest and . . .', 'In a progressive . . .': Blake,
Disraeli, p. 482. 'I have always . . .': Smith, *Disraeli*, p. 149. 'We were so
. . .', etc: Blake, *Disraeli*, p. 483. 'This has been . . .': Monypenny and
Buckle, *Disraeli*, II, p. 304. 'Parliament sitting . . .', 'you will not . . .', 'I
will not . . .', 'he and only . . .': Monypenny and Buckle, *Disraeli*, II,
pp. 317–20. 'At one . . .': *Gladstone Diaries*, 25 February 68. 'All is
sunshine . . .', etc.: Monypenny and Buckle, *Disraeli*, II, p. 326. 'Mr
Disraeli is . . .', 'I have climbed . . .': Blake, *Disraeli*, p. 487. 'Well Disraeli
. . .': André Maurois, *Disraeli* (1927), p. 188.

CHAPTER FOURTEEN: PREMIER LEAGUE (pp. 190–203)

Foreign Office. 'She can do . . .', 'Dizzy in his . . .' 'Gladstone's teeth
were . . .': W. F. Monypenny & G. E. Buckle, *The Life of Benjamin
Disraeli* (2 vols, 1929 edn), II, pp. 333–4. 'Risen from the . . .', Robert
Blake, *Disraeli* (1966), p. 487. 'The H. of . . .': Travis L. Crosby, *The Two
Mr Gladstones* (1997), p. 118. 'Too religious,' 'for success is . . .': Stanley
Weintraub, *Disraeli* (1993), p. 462. Russell's pamphlets: Spencer Walpole,
Lord John Russell (1891), II, p. 448. 'Fear and alarm . . .', 'failed to realise
. . .', 'there really . . .': Richard Shannon, *Gladstone: Heroic Minister*
(1999), pp. 48–9. 'Disraeli ambiguous and . . .', etc, 'there is great . . .':
Weintraub, *Disraeli*, pp. 465–6. 'Spoke 1(½) hours . . .': *Gladstone Diaries*,
VI, 3 April 68. 'In the most . . .', etc.: Shannon, *Heroic Minister*, p. 49.
'Under these circumstances . . .', etc: Monypenny & Buckle, *Disraeli*,
II, p. 372. 'We all agreed . . .': John Vincent, *Derby Diaries*, I, (1978), p.
333. 'In a white . . .': Monypenny & Buckle, *Disraeli*, II,
p. 375. 'At once pompous . . .': Keith Robbins, *John Bright* (1979), p.
202. 'Lost his temper . . .,' etc: Blake, *Disraeli*, p. 502. Whips advice: A.
F. Thompson, 'Gladstone's whips and the general election of 1868' in
English Historical Review, 63: 247 (1948), pp. 189–200. 'Miserable session,'
etc: Shannon, *Heroic Minister*, p. 53.
National Portrait Gallery. 'Meeting of the dead . . .': *Gladstone
Diaries*, VI, 11 July 68. 'I feel like . . .': *Gladstone Diaries*, VI, 31 December
68. 1868 election: K. T. Hoppen, *The Mid-Victorian Generation* (1998),
p. 591. 'Niagara leap of . . .': A. N. Wilson, *The Victorians* (2002), p. 334.
'All is new . . .' and Gladstone's role a modern electioneering party
leader: Thompson, 'Gladstone's whips and the general election of 1868'

in *English Historical Review* 63: 247 (1948), 189–90. 'D. says the . . .':
Vincent, *Derby Diaries*, I, p. 336. 'An evil night . . .': *Gladstone Diaries*,
VI, 2 September 68; 'There is the . . .': H. C. G. Matthew, *Gladstone*
(1997), p. 147. 'A dissolution of . . ,' 'I think I . . ,' 'Our shadows seem
. . .': Monypenny & Buckle, *Disraeli*, II, pp. 428–31. 'Nothing could
have . . .': G. E. Buckle, *The Letters of Queen Victoria 1862–1878* (1926),
I, p. 557. 'Grant those honours . . .': Monypenny & Buckle, *Disraeli*,
II, p. 439. 'The Queen can . . ,' 'the proffered coronet . . ,' Lord
Rosebery: Mollie Hardwick, *Mrs Dizzy* (1972), pp. 176–7. 'Mr Disraeli
at . . .' Theo Aronson, *Victoria and Disraeli* (1977), p. 114. 'To present
my . . .': Monypenny & Buckle, *Disraeli*, II, pp. 440–41. 'He looked
ill . . .': Vincent, *Derby Diaries*, I, p. 337. 'I said nothing . . .': Matthew,
Gladstone, p. 147. 'The lessons as . . .': *Gladstone Diaries*, VI, 1 December
68. Reginald Lucas, 'Ashley (Anthony) Evelyn Melbourne
(1836–1907)', rev. H. C. G. Matthew, *Oxford Dictionary of National
Biography* (2004).

CHAPTER FIFTEEN: DIE OR BREAK DOWN (pp. 204–217)

Hagley. 'Arrived at 10.45 . . .': *Gladstone Diaries*, VI, 29–31 December
68. 'Called on Disraeli . . .': John Vincent, *Derby Diaries*, I, (1978), pp.
339–40. 'Feeling unwell all . . . ,' 'I can't say . . .': Christopher Hibbert,
Disraeli (2004), p. 280. 'I never thought . . .': Stanley Weintraub, *Disraeli*
(1993), p. 479. 'Depressing work . . . stupor . . .' and the Commons/Lord
dispute: Travis L. Crosby, *The Two Mr Gladstones* (1997), pp. 125–7. 'In
some other . . .': D. C. Somervell, *Disraeli and Gladstone* (1926), pp.
157–8. 'The time grows . . .': *Gladstone Diaries*, VII, 12 July 69. 'A great
moral . . .': *Gladstone Diaries*, VII, 17 July 69. 'Obstinately bent . . .': A.
Hawkins & J. Powell, *The Journal of John Wodehouse, First Earl of Kimberley,
1862–1902* (1997), p. 239. 'He must I . . .' 'And no wonder': T. A. Jenkins,
'Parliamentary Diary of Sir John Trelawny, 1868–73' in *Camden
Miscellany*, XXXII (1994) pp. 370–71. 'Gladstone's own temper . . .':
Vincent, *Derby Diaries*, I, p. 341. 'Quite, quite myself . . .': Hibbert,
Disraeli, p. 280. 'My attack did . . .': *Gladstone Diaries*, VII, 23 July 69.
'Spent the morning . . .': *Gladstone Diaries*, VII, 13 August 69. 'Strange
story of . . .': Vincent, *Derby Diaries*, I, p. 346. The account of Gladstone
and Mrs Thistlethwayte is from: Roy Jenkins, *Gladstone* (1995),
pp. 307–12 and H. C. G. Matthew, *Gladstone* (1997), pp. 239–44. 'On
Monday till . . .': Jenkins, *Gladstone*, p. 310. 'Walked a little . . .': *Gladstone*

Diaries, VII, 11 December 69. 'It is like . . .': *Gladstone Diaries*, VIII, p. 563. 'Friendship with women . . .': Matthew, *Gladstone*, p. 241. 'Mrs Thistlethwayte . . .': *Gladstone Diaries*, VII, 28 October 69. 'It is difficult . . .': *Gladstone Diaries*, VIII, p. 563. 'Read a sermon . . .', 'Came to my rooms . . .': *Gladstone Diaries*, VII, 12 December 69. 'My review this . . .': *Gladstone Diaries*, VII, 29 December 69. 'And at midnight . . .': *Gladstone Diaries*, VII, 31 December 69.

Hughenden. 'Our talk was . . .': Vincent, *Derby Diaries*, I, p. 347. 'He is desponding . . .': A. E. Gathorne-Hardy, *Gathorne Hardy* (1910), I, p. 296. 'Montagu Corry . . .': W. F. Monypenny & G. E. Buckle, *The Life of Benjamin Disraeli* (2 vols, 1929 end), II, p. 489. 'My wrath against . . .': Weintraub, *Disraeli*, p. 485. Summary of *Lothair*: Paul Smith, *Disraeli* (1996), p. 158. Benjamin vii–xvii. 'Which now cover . . .': Smith, *Disraeli*, p. 158. 'If Mr Disraeli . . .', 'There is immense . . .': Disraeli (ed. Vernon Bogdanor), *Lothair*, p. vii. 'On Monday . . .,' etc.: Blake, *Disraeli*, p. 519. 'Tardy return': Weintraub, *Disraeli*, p. 482. 'Spice of Lothair': *Gladstone Diaries*, VII, 18 May 70. 'Unreadable': Jenkins, *Gladstone*, p. 183.

'There are few . . .': Benjamin Disraeli, *Lord George Bentinck* (1858 edn), pp. 7–8. On the Irish land question, see Alvin Jackson, *Ireland, 1798–1998* (1999), pp. 86–109. 'Three months of . . .': Shannon, *Heroic Minister*, p. 76. Also, Eugenio Biagini, *Gladstone* (2000), pp. 46–7. 'Rather give up . . .': K. T. Hoppen, *The Mid-Victorian Generation* (1998), pp. 595–6. 'Well received by . . .': *Gladstone Diaries*, VII, 15 February 70. Sir Roundell Palmer: David Steele, 'Palmer, Roundell, first earl of Selborne (1812–1895)', *Oxford Dictionary of National Biography* (2004). 'Gladstone looked worn . . .': Morley, Gladstone, I, p. 929. 'H of C . . .': *Gladstone Diaries*, VII, 8 April 70. 'In the best . . .': Weintraub, *Disraeli*, p. 485. 'The signal prudence . . .': Jenkins, *Gladstone*, p. 359. 'Dizzy's speeches . . .': Hibbert, *Disraeli*, p. 281. 'The premier was . . .': Monypenny & Buckle, *Disraeli*, II, pp. 475–6.

Burghley. Gathorne-Hardy, *Gathorne Hardy*, I, pp. 304–6.

CHAPTER SIXTEEN: VOLCANOES (pp. 218–226)

St Paul's Cathedral. 'An overpowering ovation . . .,' 'His face was . . .': William Fraser, *Disraeli and His Day* (1891), pp. 375–6. 'I know how . . .': A. E. Gathorne-Hardy, *Gathorne Hardy* (1910), I, p. 306. 'Injurious to . . .': W. F. Monypenny & G. E. Buckle, *The Life of Benjamin Disraeli* (2 vols, 1929 edn), II, p. 515. 'Gladstone sees that . . .,' 'He is vexed . . .': John Morley, *The Life of William Ewart Gladstone* (1905 edn), I, pp. 1022–3. 'Well pleased with . . .': John Vincent (ed.). *Derby Diaries*, II (1994), p. 101. On Gorst, see A. Hunter, *A Life of Sir John Eldon Gorst* (2001); E. J. Feuchtwanger, 'Gorst, Sir John Eldon (1835–1916)', *Oxford Dictionary of National Biography* (2004), online edn, May 2005. 'I found him . . .': Vincent, *Derby Diary*, II, p. 102. 'Was not an . . .,' and on Disraeli's style: Joseph S. Meisel, *Public Speech and the Culture of Public Life in the Age of Gladstone* (2001), p. 97. 'Disraeli's peculiar powers . . .': Vincent, *Derby Diaries*, II, p. 104. 'Fell flat . . .': ibid, p. 103. 'Oh Dizzy . . .': Mollie Hardwick, *Mrs Dizzy* (1972), p. 183. Disraeli's Manchester speech, 3 April 1872: T. E. Kebbel, *Selected Speeches of the Earl of Beaconsfield* (1882), II, pp. 490–522. Disraeli's Crystal Palace speech, 24 June 1872: Kebbel, *Speeches of Beaconsfield*, II, pp. 523–36. 'It is all . . .': Christopher Hibbert, *Disraeli* (2004), p. 284.

'Dizzy was perfect . . .': Agatha Ramm (ed.), *The Gladstone–Granville Correspondence* (1998), p. 327. On the death of Mary Anne: Hardwick, *Mrs Dizzy*, pp. 182–96. 'You and I . . .': *Gladstone Diaries*, VII, 19 January 73. ' I am much . . .': Morley, *Gladstone*, II, p. 155.

CHAPTER SEVENTEEN: AN ARTFUL DODGE (pp. 227–239)

Edwards's Hotel. 'My friends admire . . .': Christopher Hibbert, *Disraeli* (2004), p. 294. 'We found him . . .': A. E. Gathorne-Hardy, *Gathorne Hardy* (1910), p. 315. 'Found him much . . .': John Vincent, *Derby Diaries*, vol. II (1994), p. 127. The topography of political London is drawn from Michael Bentley, *Lord Salisbury's World* (2001). Rothschild breakfast: Stanley Weintraub, *Disraeli* (1993), p. 510. 'He did not . . .': Vincent, *Derby Diaries*, II, p. 127. 'As a bait . . .': Travis L. Crosby, *The Two Mr Gladstones* (1997), p. 132. Liberal division on Irish University Bill: Jonathan Parry, *The Rise and Fall of Liberal Government in Victorian Britain* (1993), p. 267. 'Overhead it is . . .': *Gladstone Diaries*, VIII, 1 March 73. 'Much coldness . . .': ibid, 4 March 73. T. A. Jenkins, 'Parliamentary Diaries of Sir John Trelawny, 1868–1873' in *Camden Miscellany XXXII* (1994), p. 479. Disraeli's speech, 11 March 73: T. E. Kebbel, *Selected Speeches of Beaconsfield* (1882), II, pp. 389–90. 'Wrapt attention': Philip Guedalla, *The Queen and Mr Gladstone* (1933), I, p. 395. 'Gladstone with the . . .,' 'It was a . . .': Morley, *Gladstone*, II, pp. 52–3. 'It seems to . . .': Jenkins, 'Trelawny Diaries,' p. 479. 'And here . . .': Morley, *Gladstone*, II, p. 55. 'You give no . . .': *Gladstone Diaries*, VIII, 13 March 73. 'As for himself . . .': J. Brooke & M. Sorensen (eds), *W. E. Gladstone IV: Autobiographical Memoranda 1868–1894* (1981), p. 32.

'Any news . . .': *Gladstone Diaries*, VIII, 13 March 73. 'Disappointed': Gathorne-Hardy, *Gathorne Hardy*, p. 320. 'That it would . . .': W. F. Monypenny & G. E. Buckle, *Life of Benjamin Disraeli* (2 vols, 1929 edn), II, p. 548. 'The artful dodger': Agatha Ramm (ed.), *The Gladstone–Granville Correspondence* (1998), p. 378. 'I decline altogether . . .': Monypenny & Buckle, *Disraeli*, II, pp. 551–2. Gladstone's correspondence with the Queen, 12–18 March 73: Guedalla, *The Queen and Mr Gladstone*, I, pp. 394–409. 'Nothing more is . . .': Brooke and Sorensen, *W. E. Gladstone*, IV, p. 28. 'A pamphlet . . .': Gathorne-Hardy, *Gathorne Hardy*, p. 324. 'Seriously unhinged by . . .': Guedalla, *The Queen and Mr Gladstone*, I, p. 406. 'He considered that . . .': Gathorne-Hardy, *Gathorne Hardy*, p. 324. 'We looked like . . .': Angus Hawkins & John Powell (eds), *Journal of John Woodhouse, First Earl of Kimberley* (1997), p. 275. 'Gladstone and D'Israeli . . .': Jenkins, 'Trelawny Diaries,' p. 480.

'Very unwell . . .': Morley, *Gladstone*, II, pp. 69–70. 'My cousin . . .': *Gladstone Diaries*, VIII, 10 March 73. 'We were enjoying . . .': ibid, 19–23 July 73. 'No manners, no . . .': Jenkins, 'Trelawny Diaries,' p. 501. 'Truly we go . . .': Hawkins & Powell, *Kimberley Journal*, p. 281. 'Sixty four years . . .,' 'the year ends . . .': *Gladstone Diaries*, VIII, 29–31 December 73.

'For nearly five . . .': Monypenny & Buckle, *Disraeli*, II, p. 602. 'Foolish and violent . . .': Vincent, *Derby Diaries II*, p. 145. Glasgow visit and reaction: Monypenny & Buckle, *Disraeli*, II, pp. 603–8. 'Paraphernalia of pheasants': Weintraub, *Disraeli*, p. 516. 'We were as . . .': Vincent, *Derby Diaries, II*, p. 133. 'We shall walk . . .,' 'the foxes have . . .': Marquis of Zetland, *Letters of Disraeli to Lady Bradford and Lady Chesterfield* (1929), I, pp. 45–6.

CHAPTER EIGHTEEN: THE JEWEL THIEF (pp. 240–251)

Benjamin Disraeli's bedroom. 'Dressing gown of . . .': A. E. Gathorne-Hardy, *Gathorne Hardy* (1910), p. 316. 'The great event . . .': Marquis of Zetland, *Letters of Disraeli to Lady Bradford and Lady Chesterfield* (1929), I, p. 49. 'Well satisfied on . . .': *Gladstone Diaries*, VIII, 24 January 74. 'The enemy will . . .': Sarah Bradford, *Disraeli* (1982), p. 303. 'Hurried me off . . .': Gathorne-Hardy, *Gathorne Hardy*, p. 334. 'To the conservatives . . .': John Vincent, *Derby Diaries*, II (1994), p. 159. 'Too late to

. . .,' 'I have never . . .,' 'I think his . . .': W. F. Monypenny & G. E. Buckle, *The Life of Benjamin Disraeli* (2 vols, 1929 edn), II, pp. 613–14. 'Where one is . . .': *The Times*, 26 January 74. 'Much said . . .': Gathorne-Hardy, *Gathorne Hardy*, p. 334. 'It is a . . .': Robert Rhodes James, 'Gladstone and the Greenwich seat' in *History Today* (1959), pp. 344–51. 'An enthusiastic meeting . . .': *Gladstone Diaries*, VIII, 28 July 74. 'We had exhausted . . .': Angus Hawkins and John Powell (eds), *Journal of John Woodhouse, First Earl of Kimberley* (1997), p. 285. 'I read something . . .,' 'we must reprobate . . .,' 'Mr Disraeli . . .': *The Times*, 2 February 74. 'Perhaps too personal . . .': Vincent, *Derby Diaries*, II, p. 160. 'A complete success' . . .': Zetland, *Letters to Lady Bradford and Lady Chesterfield*, I, p. 51 'I have been . . .': *The Times*, 3 February 74. 'The contest has . . .': *The Times*, 9 February 74. *Through the Looking Glass and What Alice Found There*: Martin Gardner, *The Annotated Alice* (2000 edn). 'A wakeful night . . .': *Gladstone Diaries*, VIII, 3 February 74. Summary of Gladstone's government: K. T. Hoppen, *The Mid-Victorian Generation* (1998), pp. 592–3. 'A dangerous man . . .,' etc.: Bradford, *Disraeli*, p. 305. 'The greatest . . .': Philip Magnus, *Gladstone* (1954), p. 228. 'It is parliament . . .,' 'I would give . . .': Agatha Ramm, *The Gladstone–Granville Correspondence* (1998), pp. 446–9. 'Is it not . . .': Bradford, *Disraeli*, p. 305. 'Disadvantage of a . . .': Philip Guedalla, *The Queen and Mr Gladstone* (1933), I, p. 446. 'To bed at . . .': *Gladstone Diaries*, VIII, 16 February 74. 'Startling announcement . . .': ibid., fn. 5. 'Perfectly demoniacal': Weintraub, *Disraeli*, p. 521. 'Very grave and . . .': G. E. Buckle, *The Letters of Queen Victoria, 1862–1878* (1926), II, p. 322.

'My dear mistress . . .,' 'He repeatedly said . . .': Monypenny and Buckle, *Disraeli*, II, p. 626. On Disraeli's relationship with the Queen: Theo Aronson, *Victoria and Disraeli* (1977), pp. 129–33. 'Cleverest woman in England . . .' is variously attributed. On Countess of Cardigan: Weintraub, *Disraeli*, p. 513. On Lady Bradford, and 'Lady Bradford seems . . .': Zetland, *Letters to Lady Bradford and Lady Chesterfield*, I, pp. 13–26. 'When you have . . .': Monypenny and Buckle, *Disraeli*, II, p. 589. 'I live for . . .': Paul Smith, *Disraeli* (1996), p. 172.

CHAPTER NINETEEN: THE OTHER GUEST (pp. 252–265)

Anthony Trollope (ed. John Sutherland), *The Way We Live Now* (1982). 'Finish *Vivian Grey* . . .': *Gladstone Diaries*, VIII, 20 March 74. Breakfast at Grillion's: Ibid, 7 March 74. 'Startled': ibid, 7 February 74. 'A civil talk . . .': ibid, 16 March 74. 'We are in . . .': Angus Hawkins & John Powell (eds), *Journal of John Woodhouse, First Earl of Kimberley* (1997), p. 285. 'How foolish and . . .': ibid, p. 286. 'I begin to . . .': Marquis of Zetland, *Letters of Disraeli to Lady Bradford and Lady Chesterfield* (1929), I, p. 66. 'I hear also . . .': John Vincent (ed.), *Derby Diaries*, vol. II (1994), p. 171. 'It was past . . .': Zetland, *Letters to Lady Bradford and Lady Chesterfield*, p. 120. . Never did the . . .': Christopher Hibbert, *Disraeli* (2004), p. 307. 'Against which as . . .': Jonathan Parry, *The Rise and Fall of Liberal Government in Victorian Britain* (1993), p. 251. 'A bill to . . .': Robert Blake, *Disraeli* (1966), p. 550. 'What has become . . .,' 'mass in masquerade,' 'master of flouts . . .': W. F. Monypenny & G. E. Buckle, *The Life of Benjamin Disraeli* (2 vols, 1929 edn), II, pp. 665–7. 'Gladstone ran away': Zetland, *Letters to Lady Bradford and Lady Chesterfield*, I, p. 116. Disraeli at Balmoral and Bournemouth: Hibbert, *Disraeli*, pp. 312–15. 'A great piece . . .': Zetland, *Letters to Lady Bradford and Lady Chesterfield*, p. 142. 'Hardly be brought . . .': Richard Shannon, Gladstone: *Heroic Minister* (1999), p. 147. On the Vatican Decrees controversy, see Josef L. Altholz & John Powell, 'Gladstone, Lord Rippon, and the Vatican Decrees, 1874' in *Albion*, 22 (1990), 449–59. 'On this my . . .': *Gladstone Diaries*, VIII, 29 December 74. 'I shall not . . .': *Gladstone Diaries*, IX, 14 January 75. 'I seem to . . .': ibid, 16 January 74. 'Mr Gladstone not . . .': Roy Jenkins, *Gladstone* (1995), p. 390. 'Rather low . . .': *Gladstone Diaries*, IX, 15 January 75.

'Never was a . . .': Zetland, *Letters to Lady Bradford and Lady Chesterfield*, I, p. 195. 'Had it never . . .,' 'Amiable, brilliant and . . .': ibid, pp. 217–18. 'In the great . . .': *Gladstone Diaries,* IX, 29 December 75.

'The thing has . . .', 'it is settled . . .', 'the whole country . . .': Bradford, *Disraeli*, pp. 327–8. 'The overland communication . . .', 'the determining influence . . .': Andrew Porter: *The Oxford History of the British Empire: The Nineteenth Century* (1999) pp. 112–13, 443. 'There is to . . .': Zetland, *Letters to Lady Bradford and Lady Chesterfield*, II, p. 15. 'It has been . . .,' 'A piece of . . .': Hawkins & Powell (eds), *Kimberley Journal*, p. 285. 'Mr Gladstone . . .,' 'White rages . . .': Zetland, *Letters to Lady Bradford and Lady Chesterfield*, II, p. 24. 'Universally disliked . . .': Vincent, *Derby Diaries*, II, p. 283. 'It would be . . .': T. A. Jenkins, *Disraeli and Victorian Conservatism* (1996), p. 109. 'Disraeli complains of . . .': Vincent, *Derby Diaries*, II, p. 294.

CHAPTER TWENTY: A CLASH OF CIVILISATIONS
(pp. 266–278)

House of Commons. Disraeli taking leave of the Commons: W. F. Monypenny & G. E. Buckle, *The Life of Benjamin Disraeli* (2 vols, 1929 edn), II, pp. 828ff. 'Now mark all . . .': Marquis of Zetland, *Letters of Disraeli to Lady Bradford and Lady Chesterfield* (1929), II, pp. 71–2. John Morley, *Life of Gladstone* (1905 edn), II, p. 156. John Vincent (ed.), *Derby Diaries,* (1994), p. 298. The classic text on the Eastern Question remains R. W. Seton-Watson, *Disraeli, Gladstone and the Eastern Question* (1972 edn) which is used extensively here. Schuyler report: ibid, p. 58. 'Foreign affairs had . . .': Stephen Gwynn, *The Life of Sir Charles Dilke* (1917), I, p. 203. 'More news of . . .': G. E. Buckle, *The Letters of Queen Victoria, 1862–1878* (1926), II, p. 475. 'It is still . . .': Marvin Swartz, *The Politics of British Foreign Policy in the Era of Disraeli and Gladstone* (1985), p. 38. 'I really hope . . .': Travis L. Crosby, *The Two Mr Gladstones* (1997), p. 153. 'Gladstone has had . . .': Monypenny and Buckle, *Disraeli* (2 vols, 1929 edn), II, p. 932. 'It is raining . . .': Zetland, *Letters of Disraeli to Lady Bradford and Lady Chesterfield*, pp. 72–3.

Blackheath. In evening saw . . .': *Gladstone Diaries*, IX, 7 September 76. Blackheath speech: Morley, *Gladstone*, II, p. 162, Seton-Watson, *Disraeli, Gladstone and the Eastern Question*, p. 81. 'The most enthusiastic . . .': *Gladstone Diaries*, IX, 9 September 76. For a less sanguine appraisal of Gladstone's liberal nationalism, see Keith Sandiford, 'W. E. Gladstone and Liberal-Nationalist movements' in *Albion*, 13: 1 (1981), 27–43. The town gave . . .': *Gladstone Diaries*, IX, 11 September 76. 'That is the . . .': Seton-Watson, *Disraeli, Gladstone and the Eastern Question*, p. 78fn. 'Posterity will do . . .': ibid, pp. 78–9. 'Generally speaking when . . .': Monypenny and Buckle, *Disraeli*, II, p. 934. 'The sphinx is . . .': Seton-Watson, *Disraeli, Gladstone and the Eastern Question*, pp. 82–3. 'He who at . . .', 'master speech': Monypenny and Buckle, *Disraeli*, II, pp. 937–9. 'A skilfully ingenious . . .': Vincent, *Derby Diaries,* II, p. 329. 'A negligence astonishing . . .', 'added to the . . .': Seton-Watson, *Disraeli, Gladstone and the Eastern Question*, p. 88. 'No doubt will . . .': Vincent, *Derby Diaries,* II, p. 328. Guildhall speech: Monypenny and Buckle, *Disraeli*, II, p. 964. 'The provocation offered . . .': Morley, *Gladstone*, II, p. 166.

St James's Hall. 'I came to . . .', 'We have never . . .': Seton-Watson, *Disraeli, Gladstone and the Eastern Question*, pp. 110–12. Spencer, Kimberley, Hartington: Swartz, *The Politics of British Foreign Policy in* *the Era of Disraeli and Gladstone*, pp. 42–3. On Canning, see Wendy Hinde, *George Canning* (1973), pp. 384–9. Gladstone's speech: Seton-Watson, *Disraeli, Gladstone and the Eastern Question*, pp. 112–3, Morley, *Gladstone*, II, p. 167. 'The meetings were . . .': *Gladstone Diaries*, IX, 8 December 76 (see fn. 7 on Mrs Thistlethwayte). Hartington: Swartz, *The Politics of British Foreign Policy in the era of Disraeli and Gladstone*, p. 43. 'When did the . . .', 'We don't want . . .': Philip Magnus, *Gladstone* (1954), pp. 243–5.

CHAPTER TWENTY-ONE: PEACE WITH HONOUR
(pp. 279–289)

High Wycombe. 'The visit of . . .': Marquis of Zetland, *Letters of Disraeli to Lady Bradford and Lady Chesterfield* (1929), II, p. 148. 'And made a . . .': *Gladstone Diaries*, IX, 15 December 77. 'The country is . . .', 'By Jingo . . .': Stanley Weintraub, *Disraeli* (1993), pp. 582–3. 'Everybody has taken . . .': Marvin Swartz, *The Politics of British Foreign Policy in the Era of Disraeli and Gladstone* (1985). Gladstone's Oxford speech and reaction: R. W. Seton-Watson, *Disraeli, Gladstone and the Eastern Question* (1972 edn), pp. 304–7. 'I said what . . .': *Gladstone Diaries*, IX, 30 January 78. 'What an exposure . . .': Zetland, *Letters to Lady Bradford and Lady Chesterfield*, II, p. 158. 'Between four and . . .': *Gladstone Diaries*, IX, 24 February 78. Whispering campaign against Gladstone: Travis L. Crosby, *The Two Mr Gladstones* (1997), p. 160. 'This is a . . .': Zetland, *Letters to Lady Bradford and Lady Chesterfield*, II, p. 162. 'Saw four . . .': *Gladstone Diaries*, IX, 19 March 78.
Kaiserhof Hotel. Assessment of Disraeli's relationship with Bismarck: Robert Blake, *Disraeli* (1966), p. 646. Disraeli quotations at Berlin Congress: W. F. Monypenny and G. E. Buckle, *Disraeli* (2 vols, 1929 edn), II, pp. 1182–1216. Zetland, *Letters to Lady Bradford and Lady Chesterfield*, II, pp. 170–82. Blake, *Disraeli*, pp. 644–54. Weintraub, *Disraeli*, pp. 591–7. Andrew Roberts, *Salisbury* (1999) pp. 196–204. Summary of Treaty of Berlin: Roberts, *Salisbury*, p. 204. 'A treaty of peace . . .': Zetland, *Letters to Lady Bradford and Lady Chesterfield*, II, p. 178. Monypenny and Buckle, *Disraeli*, II, pp. 1228–9.
Dover. Disraeli's return: Roberts, *Salisbury*, pp. 204–5. 'Which do you . . .': John Morley, *Life of Gladstone* (1905 edn), II, p. 156. John Vincent (ed.), *Derby Diaries II* (1994), p. 298. 'I was in . . .': *Gladstone Diaries*, IX, 30 July 78. 'I say sir . . .': Morley, *Gladstone*, II, p. 185. 'We

were two . . .': Weintraub, *Disraeli*, p. 603. 'Some nonsense . . .': Zetland, *Letters to Lady Bradford and Lady Chesterfield*, II, p. 181. 'Realizing all the . . .': ibid, p. 182.

CHAPTER TWENTY-TWO: MIDLOTHIAN (pp. 290–305)

Hawarden. 'Sixty nine years . . .', 'Great shifting of . . .': *Gladstone Diaries*, IX, 29 December 78. 'Under anything like . . .', 'The particular circumstances . . .', 'On a crisis . . .': ibid, 30 January 79. 'The pot is . . .': Richard Shannon: *Gladstone: Heroic Minister* (1999), p. 224. 'A great moral . . .': Leo McKinstry, *Rosebery: Statesman in Turmoil* (2005), p. 80. Rosebery and Disraeli: McKinstry, *Rosebery*, pp. 54–7; John Davis, 'Primrose, Archibald Philip, fifth earl of Rosebery and first earl of Midlothian (1847–1929)', *Oxford Dictionary of National Biography* (2004). Sport and national life: Colin Matthew, *The Nineteenth Century* (2000). 'The terrible disaster . . .': Marquis of Zetland, *Letters of Disraeli to Lady Bradford and Lady Chesterfield* (1929), II, p. 148. Summary of Isandhlwana, Kabul and economic depression: Paul Smith, *Disraeli* (1996), pp. 198, 202. 'I think the . . .': Zetland, *Letters to Lady Bradford and Lady Chesterfield*, II, p. 232. 'We have had . . .': W. F. Monypenny and G. E. Buckle, *The Life of Benjamin Disraeli* (2 vols, 1929 edn), II, p. 1305. Disraeli's Guildhall speech: Stanley Weintraub, *Disraeli* (1993), pp. 616–18, Monypenny and Buckle, *Disraeli*, II, p. 1369. 'The fogs and . . .': ibid, p. 1375.

Gladstone's Midlothian speeches: J. J. Reid (ed.), *W. E. Gladstone: Political Speeches in Scotland, November and December 1879* (1879). See also *Gladstone Diaries*, IX, November–December 1879. Philip Magnus, *Gladstone* (1954) pp. 261–5; Roy Jenkins, *Gladstone* (1995), pp. 424–8; Travis L. Crosby, *Gladstone* (1997), pp. 159–61; John Morley, *Life of Gladstone* (1905 edn), II, pp. 192–205. 'I have not . . .': Zetland, *Letters to Lady Bradford and Lady Chesterfield*, II, p. 249–50. A. E. Gathorne-Hardy, *Gathorne Hardy* (1910), 2, p. 126. 'The event of . . .': John Vincent (ed.), *Derby Diaries*, III (2003), p. 188. 'Progress has been . . .': ibid., p. 187. 'Disgracefully bitter . . .' etc.: Crosby, *The Two Mr Gladstones*, p. 160. 'One series of . . .': G. E. Buckle, *The Letters of Queen Victoria, 1879–1885* (1928), p. 75. 'Disgusted with the . . .': Weintraub, *Disraeli*, p. 620. 'Gladstone's rodomontade and rigmarole': Blake, *Disraeli*, p. 701. Cabinet meeting, 14 February 80: Blake, *Disraeli*, pp. 702–3. 'I hear that . . .': Vincent (ed.), *Derby Diaries,* III, p. 217. 'Dissolution announced': *Gladstone Diaries,* IX, 8 March 80. 'Indictment against the Government

. . .': K. T. Hoppen, *The Mid-Victorian Generation* (1998), p. 633.

'Sober men on . . .': Angus Hawkins & John Powell, *The Journal of John Wodehouse, First Earl of Kimberley* (1997), p. 314. 'Much doubt as . . .': Stephen Gwynn et al., *The Life of Sir Charles Dilke* (1917), I, p. 302. 'All is uncertain . . .': Vincent, *Derby Diaries*, III, p. 218. 'He was cheerful . . .': A. E. Gathorne-Hardy, *Gathorne Hardy, First Earl of Cranbrook* (1910), II, p. 129. 'Rarely in this . . .': Monypenny and Buckle, *Disraeli*, II, p. 1390. 'Both sides are . . .': Zetland, *Letters to Lady Bradford and Lady Chesterfield*, II, p. 263.

'We cannot reckon . . .': Magnus, *Gladstone*, p. 270. 'And so ends . . .': *Gladstone Diaries*, IX, 2 April 80. 'Was not sorry . . .', 'Lord B. spoke . . .': Monypenny and Buckle, *Disraeli*, II, p. 1397. 'It is the . . .': Zetland, *Letters to Lady Bradford and Lady Chesterfield*, II, p. 267. 'Hatred of Gladstone, Vincent, *Derby Diaries*, III, p. 224. 'All our heads . . .': Morley, *Gladstone*, II, p. 223. 'All parties wish . . .': Vincent, *Derby Diaries*, III, p. 228. 'I am stunned . . .': *Gladstone Diaries*, IX, 10 April 80. 'I vaguely feel . . .': ibid., 19 April 80.

CHAPTER TWENTY-THREE: FALCONET (pp. 306–319)

Baden-Baden. William M. Kuhn, *Henry and Mary Ponsonby* (2002), pp. 162–74. W. F. Monypenny and G. E. Buckle, *The Life of Benjamin Disraeli* (2 vols, 1929 edn), II, pp. 1396–1402. Theo Aronson, *Victoria and Disraeli* (1977), p. 202. Disraeli's audience with the Queen: Monypenny and Buckle, *Disraeli*, II, pp. 1406–10. 'The Queen has . . .': Angus Hawkins & John Powell, *The Journal of John Wodehouse, First Earl of Kimberley* (1997), p. 315. Hartington's audience with the Queen: G. E. Buckle, *The Letters of Queen Victoria, 1879–1885* (1928), pp. 81–5. Hartington: Jonathan Parry, 'Cavendish, Spencer Compton, marquess of Hartington and eighth duke of Devonshire (1833–1908)', *Oxford Dictionary of National Biography* (2004); John Morley, *Life of Gladstone* (1905 edn), II, pp. 230–32. 'It does look . . .': Roy Jenkins, *Gladstone* (1995), p. 436. Hartington's second interview with the Queen: Buckle, *Letters of Queen Victoria, 1879–1885*, pp. 82–3. Gladstone's interview with the Queen: *Gladstone Diaries*, IX, 23 April 80; John Brooke & Mary Sorensen, *W. E. Gladstone, III, Autobiographical Memoranda, 1845–1866* (1978), pp. 256–60.

'Battle of Armageddon . . .': Marquis of Zetland, *Letters of Disraeli to Lady Bradford and Lady Chesterfield* (1929), II, p. 267. 'I will keep . . .':

Monypenny and Buckle, *Disraeli*, II, p. 1412. 'There has been . . .': Robert Blake, *Disraeli* (1966), p. 715. 'Whatever philosophers may . . .': Stanley Weintraub, *Disraeli* (1993), p. 627. 'My Glad . . .': Monypenny and Buckle, *Disraeli*, II, p. 1426. 'It is like . . .': John Vincent (ed.), *Derby Diaries*, III (2003), p. 283. 'Elijah's mantle . . .': Archie Hunter, *A Life of Sir John Eldon Gorst* (2001), p. 146. 'Such was the . . .', 'O 'tis a . . .': *Gladstone Diaries*, IX, 24 and 31 July 80. Gladstone as an 'old man': Jenkins, *Gladstone*, pp. 457–8. 'C went for . . .': *Gladstone Diaries*, IX, 31 December 80. 'I see no . . .' etc.: Sarah Bradford, *Disraeli* (1986), pp. 383–4. Extracts from Falconet: Monypenny and Buckle, *Disraeli*, II, pp. 1521ff. Disraeli's last winter: Bradford, *Disraeli* (1982), pp. 386–90; Monypenny and Buckle, *Disraeli*, II, pp. 1471–89; Weintraub, *Disraeli*, pp. 650–58; Blake, *Disraeli*, pp. 744–50.

EPILOGUE: *IN MEMORIAM* (pp. 320–326)

The account of the death and funeral of Gladstone is drawn from John Wolffe, *Great Deaths: Grieving, Religion, and Nationhood in Victorian and Edwardian Britain* (2000), pp. 169–91 and H. C. G. Matthew, 'Gladstone's death and funeral' in *The Journal of Liberal Democratic History* (Autumn, 1998), 38–42. See also, Peter J. Jagger (ed.), *Gladstone* (1998), pp. 51–70. 'Just back from . . .': A. E. Gathorne-Hardy, *Gathorne Hardy* (1910), p. 363. 'Which has had . . .', 'sat quite composed . . .', 'The House showed . . .'; 'the gradual loosening . . .': H.C.G. Matthew, *Gladstone* (1997), pp. 400, 606–8. 'Ireland!'; 'Democracy [has] certainly . . .': John Morley, *The Life of Gladstone* (2 vols, 1907 edn), II, pp. 287, 713–15. 'Something totally different . . .': *Gladstone Diaries*, X, G. to Harry Gladstone, 21 April 81. 'Regret all the . . .': Andrew Roberts, *Salisbury* (1999), p. 693. 'Throughout the morning . . .': *The Times*, 30 May 98. G. E. Buckle: Stanley Weintraub, 'Buckle, George Earle (1854–1935)', *Oxford Dictionary of National Biography* (2004; online edn, May 2005). Paul Addison, 'Churchill, Sir Winston Leonard Spencer (1874–1965)', *Oxford Dictionary of National Biography* (2004). R. S. Churchill and M. Gilbert (eds), Winston S. Churchill: Companion, 5 vols (1967–79), I (ii), p. 775.

Index

Elgin, Lord 178
Eliot, George, *Daniel Deronda* 311
Ellenborough, Lord 104, 107
Ely, Lady 306
Erskine, Lord 313
Esher, Lord 217
Eton 12, 27, 114, 143, 145

Faber, Frederick 38
Farquhar, Caroline 28
Fawcett, Henry 230
Fenian Outrages 192
Ferguson, Sir James 121
Fielding, Henry 25
Football Association (FA) 292
Foreign and Colonial Quarterly magazine 34
Forster, W.E. 156, 231, 232
Fox, Charles James 320
Fraser, Sir William 70, 71, 75, 132, 218–19
Freeman, Edward 277–8, 280

George V 320
Gilbert, W.S. 288–9; *Iolanthe* 117
Gladstone, Catherine (née Glynne) 131; marriage to WG 28–9; support for husband 29–30, 127, 180, 245; pregnancies and children 52; WG confides in 74, 77; and WG's bizarre behaviour 169–70; reaction to WG's intended retirement 254; and WG's decision to retire 261; and attacks on property 282; and Midlothian campaign 295; and death of WG 324
Gladstone, Helen 55
Gladstone, Herbert 245
Gladstone, John 12
Gladstone, Sir John 54
Gladstone, Mary 6, 296
Gladstone, William, and death of BD 1–2, 4, 5, 319; political rivalry 2, 7–8; ill-health 5, 6, 7, 125, 170, 198, 207, 236–7, 237, 272, 314; portrait of 5; speech at RA annual banquet 5; at BD's memorial service 6; tribute speech to BD in House of Commons 6–7; character of 10, 12, 41, 96, 191–2, 220, 236; meets BD 10–11; as evangelical Christian 11, 12, 14, 79–80, 97; as rising man 11–12; as anti-reformist 12–13, 14; birth and early life 12–13; enters Parliament 13–14; social life 13–14; as MP 23, 24; love and marriage 27–30; offered junior post in Peel's administration 32–3; works on tariffs and trade matters 34–5; resignations of 35–7, 88, 232–3, 260–1; comment on *Sybil* 39; loss of parliamentary seats 40–1, 49, 150, 199; political rehabilitation 40–1; support for Peel 45–6; at the RA Summer Exhibition and banquet 50–1; sexual exploits 51–4, 52–3, 56, 75, 84–6, 96, 114, 125–6, 126, 131–2, 170, 194, 197, 273; and deaths of father, daughter and Peel 54–5, 96; and loss of friends through religion 55; encouraged to return to Cabinet 60–2; budget proposals 67, 70–2, 79–83, 119–22, 124–5, 126–7; enjoyment in budget attack on BD 73–5; insulted at the Carlton Club 73–4, 77; as Chancellor of the Exchequer 77–9; exposure of indiscretions 84–6; shakes hands with BD 90; unwilling to work with either Derby or Palmerston 90–4; Homeric studies 96–9; Irish debates 96, 192–4, 199, 205–7, 214–15, 229–32, 322–3; dismay at religious conversion of Manning and Hope 97; recall to politics 99; urged to join Derby administration 102, 103–7; as Lord High Commissioner Extraordinary 108–13; visit to Corfu 108–13; vows revenge on BD 114; as Liberal 116–19; life at Hawarden 128–30; relationship with Duchess of Sutherland 131–2; liking for BD's wife 135–6; and death of Albert 137–8; visit to the Northeast 142–3; as celebrity 143–6; wins South Lancashire seat 150–1; and death of Palmerston 153; and Reform Bill 157–9, 160–4, 174–80, 182–5;